D1313304

PAGANS AND CHRISTIANS IN LATE ANTIQUITY

In the third century AD, the Roman empire encompassed an enormous diversity of religious practices and creeds; by the sixth century, one of those creeds – Christianity – had become the dominant religious force in the Mediterranean world, providing a vital thread of continuity and stability as antiquity gave way to the Middle Ages.

A.D. Lee uses translated extracts from contemporary sources, and related material evidence, to document this process. The volume examines the fortunes of pagans and Christians from the upheavals of the third century, through the dramatic events associated with the emperors Constantine, Julian the Apostate, and Theodosius in the fourth, to the increasingly tumultuous times of the fifth and sixth centuries which witnessed the demise of the western empire and the survival of the eastern half. It also explores the fate of other significant religious groups – Jews, Zoroastrians, and Manichaeans – and illustrates a number of important themes in late antique Christianity, such as the growth of monasticism, the emerging power of bishops, and the development of pilgrimage.

Each extract or item is accompanied by a clear explanation of its context and significance and by guidance on further reading. By presenting contemporary material in this way, *Pagans and Christians in Late Antiquity* forms the ideal introduction to a period and subject full of interest.

Doug Lee, a former Research Fellow at Trinity College, Cambridge, is Senior Lecturer in Classics and Ancient History at the University of Wales, Lampeter. He is the author of *Information and Frontiers: Roman Foreign Relations in Late Antiquity* (1993) and is a contributor to the new edition of *Cambridge Ancient History*.

PAGANS AND CHRISTIANS IN LATE ANTIQUITY

A sourcebook

A.D. Lee

London and New York

First published 2000
by Routledge
11 New Fetter Lane, London EC4P 4EE

Simultaneously published in the USA and Canada
by Routledge
29 West 35th Street, New York, NY 10001

Routledge is an imprint of the Taylor & Francis Group

© 2000 A.D. Lee

Typeset in Garamond by Taylor & Francis Books Ltd
Printed and bound in Great Britain by Biddles Ltd,
Guildford and King's Lynn

British Library Cataloguing in Publication Data
A catalogue record for this book is available from the British Library

Library of Congress Cataloging in Publication Data
Lee, A.D.
Pagans and Christians in late antiquity: a sourcebook/A.D. Lee.
p.cm.
Includes bibliographical references (p.) and indexes.
1. Christianity and other religions–Roman. 2. Rome–Religion.
3. Church history–Primitive and early church, ca. 30–600. I. Title.
BR128.R7 L44 2000
200'.9'015–dc21   00-021697

ISBN 0–415–13892–2 (hbk)
ISBN 0–415–13893–0 (pbk)

FOR ANNA

CONTENTS

CONTENTS

ILLUSTRATIONS

Figures

Plates

PREFACE

Late Antiquity is a fascinating period of history, not least because of the seminal religious developments that occurred in it. It is the aim of this book to provide an entrée into those developments, from the third century through to the sixth, via a selection of translated extracts from contemporary sources. The envisaged audience is primarily university undergraduates and sixth formers studying ancient or early medieval history.

Such students have long had available the twin sourcebooks by J. Stevenson, *A New Eusebius* (SPCK, London, 1957) and *Creeds, Councils, and Controversies* (1966), whose value is amply attested by their being re-issued in revised editions in the late 1980s. More recently, Ramsay MacMullen and Eugene Lane have produced their sourcebook *Paganism and Christianity, 100–425 CE* (Fortress Press, Minneapolis, 1992). For the student of Late Antiquity, however, these titles have a number of disadvantages which the present volume aims to make good. Although they commence a century or more earlier than this volume, they conclude in the mid-fifth century; they offer very limited help with further reading; and they make no use of visual evidence. Stevenson's books also place heavy emphasis on doctrinal controversies, while giving limited attention to pagans and adherents of other religions – understandable when they are explicitly addressed to 'students of Early Church History', but less satisfactory for ancient history students – and he made very limited use of documentary evidence in the form of inscriptions and papyri. MacMullen and Lane are better in this respect, but their coverage of the fourth century and beyond is patchy.

By contrast, the present volume includes material from every century of Late Antiquity, though with an emphasis on the third and fourth; it uses a wide range of different types of evidence, including visual (though costs have limited the number of pictures able to be included); and it provides detailed guidance on further reading (mostly in English, but occasionally in other European languages).

The selection of sources is that of an ancient historian rather than a patristic scholar, with a focus on religious life in its political and social context. No doubt some readers will disagree with some of the choices I have made with regard to inclusion and/or omission; in particular, I am conscious that, partly in reaction to Stevenson, I have probably under-played doctrinal controversy and heresy too much, and early medievalists may feel that I have not done sufficient justice to the post-Roman west. I certainly recognise that most of the subjects of the individual chapters in this volume could have whole sourcebooks devoted to each of them (as indeed some of them already do), but I have had to work to a fairly tight word limit while trying to preserve an even balance between extended passages and shorter excerpts. I have also endeavoured to ensure the inclusion of well-known items that anyone teaching on this period and subject would expect to find, while also incorporating as much less familiar material as possible, and seeking to maintain a reasonable balance in terms of geographical spread. The modern literature is also vast, and I certainly have not read it all, but if I have omitted items of major importance, then the suggestions for further reading and useful reference works should lead readers to them.

Except where otherwise indicated, all translations are my own. I must, however, express my thanks for significant help with particular passages to Sebastian Brock (7.1), Tony Brothers (6.12, 7.12), David Johnston (15.5), and Rosemary Wright (1.13). In the transliteration of proper names, I have generally opted for the Latinised form, but I have not always been consistent. All dates are AD unless otherwise indicated. The map is intended to show locations referred to in the text.

My thanks to Richard Stoneman for inviting me to write this book, and to Rosamond McKitterick for suggesting my name as a possible candidate. Work on it began in the final weeks of a term's study leave in 1995 and was significantly advanced by a further term's leave in 1998, and I am very grateful to my hard-working colleagues at Lampeter who covered my administrative responsibilities during those periods. Those terms were spent in my city of origin, Sydney, where the kindness of Professor Kevin Lee (no relation!) and his colleagues at the University of Sydney made available work space and wordprocessing facilities, while Fisher Library at Sydney University and Macquarie University Library provided marvellous resources for work on Late Antiquity. In the United Kingdom, the hold-ings of the Hugh Owen Library and the National Library of Wales in Aberystwyth have been of great help, as have those of the Cambridge University Library. In Lampeter, Kathy Miles and Haf James have been very efficient in processing numerous Interlibrary Loan requests. Various colleagues and friends have also assisted by lending or obtaining books for me, sometimes for extended periods of time – in particular, Tony Brothers, David Noy, Keith Hopwood, Neville Morley, and Colin Stevens.

My colleagues David Noy and Emma Stafford have been especially helpful, first, through their willingness to read and comment on drafts of some chapters, and second, through their ever courteous and prompt responses to innumerable questions on everything from the Palestinian Talmud to the finer points of obtaining photographs from museums.

Others who have given valued help with matters large or small include Michel Amandry, Ian Barton, Heike Behlmer, Peter Brennan, Andrew Burnett, Jan Willem Drijvers, Günter Hansen, Greg Horsley, Chris Howgego, Anne Johnson, Erich Kettenhoffen, Stephen Mitchell, and Keith Rutter. The Department of Classics at Lampeter has helped with the costs of photographs and other research expenses, and Anne Morley kindly assisted with some of the typing in the final stages.

To all of the above go my sincere thanks, and my assurance that I alone bear the responsibility for the inevitable errors.

Richard Stoneman has shown exemplary patience as deadlines have come and gone. I can only say that it would have been finished much sooner were it not for the inordinate amounts of time entailed by the need to meet government requirements in the form of teaching quality assessments and the like. I am also grateful to Catherine Bousfield, Eve Daintith and Lauren Dallinger for the speed and care with which they have handled the production of the book.

On a personal note, thanks to Mum and Dad again for your love and help over the years, and especially during the recent times in Sydney – I hope you'll find this book more accessible than the previous one; to my brothers and sisters-in-law in Sydney – Pete and Linda, Grae and Jane – for all sorts of practical support; and not least, to my aunt Ruth, for the loan of a laptop in Sydney, and for obtaining numerous books and articles there and since – a huge help. At all times, my children – James, Philip and Naomi – have helped to keep at least one foot rooted in the realities of the present and so maintained my sanity, as also, in different ways, has my wife Anna – thank you for all your practical support, love, and forebearance.

Aberaeron
December 1999

ACKNOWLEDGEMENTS

Acknowledgement is made to the following for permission to reprint translations:

Prof. Mary Boyce for an extract from *Textual Sources for the Study of Zoroastrianism* (originally Manchester: Manchester University Press, 1984; rights now reverted to the author).

Prof. David Brakke and Johns Hopkins University Press for an extract from *Athanasius and Asceticism*, translated by D. Brakke (Baltimore, 1998).

Brill for extracts from *The Nag Hammadi Library in English*, edited by J.M. Robinson (Leiden, 1988).

Cambridge University Press for extracts from *Sallustius: Concerning the Gods and the Universe*, translated by A.D. Nock (Cambridge, 1926); *Origen: Contra Celsum*, translated by H. Chadwick (Cambridge, 1953).

The Catholic University of America Press for extracts from *St John Chrysostom: Discourses against Judaizing Christians* (Fathers of the Church vol. 68), translated by P.W. Harkins (Washington DC, 1979).

Cistercian Publications for extracts from *Pachomian Koinonia* vol. 1: *The Life of Pachomius and his Disciples*, translated by A. Veilleux (1980); *Pachomian Koinonia* vol. 2: *Pachomian Chronicles and Rules*, translated by A. Veilleux (1981); *Besa: The Life of Shenoute*, translated by D.N. Bell (Kalamazoo, MI, 1983).

The Edwin Mellen Press for extracts from *Jerome, Chrysostom, and Friends*, translated by E.A. Clark (New York, 1979).

The Egypt Exploration Society for an extract from *The Oxyrhynchus Papyri* vol. 12.

Harvard University Press for extracts from *Libanius: Selected Works*, vol. 2, translated by A.F. Norman (Cambridge, Mass., 1977).

Manchester University Press for an extract from *Catalogue of the Greek and Latin Papyri in the John Rylands Library Manchester*, vol. 3: *Theological and literary texts*, translated by C.H. Roberts (Manchester, 1938).

Oxford University Press for an extract from *Bede's 'Ecclesiastical History of the English People'*, trans. B. Colgrave and R.A.B. Mynors (Oxford, 1969).

Peeters Publishers for extracts from C. Moss, 'Jacob of Serugh's Homilies on the Spectacles of the Theatre', pp. 108–9 and 109–10 in *Le Muséon*, vol. 48 (Leuven, 1935).

Princeton University Press for an extract from *Excavations at Nessana* vol. 3: *Non-literary papyri*, translated by C.J. Kraemer (Princeton, New Jersey, 1958).

Dr Roger Tomlin for an extract from 'The curse tablets' in B. Cunliffe (ed.) *The Temple of Sulis Minerva at Bath* vol. 2: *The Finds from the Sacred Spring* (Oxford University Committee for Archaeology: monograph no. 16, 1988).

University of Chicago Press for an extract from *The Talmud of the Land of Israel: A Preliminary Translation and Explanation*, vol. 33: *Abodah Zarah* translated by J. Neusner (Chicago, 1982).

Every effort has been made to obtain permission for the use of copyright items. Author and publisher would be glad to hear from any copyright holders not so acknowledged.

Picture credits

Acknowledgement is made to the following for permission to reproduce illustrations: Amt für kirchliche Denkmalpflege Trier (16.14); Archaeological Exploration of Sardis/Harvard University (8.2); The Cleveland Museum of Art (14.12a); The Dumbarton Oaks Collection, Washington DC (13.6); The German Archaeological Institute, Rome (1.2, 14.4); The Louvre, Paris (16.6); The Menil Collection, Houston (16.12); Musée du Bardo, Tunisia (14.8); Rijksmuseum van Oudheden, Leiden (1.9); The Sinai Archive, University of Michigan (14.12b); The Society of Antiquaries of London (14.4); The Walters Art Gallery, Baltimore (13.5, 16.11); Yale University Art Gallery (1.4); Yale University Press (2.4). Every effort has been made to obtain permission for the use of copyright items. Author and publisher would be glad to hear from any copyright holders not so acknowledged.

CONVENTIONS AND ABBREVIATIONS

Conventions

In the translations, the following conventions have been used:

( )   enclose parenthetic comments by the author of the ancient text
< >   enclose words restored by the modern editor of the ancient text
< ... > indicates a damaged portion of the ancient text
[ ]   enclose words that I have added for clarification of the meaning of the ancient text
+   indicates the presence of the Christian symbol of the cross

Abbreviations

AB	*Analecta Bollandiana*
AE	*L'Année épigraphique*
AJP	*American Journal of Philology*
ANRW	*Aufstieg und Niedergang der römischen Welt*
BCH	*Bulletin de correspondance hellénique*
BE	*Bulletin épigraphique* in *Revue des études grecques*
BICS	*Bulletin of the Institute of Classical Studies* (London)
BJRL	*Bulletin of the John Rylands Library*
CCSL	*Corpus Christianorum, Series Latina* (Brepols: Turnhout, 1953–)
CIJ	*Corpus Inscriptionum Judaicarum*, eds J.B. Frey and B. Lifshitz (Pontificio Istituto di Archaeologica Cristiana: Rome and New York, 1936–75)
CIL	*Corpus Inscriptionum Latinarum*
CIMRM	*Corpus Inscriptionum et Monumentorum Religionis Mithrae*, ed. M.J. Vermaseren (The Hague: Martinus Nijhoff, 1956–60)
CMRDM	*Corpus Monumentorum Religionis Dei Menis*, ed. E.N. Lane (Leiden: Brill, 1971–8)
CPh	*Classical Philology*
CNRS	Centre National de la Recherche Scientifique, Paris
CQ	*Classical Quarterly*

CSEL	*Corpus Scriptorum Ecclesiasticorum Latinorum* (Vienna: Tempsky, 1866–)
DT	*Defixionum Tabellae*, ed. A. Audollent (Fontemoing: Paris, 1904)
FC	*Fathers of the Church* (Washington DC: Catholic University of America Press)
GCS	*Die griechischen christlichen Schriftsteller der ersten drei Jahrhunderte* (Berlin: Akademie Verlag, 1897–)
G&R	*Greece & Rome*
GRBS	*Greek, Roman and Byzantine Studies*
HTR	*Harvard Theological Review*
IEJ	*Israel Exploration Journal*
IGLT	*Inscriptions grecques et latines des tombeaux des rois ou syringes à Thebes*, ed. J. Baillet (Cairo: Imprimerie de l'Institut française d'archéologie orientale, 1920–6)
IGPhilae	*Les Inscriptions grecques et latines de Philae*, eds A. and E. Bernand (Paris: CNRS, 1969)
ILAlg	*Inscriptions latines de l'Algérie*, eds S. Gsell, H.-G. Pflaum (Paris: Librairie ancienne Honoré Champion; Algiers: Société nationale d'édition et de diffusion, 1922–76)
ILCV	*Inscriptiones Latinae Christianae Veteres*, ed. E. Diehl (Berlin: Weidmann, 1925–31)
ILS	*Inscriptiones Latinae Selectae*, ed. H. Dessau (Berlin: Weidmann, 1892–1916)
I. Sardis	*Sardis. Publications of the American Society for the Excavation of Sardis* vol. 7 (*Greek and Latin Inscriptions, Part 1*), eds W.H. Buckler and D.M. Robinson (Leiden: Brill, 1932)
I. Strat.	*Die Inschriften von Stratonikeia*, ed. M.C. Sahin (Bonn: Habelt, 1981–90)
JAC	*Jahrbuch für Antike und Christentum*
JECS	*Journal of Early Christian Studies*
JEH	*Journal of Ecclesiastical History*
JHS	*Journal of Hellenic Studies*
JIWE	*Jewish Inscriptions of Western Europe*, ed. D. Noy (Cambridge: Cambridge University Press, 1993–5)
JRS	*Journal of Roman Studies*
JTS	*Journal of Theological Studies*
MAMA	*Monumenta Asiae Minoris Antiqua* (1928–)
MEFRA	*Mélanges de l'école français de Rome* (*Antiquité*)
MGH.AA	*Monumenta Germaniae Historica, Auctores Antiquissimi*
P. Dura	*The Excavations at Dura-Europos, Final Report*, vol. 5, part I (*The Parchments and Papyri*), eds C.B. Welles, R.O. Fink and J.F. Gilliam (New Haven: Yale University Press, 1959)
PG	*Patrologia Graeca*, ed. J.P. Migne (Paris, 1857–1912)
P. Grenf.	*Greek Papyri*, eds B.P. Grenfell and A.S. Hunt (Oxford: Clarendon Press, 1896–7)

P. Ital.	*Die nichtliterarischen lateinischen Papyri Italiens aus der Zeit* 445–700, ed. J.-O. Tjäder (Lund: Gleerup, 1955–82)
PL	*Patrologia Latina*, ed. J.P. Migne (Paris, 1844–64)
PLRE	*Prosopography of the Later Roman Empire*
P. Mich 3	*Michigan Papyri* vol. 3, ed. J.G. Winter (Ann Arbor: University of Michigan Press, 1936)
P. Ness.	*Excavations at Nessana* vol.3 *The Non-literary Papyri*, ed. and trans. C.J. Kraemer (Princeton: Princeton University Press, 1958)
PO	*Patrologia Orientalis* (Paris: Firmin-Didot, 1903–)
P. Oxy.	*The Oxyrhynchus Papyri* (London: Egypt Exploration Society, 1898–)
P. Rendel Harris	*The Rendel Harris Papyri*, ed. E. Powell (Cambridge: Cambridge University Press, 1936)
P. Ryl. 3	*Catalogue of the Greek and Latin Papyri in the John Rylands Library Manchester*, vol.3, ed. and trans. C.H. Roberts (Manchester: Manchester University Press, 1938)
RAC	*Reallexikon für Antike und Christentum*
RE	*Real-Encyclopädie der klassischen Altertumswissenschaft*, eds A. Pauly, G. Wissowa and W. Kroll (Stuttgart: Alfred Druckenmüller, 1893–)
RICG	*Recueil des inscriptions chrétiennes de la Gaule* (Paris, 1976–)
Robert *NIS*	L. Robert, *Nouvelles inscriptions de Sardes* (Paris: Librairie d'Amérique et d'Orient, 1964)
SB	*Sammelbuch griechischer Urkunden aus Ägypten*
SC	*Sources chrétiennes* (Paris: Editions du Cerf, 1941–)
SCH	*Studies in Church History*
Tab. Sulis	R.S.O. Tomlin, 'The curse tablets', in B. Cunliffe (ed.), *The Temple of Sulis Minerva at Bath*, vol. 2: *The Finds from the Sacred Spring* (Oxford University Committee for Archaeology: Monograph no. 16, 1988)
TzM	*Texte zum Manichäismus*, ed. A. Adam (Berlin: de Gruyter, 1954)
TTH	Translated Texts for Historians (Liverpool: Liverpool University Press)
VC	*Vigiliae Christianae*
Wilcken	L. Mitteis and U. Wilcken, *Grundzüge und Chrestomathie der Papyruskunde* (Leipzig and Berlin: Teubner, 1912), vol. 1/2 (by U. Wilcken)
ZPE	*Zeitschrift für Papyrologie und Epigraphik*

LIST OF EMPERORS

This list presents the dates of emperors referred to in this volume from the early third to the early seventh century. The frequent over-lapping of dates is due to the common late Roman practice of having co-emperors.

Septimius Severus 193–211
Caracalla 198–217
Elagabalus 218–22
Severus Alexander 222–35
Gordian III 238–44
Decius 249–51
Valerian 253–60
Gallienus 253–68
Aurelian 270–5
Diocletian 284–305
Maximian 286–305
Constantius I 305–6
Galerius 305–11
Maxentius 306–12
Constantine 306–37
Maximinus Daia 308–13
Licinius 308–24
Constans 337–50
Constantius II 337–61
Julian 361–3
Jovian 363–4
Valentinian I 364–75
Valens 364–78
Gratian 375–83
Valentinian II 375–92

Theodosius I 379–95
Arcadius 395–408
Honorius 395–423
Constantius III 421
Theodosius II 408–50
Valentinian III 425–55
Leo 457–74
Zeno 474–91
Anastasius 491–518
Justin I 518–27
Justinian 527–65
Justin II 565–78
Tiberius II 578–82
Maurice 582–602
Heraclius 610–41

GLOSSARY

apa (lit. 'father') Coptic term of respect for bishops and clergy.

Arians Supporters of the views of the early fourth-century Egyptian clergyman Arius, condemned as heterodox at the Council of Nicaea (325), who taught that Christ the Son was inferior to the Father.

aroura (pl. *arourai*) Standard unit of area in Roman Egypt, equivalent to 0.68 acres or 0.275 hectares.

Augustus (pl. Augusti) Originally the name of the first Roman emperor (31 BC–AD 14), the term became a generic one for Roman emperors.

Coptic Late Roman version of the indigenous Egyptian language.

denarius (pl. denarii) Roman silver coin in common use in earlier centuries that fell into disuse in Late Antiquity.

Donatists Major breakaway group of Christians in fourth-century north Africa who regarded the mainstream church as tainted by compromise during the Diocletianic persecution.

drachma Greek silver coin (originally worth 6 obols) that remained in use in Roman Egypt.

epigraphic Relating to inscriptions.

freedman A former slave set free by the owner.

Monophysites Eastern Christians (especially in Egypt) opposed to the Council of Chalcedon (451) whose formulations they viewed as giving too much weight to Christ's humanity at the expense of his divinity.

praetorian prefect In earlier centuries, the praetorian prefect commanded elite units of troops based in and around Rome (the Praetorian Guard), but in Late Antiquity the office designated the most senior position in the bureaucracy, with oversight of taxation and justice; there were usually a number of praetorian prefects at any one time, responsible for different regions of the empire.

presbyter (lit. 'elder') One of the terms used in New Testament times for those in positions of church leadership, it gradually came to be distinguished from and subordinate to that of 'overseer' (*episkopos*). Although the English term 'priest' derives etymologically from 'presbyter', the latter term has been retained in this volume to avoid confusion with pagan terminology.

solidus (pl. solidi) Standard gold coin introduced by Diocletian and Constantine; the latter fixed it at a rate of 72 solidi to a pound of gold.

Syriac A dialect of the Semitic language Aramaic widely used in late Roman Syria and Mesopotamia in both spoken and written form.

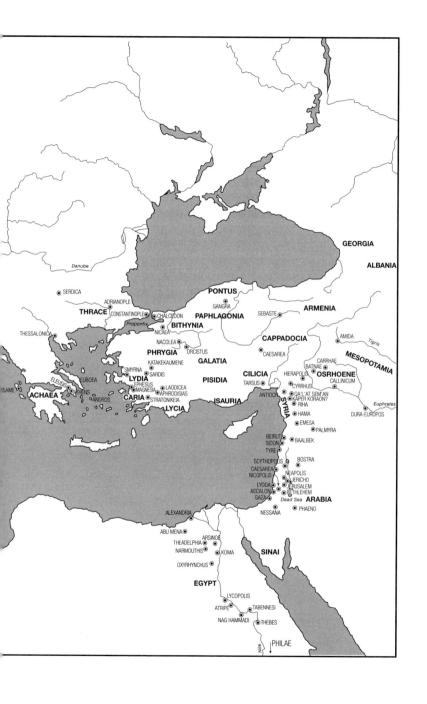

GEORGIA

ALBANIA

SERDICA

Danube

THRACE
ADRIANOPLE
CONSTANTINOPLE
Propontis

PONTUS
GANGRA

PAPHLAGONIA

ARMENIA

SEBASTE

AMIDA

Tigris

CHALCEDON

NICAEA

BITHYNIA

THESSALONICA

NACOLEA

PHRYGIA
ORCISTUS

KATAKEKAUMENE

CAPPADOCIA

CAESAREA

MESOPOTAMIA

SMYRNA
SARDIS

GALATIA

CILICIA

CARRHAE
BATNAE

OSRHOENE

HIERAPOLIS

CALLINICUM

EUBOEA

LYDIA
EPHESUS
MAGNESIA

PISIDIA

TARSUS

CYRRHUS

SAME

ELEUSIS
ATHENS

LAODICEA
APHRODISIAS

ANTIOCH

Euphrates

ACHAEA
ANDROS

CARIA
STRATONIKEIA

ISAURIA

QA'L'AT SEM'AN
KAPER KORAON?
RIHA

DURA-EUROPOS

LYCIA

HAMA

EMESA
PALMYRA

BEIRUT
SIDON
TYRE

BAALBEK

SCYTHOPOLIS

BOSTRA

CAESAREA
NICOPOLIS

NEAPOLIS
JERICHO
JERUSALEM
BETHLEHEM

SYRIA

ALEXANDRIA

LYDDA
ASCALON
GAZA

Dead Sea

ARABIA

NESSANA

PHAENO

ABU MENA

ARSINOE
THEADELPHIA
NARMOUTHIS
KOMA

SINAI

OXYRHYNCHUS

EGYPT

LYCOPOLIS

ATRIPE
NAG HAMMADI

TABENNESI
THEBES

Nile

PHILAE

INTRODUCTION

Late Antiquity: an overview

The major religious changes which took place during Late Antiquity cannot be understood without some appreciation of their broader historical context. Late Antiquity is defined here as the period from the early third century to the late sixth century (all dates in this volume are AD unless otherwise indicated), and these centuries witnessed many other significant changes in the Roman world. At the risk of oversimplifying and overschematising, this opening section of the Introduction aims to provide a succinct overview of the most important of these developments.

(a) Third-century problems

Compared with the second century, the third century was a period of considerable instability for the Roman world – militarily, economically, and politically. Militarily, the Roman empire faced greatly increased threats from both the east and the north. In the east, the Parthian regime was overthrown in the 220s by a Persian noble family who founded the Sasanian dynasty, began a centralising approach to government, and pursued a more aggressive foreign policy, invading Roman territory twice in the 250s and on the second occasion capturing the Roman emperor himself (Valerian). To the north (and at least partly as a result of their interaction with the Roman empire), the fragmented tribes of earlier centuries began coalescing into larger confederations against which Roman defences frequently proved ineffective.

The inevitable demand for larger armies to meet these threats prompted successive emperors to devalue Roman coinage to the extent that by the middle of the century it was almost worthless

1

and inflation was rampant. Soldiers and government officials were increasingly paid in kind, while these military and economic pressures together contributed to a high degree of political instability, with emperors holding office for an average of only two to three years, before either being killed in battle against foreign invaders or removed by dissatisfied troops. During the 260s and early 270s, there was a real risk of the empire fragmenting permanently as many western provinces broke away to form the so-called Gallic Empire, while many eastern provinces fell under the control of the Syrian city of Palmyra, whose leadership had emerged to fill the vacuum created by the capture of Valerian in 260.

(b) A new kind of emperor, a new style of rule

That the empire did not fragment permanently was largely due to efforts of a succession of emperors in the 270s who gradually re-established some stability and reunited the empire. But these men were rather different from the emperors of previous centuries. Until 235, emperors had almost always been drawn from the senatorial aristocracy, but the pressures of the mid-third century demanded leaders who were above all militarily competent – which opened the way for the advancement of men of much lower social rank who had spent their lives in the army. Since the army recruited particularly heavily from the Balkans, it is hardly surprising that many emperors in the second half of the third century came from this region. It is interesting to speculate whether this important change was a necessary precondition for the emergence of a figure like Constantine, who was open to the possibility of abandoning Rome's traditional religious cults; it is hard to imagine an emperor of the old senatorial variety exhibiting the same degree of flexibility.

This new kind of emperor also exercised a different style of rule. Circumstances necessitated their proximity to the frontiers, and so a number of provincial cities – Trier, Milan, Serdica, Antioch, and others – emerged as imperial bases, while, strange though it may seem, the city of Rome became almost an irrelevance. Certainly, it was now a rarity for emperors to visit the traditional capital, let alone live there. The culmination of this trend was to be Constantine's foundation of the new Rome on the better strategically located Bosporus – Constantinople.

(c) *Diocletian and the Tetrarchy*

The key figure in the re-establishment of stability was the emperor Diocletian (284–305), a man of humble origins in the Balkans who, unlike most of his recent predecessors, was to die peacefully in his bed. Diocletian took on board many of the lessons of recent decades. Above all, he appreciated that the empire's problems were too great to be dealt with by one man, so he shared power with three others in an arrangement referred to as the Tetrarchy ('rule by four'); with each emperor responsible for a different region, this amounted in a sense to a formalisation of the empire's fragmented state in the 260s.

Diocletian initiated changes in many areas, such as the empire's tax system, and when he abdicated in 305, he hoped that his power-sharing arrangements would ensure ongoing stability. This proved not to be the case, at least in the short term, as various ambitious individuals fell to competing with one another for imperial power.

(d) *The consequences of Constantine*

One of these was Constantine, the son of one of Diocletian's co-emperors. His famous defeat of another contender, Maxentius, near the Milvian Bridge at Rome in 312 convinced him of the power of the god of the Christians, as well as giving him effective control of the western half of the empire. Initially he enjoyed good relations with Licinius who ruled the eastern half, but eventually, Constantine initiated military action to gain control of the eastern provinces (324), so that the empire once more had a single ruler. The establishment of Constantinople followed soon after, reflecting a fundamental shift in the empire's strategic centre of gravity whose long-term culmination was to be the survival of the eastern half of the empire when the west succumbed in the fifth century.

Constantine's sons continued his policy of support for the church, but upon becoming emperor in 361 his nephew Julian announced that he was a closet pagan and set about trying to undo many of the changes Constantine had initiated. His early death in 363 while campaigning in Persia makes it difficult to predict whether this experiment would have been successful or not. He was the last pagan emperor, but his immediate successors did not implement an anti-pagan backlash, preoccupied as they were with other pressing problems, notably from the Goths on the lower Danube frontier.

(e) The impact of the Goths

The Goths had moved into the lower Danube basin during the third century, but under pressure from nomadic Huns to the north-east, they sought, and were granted, official permission to settle in the empire in 376, at least partly because they were seen as a potential source of recruits for the Roman army – a common practice in this period which had resulted in many Roman generals bearing very unRoman-sounding names. Once inside the empire, however, the Goths mounted an armed rising in Thrace after mistreatment by local officials, culminating in their inflicting a crushing defeat on a Roman army at Adrianople in 378, during which the emperor responsible for the eastern half of the empire, Valens, was killed.

His successor, Theodosius I (379–95), was forced by circumstances to reach an accommodation with the Goths which gave them land in the Balkans in return for their providing units for the Roman army. It was also during Theodosius' reign that more stringent measures were taken against pagan practices. His death proved to be of considerable significance for a number of reasons. He was to be the last emperor to rule the whole empire, east and west, and he was to be the last emperor until the early seventh century regularly to lead the army in person – partly because the deaths in battle of Julian and Valens had emphasised the risks involved, and partly because many of his immediate successors were too young to assume military responsibilities. In the west, this last factor opened the way for military commanders of Germanic origin to exercise political power during the fifth century, often to the detriment of the empire's interests.

(f) Dissolution in the west, survival in the east

On the death of Theodosius I in 395, the Goths settled in the Balkans rose in revolt under the leadership of Alaric in an attempt to extract further concessions from the eastern government, but thwarted in their efforts, they headed west around the turn of the century and invaded Italy, eventually sacking the city of Rome in 410 – an event of more symbolic than practical significance – before establishing themselves in southern Gaul. Of greater long-term significance for the west was the crossing of the Rhine in 406 by various Germanic groups. One of these, the Vandals, made their way through Gaul and Spain before crossing the Straits of Gibraltar into north Africa in 429 and capturing Carthage in 439. This was a fatal blow because the Vandal occupation of north Africa deprived the western empire of the substantial revenues of its wealthiest region, and attempts to recapture it during the fifth century failed. A dwindling tax base and the interference of army commanders weakened imperial authority in the west until, in 476, one general, Odoacer, deposed the emperor and instead of replacing him with another puppet, ruled as self-proclaimed king of Italy. Meanwhile, the Franks occupied Gaul, the Goths moved into Spain, and so the western half of the empire was transformed into a collage of Germanic kingdoms.

The eastern government was more successful in resisting this trend towards military dominance, though it, too, faced severe problems, notably at the hands of Attila the Hun who, during the 440s, built up a substantial empire of his own in the lower Danube basin. Attila's unexpected death in 453 delivered the east from one problem but also created another: his Hunnic empire rapidly disintegrated as subject peoples rose in revolt, including another substantial group of Goths. They then invaded the Balkans where they caused considerable instability for three decades until their leader Theoderic was induced by Constantinople to invade Italy. Theoderic duly defeated Odoacer and established the so-called Ostrogothic kingdom of Italy. Meanwhile the eastern equivalent of north Africa from the point of view of revenue – Egypt – was never under any threat, and sound financial management by the emperor Anastasius (491–518) left the eastern empire in a stronger position than had been the case for a century.

(g) *The consequences of Justinian*

Anastasius was childless, and the unexpected beneficiary from the manoeuvring for power that followed his death was a Balkan peasant named Justin who had made good as commander of the palace guard. The real winner, however, was to be Justin's ambitious nephew Justinian (527–65), who succeeded his uncle and quickly set about implementing various grandiose plans. His codification of Roman law proved to be of enduring importance for European history, but his attempt to reconquer the west was only a qualified success. His forces achieved a quick victory against the Vandals (533–4), but the next phase, against Ostrogothic Italy, turned into a lengthy war of attrition (535–54), which drained imperial resources – a problem compounded by renewed warfare with Sasanian Persia in the 540s and a devastating outbreak of bubonic plague in 542.

Moreover, Justinian's attempts to resolve the major theological controversies of his day also ended in failure. He certainly has a claim to be considered the last great Roman emperor of antiquity, but in terms of the empire's prospects, his legacy was on balance a negative one.

For the most part, Justinian's successors did a reasonable job of sustaining the empire's position in the face of a variety of problems, but a number of internal revolts in the first decade of the seventh century gave Persia the opportunity to make major territorial gains and even threaten Constantinople itself. The emperor Heraclius (610–41) eventually defeated the Persians, only to see his hard-won achievements largely undone at the hands of Arab armies marching under the banner of Islam in the 630s. The Roman empire was in fact to endure for another 800 years (although textbooks usually refer to it as the Byzantine empire), but the advent of Islam changed the parameters of life in the Mediterranean world so dramatically that there is good reason to regard it as signalling the end of (Late) Antiquity.

The sources: types, languages, and dating

(a) Types

This volume includes a wide range of types of evidence, both textual and material, and the textual evidence includes some types which may be less familiar. It is traditional to draw a distinction between 'literary' and 'documentary' texts. Literary texts most obviously include items such as poems and plays, but in antiquity also comprised genres such as histories, philosophical treatises, and letters, which usually had definite literary pretensions. In Late Antiquity there was, in addition, a profusion of Christian literature including apologetic works, theological treatises, sermons and the like, often written by highly educated men who were also conscious of the stylistic conventions of classical literature. Although the literary qualities of some of these items may have been inferior to classical standards, they are nevertheless grouped here in the literary category.

Documentary evidence, by contrast, comprises texts with a more obviously utilitarian purpose, typically recorded especially on metal or stone (inscriptions) or on papyrus. Inscriptions as a category includes records of imperial legal pronouncements (e.g., 4.9), epitaphs which sometimes include details of an individual's life and career (e.g., **5.2, 6.3, 12.1**), dedications to a deity (e.g., **1.8, 1.9**), dedications honouring an emperor (e.g., **4.3, 5.7**), commemorations of building work (e.g., **1.14, 12.7**), and curses written on lead tablets (**1.11, 6.13**). Stone is the more durable material (though still subject to chipping and other damage), since the inherent value of metal meant it was liable to be melted down in antiquity. (For further discussion of inscriptions as evidence for the ancient world, see Millar 1983; Keppie 1991.)

Literary works were certainly written on papyrus in antiquity (and many examples survive), but papyrus was also used for many more mundane purposes arising from government administration, the legal process, and private correspondence, reflecting the fact that papyrus was effectively the paper of the ancient Graeco-Roman world. Produced from the stalk of the papyrus reed – which was especially prolific in Egypt – papyrus was used throughout the Mediterranean, but being very vulnerable to damp conditions, it has survived almost exclusively in Egypt, where dry desert sands have preserved vast quantities. Papyrus documentation therefore tends to illustrate circumstances in Egypt, though small quantities have survived from other parts of the Roman empire (**15.5, 16.4**). (For further discussion of papyri as evidence for the ancient world, see Pestman 1994; Bagnall 1995.)

Besides literary and documentary sources, a third category of textual evidence must be distinguished – legal texts. In Late Antiquity, this means primarily the two great legal codes produced in the fifth and sixth centuries at the behest of the emperors Theodosius II and Justinian (though the pronouncements of church councils might also legitimately be included in this category). The *Theodosian Code* was produced in the 430s and was a compilation of imperial laws from the early fourth century onwards, grouped by subject. The *Justinianic Code* was a revision of the *Theodosian Code* that extended it down to the early 530s when it was put together. An important feature of these *Codes* is that their compilers aimed to encapsulate the essentials of each law – which meant they edited out much of their content, including preambles and epilogues. The loss of these is unfortunate since they would have provided important contextual data about the problem to which the law was a response. This is known because a small group of laws included in the *Theodosian Code* also survived separately in their full versions as a collection known as the *Sirmondian Constitutions*, of which there is one example in this volume (**12.5**). Moreover, after the publication of the *Justinianic Code*, Justinian and his successors continued to issue laws known, rather confusingly, as *Novels* (literally 'new laws'); these were subsequently gathered together and preserved in their full versions (e.g., **8.15**, **13.8**). One general feature of late Roman imperial laws warrants a word of warning: the style of expression is usually very rhetorical, prolix, and often bombastic, and the lawyers who drafted these pronouncements for the emperor had a fondness for honorific modes of address which strike the modern reader as stilted (e.g., 'Our Clemency' [used of the emperor], 'Your Wisdom' [used of the official to whom the law is directed]).

(b) Languages

The majority of the passages in this volume were originally written in either Greek or Latin – the former being the predominant language in the eastern Mediterranean, the latter that in the west. However, the linguistic profile of the Roman empire in Late Antiquity was more diverse than this. Indigenous languages continued to be used in a number of parts of the empire (for north Africa cf. **12.3**), and under the stimulus of Christianity two of these produced significant literatures in their own right – Syriac and Coptic.

Syriac was a dialect of the Semitic language Aramaic and became widely used by Christian clergy and writers in Syria and Mesopotamia (e.g., **7.9**). Perhaps equally important is the fact that many works in Greek that no longer survive were translated into Syriac and do survive in that version (e.g., **7.1**, **16.2**).

Coptic is the final stage in the development of the ancient Egyptian language and was distinguished by its use of the Greek alphabet supplemented by seven signs derived from the indigenous script; grammar and syntax, however, were predominantly Egyptian. The emergence of Coptic in the third century is closely linked with the growth of Christianity in Egypt, and much of the surviving literature is Christian (cf. **7.4**, **11.2**, **15.8** – Bohairic is a Coptic dialect), though there is also Gnostic and Manichaean material (e.g., **2.8**, **10.2**).

On the linguistic situation in Late Antiquity generally, see Mango 1980: ch. 1; for further discussion of Syriac, see Brock 1994, 1998; for Coptic, see Bagnall 1993: 235–40, 251–5; and Smith 1998.

(c) Dating

Where a literary text can be attributed to a named author, it is usually possible to assign at least an approximate chronological context for the text on the basis of what else is known about that author and/or internal references to events or people within the work in question. Where a literary text is anonymous, subject matter, linguistic features, and the history of the text itself can all help to arrive at an approximate dating. When it comes to dating documentary texts – inscriptions and papyri – it is sometimes necessary to rely on subject matter and linguistic features, though they have an additional advantage: because the actual original text is available, the shapes of the letters carved in the stone or written on the papyrus can be studied and can provide valuable clues about the century or part of a century in which the text was produced.

But documentary texts can sometimes be dated very precisely because they often include dating formulae as part of the text itself (legal texts generally include this sort of information as well). In the translations in this volume, these dating formulae have been given in both their ancient format and their modern equivalent. The ancient format has been retained deliberately, as one small way of reminding readers of the 'otherness' of the ancient world, the sense of which can be lost when reading translations. It is therefore appropriate to say a few words about these formulae.

The most common way of specifying a year in the Roman world was to give the names of the consuls for that year, a practice which continued in Late Antiquity and features in many of the passages in this volume. However, the emperor Diocletian introduced another system as well. His new tax system operated on a fifteen-year cycle known as the indiction, and an alternative method for specifying a year was to say 'in the 4th year of the indiction' and the like – but this is not nearly so helpful to modern scholars since it is by no means always clear which indiction is being referred to.

As for dates within a year, the Roman system was based around three fixed points during each month and involved specifying the date by how many days it fell before one of those fixed points. Those fixed points were the Kalends (the 1st of the month), the Nones (the 5th day, except in March, May, July and October when it fell on the 7th day), and the Ides (the 13th day, except in March, May, July and October when it fell on the 15th day). The other important feature of this system was that the Romans counted inclusively. Egypt, however, retained a different system with indigenous names for the months and a simple statement of the number of the day within that month, and this often features on papyri (for full details, see Pestman 1994).

Pagans or polytheists?

In recent years, use of the term 'pagan' has become an issue in the study of Late Antiquity, with some scholars arguing that it is an inappropriate designation for the cults and religious practices of the Graeco-Roman world, which were affiliated to neither Christianity nor Judaism (e.g., Cameron 1991: 121–2; Fowden 1991: 119). There are two particular arguments against using the term 'pagan'. First, if 'paganism was not so much a religion as a loosely-knit amalgam of cults, myths and philosophical beliefs of varying origins and even more varying levels of culture' (Jones 1964: 940), then use of the word as a catch-all term runs the risk of conveying a misleading impression of paganism as a monolithic religious entity. Second, it was a term used in Late Antiquity by Christians about their opponents. There is debate as to the connotations of the term, for the Latin word *paganus* can mean both a rural dweller and a civilian, and both senses have a certain logic from a Christian perspective: on the one hand, Christianity was above all an urban religion and its slower progress in rural areas must have reinforced the idea that paganism was especially strong in the countryside; on the other hand, since Christians saw themselves as soldiers of Christ, it would be natural to define non-Christians as non-combatants or civilians (for discussion, see O'Donnell 1977; Chuvin 1990: ch. 1). Either way, however, the fact remains that it is an 'opposition label' and there has been understandable concern that using it risks colluding with the way in which one side chose to represent the other.

The main alternative that has been proposed is 'polytheist', which would seem to meet both of the concerns mentioned above. However, arguments have also been forthcoming against the suitability of this term – e.g., that some philosophically oriented pagans were essentially monotheistic, that 'by the fourth century the challenge of Christianity had long since forced those who observed the cults of the gods into explicit philosophical reflection on their system of belief and practice – which we therefore may appropriately call paganism' (Millar 1992: 105; cf. Barnes 1994a: ix–xi). As will already be evident from its title, this volume has retained the traditional designation – because no alternative is without its own problems, and for ease of recognition – but does so in the (perhaps naive) hope that by drawing attention to the issue at this early stage, readers will be more alert to the term's problematic status. In addition, individual passages usually include details of the word in the original language being translated as 'pagan' or 'paganism'.

Further reading and useful reference works

Each of the chapters in this volume begins with an overall introduction that includes suggestions for further reading, and nearly all the passages that follow are also accompanied by suggestions for further reading relating to that specific aspect. These are usually books or articles in English, but occasionally works in other European languages have been included. There are, however, also a number of more general books and reference works which offer convenient ways to pursue topics and answer further questions.

For a succinct but authoritative overview of Late Antiquity, it is hard to beat the final third of Tim Cornell and John Matthews, *Atlas of the Roman World* (1981) which includes much more than just maps and is beautifully illustrated. Fuller introductions to Late Antiquity include Peter Brown, *The World of Late Antiquity* (London: Thames and Hudson, 1971) (which is also well illustrated) and Averil Cameron's twin volumes *The Later Roman Empire, AD 284–430* (London: Fontana, 1993) and *The Mediterranean World in Late Antiquity, AD 395–600* (London: Routledge, 1993). The early chapters of Peter Brown, *The Rise of Western Christendom* (Oxford: Blackwell, 1996) focus on Late Antiquity and, despite the title, include coverage of the eastern Mediterranean, as does the first half of Roger Collins's, *Early Medieval Europe, 300–1000* (London: Macmillan, 1991) and the first part of Judith Herrin, *The Formation of Christendom* (London: Fontana, 1987). Introductions to the early history of Christianity are also relevant. Henry Chadwick, *The Early Church* (Harmondsworth: Penguin, 1967) remains the best concise overview, while W.H.C. Frend, *The Rise of Christianity* (London: Darton, Longman and Todd, 1984) offers a rather more detailed survey.

Good dictionaries on church history are also available: F.L. Cross and E.A. Livingstone (eds), *The Oxford Dictionary of the Christian Church* (3rd edn, Oxford: Oxford University Press, 1997), A. di Berardino (ed.), *Encyclopedia of the Early Church* (Cambridge: James Clarke, 1992), and E. Ferguson (ed.), *Encyclopedia of Early Christianity* (New York: Garland, 1990). S. Hornblower and A. Spawforth (eds), *The Oxford Classical Dictionary* (3rd edn, Oxford: Oxford University Press, 1996) and A. Kazhdan (ed.), *The Oxford Dictionary of Byzantine* (Oxford: Oxford University Press, 1991) include many entries relating to Late Antiquity, while G.W.

Bowersock, Peter Brown and Oleg Grabar (eds), *Late Antiquity: A Guide to the Postclassical World* (Cambridge, Mass: Harvard University Press, 1999) combines essays on major themes with dictionary articles on key personalities and subjects. For those wishing to pursue the biographies of (some) individuals in exhaustive detail, there is A.H.M. Jones, J. Martindale and J. Morris (eds), *The Prosopography of the Late Roman Empire* (Cambridge: Cambridge University Press, 1971–92), though it explicitly excludes Christian bishops and clergy, who are being covered in a French project *Prosopographie chrétienne* (which to date has produced the volumes covering north Africa and Italy). Mention should also be made of A.H.M. Jones, *The Later Roman Empire 284–602: An Economic, Social and Administrative Survey* (Oxford: Blackwell, 1964) which, with the aid of its very good index, remains a superb reference work on many aspects of the late Roman world. The new edition of the *Cambridge Ancient History* includes full coverage of Late Antiquity: vol. 13 on the fourth and early fifth century has already appeared (Cambridge: Cambridge University Press, 1998), vol. 14 on the period to the end of the sixth century is due to appear in 2000, and vol. 12 on the third century and Constantine will follow in due course. Regular perusal of the reviews sections of periodicals such as the *Journal of Early Christian Studies*, *Journal of Theological Studies*, and *Journal of Ecclesiastical History* is a good way to keep up-to-date with the most recent work in this field.

Part I

PAGANS AND CHRISTIANS THROUGH TIME

1

PAGANS IN THE THIRD CENTURY

The aim of this chapter is to sketch some of the salient features of pagan religious life during the third century and to convey some sense of its diversity. It begins with a calendar of festivals (1.1) which, among other things, shows how religion impinged on people's lives throughout the year. This is followed by illustrative examples of important practices associated with civic cults – sacrifice (1.2) and alternatives (1.3, 1.4), the role of music (1.5, 1.6), and processions (1.7). More private expressions of devotion are exemplified by some texts relating to the goddess Isis (1.8), while the next two items highlight common motivations for individuals having recourse to the gods – ill-health (1.9) and anxieties about the future (1.10). A different type of common religious engagement is reflected in the evidence for resort to magic, exemplified here by a curse tablet (1.11). Part of a temple inventory is presented in 1.12 to show how these institutions came to acquire considerable material resources. At the same time, it is worth remembering that there was a philosophical tradition critical of some aspects of pagan religious observance, especially sacrifice, as shown in 1.13.

All these items are drawn from the third century (or occasionally the late second century), but all could be paralleled by examples from earlier centuries. The remaining items in the chapter focus on matters more specific to the third century. First, some texts are presented relating to the mystery cult of Mithras (1.14) which, though already growing in importance in the second century, particularly flourished in the third. Second, an inscription relating to the emperor Decius (249–51) is discussed (1.15), since his brief reign was marked by a concerted attempt to unite the empire in traditional religious observances. Third, some texts relating to the cult of the Sun are included (1.16) – a cult that came to prominence in the 270s and has sometimes been seen as a significant precursor of Christianity's official acceptance.

Finally, mention should be made of an overarching issue for third-century paganism, namely its vitality or otherwise. The significant decline of epigraphic evidence from the middle decades of the third century was seen by scholars in the first half of the twentieth century as reflecting a decline in people's faith in the old gods under the impact of inflation and foreign invasion on unprecedented scales (e.g., Geffcken 1978 [originally written in 1920]). More recent studies have seen a shift away from such views to an emphasis on the continuing vigour of third-century paganism in the face of testing times (MacMullen 1981: 126–30; Lane Fox 1986: 572–85). This is a contentious issue, certainly not easy to illustrate, let alone settle, in a necessarily selective anthology such as this, but it is an important question to bear in mind in relation to both the material in this chapter and that in Chapter 3 (on the late third and early fourth centuries). For further reading on (late) Roman paganism in general, see Geffcken 1978; MacMullen 1981; Lane Fox 1986: chs 2–5; Beard *et al.* 1998: vol. 1.

1.1 A religious calendar: *P. Dura* 54 (Cols 1–2)

The well-known document from which this passage comes was part of a cache of papyri found at the Roman frontier fortress of Dura-Europos on the Euphrates, and sets out the calendar of religious rites observed by the military unit stationed there in the mid-220s. Despite Dura's peripheral location, it is generally accepted that this document was not specific to this particular unit, but rather was 'a standard festival list for the army, simply one representative of a type issued to every camp and garrison' (Fink *et al.* 1940: 28; cf. Fishwick 1988). As such, despite being damaged and therefore incomplete, it provides invaluable insights into important features of Roman religious practices during the early centuries AD, notably reverence for the traditional deities of Rome, the role of regular sacrifice, the emphasis on the imperial cult, and the prominence of 'supplication' – the offering of incense and wine to a deity (on which see Fink *et al.* 1940: 193–202 and 1.4). The document dates from the reign of the emperor Severus Alexander (222–35), which is why so many of the celebrations relate to key events in his own life or the lives of earlier members, male and female, of the Severan dynasty. Even earlier emperors (denoted by the term 'deified') going back to Claudius are also included to emphasise continuity and help legitimate his rule – especially important *vis-à-vis* the army. Moreover, since the Roman army had increasingly come to be recruited from outside the Italian peninsula, the calendar also serves to illustrate how large numbers of provincials became familiar with aspects of traditional Roman religious observances. Further reading: Fink *et al.* 1940; Welles *et al.* 1959: 191–212.

[Column 1]

\<On the Kalends of January [1 **January**] ... \>

\<On the 3rd day before the Nones of January [3 **January**], because\> vows are \<discharged and pronounced\> both for the well-being \<of our Lord Marcus Aurelius Severus Alexander Augustus and for the\> perpetual continuance of the empire of the Roman people: \<to Jupiter the Best and Greatest an ox, to Queen Juno a cow, to Minerva a cow, to Jupiter the Victor\> an ox, ... \<to Mars the Father a bull, to Mars the Victor\> a bull; to Victory a cow. ...

\<On the 7th day before the Ides\> of January [7 **January**], \<because honourable discharge with enjoyment of\> privileges is given to those who have completed their service and \<pay\> is counted out \<to the soldiers: to Jupiter the Best and Greatest an ox, to Juno a cow, to Minerva\> a cow, to Well-being (*Salus*) a cow, to Mars the Father a bull. ...

On the 6th day before \<the Ides\> of January [8 **January**], for the birthday of the \<deified, ... for the deified ... \> a supplication.

\<On the ... day before the ... \> of January [9/23 **January**], for the birthday of \<Lucius ... Caesar ... \>: ... of Lucius ... Caesar. ...

On the 9th day before \<the Kalends\> of February [24 **January**], for the birthday of \<the deified Hadrian: to the deified Hadrian, an ox\>.

On the 5th day before the Kalends of February [28 **January**], for the \<Arabian, Adiabenic, and very great Parthian\> victories of the deified Severus and for \<the accession of the deified Trajan: to Victory\> over Parthia a cow, \<to the deified Trajan an ox\>.

On the day before the Nones of February [4 **February**], for \<the accession of the deified Antoninus the Great [Caracalla]\>, a supplication: to the deified Antoninus the Great, an ox.

On the Kalends of March [1 **March**], for the \<birthday observances of Mars the Father and Victor: to Mars\> the Father and Victor, a bull.

On the day before the Nones of March [6 **March**], for the accession \<of the deified Marcus Antoninus and the deified Lucius Verus\>: to the deified Marcus, an ox; \<to the deified Lucius\>, an ox.

On the 3rd day before the Ides of March [13 **March**], because the emperor \<Caesar Marcus Aurelius Severus Alexander\> was acclaimed emperor: to Jupiter an ox, \<to Juno a cow, to Minerva a cow, ... \> to Mars an ox; and because Alexander our

17

Augustus was <first> hailed as victorious general (*imperator*) by the soldiers of our lord Augustus <the emperor Marcus Aurelius Severus Alexander>: a supplication. ...

<On the day before> the Ides of <March> [14 **March**], because Alexander our <Augustus> was <acclaimed Augustus, Father of his Country, and> Chief Priest (*pontifex maximus*), a supplication: <to the guardian spirit (*genius*) of our lord> Alexander Augustus a bull. ...

[Column 2]

On the 14th day before the Kalends of April [19 **March**], for the day of the Quinquatria [in honour of Minerva], a supplication: until the 10th day before the Kalends of April [23 **March**], the same a supplication.

On the day before the Nones of April [4 **April**], for the birthday of the deified Antoninus the Great: to the deified Antoninus an ox.

On the 5th day before the Ides of April [9 **April**], for the accession of the deified Pius Severus: to the deified Pius Severus an ox.

On the 3rd day before the Ides of April [11 **April**], for the birthday of the deified Pius Severus: to the deified Pius Severus an ox.

On the 11th day before the Kalends of May [21 **April**], for the birthday of the eternal City of Rome: <to the eternal City of Rome an ox>.

On the 6th day before the Kalends of May [26 **April**], for the birthday of the deified Marcus Antoninus: <to the deified Marcus> Antoninus <an ox>.

On the Nones of May [7 **May**], for the birthday of the deified Julia Maesa: to the <deified> Maesa a supplication.

On the 6th day before the Ides of May [10 **May**], for the Rose Festival of the legionary standards, a supplication.

On the 4th day before the Ides of May [12 **May**], for the games in honour of Mars: to Mars the Father and Avenger a bull.

On the 12th day before the Kalends of June [21 **May**], because the deified Severus was hailed as victorious general (*imperator*) ... : to the deified Pius Severus. ...

On the 9th day before the Kalends of June [24 **May**], for the birthday of Germanicus Caesar, a supplication in memory of Germanicus Caesar.

On the day before the Kalends of June [31 **May**], for the Rose Festival of the legionary standards, a supplication.

On the 5th day before the Ides of June [9 **June**], for the festival in honour of Vesta: to Mother Vesta a supplication.

On the 6th day before the Kalends of July [26 **June**], because our lord Marcus Aurelius Severus Alexander was acclaimed Caesar and assumed the adult toga: to the guardian spirit (*genius*) of Alexander Augustus a bull.

On the Kalends of July [1 **July**], because Alexander our Augustus was appointed consul for the first time, a supplication.

<On the 3rd day> before the Nones of July [4 **July**], for the birthday of the deified Matidia: to the deified Matidia a supplication.

<On the 6th day before the Ides> of July [10 **July**], for the accession of the deified Antoninus Pius: to the deified Antoninus an ox.

<On the 4th day before the Ides> of July [12 **July**], for the birthday of the deified Julius: to the deified Julius an ox.

<On the 10th day before the Kalends> of August [23 **July**], for the day of the festival in honour of Neptune, a supplication and a sacrifice.

<On the Kalends of August [1 **August**], for> the birthday of the deified Claudius and the deified Pertinax: to the deified Claudius an ox, <to the deified Pertinax> an ox.

<On the Nones of August [5 **August**]>, for <the games> in honour of Well-being: to Well-being a cow.

<On the ... day before the Kalends> of September [14/29 **August**], for the birthday of Mamaea <Augusta>, mother of our Augustus: to the guardian spirit (*Juno*) of Mamaea Augusta <a cow ... >

<On the ... day before the Kalends> of September [15/30 **August**], for the birthday of the deified Marciana: to the <deified> Marciana <a supplication>

1.2 Animal sacrifice: relief from the Arch of Septimius Severus, Lepcis Magna, North Africa

This relief (1.72 m high) from the early third century (probably 203) shows an animal in the process of being slaughtered, a ritual of fundamental importance in traditional Roman cult practice (**Figure 1.2**). The relief conflates two moments in the process – one assistant, standing behind the animal, swings a mallet to stun the animal, while a second, kneeling beside the felled animal, plunges a knife into its neck. In this case, the ritual is taking place in the presence of members of the imperial family, for the female figure on the left has been identified as Septimius Severus' wife, Julia Domna, in the process of offering incense from the jar in her

Figure 1.2 Relief from the Arch of Septimius Severus, Lepcis Magna

Source: Photograph by Koppermann, InstNegNo 61.1699, Reproduced by permission of the German Archaeological Institute, Rome.

left hand. Immediately to her left is a flute-player – a reminder of the musical dimension of these rituals. For further discussion of this relief, see Ryberg 1955: 160–2, Gordon 1990: 214–15; for more general discussion of sacrifice in the Roman world, see Lane Fox 1986: 69–72; Beard *et al.* 1998: vol. 1, 350–1, vol. 2, 148–50.

1.3 Substituting for animal sacrifice: *CMRDM* I.50

This inscription comes from the lower half of a marble stele (88 cm high) found in the west Anatolian region of Lydia, where reverence for the moon-god Mēn was particularly prevalent (on the cult of Mēn generally, see Lane 1990). The stele was inscribed in the first half of the third century (the number of years in the dating formula at the end refers to the time elapsed since the region was reconquered from Mithdridates by Sulla in 85 BC), and illustrates the fundamental principle of offering a god something in return for the god's help, though here with an interesting twist. In this case, the female devotee proved unable to fulfil directly her vow to sacrifice a bull, no doubt on grounds of expense, and instead dedicated a marble stele, presumably considered an appropriate substitute because the upper half depicts the god Mēn approached by a bull (for a photograph, see Lane 1971: Plate XXII).

To Mēn Axiottenos. Tatiane, daughter of Erpos, promised a bull as an offering on behalf of her brothers and having been heard [by the god], but being unable to give the bull, she asked the god, and he agreed, to accept this stele. In the year 320, on the 10th day of the month Panemos [2 June 236].

1.4 Offering incense: Fresco from the Temple of Bel, Dura-Europos

The early third-century painting (1.75 x 1 m) of which the accompanying picture (**Figure 1.4**) is a restored drawing was found on one of the walls in the Temple of Bel in the north-west corner of the Roman fortress of Dura-Europos on the Euphrates. It depicts a Roman tribune, named on the painting (in Latin) as Julius Terentius, offering incense on an altar. He is accompanied by soldiers to the right and a standard-bearer to the left, while the man standing behind Terentius is identified in the painting (in Greek) as 'the priest Themes, son of Mokimos'. The female figures with turreted crowns in the lower left-hand corner are named as the guardian deities of Palmyra and of Dura, below whom are personifications of Palmyra's underground springs (female) and of the Euphrates (male) (the military unit stationed at Dura in the third century was recruited from Palmyra). In the upper left-hand corner are three statues which are the object of reverence on the part of Terentius and his men. Traditionally these have been identified as Palmyrene deities, but it has been persuasively argued more recently that they are representations of Roman emperors, probably Pupienus, Balbinus and Gordian III who briefly reigned together in 238 (Pekáry 1986). On this interpretation, the

ΘΕΜΙC
ΜΟΚΙΜΟC
ΙΕΡΕΥC

IVLTERN
TIVSTR

TYXH
ΔΟΥΡΑ

TYXH
ΠΑΛΜΥ
PΩN

Figure 1.4 Sacrifice of Julius Terentius (copy by L. North). Temple of Bel, Dura-Europos

Source: Yale University Art Gallery, Dura-Europos Archive.

picture shows the imperial cult in action, more specifically an act of supplication such as referred to at many points in 1.1. The advantage of this sort of cult offering over animal sacrifice was that it 'was in every man's power, practically whenever and wherever he pleased. Its cheapness and convenience allowed many more to take a personal part in religious observances – which was felt to be particularly desirable in the case of emperor-worship' (Fink *et al.* 1940: 195). (For a colour picture of the original fresco, see Breasted 1922: Plate XLVIII.)

1.5 Arrangements for honouring the gods through music: *I. Strat.* 1101

In addition to animal sacrifice and other offerings, reverence for the gods could be expressed through music (Bremmer 1981). The following inscription, probably dating to the end of the second century (Robert 1937: 521), sets out detailed regulations on this subject with reference to the chief deities of the Carian community of Stratonikeia, in south-western Asia Minor. The deities in question, Hellenised versions of indigenous deities, comprised Hekate, whose temple was situated at Lagina, six miles to the north of Stratonikeia, and Zeus Panamaros, whose sanctuary lay a similar distance to the south-east at Panamara. Although not well known, these cults are epigraphically very well documented – 'indeed, [the cult of Zeus Panamaros] may be known in fuller detail than any other in ancient times save Judaism' (MacMullen 1981: 46). As so often, the priesthoods associated with their cults were one of the ways in which members of the local elite exercised munificence and gained prestige (cf. **3.10**). The 'ephebes' referred to in line 10 and later belonged to the *ephebeia*, the institution found in Greek communities in the eastern Mediterranean through which adolescent males were inducted into the gymnasium and trained in civic values. Further reading: MacMullen 1981: 46–8; Laumonier 1958: 401–3; Robert 1937: 516–23.

When Ptolemaios was chief magistrate (*stephanephoros*, lit. 'wreath-wearer'), in the month of Artemisios [late February/March], with Sosandros, son of Diomedes, secretary to the town council, proposing:

In former times the city has been saved from many great and constant dangers by the providence of its protective and mighty deities, Zeus of Panamara and Hekate, whose sanctuaries were recognised by a decree of the sacred [Roman] Senate as being inviolable and possessing the right to receive suppliants, on account of the manifest miracles which they performed for the safety of the eternal empire of our lords the Romans. It is right to apply all possible zeal to honouring them [Zeus and Hekate] and not to neglect any opportunity to honour (5) and entreat them. Statues of the aforementioned deities stand in the august council-chamber, producing miracles which manifest their divine power. On account of these miracles, the whole populace offers sacrifice, burns incense, prays and gives thanks, without ceasing, to these deities who so manifest themselves, and it is right to honour them also with this religious observance, namely a hymn-singing procession.

The council has decided to select now thirty boys from among the well-born, whom the supervisor of education (*paidonomos*), together with the public guardians of boys (*paidophylakoi*), shall lead each day to the council-chamber, dressed in white, wearing crowns made of olive branches, likewise carrying olive branches in their hands, and, accompanied by a lyre-player and a herald, they shall sing a hymn which (10) the secretary Sosandros, the son of Diomedes, shall compose. If any of the selected boys are admitted to the ephebes, or – may none of the gods bring it about – they die without having been admitted to the ephebes, others are to be selected as soon as possible for the same singing of hymns. The supervisor of education and the public guardians of boys are to make this clear in written form so that the same procedure for succession, and the worship and honouring of the deities, continues for all time (with permission [for absence] to the boys if any of them is unwell or they are prevented by mourning in the family). But if any of these things is not done, the officials and the supervisor of education shall be guilty of impiety (*asebeia*), and the (15) public guardians of boys shall be imprisoned.

Moreover the annually chosen priest of Hekate is to select boys from within the precinct [of the temple] of the goddess and from the neighbourhood every <tenth?> year and they are to sing the customary hymn to the goddess, as happened in former times. [The priest] shall have authority against both the fathers and the boys, if the fathers do not provide them for the hymn-singing and worship or the boys do not attend, to lay a charge of misconduct or another [charge] which he prefers. The priest and the staff-bearing eunuch shall provide the names (20) of the boys in writing through the council, as was also stated earlier for the boys chosen in the town. But if the priest or the eunuch does not do this, they are to be subject to the same penalties as the boys. But any of the boys participating in the hymn-singing who is admitted to the ephebes of the city < ... > a painted image bearing the name of his father. The supervisor of education is to write up (25) the decree in the courtyard of the temple of Serapis, in [the portico] designated for boys, and the priest of the goddess is to set up a stone stele in the temple of the goddess containing the relevant words of the decree. The decree is to be inscribed in the entrance of the council-chamber (30) on the right-hand side so that the deities may continue to be honoured in perpetuity, with the cost of the inscription being defrayed by the officials responsible for the council-chamber.

1.6 An example of a hymn: Ariphron of Sicyon, *Hymn to Hygieia*

The following item is an example of a hymn used in pagan worship, in this case addressed to and honouring the personification of Health (*Hygieia*), usually worshipped alongside the healing god Asklepios – an appropriate example, given that health was a major preoccupation in individuals' relations with the gods (cf. 1.9). Although originally written in the fourth century BC, it is included in this volume because it clearly remained in use in Late Antiquity, since it is preserved in a number of inscriptions from the third century AD and later. In view of the previous passage, it is worth adding that there was an image of Hygieia in the council-chamber at Stratonikeia in the third century (*I. Strat.* 289, lines 10–11). For the emperor Julian's concern with hymns as an integral part of pagan worship in the fourth century, see 5.3b. Further reading: Bremer 1981; Stafford 2000: ch. 5.

Health, most important of the blessed gods for humans, with you
May I dwell for the rest of my life, and may you graciously be with
    me.
For if there is any enjoyment in wealth, or in children,
Or in godlike royal power over men, or in the desires
Which we pursue with the stealthy nets of Aphrodite,
Or if any other delight, or relief from troubles,
Has been made known by the gods to men –
With you, blessed Health,
It is enriched and shines in the words of the Graces:
Without you, no-one is happy.

1.7 Processions: A coin from Magnesia-on-the-Maeander, Asia Minor

An important aspect of some pagan cults was public processions, particularly when sanctuaries lay some distance from the relevant urban centre, as, e.g., was the case with Panamara and Lagina in relation to Stratonikeia (1.5). 'In Greece and Asia Minor, specifically attested, regularly recurrent religious parades number in the hundreds, in some towns taking place several times a year on behalf of different cults' (MacMullen 1981: 28). Such processions often involved the carrying of the cult statue from the sanctuary to the city to the accompaniment of general public rejoicing and festivities (cf. 3.10), as illustrated on the following coin from Magnesia-on-the-Maeander in western Asia Minor (**Figure 1.7**). Issued during the reign of the emperor Gordian III (238–44), whose bust and name feature on the obverse side, the coin's reverse side shows the statue of the god Hephaestus being paraded on a litter by four men. 'It was a great honour to carry sacred objects in a

Figure 1.7   Coin from Magnesia-on-the-Maeander, Asia Minor

Source: Photograph of a cast (original coin in the Bibliothèque nationale, Paris).

civic procession, and, like other great honours, it fell to the most distinguished families' (Lane Fox 1986: 67). The text around the edge of the reverse side indicates that the coin was issued during the year when a certain Antiochus was secretary to the city council.

1.8 Devotion to the goddess Isis: *IGPhilae* 168, 178, 180

One of the most popular deities in the Roman world during the early centuries AD was the goddess Isis, a guarantor of fertility, protection and healing, whose relevance to diverse situations led to her being known as 'Isis of the innumerable names'. Originally Egyptian, her cult spread widely throughout the Mediterranean during the Hellenistic period (Solmsen 1979), but her temple on the island of Philae below the first cataract of the Nile in southern Egypt remained an important cult centre, visited by pilgrims both from within and outside the Roman empire. The following three texts reflect various dimensions of this activity at the end of the second century and during the third century. The first, painted on the Gateway of Hadrian adjacent to the temple of Isis by a group of friends from Alexandria, provides the fullest expression of the religious sentiments which motivated such visits. The second was inscribed on a votive offering in the form of a cone-shaped stone, presented by the wife of a Roman army officer whose unit was stationed nearby at Syene. The third, also painted on the Gateway of Hadrian, is an example of the external interface of the cult, having been left by a member of the ruling family of the Ethiopian kingdom of Meroe, for whom the cult of Isis was also important. (The Abaton referred to here was a cult centre associated with Isis' husband Osiris on the neighbouring island of Bigeh.) For an excellent overview of the history and significance of Philae, see Rutherford 1998; for further discussion of the texts below, including their dating, see Bernand 1969: 11–12, 166–74, 190–7; for the continuing attractions of the cult at Philae during Late Antiquity, and for the eventual conversion of the temple into a church, see 7.6 and 7.7.

(a) IGPhilae 168

He who has worshipped Isis of Philae is fortunate, not only because he becomes wealthy, but because at the same time he enjoys a long life. I, who grew up near Isis of Pharos [in Alexandria] have come here – I am Serenus, assistant to the illustrious Ptolemaios – (5) together with Felix and Apollonios the painter. We have come here, in accordance with the oracles of the invincible lord Apollo, to offer libations and sacrifices, desiring also to share in these, for this was appropriate. You will find nothing to reproach.

(10) The act of worship of Felix, on behalf of Licinius and of Sarapion <and> of Pous, and of their household, and of Pompeianus, friend for all time. The year 31 [of the emperor Commodus], 29th [day of the month] Phamenoth [25 March 191]. For a blessing.

The act of worship of Harkinis (15) also called Apollonios, on behalf of his wife and of their children and of all his household, to Isis of the innumerable names, today, for a blessing. The year 31 [of the emperor Commodus], 29th [day of the month] Phamenoth [25 March 191].

(b) IGPhilae 178

To Isis, very great goddess: Kasyllos, wife of Herculanus, centurion of the cohort (5) Flavia Cilicum, with her children, has dedicated [this offering] for a blessing.

(c) IGPhilae 180

This act of worship I, Abratoeis, viceroy, am performing on behalf of the king of the Ethiopians before the goddess of the innumerable names, Isis of Philae and of Abaton, and to the gods sharing the same temple, and on behalf of all his household. [The year] 8 [of the emperors Valerian and Gallienus], 1st [day of the month of] Tybi [27 December 260].

1.9 Votive offering for healing: a stele from Lydia, Asia Minor

The previous set of texts indicated a desire for divine blessing, but were non-specific about the nature of that blessing. When there is an indication of a specific reason for seeking divine help, one of the most common reasons is, unsurprisingly, healing – as in this marble stele (85 cm high) of the early third century from the temple of Artemis Anaeitis at Katakekaumene (Aivatlar) in Lydia (**Figure** 1.9). The inscription on the lower half reads: 'Stratoneike, the daughter of Meltine, dedicated this votive offering to Artemis Anaeitis for the health of her eyes', while to the right of the dedicatee above has been carved, appropriately, a pair of eyes – a variation on the common practice of presenting actual models of the afflicted part of the body as a votive offering to the relevant deity. Further reading: Van Straten 1981 (for this particular item and its date, see p. 136, no. 42.2).

1.10 Questions to an oracle: *P. Oxy.* 1477

Another understandable concern brought by individuals to the gods was the future, well-illustrated by this papyrus text. As will be readily apparent, it is the surviving portion of a larger document, comprising a series of numbered questions. Since the original publication of the papyrus in 1916, detective work by a number of scholars has provided a much clearer context for this document, revealing that it is a fragment of the original version of a work better known in its popular medieval incarnation, the *Sortes Astrampsychi* or 'Responses of Astrampsychus' (Astrampsychus supposedly being an ancient Persian wise man). The medieval version together with further papyrus discoveries show that in addition to a numbered list of nearly one hundred questions, the oracular expert would have had at his disposal a set of numbered answers and a mathematical formula for selecting, in an apparently baffling and mysterious manner, an answer appropriate to the question chosen by the enquirer. As for the document's substantive content, it has been well-observed that 'its questions suit the various social classes, high and low alike. While matters of marriage and health, love and inheritance interested everyone, others varied with the client's rank' (Lane Fox 1986: 211). The translation below is of the corrected edition in Browne 1974: 19–20. Further reading: Browne 1970, 1974, 1976.

< ... >

72. Shall I receive the wages?
73. Am I to remain where I am going?
74. Am I to be sold?
75. Am I to receive help from my friend?
76. Has it been granted to me to make a contract with another?
77. Am I to be restored to my position?
78. Am I to receive leave?
79. Shall I receive the money?
80. Is the one who is abroad alive?

Figure 1.9   Stele from the temple of Artemis Anaeitis, Katakekaumene,
            Lydia, Asia Minor
Source: ©Fotografie Rijksmuseum van Oudheden, Leiden.

81. Am I to profit from the business transaction?
82. Is my property to be sold at auction?
83. Shall I be able to sell?
84. Can I buy what I desire?
85. Am I to become successful?
86. Shall I run away?
87. Shall I be an envoy?

88. Am I to become a member of the town council (*bouleutēs*)?
89. Shall my flight go unnoticed?
90. Am I to be divorced from my wife?
91. Have I been poisoned?
92. Am I to receive a legacy?
<...>

1.11 Curse tablets and magic: *DT* 286 (= *ILS* 8753)

Although magic has often been categorised as an activity separate from religion (see Betz 1991 for discussion), it was a significant area in antiquity where ordinary people had some sort of engagement with spiritual matters, however material their motives. The many surviving examples of magical papyri are one reflection of this (for which, see Betz 1992), while curse tablets are another. The curse tablet depicted in **Figure 1.11** is one of many found in tombs at Hadrumentum in north Africa and was dated by its editor to the third century on the basis of its letter forms. It was inscribed on both sides of a lead tablet (11 x 8–9 cm), a common practice because lead was relatively cheap and, being cold and heavy, was associated with the underworld where the relevant spiritual powers were thought to reside. Such tablets typically sought to harness these powers in an attempt to achieve objectives such as gaining revenge, securing a lover, or (as here) winning at sport – chariot-racing was a popular form of public entertainment, with teams being managed by one of four 'factions' (Reds, Whites, Blues and Greens). The translation below is of Side B of the tablet. Side A depicts the demon invoked standing on a boat. The words on his chest and to the left of him are 'magical' nonsense words believed to be essential for communication with the spirit world; the words in Greek script at the end of Side B serve a similar purpose, though the first of them,

Figure 1.11   Curse tablet, Hadrumentum, north Africa

Source: A. Audollent, *Defixionum Tabellae* (Paris: Fontemoing, 1904).

IAO, is intelligible, a corruption of Yahweh which reflects the influence of Jewish traditions. On the boat itself are the words Nightwanderer, Tiber, and Oceanus, assumed to be the names of the horses concerned (the last occurs on a number of tablets from this region, while river names were also common). Further reading: Tomlin 1988: 59–81; Gager 1992.

I call upon you, demon, whoever you are, and I charge you from this hour, from this day, from this moment – torment and strike down the horses of the Green and White [factions]. Strike down the charioteers Clarus and Felix and Primulus and Romanus, and cause them to crash, and leave no life in them. I call upon you by the one who loosed you for periods of time, the god of sea and air. [Greek letters] IAO IASDAO OORIO AEIA.

1.12 An inventory of temple property: *P. Oxy.* 1449

The damaged papyrus from which this passage is extracted is a return, submitted to local government authorities in the period 213/17 by priests in the Egyptian town of Oxyrhynchus, listing the cult objects and votive offerings in the possession of various temples. Despite its fragmentary nature, it illustrates the sheer number and range of dedications and offerings which temples could accumulate over the years, as well as giving some idea of the wealth which accrued to temples in this way. The extract focuses on items in the temple of Neotera (a local version of the syncretic deity Hathor–Aphrodite: *RE* XVI.2: 2478), the significance of whose inventory is heightened by the fact that it was by no means one of the major sanctuaries in Oxyrhynchus. Further reading: Baratte 1992.

List of offerings (*graphē anathēmatōn*) for the 2<.> year of Marcus Aurelius Severus Antoninus Parthicus Maximus Britannicus Maximus Germanicus Maximus Pius Augustus, as follows. Objects in the temple of Neotera: a representation of our lord the Emperor Marcus Aurelius Severus Antoninus Felix Pius Augustus and Julia Domna the lady Augusta and his deified father Severus, some of the offerings being inscribed with the names of the dedicators, < ... > while in other cases we are ignorant of the dedicators, because the offerings have been in the temple from antiquity; a statue of Demeter, most great goddess, of which the bust is of Parian marble and the other parts of the body of wood, < ... > was not disclosed to us. And with regard to other offerings, which were dedicated in accordance with ancient customs for vows or pious reasons, < ... > dedicated by Phragenes (?) son of Horion, a small bronze statue of Neotera, five rings dedicated by < ... > son of Didymus, a green robe dedicated by the mother of An< ... >, < ... > dedicated by

(a) CIMRM 2350 (*Palaiopolis, Andros, Cyclades: 198/209*)

For the well-being of the Augusti, the emperor Caesar Lucius Septimius Severus and Marcus Aurelius Antoninus [Caracalla], and of the Caesar, Publius Septimius Geta, Marcus Aurelius Rufinus, re-enlisted veteran of our emperors, built a cave (*speleum*) for the holy and unconquerable god, with the praetorian soldiers Flavius Clarinus, Aelius Messius, Aurelius Julianus.

(b) CIMRM 1438 (= CIL 3.4800, ILS 4198) (*Virunum, Noricum*)

For the well-being of the emperor, in honour of the divine house-hold, to the Sun, unconquerable Mithras, Hilarus, freedman of the emperor, accountant (*tabularius*) for the estates of the [former] kingdom of Noricum, and Epictetus, a treasurer (*arkarius*) of the emperor, restored the temple which had fallen down from old age, and its painting, at their own expense, when the emperor, our lord Gordian Augustus, and Aviola were consuls [239], and the priest Licinius Marcellus was father of the rites (*pater sacrorum*). Dedicated on the 7th day before the Kalends of July [25 June]< … >

1.15 The emperor Decius as 'restorer of the cults': *AE* (1973) 235

The brief reign of the emperor Decius (249–51) was one of considerable impor-tance in the religious history of the Roman empire. Decius apparently believed the problems facing the empire in this period were a consequence of failure to honour the gods adequately, and he therefore instigated an empire-wide programme of sacrifices to remedy this situation (Clarke 1984–89: vol. 1, 21–39; Pohlsander 1986; Rives 1999). This was to have significant ramifications for Christians in the empire which will be investigated in the next chapter. At this point, however, it is worth noting the following short inscription from the Italian town of Cosa, with its description of Decius as 'restorer of the cults' – an expression otherwise attested only with reference to the emperor Julian in the fourth century (cf. 5.7b) (though a word of caution has been sounded: 'Care is needed with the interpretation of the Decian inscription: found in a temple at Cosa in Etruria, it may have local rather than general significance (Decius' wife had Etruscan connections)' (Smith 1995: 281 n.134)).

To the emperor Caesar Gaius Messius Quintus Trajanus Decius, devout, blessed Augustus, chief priest, with tribunician power, consul for the third time [251], father of his country, restorer of the cults (*restitutor sacr<o>rum*) and of freedom: the community of the Cosani dedicated this to his divinity and majesty.

1.16 The emperor Aurelian and the cult of the Sun: Zosimus *New History* 1.61.2 and *CIL* 6.31775

Early in the third century the emperor Elagabalus (218–22) had actively promoted a Sun cult derived from his native Syria, with himself as chief priest, but the unpopularity of his brief reign had ensured that his immediate successors discontinued official support. Half a century later, however, the emperor Aurelian (270–5) gave renewed prominence to the Sun god (*Sol*), issuing coinage bearing the words 'Sol, master of the Roman empire', building a temple in Rome (see **1.16a** below and Richardson 1992: 363–4 for a summary of the possible archaeological evidence), and establishing games and a special priesthood (of whom Virius Lupus, below, is the earliest known example). The generally patchy evidence for the mid-third century increases the difficulties of interpreting Aurelian's actions: they have been variously interpreted as a conscious attempt to unify the empire and as part of a trend towards monotheism which prepared the ground for Christianity. Certainly, Constantine's father appears to have had a special regard for Sol and it is of interest that 25 December held a special place in cult celebrations, but other scholars remain sceptical about its broader significance. Further reading: Halsberghe 1972: ch. 6; MacMullen 1981: 84–94; Lane Fox 1986: 593.

(a) Zosimus New History 1.61.2

Here [Rome] Aurelian also constructed a temple of the Sun which he adorned magnificently with votive offerings from Palmyra, and in which he placed statues of the Sun and of Bel.

(b) CIL 6.31775 (= ILS 1210) (Rome)

< ... > to <Viri>us Lupus, man of illustrious memory, consul ordinary [278], prefect of the city [of Rome], priest of the sun god (*pontifex dei Solis*), judge hearing imperial appeals in Asia and the East, governor of Coele Syria and Arabia < ... >

2

CHRISTIANS IN THE
THIRD CENTURY

This chapter aims to outline some of the key features of Christianity in the period when it was still a minority religion, sometimes subject to persecution by the authorities. The opening passage presents some of the significant distinguishing features of church organisation and practices (2.1), while the second amplifies one of those features which helps to explain Christianity's attractiveness, namely charitable work of a very practical kind (2.2). The issue of the number of Christians during the first half of the third century is raised (if not answered) by the next two items (2.3, 2.4), and that of the social profile of adherents is highlighted through the evidence presented in 2.5, 2.6 and 2.7. Gnostic teachings, an important facet of the Christian scene during the second century but exercising ongoing influence in the third, are illustrated in 2.8, before turning to pagan reactions to Christianity, first, in the form of philosophical critiques (and Christians responses) (2.9), and second, in the form of persecution. An instance of localised persecution in the 230s, and its intriguing consequences, is described in 2.10, followed by some of the evidence arising from the first empire-wide persecution during the reign of the emperor Decius in 250, including a detailed account of a martyrdom (2.11, 2.12). The chapter concludes with an important item relating to the persecution initiated by the emperor Valerian in the late 250s (2.13).

There are many indications within this material as to why Christianity proved an attractive religious option during the third century, but it leaves unanswered the important underlying question of just how successful it was during this century, before the advent of Constantine introduced an imponderable new factor into the equation. Part of the difficulty here is uncertainty about what happened during the decades after the end of the Valerianic persecution in 260. Some scholars have seen this as a period of rapid growth for the church, while others have argued that Christians still constituted only a small minority of the empire's population by the end of the century – with the view one takes on this issue having implications for the significance of Constantine. For discussion and further references, see Chadwick 1981; Lane Fox 1986: 585–95; Praet 1992–93; Galvao-Sobrinho 1995.

2.1 Christian organisation and activities: Tertullian *Apology* 39.1–6

The great north African Christian apologist Tertullian (*c.* 160–*c.* 240) here gives an account of the character of Christian organisation and activities at the end of the second century (*c.* 197), with a view to rebutting common misconceptions about the group. His description makes clear the importance of communal prayer and the reading of Scripture in the life of the church (on which, see further Gamble 1995: ch. 5), the existence of disciplinary procedures, and the central role of charity. In order to make his comments accessible to non-Christians, he deliberately uses terminology that would have been familiar from the widespread common-interest associations, clubs and philosophical schools of the Roman world, while at the same time highlighting the significant ways in which the Christians differed from these non-Christian social groupings (Wilken 1984: 45–7).

(1) I will now tell you about the activities of the Christian club (*Christiana factio*): having proved they are not bad, I will show they are good, if I have indeed revealed the truth. We are an association (*corpus*) based on shared religious conviction, the unity of our way of life, and the bond of a common hope. (2) We come together in meetings and assemble to assail God with prayers as if drawn up for battle. Determination of this sort pleases God. We also pray for the emperors, for their officials and those in authority, for the well-being of the world, for peace in human affairs, for postponement of the end of the world. (3) We come together to read the divine writings, to see if the nature of the present times requires us to look there for warnings of what is to come or for explanations of what has happened. We nourish our faith with these holy words, we strengthen our hope, we consolidate our trust, and likewise we reinforce our discipline by the instilling of divine precepts. (4) In the same place there is also encouragement, chastisement, and censure in the name of God. Judgement is undertaken with great seriousness, as is appropriate among those who are confident they are in the presence of God, and it is a grave foreshadowing of the judgement to come if anyone has sinned to such an extent that they are excluded from participating in prayers, from gatherings and from

all holy communion with God. (5) Older men of proven character are in charge, men who have achieved this rank not by payment, but by proof of their merit, for nothing of God's can be bought for a price. Even if there is a money chest (*arca*) of sorts, it does not accumulate from payments for membership (*honoraria*), as though true religion were a commercial commodity. Each person deposits a modest sum once a month, or when they wish – and only if they wish and are able. For no-one is forced to give, but does so voluntarily. (6) These gifts are like deposits of devotion. For the money is not spent on feasting or heavy drinking or worthless taverns, but on feeding the poor, and burying them, on boys and girls deprived of means and of parents, on elderly slaves who have outlived their usefulness, on the shipwrecked, and on any who are in the mines or on islands or in prison because, for the sake of the school of God (*Dei sectae*), they have become charges of the faith they profess.

2.2 Christian charity in action: Eusebius *Church History* 7.22.7–10

This passage – part of a letter by Dionysius, bishop of Alexandria (247–*c*. 264) (on whom see Clarke 1998), reproduced by the church historian and bishop Eusebius (*c*. 260–339) – provides a graphic and striking illustration of the church's charitable activities referred to in the previous extract – 'probably the most potent single cause of Christian success' (Chadwick 1967: 56). Here, Dionysius reports the responses of the Christian and pagan communities of Alexandria to a severe bout of plague in 262. From the perspective of contemporaries, the contrasting treatment of the dead would have been as significant as that of the sick. For intriguing suggestions about the wider implications of all this, see Stark 1996: ch. 4.

(7) The vast majority of our brethren were, in their very great love and brotherly affection, unsparing of themselves and supportive of one another. Visiting the sick without thought of the danger to themselves, resolutely caring for them, tending them in Christ, they readily left this life with them, after contracting the disease from others, drawing the sickness onto themselves from their neighbours, and willingly partaking of their sufferings. Many also, in nursing the sick and helping them to recover, themselves died, transferring to themselves the death coming to others and giving real meaning to the common saying that only ever seems to be a polite cliché, 'Your humble servant bids you farewell'. (8) The best of our brethren departed life in this way – some presbyters and deacons and some of the laity, greatly esteemed, so that, on account of the great devotion and strong faith it entails, this kind of death does

not seem inferior to martyrdom. (9) Gathering up the bodies of the saints with open hands into their laps, they closed their eyes and shut their mouths before carrying them on their shoulders and laying them out; they clasped and embraced them, washed and dressed them in grave clothes – then before long, the same would happen to them, since those left behind were continually following those who had preceded them. (10) But the pagans (*ta ethnē*) behaved completely the opposite. They shunned those in the early stages of the illness, fled from their loved ones and abandoned them half-dead on the roads, and treated unburied corpses like garbage, in their efforts to avoid the spread and communication of the fatal disease – which was not easy to deflect whatever strategy they tried.

2.3 The number of Christians in third-century Rome: Eusebius *Church History* 6.43.11–12

How many Christians were there in the third century? The only item of statistical evidence occurs in the following passage, in which Eusebius reproduces part of a letter written by Cornelius, bishop of Rome, to Fabius, bishop of Antioch, in 251. Cornelius' purpose in writing was to give Fabius a report on the so-called Novatian schism, which arose from Novatian's rigorist line against Christians who lapsed during persecution, but in doing so he provides interesting incidental detail about the numbers of various categories of individual in the church at Rome in the mid-third century. Because of the rarity of such statistics, attempts have been made to extrapolate the overall size of the church at Rome and even the approximate number of Christians in the Roman empire at this time, but there are problems in doing so. On the basis of Eusebius' figures, Edward Gibbon 'venture[d] to estimate the Christians at Rome at about fifty thousand', from which he deduced that they might have constituted at most 'a twentieth part' of the population of the city and hence of the empire (Gibbon 1994: vol. 1, 504, 507). But 'the guess was too high, not least because widows and the poor were strongly represented in the Church's membership. Even if the figure is more or less right, we cannot project a total for Rome, the capital, onto other populations in the Empire. Rome was an exceptional city, a magnet for immigrants and visitors, where Christians had rapidly put down roots' (Lane Fox 1986: 268–9). For this issue more generally, see Stark 1996: 2–12; Hopkins 1998.

(11) So this champion of the gospel [Novatian] did not know that there should be only one bishop in a catholic church where he knew full well that there are forty-six presbyters, seven deacons, seven sub-deacons, forty-two assistants (*akolouthoi*), fifty-two exorcists, readers and door-keepers, and more than 1500 widows and poor, all of whom the grace and charity of the Lord supports. (12) But this multitude, so necessary in the church, a number rich and increasing through the providence of God, together with the great and

innumerable laity, did not turn him from such desperate and doomed action and recall him into the church.

2.4 An early Christian house church: Dura-Europos, Syria

The town of Dura-Europos on the Euphrates not only preserves much evidence relating to pagan religious practices (1.1, 1.4), it is also the site of the earliest surviving example of a Christian meeting place. The building (**Figure 2.4**) lies in a residential quarter of the town and is itself 'simply a typical private house ... modified slightly to adapt it to religious use' (Kraeling 1967: 3). The house was built *c.* 232–3, so its conversion to a Christian meeting place must have taken place between that date and the capture of Dura by the Persians in 256 (probably in the 240s: Kraeling 1967: 38). The two most significant rooms are the assembly hall (4) and the baptistery (6). The former was created by knocking down a wall between two smaller rooms and placing a low platform at the eastern end of the room, which could now hold perhaps sixty people (Lane Fox 1986: 269–70). The latter incorporates at its western end a basin surmounted by a heavy vaulted canopy supported by columns and the room is entirely painted, its walls decorated with Biblical scenes from both Old and New Testaments – Adam and Eve, David and Goliath, the good shepherd and his sheep, the healing of the paralytic, the woman at the well, and Jesus walking on the water (for colour pictures of these paintings, see Kraeling 1967; Grabar 1967: 69–71). By contrast, the assembly hall is undecorated, implying that 'for the Christians of Dura the room devoted to the initiatory rite had a character and importance not shared by the Assembly Hall' (Kraeling 1967: 40). Further reading: Kraeling 1967; Snyder 1985: ch. 5; White 1990: ch. 5; 1997: 18–24, 123–34.

2.5 Christians in the imperial palace: *ILCV* 3332 and 3872

Another important issue besides that of numbers is the social profile of Christianity. The final item in this chapter (2.13) includes a statement implying that there were adherents of Christianity among the Roman social elite – senators and equestrians – by the 250s. The following inscriptions from Rome point to Christianity having penetrated the administrative ranks of the imperial palace rather earlier in the century, and to quite a high level in the case of the first text. Its first paragraph was inscribed on the front of a sarcophagus and presents a normal career summary without any hint of religious affiliation (the expedition from which Prosenes was returning must have been the Mesopotamian campaign of 217 in which the emperor Caracalla was killed). However, the phrase 'received to God' in the second paragraph, inscribed in a much less conspicuous place, has widely been interpreted as a veiled profession of Christian allegiance (for residual doubts see Pietri 1983: 556). Such a conclusion is certainly consistent with statements by a number of Christian writers during this period (e.g., Tertullian *To Scapula* 4.5–6), while there is other epigraphic evidence, such as the second text below with its less ambiguous Christian references (probably from the early third century: McKechnie 1999: 438), suggesting Prosenes was by no means unique. For

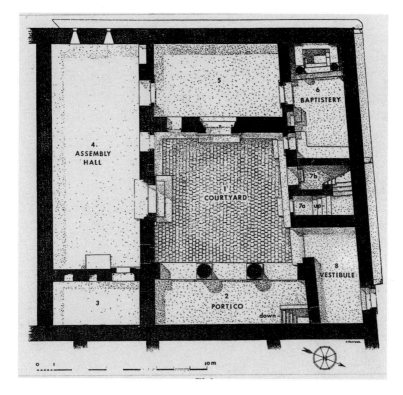

Figure 2.4   The house church at Dura-Europos

Source: *The Excavations at Dura-Europos, Final Report VIII, Part II: The Christian Building*, edited by C.H. Kraeling (New Haven: Yale University Press, 1967): Figure 1.

further discussion of the second inscription, see Clarke 1971, and for all the relevant evidence, see McKechnie 1999.

(a) ILCV 3332 (= CIL 6.8498)

[on the front of the sarcophagus] For Marcus Aurelius Prosenes, freedman of the emperors, imperial chamberlain, supervisor of the treasury, supervisor of the imperial estate, supervisor of the gladiatorial shows, supervisor of wines, appointed to the imperial administration by the deified Commodus: his freedmen had this sarcophagus adorned for their most devoted and well-deserving patron from their own resources.

[on the upper edge of the right-hand end of the sarcophagus] Prosenes was received to God (*receptus ad deum*), on the 5th day

41

before the Nones of <May/July?> [3 May/July] at S<ame in Cephalle?>nia, when Praesens was consul and Extricatus consul for the second time [217], while returning to the city [of Rome] from campaign. Ampelius, his freedman, wrote this.

(b) ILCV 3872 (= CIL 6.8987)

Alexander, slave of the emperors, set up [this epitaph] while he was still alive for his dearest son, Marcus, a student at the Caput Africae school [for training imperial slaves], who was assigned to the tailors and who lived for 18 years, 8 months, and 5 days. I ask you, good brothers (*boni fratres*), by the one God (*per unum deum*), not to damage this inscription after my death.

2.6 Christians in local administration: *SB* 16.12497

The (damaged) papyrus from which the following passage is extracted comprises a list of individuals nominated, at some point in the first half of the third century, for liturgies in Arsinoe, a district capital in Egypt. In the context of Roman Egypt, a liturgy was a compulsory public service, which could involve anything from serving as village policeman, to collecting taxes, to being official banker for the district. Many liturgies involved financial responsibilities, so individuals nominated for such liturgies by the local authorities had to satisfy property requirements so that they could make good any shortfall out of their own pocket; needless to say, liturgies were not a very popular feature of Roman rule (Lewis 1983: 177–84; Lewis 1982). (It is clear from earlier sections of this papyrus that the damaged right-hand side of our extract listed details of each individual's property qualification.) If the dating of this papyrus to the first half of the third century is correct (it is based on the styles of handwriting: Sijpesteijn 1980: 341), then this seemingly innocuous item of routine administration is of great significance, since it is 'the earliest example of a Christian in an official text from Egypt' (Van Minnen 1994: 74). It has been deduced from the two different styles of handwriting used in compiling the list that 'a second clerk went over the list and added some personal detail about each candidate, presumably to give the reviewer of the list, his superior no doubt, some idea of the suitability of the candidate' (Van Minnen 1994: 75). It is the final name on the list which is of interest, for Antonius Dioskoros is described as being a Christian, showing that in this period 'Christians were at least considered for minor public offices in Egypt' (Van Minnen 1994: 76). If the social background of the other nominees is anything to judge by, then Antonius probably came from the same milieu of 'urban shopkeepers and craftsmen of moderate means', though the Alexandrian origin of his father and the Roman element in his name may have given him enhanced social status; at any rate, a third official who went down the left-hand margin ranking the nominees seems to have rated him highly against the others, despite the potential disadvantage of his religious affiliation (Van Minnen 1994: 76). His family's Alexandrian origin is also consistent with what might be expected about the manner in which Christianity spread within Egypt, namely by migration from the capital up the Nile valley (Van Minnen 1994: 76).

For responsibility for the water-reservoir and the fountains of the district capital < ... >

4th [1st hand] Sarapammon, also known as Arios, son of Nilos, son of Zoilos, from < ... >
[2nd hand] He is the < ... > of the new landowner < ... >
8th [1st hand] Isidoros, also known as Herakleides, son of Heron, son of Socrates < ... >
[2nd hand] He is a good man and a manufacturer of oil in < ... >
5th [1st hand] Theodoros, son of Isidoros, son of Ischyrion, from < ... >
[2nd hand] He is the son of the Isidorus who lives in the < ... >
7th [1st hand] Ammonios, son of Magnus, also known as Menouthes, from the gymnasium quarter < ... >
[2nd hand] Ammonios is a chatterbox and a labourer < ... >
2nd [1st hand] Antonius Dioskoros, son of Horigenes from Alexandria < ... >
[2nd hand] Dioskoros is a Christian < ... >

2.7 Women in the church: Porphyry *Against the Christians* fr. 97 (= Jerome *Commentary on Isaiah* 3.12)

In addition to philosophical works such as *On Abstinence* (cf. 1.13), the Neoplatonic philosopher Porphyry (234–*c*. 305) wrote a work entitled *Against the Christians* (debate continues as to whether it was written in the 270s or *c*. 300: Croke 1984–5; Barnes 1994b). As a result of official book burnings by Christian emperors in the fourth and fifth centuries, however, it survives only in the form of quotations by later writers, usually Christian authors seeking to refute Porphyry's arguments. In this case, the fourth-century scholar Jerome refers to one of Porphyry's claims in the course of commenting on a passage from Isaiah 3.12, 'My people have been robbed by their own tax-collectors and are ruled by women'. Porphyry is obviously not an unbiased source, but his jibe is nevertheless evidence for the prominence of women in the third-century church, and particularly women of high social status. Further reading: Meredith 1980: 1123–37; Wilken 1984: ch. 6; Demarolle 1970; Eck 1971: 399–401.

Let us therefore also take care that we are not extortioners among our people, that, as the godless Porphyry claimed, married ladies (*matronae*) and [other] women do not constitute our ruling body (*senatus*), exercising authority in church congregations, and that the prejudice of women does not determine priestly rank.

2.8 An example of Gnostic literature: Extracts from *The Gospel of Philip* (Nag Hammadi Codex II,3)

'Gnostics' is the catch-all term that has been used by modern scholars for a range of early Christian groups who placed particular emphasis on the importance of special knowledge (*gnōsis*) as the key to salvation. This knowledge typically included a dualistic understanding of the universe which set a perfect spiritual world against an imperfect material world (complete with complex mythologies to explain how this came about), with the human goal being to reunite the spiritual element within with the perfect spiritual world. Gnosticism has provoked widely divergent views from modern scholars, ranging from those who see it as the predominant trend within Christianity for much of the second century, to those who regard it as diverging so far from fundamental Christian tenets that it must be regarded as essentially a separate religion. All would agree, however, that modern under-standing of Gnosticism, previously reliant primarily on information derived from anti-Gnostic writers in antiquity, has been revolutionised by the discovery in 1945, at Nag Hammadi in southern Egypt, of a major cache of texts written by Gnostics themselves. Many of the Nag Hammadi texts are fourth-century Coptic transla-tions of earlier Greek works, including the example below, originally written 'perhaps as late as the second half of the third century' (Isenberg 1988: 141). Despite its title, the *Gospel of Philip* does not present a narrative of the life of Jesus, but rather a somewhat disjointed collection of sayings. The extracts chosen here reflect various aspects of Gnostic thought, more specifically the strand associated with one of the most influential Gnostic exegetes, Valentinus, active in both Egypt and Italy in the mid-second century. The *Gospel of Philip* itself was not written by Valentinus, but reflects the ongoing influence of his ideas. It is noteworthy that, while New Testament scriptures are quoted (77), the designation 'Christians' is used (74), and there is reference to rites of baptism and eucharist (67), yet it is also asserted that the creation of the world was a mistake (75). An ascetic tendency is also evident in the reference to virgins (69), at odds with the frequent portrayal of Gnostics as libertarians by anti-Gnostic contemporaries. The literature on Gnosticism is vast: for general discussions, see Rudolph 1990; Filoramo 1990; Pagels 1979; Pearson 1990; McKechnie 1996; for specific treatments of the *Gospel of Philip*, see Segelberg 1960, 1983; Pagels 1991.

(67) ... Truth did not come into the world naked, but it came in types and images. The world will not receive truth in any other way. There is a rebirth and an image of rebirth. It is certainly necessary to be born again through the image. Which one? Resurrection. The image must rise again through the image. The bridal chamber and the image must enter through the image into the truth: this is the restoration. ...

The Lord <did> everything in a mystery, a baptism and a chrism and a eucharist and a redemption and a bridal chamber. ...

(68) ...When Eve was still in Adam death did not exist. When she was separated from him death came into being. If he enters again and attains his former self, death will be no more. ...

(69) A bridal chamber is not for the animals, nor is it for the slaves, nor for defiled women; but it is for free men and virgins.

Through the holy spirit we are indeed begotten again, but we are begotten through Christ in the two. We are anointed through the spirit. When we were begotten we were united. None can see himself either in water or in a mirror without light. Nor again can you see in light without water or mirror. For this reason it is fitting to baptize in the two, in the light and the water. Now the light is the chrism. ...

(70) ... If the woman had not separated from the man, she should not die with the man. His separation became the beginning of death. Because of this Christ came to repair the separation which was from the beginning and again unite the two, and to give life to those who died as a result of the separation and unite them. But the woman is united to her husband in the bridal chamber. Indeed those who have united in the bridal chamber will no longer be separated. Thus Eve separated from Adam because it was not in the bridal chamber that she united with him. ...

(74) ... The chrism is superior to baptism, for it is from the word 'chrism' that we have been called 'Christians', certainly not because of the word 'baptism'. And it is because of the chrism that 'the Christ' has his name. For the father anointed the son, and the son anointed the apostles, and the apostles anointed us. He who has been anointed possesses everything. He possesses the resurrection, the light, the cross, the holy spirit. The father gave him this in the bridal chamber; he merely accepted <the gift>. The father was in the son and the son was in the father. This is <the> kingdom of heaven. ...

(75) ... The world came about through a mistake. For he who created it wanted to create it imperishable and immortal. He fell short of attaining his desire. For the world never was imperishable, nor, for that matter, was he who made the world. ...

(77) ... He who has knowledge of the truth is a free man, but the free man does not sin, for 'he who sins is the slave of sin' [Jn. 8.34]. Truth is the mother, knowledge the father. Those who think that sinning does not apply to them are called 'free' by the world. 'Knowledge' of the truth merely 'makes such people arrogant',

which is what the words 'it makes men free' mean. It even gives them a sense of superiority over the whole world. But 'love builds up' [1 Cor. 8.1]. In fact, he who is really free through knowledge is a slave because of love for those who have not yet been able to attain to the freedom of knowledge. Knowledge makes them capable of becoming free. ...

(tr. W.W. Isenberg)

2.9 Christian responses to pagan criticisms: Origen *Against Celsus* 5.25, 35, 8.73, 75

Origen (*c.* 185–*c.* 255) was a leading Christian intellectual and theologian of the third century. In his youth he studied philosophy in his native city of Alexandria, where his teacher may have been the man who also taught the Neoplatonic philosopher Plotinus. One of the best-known works in Origen's prodigious output is his *Against Celsus*, probably written in the late 240s, in which he responded to the critique of Christianity contained in a work entitled *The True Doctrine* by a certain Celsus, probably written in the late second century (there is much uncertainty and debate about Celsus' identity). In order to answer Celsus' criticisms, Origen quotes extensively from *The True Doctrine*, so that in addition to being a good example of Christian apologetic literature, the *Against Celsus* also provides particularly clear insights into why Christianity was a cause of concern for a well-educated pagan in this period. The excerpts presented here highlight Celsus' worries about Christianity's apparent indifference, first, to tradition, and second, to public service, whether in the army or civil administration. (The first also has interesting implications for pagan attitudes to Jews.) Origen's responses are of interest, in the first case, for his use of philosophical argument to highlight the inconsistencies in Celsus' argument, and on the second issue, for what they reveal about one possible approach to a matter of central and increasing importance for Christians (cf. 12.1 and Tomlin 1998: 23–5 for Christians in the army). Further reading: Chadwick 1953: Introduction; Wilken 1984: ch. 5.

5. (25) Let us also look at Celsus' next passage which reads as follows: 'Now the Jews became an individual nation, and made laws according to the custom of their country; and they maintain laws among themselves at the present day, and observe worship which may be very peculiar, but is at least traditional. In this respect they behave like the rest of mankind, because each nation follows its traditional customs, whatever kind may happen to be established. This situation seems to have come to pass not only because it came into the head of different people to think differently and because it is necessary to preserve established social conventions, but also because it is probable that from the beginning the different parts of the earth were allotted to different [divine] overseers, and are governed in this way by having been divided between certain

authorities. In fact, the practices done by each nation are right when they are done in the way that pleases the overseers; and it is impious to abandon the customs which have existed in each locality from the beginning'. ...

5. (35) From these facts the argument seems to lead Celsus to the conclusion that all men ought to live according to their traditional customs and should not be criticized for this; but that since the Christians have forsaken their traditional laws and are not one individual nation like the Jews they are to be criticized for agreeing to the teaching of Jesus. Let him tell us, then, whether philosophers who teach men not to be superstitious would be right in abandoning the traditional customs, so that they even eat of things forbidden in their own countries, or would they act contrary to moral principle in so doing? For reason persuades them not to busy themselves about images and statues or even about the created things of God, but to ascend above them and to present the soul to the Creator. If Celsus or those who approve of his views were to try to defend the view which he has set forth by saying that one who has read philosophy would also observe the traditional customs, that implies that philosophers, for example, among the Egyptians would become quite ridiculous if they took care not to eat onion in order to observe traditional customs or abstained from certain parts of the body such as the head and shoulders in order not to break the traditions handed down to them by their fathers. And I have not yet said anything of those Egyptians who shiver with fear at the trivial physical experience of flatulence. If one of their sort became a philosopher and were to keep the traditional customs, he would be a ridiculous philosopher because he would be acting unphilosophically. ...

8. (73) Then Celsus next exhorts us to 'help the emperor with all our power, and co-operate with him in what is right, and fight for him, and be fellow-soldiers if he presses for this, and fellow-generals with him'. We may reply to this that at appropriate times we render to the emperors divine help, if I may so say, by taking up even the whole armour of God [Eph. 6.11]. And this we do in obedience to the apostolic utterance which says, 'I exhort you, therefore, first to make prayers, supplications, intercessions, and thanksgivings for all men, for emperors, and all that are in authority' [1 Tim. 2.1–2]. Indeed, the more pious a man is, the more effective he is in helping the emperors – more so than the soldiers who go into the lines and kill all the enemy troops they can. ...

8. (75) Celsus exhorts us also to 'accept public office in our

country if it is necessary to do this for the sake of the preservation of
the laws and of piety'. ... If Christians do avoid these responsibilities, it is not with the motive of shirking the public services of life.
But they keep themselves for a more divine and necessary service in
the church of God for the sake of the salvation of men. Here it is
both necessary and right for them to be leaders and to be concerned
about all men, both those who are within the Church, that they
may live better every day, and those who appear to be outside it,
that they may become familiar with the sacred words and acts of
worship. ...

(tr. H. Chadwick)

2.10 Localised persecution and church divisions: Cyprian *Letter* 75.10

This passage, part of a letter written in 256 by Firmilian, bishop of Cappadocian
Caesarea (early 230s–268), to Cyprian, bishop of Carthage, on the general subject
of baptismal procedure, describes events in Cappadocia more than twenty years
earlier, in 235. It is of interest, first, because it presents an example of the sort of
localised persecution of Christians which was characteristic of the church's experience prior to the mid-third century when the emperor Decius initiated the first
empire-wide persecution (see below), and shows the sort of circumstances which
might prompt such an occurrence. Second, it provides an intriguing example of
ecclesiastical authorities having to deal with a serious internal challenge – in this
instance, a female prophetess. Certain features are reminiscent of the so-called
Montanist movement of the second half of the second century, known for the high
profile role of female prophetesses and for designating their centre in western
Anatolia as the 'New Jerusalem'. 'It is possible the extraordinary distress caused by
a series of natural disasters [in 235] led to the resurgence of this eschatological
movement' (Elm 1994: 32). Further reading: Clarke 1984–89: vol. 4, 246–52,
263–8.

(1) I want to tell you the story of what happened among us, relevant
as it is to this subject. About twenty years ago in the period after
the emperor Alexander [Severus], many adversities and misfortunes
occurred, both to everyone in general and to Christians in particular. There were numerous frequent earthquakes throughout both
Cappadocia and Pontus which destroyed many buildings; some
towns were even swallowed up by cracks opening in the ground and
taken down into the depths. As a result of this, a serious persecution
of the Christian name took place against us. Arising suddenly after
the previous lengthy period of peace, it was an unexpected and
unfamiliar calamity and so disconcerted our people all the more
severely. (2) Caught up in this confusion, the faithful fled hither and

thither in fear of persecution, departing from their homelands and crossing into neighbouring regions (such movement was an option since this persecution was localised, not universal). Suddenly a woman came to the fore who presented herself as a prophetess experiencing states of ecstasy and acted as though filled with the Holy Spirit. But she was so overwhelmed by the onset of the leading demons that for a long time she seduced and deceived the brethren, performing certain monstrous marvels, and promising to make the earth quake. Not that the demon had the power to cause earthquakes or was able to upset the elements by its own strength; rather, that evil spirit, being able to foresee that an earthquake was about to happen, sometimes pretended that it was going to bring about what it saw would happen anyway.

(3) By these deceptions and displays, he gained control over the minds of some individuals, who obeyed him and followed him wherever he commanded and led. He also made the woman go barefooted through the freezing snow in the harsh winter, without her being troubled or harmed in any way by the outing. She also said she was in a hurry to get to Judaea and Jerusalem, pretending that it was from there that she had come. (4) The demon also deceived one of the presbyters, of rural origin, and another man, a deacon, so that they had illicit relations with this same woman, as was revealed a little later. For suddenly there appeared before him one of the exorcists, a man of proven character who always conducted himself properly with respect to church teaching. After being encouraged and stirred to action by several of the brethren who were themselves strong and praiseworthy in their faith, he set himself against that evil spirit to subdue it. By subtle deceit, the demon had even foretold shortly beforehand that an unbelieving assailant would come against him. But inspired by the grace of God, that exorcist resisted steadfastly and showed that that spirit which had previously been thought holy was in fact very evil.

(5) And in fact that woman who was already influenced by the deceits and tricks of the demons to deceive the faithful in many ways even dared often to do this (among the other things by which she misled many): she would pretend to sanctify the bread with a not unrespectable invocation and celebrate the eucharist, and she would offer the sacrifice to the Lord not without reciting the customary eucharistic prayer, and she would also baptise many, using the traditional and authentic words of enquiry, so that in no way did she appear to be at odds with church requirements.

2.11 Certificates of sacrifice from the Decian persecution: *P. Mich.* 3.157 and Wilcken no. 125

The following papyri are two of many examples of so-called *libelli* or certificates of sacrifice generated by the persecution which the emperor Decius initiated in late 249/early 250 (a total of forty-six have been recovered to date: Knipfing 1923 assembled forty-one; for details of a further four, see Horsley 1982: 181, to which can now be added *P. Oxy.* 3929, published in 1991). The immediate purpose of the certificates is clear – to prove that individuals had publicly sacrificed – but there is some uncertainty as to who was required to obtain them. The traditional view has been that all inhabitants of the empire had to have certificates (for a recent restatement, see Clarke 1984–9: vol. 1, 21–39; cf. also the introductory comments of J.R. Rea to *P. Oxy.* 3929, drawing (tentative) comparisons between the numbers of surviving certificates and census returns), but doubts have been raised about this. It has been observed that administering such a process for all inhabitants of the empire would have been 'a bureaucratic nightmare' (Lane Fox 1986: 455). Furthermore, all the surviving *libelli* with dates fall in June/July 250 – six months after the start of the persecution – and there is no reference to *libelli* in other contemporary sources before May 250 (lack of any reference to them in the *Martyrdom of Pionius* (2.12), which occurred during February/March 250, may be particularly significant (Lane Fox 1986: 754 n. 20), though it has also been noted that the actions required of Pionius are consistent with the *libelli* (Robert 1994: 53)). Given all this, a two-phase persecution has been suggested: the general requirement to sacrifice was published in late 249/early 250 (Clarke 1984–9: vol. 1, 25–6 for the date), but only when it became clear, after some months, that many Christians were not doing so were the *libelli* introduced as a way of monitoring the adherence of those suspected of non-compliance (Keresztes 1975: 778; Lane Fox 1986: 456). However, this alternative scenario is not without its problems. The six-month time-lag is not necessarily decisive in the light of the notorious slowness of imperial communications, and the second *libellus* translated below presents a particular difficulty, since it seems unlikely that suspicion can have attached to a pagan priestess. This difficulty has in turn prompted speculation that Aurelia Ammonous may have been 'a secret Christian, just as weak as the others who availed themselves of *libelli* without actually having to sacrifice' (Keresztes 1975: 777) or 'may have had Christians in her family or a Christian phase in her earlier life' (Lane Fox 1986: 456), but it is not clear that either of these suggestions resolves the problem satisfactorily.

More generally, the certificates are of course a reminder of the importance of sacrifice in pagan cult. Moreover, a high proportion of women is represented in the surviving certificates, consistent with what is known about Christianity's social catchment in its early centuries (Lane Fox 1986: 456). With regard to the specific detail in the *libelli* below, Theadelphia is a village in the Arsinoite district, from where the largest number have been recovered. The Moeris quarter was an area within the district-capital of Arsinoe, while Petesouchos was the local manifestation of the crocodile deity widely revered in this area of Egypt. The initial number in the second papyrus is assumed to have been added for filing purposes; other *libelli* survive in duplicate, so it is likely that one was kept by officials for their records, while a copy was retained by the individual as proof.

(a) P. Mich. 3.157

To those appointed to oversee the sacrifices, from Aurelius Sakis, from the village of Theoxenis, with his children Aion and Heras, staying in the village of Theadelphia. We have always sacrificed to the gods and now too in your presence in accordance with the decree we have offered sacrifice and we have poured a libation and we have eaten of the sacrificial offering and we ask you to undersign. May you continue to prosper.

[2nd hand] We, Aurelius Serenus and Aurelius Hermas, saw you sacrificing.
[1st hand] The Year 1 of the Emperor Caesar Gaius Messius Quintus Trajan Decius, devout, blessed, Augustus, Pauni 23 [17 June 250].

(b) Wilcken no. 125

433: To those appointed to oversee the sacrifices, from Aurelia Ammonous, daughter of Mystos, of the Moeris quarter, priestess of the great, mighty and everliving god Petesouchos and of the gods in the Moeris [quarter]. I have always sacrificed to the gods throughout my life, and now again in accordance with the edict and in your presence, I have offered sacrifice and I have poured a libation and I have eaten of the sacrifical offering, and I ask [you] to undersign< ... >

2.12 A martyrdom during the Decian persecution: *The Martyrdom of Pionius*

Among the surviving accounts of Christian martyrs, one of the best known and most interesting is that of a presbyter from Smyrna in Asia Minor named Pionius, who was executed during the persecution initiated by the emperor Decius (249–51). The fact that a magisterial new edition of this account by the famous epigrapher and classical scholar, Louis Robert, has recently been (posthumously) published gives added reason to include it in this collection. Martyr acts are notoriously prone to elaboration and interpolation by subsequent 'editors' keen to enhance their edificatory value, but Robert argues that archaeological, epigraphic and numismatic evidence from Smyrna confirms the authenticity of this account, even proposing that much of it derives from an eyewitness of the events reported (Robert 1994: 1–9). In addition to its obvious value for understanding the process of arrest, trial and execution, the account contains many other cardinal points of interest, among which are Pionius' good education and the implications of this for the social make-up of the Christian community in Smyrna, the way in which the Jewish community of Smyrna features so prominently, and the fact that Pionius had previously travelled to Palestine (cf. 16.1–2). For detailed discussion and commentary, see Robert 1994 (in French) and Lane Fox 1986: 250–92. Among points of detail, the significance of the term 'grand sabbath' remains a matter for debate (Lane Fox 1986: 486–7; Robert 1994: 50; Bowersock 1995: 82–4), while the two goddesses Nemeseis (the plural form of Nemesis) were the tutelary deities of the city of Smyrna (Robert 1994: 65). Due to constraints of space, a few chapters have been omitted – the opening one, ch. 6 in which Pionius has an exchange with a merchant, and the second and longer of Pionius' two speeches (12.3–14.15).

2. On the second day of the sixth month [23 February 250], at the beginning of the 'grand sabbath', on the anniversary of the blessed martyr Polycarp, in the time of the persecution of Decius, there were arrested Pionius, presbyter, Sabina, confessor, Asclepiades, Macedonia, and Limnus, a presbyter of the catholic church. (2) Now on the eve of the anniversary of Polycarp, Pionius foresaw that they were to be arrested on that day. (3) He was with Sabina and Asclepiades, fasting, when he foresaw that they were be arrested the following day, so he took three woven cords and fastened them around his own neck and those of Sabina and of Asclepiades, and they waited in the house. (4) He did this so that when they were arrested no-one should suppose that they were being led away, like the rest, to partake of the defiled meats, but so that all would know that they had decided to be taken immediately to prison.

3. When, on the day of the sabbath, they had prayed and taken the consecrated bread and the water, the temple warden (*neokoros*) Polemon came for them, together with the others assigned to search out the Christians and drag them away to sacrifice and partake of the defiled meats. (2) And the temple warden said, 'You know, of course, of the emperor's edict commanding you to sacrifice to the gods.' (3) And Pionius said, 'We know the commandments of God, which require that we worship him alone.' (4) Polemon said, 'In any case, come to the main square (*agora*) and there you will obey.' Both Sabina and Asclepiades said, 'We obey the living God.' (5) Then they took them away without having to use force. And on the way, everyone saw that they bore cords, and as happens when there is something unusual to be seen, a crowd quickly gathered, pressing on one another. (6) When they reached the main square, at the eastern portico, by the double entrance, the whole area and the upper stories of the porticoes were full of Greeks and Jews, and of women also; for they were on holiday, because it was the 'grand sabbath'. (7) They climbed up on the benches and booths to watch.

4. They placed them in the middle, and Polemon said, 'It is a good idea, Pionius, for you to obey like everyone else and sacrifice,

and thereby avoid punishment.' (2) Then holding out his hand, Pionius, with a radiant face, spoke in his defence as follows: 'You men who pride yourselves on the beauty of Smyrna, who glory in Homer, son of the [River] Meles, as you say, and those of the Jews who are present among you, listen to me for a moment while I speak to you. (3) For I understand that you laugh and rejoice at those who abandon the faith, and find their failure amusing, namely when they offer sacrifice of their own free will. (4) But you Greeks ought to pay attention to your master (*didaskalos*) Homer, who warns you that it is not right to pride yourselves on those who die [*Odyssey* 22.412]. (5) As for you Jews, Moses gives this command: 'If you see your enemy's donkey sink under its burden, don't pass by but go and help it up' [Ex. 23.5, Deut. 22.4]. (6) You should likewise give heed to Solomon: 'If your enemy stumbles,' he says, 'don't rejoice, and don't be glad at his downfall' [Prov. 24.17]. (7) For out of obedience to my master (*didaskalos*) I prefer to die rather than disobey his teaching and I am engaging in the contest so as not to abandon what I first learned and then taught. (8) Whom do the Jews mock mercilessly? Even if we are their enemies, as they say, we are humans and, what's more, are mistreated. (9) They say that we have opportunities to speak freely. Maybe so, but whom have we mistreated? Whom have we killed? Whom have we persecuted? Whom have we forced to worship idols? (10) Do they think that their wrongdoings are the same as those now being done by some out of human fear? But there is a big difference between wrongdoings done willingly and those done against one's will. (11) For who forced the Jews to worship Beelphegor and eat sacrifices to the dead [Ps. 106.28]? or to fornicate with the daughters of other peoples [Num. 25.1 etc.]? to burn their sons and daughters before idols [Num. 14.27 etc.]? to murmur against God and speak against Moses [Ex. 6.2–3]? to be ungrateful for blessings? to return in their hearts to Egypt? to say to Aaron when Moses had gone up to receive the law, 'Make gods for us and fashion the calf' [Ex. 32.1ff.]? – and all the other things they did. (12) For they can deceive you. But let them read you the Book of Judges, of Kings, of Exodus and all those where they are put to shame. (13) But do they ask why some came forward to sacrifice without being forced, and do they condemn all Christians on account of them? (14) Think of the present situation as being like a threshing floor: which forms the larger pile, the chaff or the grain? When the farmer comes to clear the threshing floor with his winnowing fan, the chaff, being light, is easily carried away by the movement of the air, but the grain remains there. (15)

Consider also the net which is cast into the sea: not everything it catches is useful. So it is with the present situation. (16) How then do you wish us to suffer these things – as those who have done right or as wrongdoers? If as wrongdoers, how will you who, by your own deeds, are also proven to be wrongdoers not be subject to the same punishments? But if as those who have done right, what hope do you have when the righteous suffer? 'For if the righteous man is scarcely saved, where will the impious and sinner appear?' [1 Pet. 4.18] (17) For judgement is hanging over the world, of which we are convinced by many considerations. (18) I have travelled abroad and been throughout the whole land of Judaea; I have crossed the Jordan and seen the land which testifies, even to this day, to the divine anger it has experienced because of the sins of its inhabitants, who killed foreigners and drove them out with violence. (19) I have seen the smoke rising from it even to this day and the land reduced to ashes by fire, unproductive and waterless. (20) I have also seen the Dead Sea, whose water has changed and lost its natural powers through fear of God and is unable to support life; anyone who jumps into it is pushed out upwards by the water which is unable to retain a human body – for it does not want to receive a human, to avoid being punished again on account of a human. (21) I am talking about places a long distance from you. But you yourselves see and talk about the land of the Ten Cities in Lydia, burnt by fire and lying exposed even to this day as an example for the sacrilegious – fire which bursts forth from Etna and Sicily and also from Lycia. (22) If this is also distant for you, think about your familiarity with hot water, I mean the sort which gushes out of the ground, and consider where it is warmed and heated if it does not issue from an underground fire. (23) Think also about the partial conflagrations and the floods, under Deucalion according to you and under Noah according to us: they were partial so that from the parts one might understand the totality. (24) This is why we testify to you about the coming judgement of God by fire through his Word, Jesus Christ. And because of this, we do not worship your so-called gods and we do not bow down before the golden image [Dan. 3.18].'

5. Pionius said these and many other things, and did not fall silent for a long time; the temple warden with his attendants and the whole crowd strained their ears to listen, and the silence was such that no-one even whispered. (2) While Pionius was saying again, 'We do not worship your gods and we do not bow down before the golden image', they were led into the open air, into the middle, and some of those who frequented the main square,

together with Polemon, surrounded them, earnestly entreating them and saying, (3) 'Listen to us, Pionius, because we love you and you deserve to live for many reasons, because of your character and your reasonableness. It is good to be alive and to see this light', and a great many other such things. (4) But he said to them: 'I agree that it is good to be alive, but that which we desire is even better. Yes, the light, but the true light. (5) Yes, indeed, all these things are good. We do not have a liking for death, nor do we despise the works of God and seek to flee them. But it is the superiority of other great blessings which makes us disregard these, which are snares.' [In ch. 6, Pionius has a brief exchange with a merchant named Alexander.]

7. When the people wanted to hold an assembly in the theatre in order to hear more there, some men, concerned on behalf of the city general (*stratēgos*), went to the temple warden Polemon and said, 'Do not allow him to speak, lest they go into the theatre and there is an uproar and an inquiry concerning the bread.' (2) When he heard this, Polemon said, 'Pionius, if you do not wish to sacrifice, at least come to the temple of the two goddesses Nemeseis.' Pionius replied, 'But it will not do your idols any good if we go there.' (3) Polemon said, 'Do as we say, Pionius.' Pionius replied, 'Would that I could persuade you to become Christians.' (4) But laughing loudly, the men said, 'You cannot make us burn alive!' Pionius said, 'It is much worse to burn after you have died!' (5) When Sabina smiled at this, the temple warden and his assistants said, 'You laugh?' She replied, 'If God wishes it, yes; for we are Christians. Whoever trusts in Christ will laugh unhesitatingly with everlasting joy.' (6) They said to her, 'You are going to undergo something you won't like: for women who do not sacrifice are put in the brothel.' But she said, 'The holy God will look after me in this.'

8. Polemon spoke to Pionius again, 'Listen to us, Pionius.' Pionius replied, 'You have instructions to persuade or to punish; you are not persuading us, so punish us.' (2) Then the temple warden began the formal enquiry, saying, 'Sacrifice, Pionius.' Pionius replied, 'I am a Christian.' (3) Polemon said, 'Which god do you worship?' Pionius replied, 'The all powerful God who made the heavens and the earth and all that is in them including all of us, who abundantly provides us with everything and whom we know through Christ his Word.' (4) Polemon said, 'Then at least sacrifice to the emperor.' Pionius replied, 'I will not sacrifice to a man, for I am a Christian.'

9. Then he continued the enquiry with a written report, saying:

taken to Ephesus.' (5) Pionius said, 'Let the man sent to take charge of us come here.' The cavalry commander replied, 'But it is a centurion, a person of considerable importance. If you refuse, I am a magistrate.' (6) And seizing Pionius' cloak he pulled it tight around his neck and passed it to one of the troops, almost strangling him in the process. (7) They arrived in the main square, together with Sabina and the others with them. They cried out loudly, 'We are Christians!' They threw themselves in the ground so as not to be taken to the place of the idols. Six of the local troops were carrying him head first, since they could not stop him from kicking them in the ribs with his knees and interfering with their hands and feet.

16. He shouted while those carrying him brought him and placed him on the ground near the altar, near which Euctemon remained in an attitude of worship. (2) And Lepidus said, 'Why do you not sacrifice, Pionius?' Pionius and those with him said, 'Because we are Christians.' (3) Lepidus said, 'Which god do you worship?' Pionius said, 'The one who made the heavens, the earth, the sea, and all that is in them.' (4) Lepidus said, 'Is this the one who was crucified?' Pionius said, 'He whom God sent for the salvation of the world.' (5) The magistrates let out great cries and laughed, and Lepidus cursed him. (6) But Pionius cried, 'Respect piety, honour justice, acknowledge that which is of the same nature; obey your own laws. You punish us for disobedience, but you yourselves are disobedient; you have instructions to punish, not to treat with violence.'

17. A certain Rufinus who was present and had a reputation for being one of the better rhetors, said to him, 'Stop, Pionius, don't espouse these empty theories!' (2) Pionius replied to him, 'Are these your speeches? Are these your books? Socrates didn't suffer these things from the Athenians. But now everyone is an Anytus and a Meletus. (3) Were Socrates, Aristides, Anaxarchus, and the rest espousing empty theories, according to you, because they practised philosophy, justice and steadfastness?' (4) Hearing this, Rufinus was silent.

18. One of the people of eminent station and of grand repute in worldly terms, and Lepidus, said to him, 'Do not cry out, Pionius.' (2) He replied to him, 'And you – do not use violence. Light the fire and we will climb onto it of our own accord.' (3) A certain Terentius shouted from the crowd, 'Are you saving one who is preventing others from sacrificing?' (4) Finally they placed crowns on them, but they tore them to pieces and threw them away. (5) A public slave was standing by holding meat sacrificed to the idols. However,

he did not dare to approach any of them, but ate it himself in front of everyone, he the public slave. (6) As they kept shouting, 'We are Christians', so that they could find nothing to do with them, they sent them back to the prison, and the crowd insulted them and beat them. (7) Someone said to Sabina, 'Can't you go and die in your home town?' She said, 'Where is my home town? I am the sister of Pionius.' (8) Terentius, who at that time was staging the wild beast hunts in the amphitheatre, said to Asclepiades, 'When you are condemned I will ask for you for my son's gladiatorial shows.' (9) Asclepiades replied to him, 'You don't scare me with that.' (10) And so they were led back to the prison. As Pionius was entering the prison, one of the local troops struck him heavily on the head and wounded him, but Pionius said nothing. (11) But the hands of the one who had struck him, and also his sides, became swollen to the point where he could hardly breathe. (12) After they entered, they glorified God that they had remained unharmed in the name of Christ and that neither the enemy nor Euctemon the fraud had prevailed over them, and they did not stop encouraging themselves with psalms and prayers. (13) It was said that later Euctemon had demanded that he be compelled, and that he himself had taken a lamb to the temple of the two goddesses Nemeseis, and that after eating some of it, he had wanted to carry all of it, cooked, to his own house. (14) So he became an object of ridicule through his false oath, because he had sworn by the Fortune of the emperor and by the goddesses Nemeseis, crown on his head, that he was not a Christian, and, unlike the rest, he neglected nothing by way of denial.

19. Later, the proconsul came to Smyrna, and Pionius was brought before him and gave testimony, according to the official record that follows, on the 4th day before the Ides of March [12 March 250]. (2) When Pionius was brought before the tribunal, Quintillianus the proconsul began the enquiry. 'What is your name?' Reply: 'Pionius'. (3) The proconsul said, 'Are you going to offer sacrifice?' He replied, 'No.' (4) The proconsul asked, 'To what cult or sect do you belong?' He replied, 'That of the catholics'. (5) He asked him, 'Of which catholics?' He replied, 'I am a presbyter of the catholic church'. (6) The proconsul: 'You are their teacher?' He replied, 'Yes, I teach them.' (7) He asked, 'You are a teacher of foolishness?' Reply: 'Of piety.' (8) He asked, 'What sort of piety?' Reply: 'Towards the God who created everything.' (9) The proconsul said, 'Sacrifice.' He replied, 'No, for I can pray only to God.' (10) The other said, 'We all worship the gods and the heavens

and the gods who are in the heavens. Why are you giving your attention to the air? Sacrifice to it!' (11) Reply: 'I am not giving my attention to the air, but to him who made the air, the heavens, and all that is in them.' (12) The proconsul said, 'Tell me, who made them?' He replied, 'It is not possible to describe him.' (13) The proconsul said, 'Certainly it is God, that is to say Zeus, who is in the heavens; for he is the king of all the gods.'

20. Pionius remained silent and was strung up. He was asked, 'Now then, are you going to offer sacrifice?' He replied, 'No.' (2) Again he was asked when he was being tortured with the 'talons': 'Change your mind; why have you lost your senses?' He replied, 'I have not lost my senses, but I fear the living God.' (3) The proconsul: 'Many men have offered sacrifice and they are alive and of sound mind.' He replied, 'I am not sacrificing.' (4) The proconsul said, 'Having been questioned, reflect a little within yourself and change your mind.' He replied, 'No'. (5) He was asked, 'Why do you seek death?' He replied, 'Not death, but life.' (6) Quintillianus the proconsul said, 'You're not performing a great feat, striving after death, for those who find employment for small sums of money fighting against the wild beasts despise death; you too are just one of them. Ah well, since you are striving after death, you will be burned alive.' (7) And from a wooden tablet was read in Latin, 'Since he has confessed to being a Christian, we order Pionius to be burned alive.'

21. Pionius then came in haste to the arena, in the ardour of his faith, and when the secretary (*commentariensis*) arrived, he stripped himself. (2) After establishing that his body was unspoiled and of good bearing [i.e., despite his tortures], he was filled with a great joy. Raising his eyes to the heavens and thanking God that he had preserved him, he extended himself on the cross, and allowed the soldier to drive home the nails. (3) When he was nailed on, the executioner said to him once more, 'Change your mind, and the nails will be removed.' (4) But he replied, 'I felt that they are there to stay.' Then after reflecting a little, he said, 'I am hurrying so as to awake more quickly', meaning the resurrection of the dead. (5) Then they raised him on the cross, and afterwards also a presbyter named Metrodorus from the sect of the Marcionites. (6) It happened that Pionius was on the right and Metrodorus on the left, though both of them faced the east. (7) When they brought the wood and had piled it all around them in a circle, Pionius closed his eyes so that the crowd thought he had died. (8) But he was praying silently, and he opened his eyes when he had reached the end of his prayer.

(9) And as the flames rose, his face was jubilant as he spoke the final amen and said, 'Lord, receive my soul', then, as if with a rattle, he died gently and without effort, and he entrusted his spirit to God, who has promised to watch over all blood and every soul unjustly condemned.

22. The blessed Pionius, having spent such a life, without fault, without reproach, without blemish, with his spirit always turned towards the all powerful God and towards the mediator between God and men, Jesus Christ our Lord, was judged worthy of such an end, and after having overcome in the great combat he entered by the straight gate into the vast and great light. (2) The crown was also manifested physically. For after the fire had gone out, we approached him and saw the body of an athlete in its strength and dignity. (3) Indeed his ears had not been deformed, his hair remained firmly on the scalp of his head, and his chin was adorned as if with the first flush of a youthful beard. (4) Moreover his face was radiant with a marvellous grace, so that the Christians were strengthened again in their faith, but the unbelievers returned home fearful, with deeply disturbed consciences.

23. These events took place under the proconsul of Asia, Julius Proclus Quintillianus, when the consuls were the emperors Gaius Messius Quintus Trajanus Decius Augustus, for the second time, and Vettius Gratus, on the 4th day before the Ides of March according to the Romans [12 March 250], and according to the calendar of the province of Asia, on the 19th day of the sixth month, on the day of the sabbath, at the tenth hour, and according to our reckoning under the kingship of our Lord Jesus Christ, to whom be glory for ever and ever. Amen.

2.13 Persecution by the emperor Valerian: Cyprian *Letter* 80

This letter from the bishop of Carthage to a fellow north African bishop is justly famous for providing valuable insights into the persecution of the church by the emperor Valerian. His first move, in 257, was to exile clergy who refused to sacrifice and to forbid Christians to meet or enter cemeteries. This letter, from mid-258, shows how the emperor reacted as it became clear that these sanctions were proving insufficient, namely the introduction of much more severe penalties for the church's leadership and its most socially prominent supporters. It is also important for what it implies about the extent to which Christianity had by this stage penetrated into the upper echelons of Roman society, while the fact that Cyprian was able to obtain forewarning of Valerian's measures confirms the presence of Christians in high places at Rome. Like Xistus, the bishop of Rome referred to in the letter, Cyprian himself was soon to suffer martyrdom (for a contemporary account of which, see Musurillo 1972: 168–75). This persecution continued until 260, when Valerian's capture by the Persians led his son and co-emperor Gallienus to call a halt, thereby initiating a period of peace for the church which lasted until the commencement of the Diocletianic persecution in 303. Further reading: Clarke 1984–9: vol. 4, 8–14, 296–310.

Cyprian to his brother Successus

1. (1) The reason I did not write to you immediately, dearest brother, is because all the clergy have been under the threat of the contest [of persecution] and have been unable to leave here at all. Consistent with the dedication of their souls, all are ready for the divine and heavenly crown [of martyrdom]. But you should know that those whom I sent to the city [of Rome] for this reason – namely that they should find out and convey to us the truth about whatever has been decreed concerning us – have returned. For many different unconfirmed reports have been current. (2) But the real situation is actually as follows: Valerian has sent a rescript to the senate to the effect that bishops, presbyters and deacons are to be punished immediately, but that senators, leading officals and Roman equestrians should be deprived of their rank and stripped of their property and if after the confiscation of their assets they persist in being Christians, they also are to undergo capital punishment; women of this status are to lose their property and be sent into exile, and any members of the imperial household who have either previously confessed or do so now are to have their property confiscated and be sent in chains to the imperial estates. (3) The emperor Valerian also appended to his decree a copy of the letter which he has produced for provincial governors concerning us. We are daily expecting this letter to arrive, standing firm in the faith, ready to undergo suffering, awaiting the crown of eternal life from the bounty and favour of the Lord. (4) Moreover you should know that Xistus was executed in the cemetery on the 8th day before the Ides of August [6 August], together with four deacons. But the authorities in the city [of Rome] daily press on with this persecution, so that anyone brought before them is punished and their possessions are claimed by the imperial treasury.

2. I ask you to make these facts known to our other colleagues also, so that our brethren everywhere can be strengthened by their encouragement and be prepared for the spiritual struggle, so that every one of our people reflects on immortality rather than on death and, devoted to the Lord with complete trust and absolute courage,

they may rejoice rather than be afraid in this confession, in which they know the soldiers of God and of Christ are not killed but crowned. I pray for your well-being in the Lord always, dearest brother.

3

PAGANS AND CHRISTIANS DURING THE TETRARCHY

Unlike the emperor Decius who, in the mid-third century, seems to have thought that an empire-wide expression of piety towards the gods in the form of sacrifices was an urgent priority in putting the Roman world right, Diocletian and his colleagues initially directed most of their energies towards stabilising the frontiers, re-organising the imperial tax system and suppressing internal revolts. This is not to say that they neglected their religious responsibilities. Indeed they harnessed the gods to enhance the solidarity and prestige of the Tetrarchy by presenting the two senior emperors as the earthly deputies of Jupiter and the two junior emperors as those of Hercules (3.1).

However, it was only after Diocletian had been emperor for nearly two decades, when these other more pressing problems had been dealt with, that religious policy became a central issue. The first sign of this was a notorious edict issued against a new, expanding sect known as the Manichaeans, in which the Tetrarchs' commitment to traditional Roman religious practices was articulated with great vigour and their hostility to perceived challenges to those practices was made very clear (3.2). Against this background, it is hardly surprising that they soon turned their attention to the Christians. Initially, in February 303, Diocletian issued an edict ordering officials to destroy church buildings and burn copies of the scriptures. Its implementation is reflected in a record of a house-to-house search for Christian writings in a north African community (3.3), a papyrus declaration from a church reader (apparently illiterate) in Egypt (3.4), and the martyrdom of a north African bishop who refused to comply (3.5). This was followed by an order for the arrest and imprisonment of church leaders everywhere, though this placed such strains on available prison capacity that they soon had to be released, even if they refused to offer sacrifice. In a move reminiscent of Decius' persecution, a further order went out in 304/5 requiring all inhabitants of the empire to offer sacrifice, though enforcement of this must have entailed enormous administrative problems. Interestingly, the Jews appear to have been exempted (**8.3**).

Diocletian's retirement from imperial office in 305 by no means meant the end of persecution, but this is an appropriate point to raise the issue of why he initiated the persecution in the first place. One ancient source suggests that the prime mover was in fact the junior emperor Galerius, but there is also good reason to think that Diocletian was no less committed to upholding traditional religious practices and that the apparent delay in moving against the Christians was only a matter of timing. The persecution certainly implies that Christians had a high profile in Roman society, a feature reflected in some of the provisions of a church council from this period (**3.6**).

With Diocletian's departure from public life, the key figures in continuing harassment of Christians were Galerius and Maximinus Daia, with responsibility for the Balkans and the eastern provinces, respectively. Galerius eventually relented and in April 311 issued a deathbed edict of toleration (**3.7**), but Maximinus effectively ignored this while also proceeding with reforms to the organisation of pagan cult (**3.8**). The following year he gave approval for the expulsion of Christians from cities in the east (**3.9**), while a wider sense of renewed enthusiasm for traditional cults is apparent in an intriguing inscription from this same year (**3.10**). Developments in the west, however, were to make this short-lived.

Further reading: de Ste. Croix 1954; Millar 1977: 573–84; Liebeschuetz 1979: 235–52; Barnes 1981: chs 2, 9; Williams 1985: chs 12, 14; Lane Fox 1986: 592–608; Mitchell 1988: 111–16; Davies 1989.

3.1 Tetrarchic 'theology': *CIL* 3.4415 (= *ILS* 659)

The following short inscription, found on an altar at Carnuntum on the Middle Danube, resulted from a meeting there in November 308 of Diocletian and Maximian (the Jovians/Augusti of the inscription) and Galerius and Licinius (the Herculians/Caesars) (Barnes 1981: 32). Although deriving from the final years of the Tetrarchy, it is a convenient reminder of their commitment to maintaining pagan cults – and Mithras is a particularly appropriate deity for the soldier emperors of this period – and also of the special 'theology' of Tetrarchic rule, whereby the emperors presented themselves as descended from Jupiter (Jove) and Hercules. It implied close co-operation by the emperors with the gods, as well as co-operation between the emperors. Indeed, the analogy of the Caesars (junior emperors) implementing the policies of the Augusti (senior emperors) with Hercules acting at the behest of his father Jupiter has interesting parallels with

Christian beliefs, prompting one scholar to observe that 'the pagan state religion and Christianity were never closer in theology than at the time of the Great Persecution' (Liebeschuetz 1979: 240–3).

To the unconquered sun god, Mithras, supporter (*fautor*) of their empire, the Jovians and the Herculians, most devout Augusti and Caesars, restored the shrine.

3.2 Diocletian's edict against Manichaeans:
Comparison of the Laws of Moses and the Romans
15.3

This important and well-known text, preserved in an unusual fourth-century compilation which attempted to compare Roman and Jewish law, is of relevance to a number of subjects. First and most obviously, it illuminates the emergence of Manichaeism in the Roman empire (on which see further ch. 10, this volume). By this stage, Manichaeism had clearly penetrated from the east as far as north Africa, and the proconsul's report shows awareness of its hierarchical structure (6). Second, the vehemence of the rescript's language highlights Diocletian's firmly held views about the importance of upholding traditional Roman religious practices. Third and closely related, despite disagreement about the precise date of issue (297 or 302?: Chadwick 1979, 137–44; Barnes 1982: 55 n. 41; Corcoran 1996: 135 n. 49), it clearly has important implications for understanding the initiation of a new round of persecution of Christians in 303. The use of epithets such as 'Your Sagacity' and 'Our Serenity' usually strikes the modern reader as mannered and awkward, but was normal in imperial pronouncements during Late Antiquity. Further reading: Brown 1969; Lieu 1992: 121–5.

The senior emperors Diocletian and Maximian, and junior emperors Constantius and Maximianus [Galerius], to Julianus, proconsul of Africa. (1) Excessive idleness sometimes encourages people of a troublesome disposition to exceed the proper bounds of human nature and induces them to introduce certain kinds of credulous teaching of the most worthless and shameful kind, so that they may be deemed to be leading on many others in the caprices of their mistaken ideas, our dearest Julianus. (2) But the immortal gods in their foresight have deigned to lay down and prescribe what is good and true, approved and confirmed by the utterance of many good and distinguished men and by the deliberation and unimpaired consideration of the wisest. It is not right to oppose or resist these, nor ought a new cult to find fault with traditional practices (*vetus religio*). For it is a most serious offence to re-examine matters decided and fixed once and for all by our ancestors which retain their standing and contain the path to be followed.

(3) For this reason we are very keen to punish the obstinate and perverse thinking of these utterly worthless people. For they introduce strange new creeds in opposition to the traditional cults, excluding by their own perverse judgement the practices which divinity granted to us in former times. (4) Your Sagacity has informed Our Serenity about these people. We have heard that, like some new and unexpected portent, these Manichaeans have recently emerged and arisen in this part of the world from among our enemies the Persians, and have been responsible for many misdeeds there; for they have disrupted peaceful peoples and been the cause of very great damage in communities, and there must be grave cause for concern that perhaps, as usually happens, they will in due course try to infect men of a more blameless character, namely the orderly and peaceful Roman people, and our whole world, with the accursed customs and savage laws of the Persians, as though with the poisons of a malevolent serpent.

(5) And because you have set out all the kinds of very clear evil-doing discovered in their religion and all the falsehoods contrived, as disclosed in Your Wisdom's report, we have prescribed hardships and penalties appropriate and suitable for them. (6) For we decree that the originators and leaders, together with their detestable writings, be subjected to a more stringent penalty, namely that they be consumed by fire, while we command that followers who persist in their adherence receive capital punishment, and we sanction the claiming of their property by our treasury. (7) If anyone holding public office or individuals of any rank or social standing have also changed their allegiance to this strange, shameful and utterly disreputable creed, or to the teaching of the Persians, you shall ensure that their property is incorporated into our treasury, and they themselves are delivered to the [copper] mines at Phaeno [in southern Palestine] or the [marble] quarries on [the island of] Proconnesus [in the Propontis]. (8) Let Your Devotion hasten to comply with these orders and decisions of Our Tranquillity, so that this iniquitous defect can be rooted out from our most fortunate age. Issued on the day before the Kalends of April [31 March] in Alexandria.

3.3 The impact of persecution at the local level: Optatus, *Against the Donatists*, Appendix 1, pp. 186–88

The first step in Diocletian's persecution of the Christians was the issuing of an edict (24 February 303) requiring that they surrender all their writings to the imperial authorities, a measure reflecting government awareness of the importance of the written word in Christian life. The following passage describes the implementation of the edict in one community, in the north African region of Numidia, from an official record preserved by a fourth-century bishop from the region. At the same time, it provides the background to the so-called Donatist controversy, which was to be an ongoing cause of serious and often violent division within the north African church throughout the fourth century: Donatists took the view that *traditores* – those who had 'handed over' Christian writings to the authorities – had compromised the faith, and that clergy in particular who had done so should not be permitted to hold the office of bishop. This passage in fact comes from the record of a case brought by Donatists against one such 'collaborator', Silvanus, in 320. The passage also contains much interesting detail, such as the number of books and other writings that an individual church possessed at this stage (37 items in total), the quantities of clothing in its keeping (presumably for distribution to the poor), and the social status of some of those who held the office of reader. Further reading: Lane Fox 1986: 310; Gamble 1995: 147–50.

From the records of Munatius Felix, priest [of the provincial imperial cult] for life (*flamen perpetuus*) and senior magistrate (*curator rei publicae*) of the colony of Cirta, on the 14th day before the Kalends of June when Diocletian was consul for the eighth time and Maximian for the seventh [19 May 303]. When he came to the house in which the Christians were accustomed to meet, Felix, priest for life and senior magistrate, said to Paul the bishop, 'Bring out the writings of the law and anything else you have here, as has been decreed, so that you can obey the edict.' Paul the bishop said, 'The readers have the writings. But we give what we have here.' Felix, priest for life and senior magistrate, said to Paul the bishop, 'Point out the readers or send for them.' Paul the bishop said, 'You know them all.' Felix, priest for life and senior magistrate, said, 'We do not known them.' Paul the bishop said, 'The public office knows them, that is the notaries Edusius and Junius.' Felix, priest for life and senior magistrate, said, 'Leaving aside the matter of the readers, whom the public office will identify, give what you have.'

Paul the bishop presided, along with the presbyters Montanus, Victor (p. 187) Deusatelius and Memorius, and the deacons Mars and Helius helped, together with the subdeacons Marcuclius, Catullinus, Silvanus and Carosus, and Januarius, Meraclus, Fructuosus, Miggo, Saturninus, Victor and the other grave-diggers, and Victor son of Aufidus kept a record, which was, in brief, as follows: 2 gold cups, 6 silver cups, 6 silver jugs, a silver container, 7 silver lamps, 2 candle-holders, 7 short bronze lampstands with their lamps, 11 bronze lamps with their chains, 82 women's tunics, 38 cloaks, 16 men's tunics, 13 pairs of men's shoes, 47 pairs of women's shoes, 19 thongs.

Felix, priest for life and senior magistrate, said to Marcuclius, Silvanus and Carosus, the grave-diggers [*sic* – read 'subdeacons'], 'Bring out what you have.' Silvanus and Carosus said, 'We have turned out everything that was here.' Felix, priest for life and senior magistrate, said to Marculius, Silvanus and Carosus, 'Your answer is preserved in the record.' After empty bookcases were found in the library there, Silvanus brought out a silver container and a silver lamp which he said he had found behind a large pot. Victor son of Aufidus said to Silvanus, 'You would have been dead if you hadn't found those.' Felix, priest for life and senior magistrate, said to Silvanus, 'Look more carefully, to ensure that nothing else remains here.' Silvanus said, 'Nothing else remains, we have brought out everything.' When the dining room was opened, 4 containers and 6 large pots were found there.

Felix, priest for life and senior magistrate, said, 'Bring out the writings which you have, so that we can obey the edicts of the emperors and their decree.' Catullinus brought out one very large book. Felix, priest for life and senior magistrate, said to Marcuclius and Silvanus, 'Why have you produced only one book? Bring out the writings which you have.' Catullinus and Marcuclius said, 'We do not have any more, because we are subdeacons; but the readers have the books.' Felix, priest for life and senior magistrate, said to Marcuclius and Catullinus, 'Point out the readers!' Marcuclius and Catullinus said, 'We don't know where they live.' Felix, priest for life and senior magistrate, said to Marcuclius and Catullinus, 'If (p. 188) you don't know where they live, tell me their names.' Catullinus and Marcuclius said, 'We are not traitors. Here we are – order us to be killed.' Felix, priest for life and senior magistrate, said, 'Arrest them' …

And when they came to the house of Felix the tailor, he brought out five books, and when they came to the house of Victorinus, he produced eight books; and when they came to the house of Projectus, he brought out five larger and two smaller books; and when they came to the house of the grammarian, Felix, priest for life and senior magistrate, said to Victor the grammarian, 'Bring out the writings you have, so that you can obey the edict.' Victor the grammarian brought out two books and four notebooks. Felix, priest for life and senior magistrate, said to Victor, 'Bring out the writings, for you have more.' Victor the grammarian said, 'If I had more, I would have handed them over' …

3.4 Documentary evidence from the first phase of persecution: *P. Oxy.* 2673

The following declaration is, somewhat surprisingly, one of the few papyri which can confidently be related to the Diocletianic persecution (cf. *P. Oxy.* 2601, for which, however, the argument is more circumstantial), and reflects the implementation of the first phase during which churches were destroyed. Interestingly, it was found in triplicate. It is a moot point whether the church was really this poor – the reader may have been lying. In the original publication of this papyrus, the 'bronze objects' (*chalken hulen*) was thought to read 'bronze door' (*chalken pulen*), which would have had interesting implications for our understanding of pre-Constantinian church buildings, but the editor subsequently revised his reading as translated below (Rea 1979: 128). The papyrus is also of interest for its puzzling reference to the declarant being a church reader, yet illiterate. The most likely resolution to this apparent paradox is that he did not know how to read or write in Greek, but was competent in the indigenous Coptic language which one would expect to be the main means of communication in rural villages of Egypt such as Chysis. On this issue, see Clarke 1984.

In the ninth consulate of our lord emperor Diocletian Augustus and the eighth of our lord emperor Maximian Augustus. To Aurelius Neilus also called Ammonius, gymnasiarch, councillor and chief magistrate, and to Aurelius Sarmates and Aurelius Martinus, both gymnasiarchs, councillors and judges (*syndikoi*), all from the illustrious and most illustrious city of the Oxyrhynchites – Aurelius Ammonius, son of Kopreos, reader of the former church of the village of Chysis.

Since you commanded me in accordance with the letter from Aurelius Athanasius, overseer of the imperial account (*procurator rei privatae*), as a result of a command of the most distinguished master of the imperial account (*magister rei privatae*), Neratius Apollonides, concerning handing over everything in the former church, and since I declared that the church had no gold, silver, or coin, no clothing, no animals, slaves, or land, no possessions whether from gifts or from inheritances, with the sole exception of the bronze objects found and handed over to the auditor (*logistes*) for transport to the most illustrious Alexandria in accordance with the letter from our most distinguished prefect Claudius Culcianus, I also swear by the guardian spirit (*tychē*) of our lords the emperors Diocletian Augustus and Maximian Augustus and of the most renowned Caesars Constantius and Maximianus [Galerius] that these things are so and that I have not deceived you, otherwise may I be liable to the sacred oath. In the 20th and 12th year of our lords Diocletian Augustus and Maximian Augustus and of the most renowned

Caesars Constantius and Maximianus [Galerius], Mecheir 10 [5 February 304].

I, Aurelius Ammonius, swore the oath as stated above. I, Aurelius Serenos, wrote on his behalf since he is illiterate.

3.5 The consequences of resistance:
The Martyrdom of the holy bishop Felix

The following passage complements the previous two, showing that there were some Christian leaders prepared to stand firm and what happened to them when they did so. Further reading: Lepelley 1979–81: vol. 2, 192–3.

(1) When Diocletian was consul for the eighth time and Maximian for the seventh [303], an edict of the emperors and junior emperors went out over all the face of the earth; and it was posted up by leaders and magistrates in the colonies and cities, by each in his own place, to the effect that they were to seize the holy books from the hands of the bishops and presbyters. The document was put up in the town of Thibiuca on the Nones of June [5 June]. Then Magnilianus the magistrate (*curator*) ordered the elders of the people [i.e., the Christians] to be brought before him, since the bishop Felix had that same day set out for Carthage. So he ordered Aper the presbyter and Cyril and Vitalis the readers to be brought before him. (2) Magnilianus the magistrate said to them, 'Do you have holy books?' (3) Aper said, 'We do.' (4) Magnilianus the magistrate said, 'Hand them over to be burned in the fire.' (5) Then Aper said, 'Our bishop has them on his person.' (6) Magnilianus the magistrate said, 'Where is he?' (7) Aper said, 'I do not know.' (8) Magnilianus the magistrate said, 'Then you will be detained until you can give an account to the proconsul Anulinus.'

(9) The following day, however, the bishop Felix returned from Carthage to Thibiuca. Then Magnilianus the magistrate ordered his staff to bring Felix the bishop before him. (10) Magnilianus the magistrate said to him, 'Are you Felix the bishop?' (11) Felix the bishop said, 'I am.' (12) Magnilianus the magistrate said, 'Hand over whatever books or parchments you have.' (13) Felix the bishop said, 'I have some, but I will not hand them over.' (14) Magnilianus the magistrate said, 'Hand over the books so they can be burned.' (15) Felix the bishop said, 'It would be better for me to be burned than the holy writings, for it is better to obey God rather than men.' (16) Magnilianus the magistrate said, 'The emperors' orders are more important than anything you say.' (17) Felix the bishop

said, 'The command of the Lord is more important than that of men.' (18) Magnilianus the magistrate said, 'Reconsider your thoughts on this for three days, for if you fail to carry out what has been decreed in this city of mine, you will go to the proconsul and continue what you are now saying in his court.'

(19) After three days had elapsed, the magistrate ordered Felix the bishop to be brought before him and he said to him, 'Have you reconsidered?' (20) Felix the bishop said, 'I repeat what I said previously, and I will say it before the proconsul.' (21) Magnilianus the magistrate said, 'Then you will go before the proconsul and give an account there.' (22) Then Vincentius Celsinus, councillor of the town of Thibiuca, was assigned to escort him.

(23) Felix set out from Thibiuca for Carthage on the 18th day before the Kalends of July [14 June]. When he arrived there, he was brought before the legate, but the legate ordered him to be thrown into prison. But on the next day, before dawn, Felix the bishop was brought out. (24) The legate said to him, 'Why do you not hand over these worthless writings?' (25) Felix the bishop said, 'I have them, but I will not hand them over.' (26) Then the legate ordered him to be sent to the deepest part of the prison. Sixteen days later, however, Felix the bishop was brought out of the prison in chains before the proconsul Anulinus, at the fourth hour of the night. (27) Anulinus said to him, 'Why do you not hand over these worthless writings?' (28) Felix the bishop replied, 'I am not going to hand them over.' (29) Then Anulinus the proconsul ordered him to be executed by the sword; it was the Ides of July [15 July]. (30) Felix the bishop raised his eyes to heaven and said in a clear voice, 'I thank you, God: I have had 56 years in this world, I have preserved my chastity, served the gospel, and proclaimed the true faith. Lord God of heaven and earth, Jesus Christ, I bow my neck as a sacrifice to you, who lives forever.' (31) When he finished praying, he was led away by soldiers and beheaded. He was buried beside the road called the Scillitan, on the property of Faustus.

3.6 Christianity and local elites: *The Council of Elvira* Canons 2–3, 55–57, 59–60

The deliberations of the Council of Elvira, which met in southern Spain in the early fourth century, shed light on a wide range of issues (cf. 8.6, 14.12). The canons selected below provide interesting evidence for the penetration of Christianity among local elites. The priests alluded to in the first three canons were responsible for the imperial cult in their locality, which could entail not only making sacrifice but also putting on gladiatorial contests and theatrical shows (hence the allusions to murder and immorality, respectively in Canon 2). These priesthoods were often hereditary, so that members of those families who became Christians found themselves in a predicament, for which the church authorities do not seem to have had much sympathy. Those holding political office would necessarily also find themselves participating in public religious ceremonies – hence the insistence that they stay away from the church for the duration of time in office (56). Canons 57 and 59 try to discourage ordinary Christian citizens from involving themselves in any public occasions with a religious element. Canon 60 is included here partly because it presents an interesting contrast with later Christian attitudes to the destruction of cult statues (cf. 6.6; Thornton 1986), and partly because it bears on the issue of the date of the council, traditionally placed in the first decade of the fourth century. More recently it has been argued that this canon must imply a date after 312, since there was a much greater likelihood of Christians smashing idols once Constantine had lent his support to the church (Lane Fox 1986: 664–5). On the other hand, Constantine had shown some favour towards Christians as early as 306 (Lactantius *On the Deaths of the Persecutors* 24.9) and Spain fell under his jurisdiction before 312. But even if the council was convened in the second decade of the century, the revision of the date does not seriously weaken the main point being made above.

2. It was decided that priests (*flamines*) who, after the faith of baptism and rebirth, have sacrificed, and have doubled their offence by adding murder or trebled it by including immorality, shall not be received into communion, even on the point of death.

3. Likewise it was decided that priests (*flamines*) who have not sacrificed but have merely given games (*munus*) shall receive communion after they have performed appropriate penance, because they have kept themselves from polluted sacrifices. It was also decided that if they engage in immoral actions after their penance, they shall no longer receive communion, to ensure they are not seen to have made a mockery of the Lord's communion …

55. It was decided that priests (*sacerdotes*) who only wear crowns but do not sacrifice or offer anything from their own resources to idols shall receive communion after two years.

56. It is decided those who hold the annual office of senior magistrates (*duumviri*) are forbidden to enter the church for one year.

57. Respectable women or their husbands are not to lend their clothing for the adorning of a pagan procession (*pompa*); if they do so, they are to be excommunicated for three years …

59. Christians are forbidden to go to the idols in the main civic temple (*Capitolium*) to sacrifice like a pagan (*gentilis*) and observe. If they do so, they are to be regarded as equally guilty. If a baptised Christian does so, they are to be received back into the church after ten years' penance.

60. If anyone is killed on the spot while destroying idols, it was

decided that they shall not be numbered among the martyrs, since this is not written about in the gospel and is never found being done in the times of the apostles.

3.7 Galerius ends the persecution: Lactantius *On the Deaths of the Persecutors* 34

This edict, issued by the dying emperor Galerius on 30 April 311, is preserved by the Christian scholar Lactantius (*c.* 240–*c.* 320) in his account of the Diocletianic persecution and its failure. Galerius' edict formally ended the period of persecution which had begun in 303 and gave legal recognition to the Christians and to the church's right to own property. It also shows how one of their most committed persecutors (despite the euphemistic language at the end of (3)) sought to justify publicly his reversal of policy: 'Galerius' interesting line of thought here [the opening of (4)] is that, while the persecution had originally been planned to ensure that everyone worshipped the gods who protected the empire, an even worse situation had developed; it would have been better, he admits, for the Christians to be at least worshipping their own god than for them to be worshipping none at all' (Creed 1984: 113 n.7). (The reference to Christians not worshipping their own god presumably alludes either to their lapsing or to their not attending church meetings for fear of arrest.) In theory, this edict applied to the whole empire, but because of the effective division of power among emperors of the Tetrarchic period, its significance varied from region to region. It was of little practical consequence in the west because Constantine had already extended toleration to the Christians when proclaimed emperor in July 306 (Lactantius *On the Deaths of the Persecutors* 24.9), as also had Maxentius in October of the same year (Eusebius *Church History* 8.14.1). On the other hand, another committed opponent of Christianity, Maximinus Daia, controlled much of the east and soon resumed persecution there (**3.8**), which meant that it was Christians living in the Balkan provinces who stood to gain most from Galerius' decision.

(1) Among other measures which we are continually putting in place for the benefit and advantage of the state, we had previously wished to rectify everything in accordance with the long-established laws and public order of the Romans, and to see to it also that the Christians, who had abandoned the principles of their forebears, returned to their right minds. (2) For somehow such great wilfulness gained control of these Christians and such great folly took a hold of them that they did not adhere to traditional practices first established by, perhaps, their very own forebears, but they decided on their own initiative to make rules for themselves to observe and to hold gatherings of various groups of people in different places. (3) Then when our law came into being to this effect – that they were to return to traditional practices – many of them were exposed to danger, and many were struck down. (4) But when many more

persisted in their way of life and we realised that they were neither offering the ritual observances due to the gods nor worshipping the god of the Christians, we reflected on our most mild mercy and our long-standing practice of showing leniency to all people, and decided that our very prompt pardon should also be extended to these people. As a result, they may once more be Christians and construct their own meeting places, provided they do nothing contrary to public order. (5) Furthermore, we intend to make known to governors in another letter what course of action they should adopt. Therefore, in accordance with our mercy, the Christians should pray to their god for our well-being and that of the state as well as their own, so that the state may be kept safe on all sides and they can live free from fear in their own homes.

3.8 Continuing persecution in the east: Lactantius *On the Deaths of the Persecutors* 36

This passage summarises developments in the east following the death of the emperor Galerius in April 311. As noted above, Maximinus Daia ignored Galerius' edict of toleration in the eastern provinces under his control, where persecution effectively continued. Lactantius' account is of particular interest, first, for the detail it provides about some of Maximinus' measures in this respect (Eusebius *Church History* 9.1–8 provides a more detailed account with some differences), and second, for its description of Maximinus' attempts to revive the pagan priesthood – a move which may have inspired some of Julian's measures in the mid-fourth century (5.3; for a dissenting view, see Nicholson 1994). This is also the context in which Julius Eugenius underwent persecution (12.1). Further reading: Grant 1975.

(1) When he heard the news [of Galerius' death], Maximinus made his way rapidly from the east via the courier relays he had organised, so as to take control of Galerius' provinces, and while Licinius was delaying, he laid claim to all the territory right up to the straits of Chalcedon. Entering Bithynia, he won popular support there for the time being by doing away with the [tax] census amidst great rejoicing by all. (2) The resulting disagreement between the two emperors almost led to war, as armed forces occupied the opposing shores of the straits. But peace and friendship were arranged on specified terms, and the agreement was formalised with the shaking of hands at the straits themselves. (3) Maximinus returned free from anxiety and behaved as he had in Syria and Egypt. To begin with, he abrogated the toleration extended to Christians in the general edict by arranging for embassies from the cities to request that Christians be banned from building meeting places within the

cities, so that he would appear to be pressured and compelled by their insistence into doing what he intended to do without any prompting. (4) Granting their requests, in a move without precedent he then appointed high priests (*sacerdotes maximi*) for each city from among its leading citizens, who were to offer sacrifice every day to all the gods and, with the assistance of the traditional priesthood, were to ensure that the Christians did not construct any buildings or meet together in public or private; they were also authorised to arrest Christians and force them to sacrifice or bring them before the magistrates. (5) Not content with this, he established as chief priests (*pontifices*) for each province individuals drawn from the more elevated ranks of society, and instructed both types of priest to appear in public dressed in white cloaks. (6) Moreover, he was preparing to do what he had already done in the eastern provinces. For on the pretext of claiming to exercise mercy, he forbade the killing of the servants of God, instead ordering that they be mutilated. As a result, the eyes of those professing the faith (*confessores*) were gouged out, hands were amputated, feet were severed, noses and ears were lopped off.

3.9 Maximinus' new strategy: Eusebius *Church History* 9.7.6–14

This passage presents most of an important document issued by the emperor Maximinus Daia in 312 (the very wordy preamble has been left out, and Eusebius himself omitted a section in the middle), in which the emperor claims to be responding to requests from communities that they be allowed to expel Christians living among them – a request which Maximinus is only too happy to approve (cf. 8.16). In doing so, he also offers a fascinating statement of the rationale for adherence to paganism. Eusebius says he read an inscribed copy in Tyre, which he then translated from Latin into Greek. In modern times, two inscriptions with portions of the Latin version addressed to communities in Asia Minor have been discovered, one as recently as 1986 (Mitchell 1988); however, since neither presents as much of the text as Eusebius' version, it is the latter which is given here. The inscriptions are important, however, not only for confirming the essential reliability of Eusebius' translation of the document, but also for confirming the allegations of Eusebius and Lactantius that Maximinus was orchestrating the whole process (for detailed argument on this point, see Mitchell 1988: 117). As for the final part, it has been plausibly argued that its enigmatic language about a reward was in fact a promise by Maximinus to abolish the much-resented poll-tax which Galerius had in 306 extended from rural to urban inhabitants of the empire, which in turn shows that 'Maximinus was, in a literal sense, prepared to pay a high price for his [religious] convictions' (Mitchell 1988: 123, with response to criticisms of this argument in Mitchell 1993: vol. 2, 64, n. 68).

(6) 'Your city gave no thought to the many concerns of its own and disregarded its previous requests relating to its own affairs when it again realised that the adherents of that accursed folly were beginning to spread, like an unattended, smouldering funeral pyre which, when its flames are stirred to life, becomes once more a huge conflagration. Immediately and without delay, your city fled for refuge to our piety, as if to a mother city of all religious devotion, asking for a remedy and for help. (7) It is clear that the gods have prompted this wholesome thinking in you because of your reverent confidence in them. It was he – most exalted and mighty Zeus, defender of your illustrious city and protector of your ancestral gods, women, children, households and homes from every deadly danger – who inspired this salutary plan in your hearts, and made very clear how special, splendid and healthful it is to approach with due reverence the adoration and divine worship of the immortal gods. (8) For can anyone be found who is so stupid or to whom rational thought is so completely alien that they do not realise that it is because of the benevolent goodwill of the gods that the earth does not reject the seeds committed to it and so disappoint the expectations of farmers with false hopes? Or again, that ungodly war does not establish its presence unhindered on the earth, upsetting the heaven-ordained order and carrying squalid corpses off to death? Or indeed that the surging sea is not whipped up by the blasts of incessant winds, or that unanticipated tempests do not rush down and stir up destructive storms? Or yet further, that the earth, the nurse and mother of all, does not subside from her deepest hollows with alarming tremors, while the mountains resting on it collapse into the resulting chasms? All these catastrophes, and others even more serious, have often happened in the past, as everyone is aware. (9) They all happened together because of the destructive error arising from the empty folly of these lawless people, when it took control of their souls and nearly crushed the whole world with its shameful deeds.'

(10) After other comments, he adds the following: 'Let them look out over the broad plains where the wheat is already ripening and waving its ears of grain, the well-watered meadows are bright with blooming flowers, and the weather granted us is temperate and very mild. (11) Let all of them rejoice that, through our reverent worship and honouring, the all powerful and resolute air has been appeased, as a result of which they are able to enjoy secure, settled peace and the leisure that goes with it. And all those who have been brought back from that blind error and wandering and have returned to a

right and favourable state of mind – let them rejoice all the more as though they had been rescued from an unexpected storm or an oppressive illness, and were hereafter benefiting from the pleasant enjoyment of life. (12) But if they persist in their accursed folly, let them be separated out and driven far away from your city and its territory, as you have asked, so that, consistent with your praiseworthy enthusiasm in this matter, your city may be freed from all defilement and godlessness, and in accordance with its innate resolve, may comply with the worship of the immortal gods through the reverence owed to them. (13) But so that you know how pleasing your request in this matter has been to us, and how willing and benevolent our heart is, of its own accord, without any resolutions or petitions [on your part], we grant to Your Devotion whatever act of munificence you wish, in return for this devout resolve of yours. (14) And now may you deem this a thing worth doing and receiving, for it will be yours without any delay – something that, once granted to your city for all time, will bear witness to our devout reverence for the immortal gods and will demonstrate to your children and descendants that you have obtained due reward from our benevolence for the manner in which you conduct your life.'

3.10 Celebrating the gods: *I. Strat.* 310

The recently discovered inscription containing part of 3.9 in its original Latin version includes important information, lacking in Eusebius, about its precise date and place of issue – 6 April 312 at Sardis in western Asia Minor. The following inscription must have been put up soon after, for it shows Maximinus further south in Caria, suppressing brigands at Stratonikeia and participating in religious festivities at nearby Panamara (cf. 1.5), before moving on to Syrian Antioch which he had reached by July (Mitchell 1988: 118–19). It therefore illuminates the wider context of 3.9, showing the emperor advertising his cause and the willingness of members of the local elite to offer extravagant expressions of support. It has also been observed, apropos the wider issue of pagan morale, that the donors commemorated here 'showed no disillusionment, no loss of heart in a time of hardship' (Lane Fox 1986: 584), though of course it would hardly have done to show a lack of enthusiasm when the emperor himself was present. For details of the various festivals referred to, see Deschamps and Cousin 1891: 172–81, Magie 1950: 997–8, Laumonier 1958: 292–333; for interpretation of the opening phrase, see Deschamps and Cousin 1891: 170, Laumonier 1958: 367.

Priests descended from priests, in the festival of Hera, Marcus Sempronius Arruncius Theodotus, son of Arrianus, and Sempronia Arruncia Arriane, his sister – children, grandchildren and great-grandchildren of priests and of chief-priests and of asiarchs [priests of the imperial cult in the province of Asia] of the temples at Ephesus. They were priests for the whole year, with reverence towards the gods and with liberality towards the people, providing oil for the procession and the festival of the Panamareia, and for the conducting of the sacred key and the storing away of the crowns, for all thirty-four days. They provided oil not only for the citizens and guests, but also for all the visiting soldiers. When they were priests, the divinity of our Lord, the invincible Augustus Jovius Maximinus, shone on our native city and destroyed brigandage. Although a container of oil cost 10,000 *denarii* because of the continued unfruitfulness of the olive trees, they gave feasts for all the councillors and citizens in the festival of Dionysus and the festival of Hera; they did not neglect any of the mysteries during the whole year, nor did they omit a single sacrifice or end-of-month feast. With liberality and magnanimity, they gave gifts to the men and women of every rank and age in the processions. They set up the memorial of stone in the portico their father built from the foundations, beside the monuments and inscribed memorials and the statue of their grandfather Sempronius Clemens, while Marcus Aurelius, son of Diophantos, < ... philosopher?> from the Mouseion, priest of the gods, acted as guide to the mysteries for the priest and conducted the mysteries without interruption throughout the whole year.

4

CONSTANTINE

The fact that only one chapter in this volume focuses on an individual reflects the fundamental importance of Constantine in the religious history of Late Antiquity. Even if one takes an optimistic view of the growth of Christian numbers during the second half of the third century, his decision to throw his support behind the church still had enormous ramifications which are reflected in much of the content of this volume (cf., e.g., 11.4, 12.5, 13.1). Although Constantine exhibited a tolerant attitude towards Christians from the time of his proclamation as emperor in 306, this did not mean he himself had embraced Christianity at this stage, as implied by his apparent encounter with the god Apollo in 310 (4.1). The formative event for Constantine was his victory, against the odds, over Maxentius at the Milvian Bridge outside Rome in 312 (4.2). Since the god of the Christians had evidently given him assurance of this outcome beforehand, his success persuaded Constantine of the power of that god and from this point onwards he began giving his support to the church. Whether 'conversion' is the appropriate term for what happened remains a moot point. There is no doubting his commitment to the Christian cause from 312, but his knowledge of what the Christian faith entailed must still have been sketchy and it is more realistic to think in terms of a gradual evolution of his understanding of the full implications of his decision (Cameron 1983). Meanwhile, the inscription placed by the senate on Constantine's victory arch in Rome provides an intriguing glimpse of how this overwhelmingly pagan body coped with the novel situation of an emperor who supported Christianity (4.3).

Constantine's new religious allegiance did not at this stage imply discrimination against pagans, as he and his colleague Licinius made clear in their famous declaration of 313 (4.4). If nothing else, political commonsense demanded an even-handed approach, since the Christian population of the empire was still in the minority. A decade later, however, a shift in Constantine's attitudes can be detected (4.5), though his theological understanding seems to have remained limited, judging by his initial reaction to the doctrinal controversy provoked by the views of Arius (4.6). Ambiguities persist during the final decade of his reign. On the one hand, he can be found giving assistance or attention to prominent pagans (4.7, 4.8), while on the other, Christianity proves to be the decisive factor in a decision about the legal status of a community (4.9). This ambiguity is epitomised above all by his willingness to endorse the continuation of the imperial cult at the same time as he prohibits certain associated rites (presumably sacrifice) (4.10).

Further reading: Chadwick 1978; Liebeschuetz 1979: 277–304; Barnes 1981: chs 3–5, 12–15; Cameron 1983; Lane Fox 1986: ch. 12; Lieu and Montserrat 1998.

4.1 Constantine's vision of Apollo: The *Latin Panegyrics* 6 (7).21.3–6

The story of Constantine's vision before the battle of the Milvian Bridge (4.2) is famous. Less well-known, but none the less significant, is the report that he had a vision of Apollo a few years earlier (310) in Gaul, probably during a visit to a shrine at Grand. The episode is important for a number of reasons. It implies that, despite his conciliatory move of restoring Christian property in 306 (Lactantius *On the Deaths of the Persecutors* 24.9), Constantine had not yet embraced Christianity himself, and it serves as a reminder that divine epiphanies were not the exclusive preserve of the Christian God. Further reading: MacMullen 1968; Rodgers 1980; Barnes 1981: 36; Lane Fox 1986: 611; Nixon and Rodgers 1994: 248–51 nn. 91–3.

You turned aside to the most beautiful temple in the whole world, or rather, to the god present there, as you saw. For you, O Constantine, saw, I believe, your Apollo, accompanied by Victory, offering you laurel crowns, each of which bears assurance of thirty years. For this is the number of human ages which are assuredly owed to you, beyond the old age of Nestor. And – why indeed do I say 'I believe' – you *saw* and you recognised yourself in the appearance of him to whom the divine hymns of the poets proclaimed the rule of the whole world to be due. I think this has now happened, since you are, O emperor, as he is, young, joyful, a bearer of good health, and most handsome.

4.2 Constantine's formative experience: Lactantius *On the Deaths of the Persecutors* 44.1–10

This is one of two accounts of the battle of the Milvian Bridge and the events preceding it. The version of Lactantius (*c.* 240–*c.* 320), who in his final years was tutor to Constantine's son Crispus, was written within a few years of the event, while the other was recorded more than twenty-five years later in Eusebius *Life of Constantine* 1.27–38, albeit on the basis of Constantine's own sworn statement in 324. Not surprisingly there are important differences between the two accounts, no doubt partly explicable in terms of Constantine's memory of events undergoing changes with the passage of time (see Cameron and Hall 1999: 204–15 for discussion). There is also more specific uncertainty about the precise configuration of the symbol inscribed on the shields of Constantine's troops (on which see Black 1970; Cameron and Hall 1999: 208–11). Despite all this, however, there can be no doubting the long-term significance of what happened. Although not alluded to below, the fact that there must have been Christians in his entourage by this stage, including the Spanish bishop Ossius, was presumably another factor that contributed to the outcome. Further reading: Barnes 1981: 42–3; Lane Fox 1986: 612–19.

(1) Civil war had already begun between them. Although Maxentius remained inside Rome, because he had received an answer from an oracle that he would die if he went beyond the gates of the city, he nevertheless waged war through competent commanders. (2) Maxentius' forces were greater because he had retrieved his father's army from Severus, and had recently fetched his own troops from the Mauri and Gaetuli. (3) There was an encounter in which Maxentius' troops prevailed, after which Constantine, regaining his resolve and ready for either victory or death, moved all his forces nearer to the city and camped in the neighbourhood of the Milvian bridge. (4) The anniversary approached of the day on which Maxentius had seized power, that is the 6th day before the Kalends of November [27 October], and the celebrations of five years of rule were drawing to a close. (5) Constantine was enjoined in a dream to mark the heavenly symbol of God on the shields of his men and so to engage in battle. He did as commanded, and marked Christ on the shields in the form of a letter X placed sideways with the top bent around. (6) Armed with this symbol, his army took up their weapons. The enemy issued forth to meet them without their commander-in-chief, and crossed the bridge. The battle lines, equal in length, engaged one another, both sides fighting with the greatest vigour – 'there was no sign of flight on either side' [Virgil *Aeneid* 10.757]. (7) Discord arose within the city, and the emperor was upbraided for abdicating responsibility for the safety of the people. Then suddenly the people shouted in one voice (for he was

holding games in honour of the anniversary of his accession), 'Constantine cannot be defeated!'. (8) Disconcerted by this cry, he hurried away and, summoning some senators, he ordered the Sibylline books to be consulted. In them was found the statement that on that day the enemy of the Romans would perish. (9) Induced by this prophecy to expect victory, he went forth and joined the fray. The bridge was torn down behind him. At the sight of this, the fighting became more intense and the hand of God was over the battle. Maxentius' troops were seized by panic. He himself turned in flight and hurried back towards the bridge, which had been broken down, and under the pressure of the fleeing masses, he was pitched into the Tiber. (10) When this very bitter war had finally drawn to a close, Constantine was welcomed as emperor with great joy by the senate and people of Rome.

4.3 Constantine's arch in Rome: *CIL* 6.1139 (= *ILS* 694)

This dedication of the famous arch erected in Rome *c.* 315 to commemorate Constantine's defeat of Maxentius in 312 is chiefly of interest here for the studied ambiguity of its language concerning 'divinity', acceptable both to a Constantine who has begun to embrace Christianity and to a pagan senate (for the likely classical resonances of the phrase *instinctu divinitatis*, see Hall 1998). Similarly, the representations of Constantine's soldiers on the reliefs adorning the arch do not show them bearing shields with any sort of Christian symbol (Lane Fox 1986: 620).

To the emperor Caesar Flavius Constantine the greatest, dutiful and blessed, Augustus, the Senate and people of Rome dedicated this arch, distinguished by [representations of] his victories, because, by the inspiration of divinity and by greatness of mind (*instinctu divinitatis mentis magnitudine*), with his army he avenged the state with righteous arms against both the tyrant and all of his faction at one and the same time. To the liberator of the city, and the establisher of peace.

4.4 Licinius and Constantine proclaim toleration: Lactantius *On the Deaths of the Persecutors* 48.2–12

This famous document has long been known as the 'Edict of Milan' despite the fact it is neither technically an edict nor was it issued at Milan. Constantine and Licinius had met at Milan in early February 313 in a show of solidarity prior to Licinius' campaign against Maximinus Daia in the east, but it was only after Licinius' defeat of the latter in early June that this letter was issued to governors of those provinces formerly under Maximinus' control where Galerius' grant of toleration (3.7) had been ignored. These circumstances diminish the significance often attached to the document, yet there are also important differences compared with Galerius' edict. It adopts a much more positive tone towards the Christians, no doubt due to Constantine's influence, and it makes provision for restoration of Christian property, as opposed to Galerius' grudging concession of their right to contruct meeting places. Clearly, however, despite what one still occasionally finds stated, it does not mark the establishment of Christianity as the official religion of the empire. The vicar referred to in (8) is an imperial official (the deputy of the Praetorian Prefect), not an ecclesiastical post. Further reading: Creed 1984: 121–2.

(2) When with good fortune both I, Constantine Augustus, and I, Licinius Augustus, met in Milan and discussed everything relevant to the public advantage and safety, we considered that, among those things which we saw would be beneficial to many people, priority should be given to setting in order those matters involving reverence for the divinity, in order that we might give both to Christians and to everyone the freedom to follow whatever religion they wish, so that whatever divinity resides in the heavens might be well-disposed and favourable towards us and all who have been placed under our authority. (3) With salutary and very sound reasoning we thought we should embark upon this considered policy of not denying anyone at all the opportunity to devote their mind either to the religion of the Christians or to that religion which they consider most appropriate to themselves, so that the highest divinity (*summa divinitas*), to whose worship we yield ourselves with free minds, might be able to show us his accustomed favour and benevolence in all matters.

(4) For this reason Your Devotion should know we have decided that, after doing away completely with all the stipulations previously written to your office on the subject of the Christians, provisions which seemed to us very harmful and incompatible with our clemency should be cancelled, and every person who wishes to adhere to the religion of the Christians may now earnestly do so, freely and openly, without any disturbance or interference. (5) We believed these decisions should be communicated fully to Your Solicitude, so you know we have given to these Christians the freedom and absolute right to practise their own religion. (6) When you realise that we have granted this favour to these people, Your Devotion will also understand that we have likewise granted to others the open and free right to observe their own religion in accordance with the peace of our time, so that everyone may have the free opportunity to worship whatever they have chosen. We have done this so that we do not appear to have acted to the detriment of any cult or religion.

(7) Moreover we have decided that the following should be decreed with regard to the community of the Christians, namely that if anyone appears in the past to have purchased from our treasury or from anyone else those same places in which the Christians used to meet before (about which letters previously sent to your office contained specific instructions), they are to restore to the Christians those same places without payment or any request for recompense, and without any prevarication or double-dealing. (8) Those who acquired them as a gift should likewise return them to these same Christians as quickly as possible. Moreover if those who bought them or who acquired them as a gift seek something [by way of compensation] from our benevolence, they should submit a request to the vicar who will look after their interests in accordance with our clemency. All these places should be handed over to the community of the Christians by your intervention immediately and without delay. (9) And since these same Christians not only had places in which they were accustomed to meet, but are known also to have had other places belonging to them in law as a community, that is, to the churches and not to individuals, you will order that all these properties be restored, in accordance with the aforementioned law, to these same Christians, that is to their community and assemblies, without any double-dealing or disagreement whatsoever, while of course observing the principle explained above, that those who restore these properties without charge, as we have specified, may expect recompense from our benevolence.

(10) In all of these matters, you should provide your most effective intervention on behalf of the aforementioned community of the Christians, so that our command may be fulfilled as quickly as possible, and public order in this matter is looked after in accordance with our clemency. (11) As indicated above, to the extent that this happens, the divine favour towards us, which we have experienced in such great matters, will continue to ensure the ongoing success of our endeavours and the public well-being. (12) Moreover, so that the purport of this decision and of our benevolence can be brought to the attention of everyone, it will be appropriate for you, after promulgating the decree, to post it up everywhere and bring it to everyone's attention, so that there is no possibility of this decree of our benevolence remaining unknown.

4.5 Constantine's changing attitude to paganism: Eusebius *Life of Constantine* 2.55–6, 60.2

Constantine's final defeat of Licinius in 324 gave him control of the eastern provinces of the empire, to whose inhabitants he addressed the letter from which this passage comes (though at 55–6 he is actually directing his remarks to God). There has been much debate about the genuineness of the documents which the church historian and bishop Eusebius (*c.* 260–339) claims to be quoting in his biography of Constantine, but the weight of argument favours a positive assessment (Cameron and Hall 1999: 16–21). It is apparent that part of Constantine's concern here is to prevent a backlash against pagans by vengeful Christians, but at the same time he displays a more contemptuous attitude to pagan beliefs and practices than previously. This may reflect his growing understanding of the implications of his faith, or possibly his awareness that he no longer needs to be so even-handed now that he controls the whole empire. The 'holy dwelling place' at 55.2 refers not to any physical structure, but to the universal church (Cameron and Hall 1999: 247). His concluding assertion that he has not banned pagan practices appears to contradict other reports that he did prohibit sacrifice (cf. **5.1a**), but a satisfactory resolution of the conflicting and ambiguous evidence remains elusive; for recent discussions, see Barnes 1984, Errington 1988, Bradbury 1994, Curran 1996; Cameron and Hall 1999: 243–4.

55. (1) I entreat you now, O almighty God – be gentle and kind to your people in the regions of the east, to all your people in these provinces worn down by prolonged misfortunes, and bring them healing through me, your servant. I do not ask these things without good reason, O Lord of all, holy God. For by your direction I have put in place and effected measures conducive to salvation, I have led my victorious army everywhere with your symbol [the cross] in the vanguard, and wherever any public need demands, I advance against the enemy accompanied by the same signs of your righteousness. (2) For these reasons I have entrusted my soul to you with a genuine combination of love and fear. For I love your name with true affection, and I fear the power which you have demonstrated with many proofs and have used to increase the strength of my faith. So I also hasten to apply my energies to the restoration of your most holy dwelling place which those loathsome and ungodly men mistreated by offensive violence.

56. (1) It is my earnest desire that, for the well-being of the world and for the benefit of all, your people should enjoy peace and remain undisturbed. Let those who are in error joyfully receive the benefits of peace and tranquillity in the same way as the believers. For the sweet taste of shared benefits itself has the power to restore them and lead them to the right path. No one is to disturb another – let each person hold fast to what their soul desires, and live by it.

(2) But right-thinking people should be confident that only those whom you call to rest their hopes on your sacred laws will live holy and upright lives. As for those who draw back, let them have the temples of falsehood they desire – we have the most radiant dwelling place of your truth which you have given in accordance with your nature. We pray this for them, that they too may gain gladness of heart through the general harmony. ...

60. (2) I have said these things and set them out at greater length than the aim of my clemency requires, because I did not wish my belief in the truth to be concealed, especially since I hear that some people are saying the traditional practices of the temples and the authority of darkness have been removed. I would have recommended this very thing to all people, were it not that the violent rebelliousness of villainous error is so deeply ingrained in the souls of some, to the detriment of the common good.

4.6 Constantine and the Arian controversy: Eusebius *Life of Constantine* 2.70–71.1

When Constantine defeated Licinius in 324, he not only acquired the wealthy eastern provinces of the empire – he also inherited the less welcome consequences of divisive theological controversy arising from the views of an Alexandrian presbyter, Arius. Arius had posed awkward questions about the character of the Trinity in a way which implied Christ was inferior to the Father, and his views struck a chord with many Christians in the east, both educated and not so well educated (cf. 5.10). So when Alexander, bishop of Alexandria, excommunicated him, Arius was able to fall back on powerful support outside of Egypt. The extract below, from a letter Constantine wrote to Alexander and Arius in 324 in an initial attempt to reconcile the two men, makes clear the emperor's concern to ensure unity within the church. It also implies limited understanding of the theological issues at stake, unless he was perhaps deliberately minimising them in his efforts to achieve agreement. At any rate, the letter failed in its purpose and the eventual upshot was Constantine's convening in 325 of a major church council at Nicaea which condemned Arius and produced the famous statement of belief. However, this did not ultimately solve the problem, which was to rumble on until the 380s. Further reading: Barnes 1981: chs 11–12; Williams 1987; Hanson 1988.

70. So let both the careless question and the ill-judged response receive mutual forgiveness from both of you. For the cause of your disagreement does not relate to the central doctrines in [God's] law, nor involved substituting new teaching about the worship of God. Rather, your thinking [on these matters] is identical – so you can come together in mutual agreement. 71. (1) For it is not considered appropriate or at all right for so many of God's people, who ought

to be guided by your views, to be in disagreement because of your squabbling with one another over small, inconsequential matters.

4.7 Constantine helps a prominent pagan: *IGLT* 1265 and 1889

These texts are two of the many hundreds of graffiti left by ancient visitors to the tombs in the Valley of the Kings near Egyptian Thebes. Their particular interest lies in their revealing one of the leading personnel responsible for the Eleusinian mysteries receiving assistance of some sort in his travels from Constantine as late as 326, even if the nature of the assistance (free use of the imperial transport system?) and the reasons for Constantine's aiding him (conciliating an important pagan constituency in the recently acquired east?) remain the subject of debate. They also provide an intriguing example of pilgrimage in the footsteps of Plato (though it is unlikely Plato actually went there – the earliest authority is Cicero (*Republic* 1.10.16)). Further reading: Fowden 1987.

(a) IGLT *1265*

I, the torchbearer (*dadouchos*) of the most sacred mysteries at Eleusis, <Nicagoras>, son of Minucianus, an Athenian, investigated the tombs many lifetimes after the divine Plato from Athens, and I marvelled and gave thanks to the gods and to the most devout emperor Constantine who made this possible for me.

(b) IGLT *1889*

When the most devout Constantine was consul for the seventh time and Constantius Caesar for the first [326], I, the torchbearer of the Eleusinians, Nicagoras, son of Minucianus, an Athenian, investigated the sacred tombs and marvelled.

4.8 A philosopher at Constantine's court: Eunapius *Lives of the Philosophers and Sophists* 6.2.1–12 (462–3)

Eunapius of Sardis (*c.* 347/8–*c.* 415) was a leading pagan intellectual in the late fourth century; educated in rhetoric, philosophy, and medicine, he was also a historian and biographer. Here he gives an account of the influence of the eminent Neoplatonic philosopher Sopatros at Constantine's court, and his subsequent downfall. The precise chronological context is uncertain, but it clearly postdates the foundation of Constantinople in 324. Although it has been argued that there is no explicit reference to a religious dimension in the events described (Penella 1990: 49–53), it seems unlikely that this was not a factor. But even if not, Sopatros' prominence at Constantine's court remains of interest for what it implies about

Constantine's willingness to retain a known pagan as an adviser in the latter stages of his reign. The passage also warrants attention as an example of pagan polemic against Constantine. Sopatros' teacher, Iamblichus, was himself taught by Porphyry, and his ideas were influential in the fourth century (cf. 5.4). Ablabius was a Christian who held senior government posts during the latter half of Constantine's reign (cf. 4.9, 12.5).

Sopatros was more eloquent than the rest [of Iamblichus' students]. Due to his sublime nature and greatness of soul, he was not prepared to associate with other people, and instead hurried quickly to the imperial palace to gain a controlling influence over Constantine's impulsive urges, and change them for the better by persuasive argument. (2) He achieved such great wisdom and power that the emperor was won over by him and retained him publicly as his adviser seated at his right hand – something incredible to hear about and see. (3) But Constantine's officials, bursting with resentment that the imperial court had now shifted its interest to philosophy, waited for their opportunity ... and held clandestine gatherings, overlooking no aspect of their evil plot ... [Eunapius then presents an extended analogy between Sopatros and Socrates.]

(7) ... Long ago, Constantinople – originally called Byzantium – used to provide Athens with grain, and an abundant supply came from there. (8) But in our time, the great number of ships from Egypt, the whole of Asia, Syria, Phoenicia and other peoples, which between them carry an enormous quantity of grain as payment of taxes, do not suffice to satisfy and meet the needs of the inebriated populace which, by stripping other cities of their inhabitants, Constantine transplanted to Byzantium and settled near him so as to have the applause in the theatres of people who vomit up their drink. He loved it when these people, unsteady on their feet, praised him and recited his name – which, in their ineptitude, they could barely enunciate.

(9) It happens that ships laden with cargo cannot touch land where Byzantium is located unless a strong wind is blowing directly from the south. At that time, there occurred what often happened in accordance with the character of the seasons, and the populace, weakened by hunger, gathered in the theatre; applause from the drunken crowd was in short supply and the emperor became despondent. (10) Sopatros' long-time detractors thought they had found the perfect opportunity, and said, 'Sopatros, whom you honour, has imprisoned the winds through the superiority of his wisdom which you yourself praise and by which, moreover, he sits

on the imperial throne.' (11) When Constantine heard these words, he was persuaded and ordered Sopater to be beheaded; his detractors ensured that it was carried out without delay. (12) The instigator of all these evils was Ablabius who, though Praetorian Prefect, felt obstructed by Sopatros when he was favoured more highly than himself.

4.9 Imperial favour for a Christian community: *MAMA* 7.305

Orcistus was a community in Phrygia, Asia Minor, which at some point in the preceding century, and for reasons unknown, had been demoted from the status of an independent city to that of a village governed – and exploited – by the neighbouring city of Nacolea. Soon after his defeat of Licinius (324) and acquisition of the eastern provinces, Constantine received a petition from the Orcistans seeking restoration of their former status. The emperor's responses to this and a subsequent petition concerning continuing financial obligations to Nacolea shed light on many aspects of late Roman administration and society, but are of particular interest here because the arguments deployed by the Orcistans in their efforts to regain their status as an independent city included an appeal on the basis of their Christianity. The community claims to be wholly Christian and is aware that this is likely to carry weight in the emperor's deliberations – an expectation that proves to be fully justified. Although the claim to be wholly Christian should not be taken literally, there must have been substantial numbers of Christians in the community, while their appeal to this feature implies that it was unusual compared with other communities in central Asia Minor at this time (Mitchell 1993: vol. 2, 58–61). Chastagnol (1981: 410–11) has raised the possibility that Orcistus may be the unnamed Christian community in Phrygia with which Diocletian dealt severely during his persecution (Eusebius *Church History* 8.11.1; Lactantius *Divine Institutes* 5.11.10), which would then be a likely context for Orcistus to lose its city status. (The translation below omits two sections of the inscription – a covering note from Ablabius to Orcistus, and the surviving portion of the Orcistans' original petition.)

(a) Imperial response to the Praetorian Prefect Ablabius (328–30?)

Greetings, Ablabius, most dear to us. The inhabitants of Orcistus, henceforth a town and city, have presented a pleasing opportunity for our munificence, most dear and pleasing Ablabius. For to those [like us] who are eager to establish new cities, to improve long-established ones or to restore lifeless ones, what they were seeking was most welcome. For they declared that their village flourished with the splendour of a town in the period of a former age so that it was adorned with the symbols of authority (*fasces*) of annual magistrates, had numerous city-councillors, and was filled with a multitude of citizens. Its location is said to be so fortunate in terms of position and natural attributes that roads converge on it from four directions, from which it may be said to be advantageous and suitable as a resting point (*mansio*) for all those on public business. An abundance of waters flows there, there are baths public and private, a forum decorated with statues of leading citizens of old, a population of inhabitants so numerous that the seating which is in this same place is easily filled. Moreover due to the downward rush of excess water there is an abundant number of water mills.

Although it is stated that the aforementioned place abounds in all these things, it came about, they have declared, that the Nacoleans demanded before the present time that they be annexed to them. It is unworthy of our times that so fortunate a location should lose the title of city and it serves no good purpose for those dwelling there that they should lose all their benefits and advantages through being plundered by a more powerful people. Added to all these considerations, the crowning detail as it were, is the fact that all the inhabitants of this same place are said to be followers of the most holy religion (*sectatores sanctissimae religionis*).

Since they beseeched that the ancient right and name of city be granted to them by our clemency, we have given the following decision, as shown by the copies of our annotated response (*adnotatio*) and their request appended below. For that which they have proposed in their petition – the re-establishment of their name and status – they have rightly sought to obtain. Accordingly, by the intercession of Your Gravity, we have decided that those things which were damaged should be restored to the wholeness of their former honour so that they and their town, protected by their diligence, may enjoy the splendour of the laws and the name which they have sought. For it is right that Your Sincerity should hasten to fulfill for these suppliants that which we have promptly granted in accordance with the dignity of our times. Farewell, Ablabius, most dear and pleasing to us.

(b) Imperial response to Orcistus (331)

Written on the day before the Kalends of July [30 June] at Constantinople. The emperor Caesar Constantine, the greatest, conqueror and triumpher over the Goths, Augustus, and Flavius Claudius Constantine, victor over the Alamanns, and Flavius Julius Constantius, most noble Caesars, send greetings to the town council of Orcistus. It has been decided by the gift of our indulgence to protect not only your right to city status, granted to you as an honour, but also the privilege of freedom. And so in this present response we remove the injustice of the Nacoleans, of longer standing than the benefits of our indulgence, and we grant your prayers and request, so that hereafter you no longer pay any of the money which you used to contribute previously to their cults. Our leniency has therefore written this to the most eminent treasurer (*rationalis*) of the diocese of Asia who, in accordance with the purport of the favour granted to you, will ensure that the money is not hereafter sought and demanded from you for the above-stated purpose. We wish you well. In the consulates of Bassus and Ablabius [331].

4.10 The imperial cult in Constantine's final years: *CIL* 11.5265 (= *ILS* 705)

This inscription, recording an imperial response to a petition from an Italian community in 333/5, is of particular interest for the evidence it provides for the continuation of the imperial cult well after Constantine's conversion to Christianity, for the emperor's active approval of that continuation (including construction of a temple), and for his somewhat allusive restriction on certain cult practices – almost certainly a reference to sacrifices (e.g., Curran 1996: 76). It looks like Constantine is trying to maintain a delicate balancing act: 'He cannot contemplate suppressing a useful institution which allows the reinforcement of sentiments of loyalty towards himself and his sons in the pagan part of the population, but, driven by the scruples which his faith inspired in him, he tries to strip the manifestations of the imperial cult of all religious significance' (Gascou 1967: 655–6). Umbria, one of the regions of Italy, was at this time administered jointly with the region of Tuscia, in whose leading city, Volsinii, the seat of regional government was probably located. This no doubt explains the situation alluded to in this inscription whereby the priest of the imperial cult whom the Umbrians chose in alternate years had to travel to Volsinii to perform his duties. Further reading: Gascou 1967 (whose minor textual emendations are adopted below); Bowersock 1982.

Copy of the sacred imperial response. The emperor Caesar Flavius Constantine, the greatest, conqueror and triumpher over the Germans, Sarmatians and Goths, Augustus, and Flavius Constantinus and Flavius Julius Constantius and Flavius Constans. Our ever-watchful oversight of affairs embraces in its thinking all things which protect the community of the human race, but the most important responsibility of our foresight is to ensure that all cities, which splendour and beauty distinguish in the eyes of all the provinces and regions, should not only maintain their standing of old but should also be raised to a better status by the favour of our beneficence.

You Umbrians assert that you are joined to Tuscia, so that according to long-established custom priests are chosen by yourselves and the aforesaid Tuscians in alternate years, and these priests put on theatrical shows and a gladiatorial contest at Volsinii, a city in Tuscia; but on account of the steepness of the mountains and the difficulties of the routes through the wooded terrain, you earnestly ask that a remedy be granted so that your priest will not be obliged to journey to Volsinii to put on the shows. You ask that on the city currently called Hispellum, which you say is adjacent to and adjoins the Flaminian Way, we bestow a name derived from our family name; that a temple to the Flavian family may be raised up in that city in a magnificent style entirely appropriate to the greatness of that name; and that the priest whom Umbria has chosen in alternate years should put on in this same place a spectacle, both theatrical shows and gladiatorial contests, while traditional practice is maintained in Tuscia, so that a priest chosen from that region celebrates in Volsinii as usual the spectacles of the aforesaid shows.

We have willingly given our consent to your request and desire. To the city of Hispellum we have granted the eternal name and revered title derived from our appellation, so that hereafter the aforesaid city shall be called Flavia Constans, in whose centre we wish the construction of a magnificent temple in honour of the Flavian family (in other words, our family) to be seen through to a successful conclusion, as you desire, on the express condition that this temple dedicated to our name should not be defiled by the deceits of any contagious superstition (*cuiusquam contagiose superstitionis fraudibus polluatur*). As a result we have also granted to you permission to stage shows in the aforesaid city, provided that, as has been stated, the ritual observance of shows continues to take place periodically at Volsinii also, where the aforementioned shows should be put on by the priests chosen from Tuscia. In this way long-standing practices will not appear to have suffered serious detraction, and you, who have come forward to us as suppliants for the aforesaid reasons, will rejoice in having obtained those things for which you earnestly asked.

5

PAGANS AND CHRISTIANS IN THE MID-FOURTH CENTURY

The religious history of the mid-fourth century is dominated by the emperor Julian. Despite the brevity of his reign (361–3), his attempt to reverse the changes initiated by Constantine was bound to be the focus of attention for contemporaries, and this is reflected in the available source material, which includes much written by Julian himself. By contrast, the much longer reign of his predecessor Constantius II (337–61) has been described as 'peculiarly elusive for the historian of religion: unlike his predecessor and successor, Constantius neither chose nor rejected Christianity, so that his personal spiritual history lacks a dramatic turning-point' (Fowden 1998: 539), and the sources are not as plentiful – hence the emphasis in this chapter on Julian.

Two laws from the reigns of Constantius and his brother Constans (337–50) reflect, on the one hand, the need to (be seen to) denounce pagan practices, and on the other, the need to maintain a careful balance in the practical implementation of anti-pagan measures (5.1). At the same time, Christianity's infiltration of the senatorial aristocracy at Rome can also be detected during this period (5.2). Meanwhile, Constantius' young cousin, Julian, had no difficulty gaining access to teaching by a variety of pagan philosophers who continued to be active in the cities of western Asia Minor in the 340s and 350s. Although brought up as a Christian, the experiences of his childhood served to alienate him from the prevailing ethos at the imperial court: he believed Constantius had been responsible for the murder of his father during the transfer of power to Constantine's sons in 337, and his suspicions were not eased by the way Constantius kept the movements of Julian and his brother closely controlled during their youth. Reading classical literature aroused Julian's interest in the traditional deities of Graeco-Roman religion, and as he moved towards adulthood he exploited the greater freedom he was given to pursue that interest, culminating in his (secret) conversion to paganism in the early 350s.

On his accession to the imperial throne in 361, he set about trying to redress the balance between Christianity and paganism in favour of the latter, through a two-pronged strategy. First, he endeavoured to reform paganism. He showed a keen appreciation for the way Christianity had grown as a result of its charitable activities, and sought to establish a similar system based around the temples; he appointed suitable individuals to a hierarchy of provincial priesthoods and encouraged the incumbents to take their responsibilities seriously (5.3); and he gave renewed emphasis to the role of sacrifice, reflected in a treatise from this period which has been plausibly attributed to one of his close associates (5.4). Second, he aimed to disadvantage Christianity without resorting to physical persecution (5.5). He removed the various privileges Constantine had extended to the church; he required churches to return property appropriated from pagan shrines; and, notoriously, he forbade Christians to earn a living as teachers (5.6) – a move of greater significance than might at first seem the case. (At least partly with a view to antagonising Christians, he also showed favour towards the Jews (8.4, 8.5)). The brevity of Julian's reign, following his premature death during the ill-fated Persian campaign of 363, makes it difficult to judge whether all these measures would have been sufficient to turn the tide. His religious reforms certainly elicited some positive responses in different parts of the empire (5.7; cf. Brown 1982b). On the other hand, the evident lack of enthusiasm on the part of many inhabitants of Christianised Antioch, where he spent nearly a year prior to his Persian expedition, suggests a more pessimistic outlook, while the emperor's interest in the more magical and esoteric branch of pagan practice known as theurgy was not calculated to win him wider pagan support (Matthews 1989: ch. 7).

Julian's reign gave Christians a short but sharp shock which fuelled a determination in some church leaders to ensure that it could never happen again. Julian's immediate successors, however, though themselves Christian, refused to countenance any officially sanctioned backlash against pagans. Jovian (363–4) issued some sort of declaration of tolerance, a move endorsed by the eminent orator and philosopher Themistius (5.8), while his successor, Valentinan I (364–75), apparently did likewise and for the most part abstained from interfering in religious matters (5.9). This was also a period when internal church wranglings, in the form of the

Arian controversy, continued to be a preoccupation for many (5.10). Hard-line anti-pagans would have to wait until the 380s.

Further reading: Cameron and Garnsey 1998: chs 1–3; Barnes 1989b, 1993; Fowden 1998: 538–49; Bowersock 1978; Athanassiadi 1992; Smith 1995; sourcebooks: Lieu 1989; Lieu and Montserrat 1996.

5.1 Laws on pagan practices in the 340s: *Theodosian Code* 16.10.2–3

These two laws issued by Constantine's sons reveal the difficult position in which they found themselves *vis-à-vis* paganism. The first shows them denouncing sacrifice with a rhetoric whose very passion somehow betrays tacit recognition of the difficulty of enforcing such a prohibition (for the debate about the law of Constantine, unfortunately not itself preserved in the *Theodosian Code*, see 4.5). The second shows them confronting the potential for disorder on a grand scale should they deprive the public of the entertainments associated with the temples, and opting for the pragmatic course of action (for the issue of public entertainments at a later stage, see 7.9).

(a) Theodosian Code 16.10.2

The emperor Constantius [II], Augustus, to Madalianus, deputy praetorian prefect: Let there be an end to superstition, let the madness of sacrifices be done away with. For anyone who dares to perform sacrifices in contravention of the law of the holy emperor our father [Constantine] and this decree of Our Clemency shall experience an appropriate penalty and an immediate sentence of judgement. Received by the consuls Marcellinus and Probinus [341].

(b) Theodosian Code 16.10.3

The Emperors Constantius [II] and Constans, Augusti, to Catullinus, Prefect of the City [of Rome]: Although every superstition is to be rooted out completely, nevertheless it is our wish that the temple buildings located outside the city walls should remain untouched and undamaged. For since certain plays, circus spectacles, and competitions have their origin from some of these temples, it is not appropriate to pull them down when they provide the Roman people with performances of traditional entertainments. Issued on the Kalends of November in the third consulate of Constantius Augustus and the second of Constans Augustus [1 November 342].

5.2 A Christian senator in the 350s: *CIL* 6.32004 (= *ILS* 1286)

This inscription comes from a mid-fourth-century sarcophagus whose iconography, with its intriguing mix of Christian and non-Christian subject matter, is of interest in its own right (for discussion see Malbon 1990). The inscription itself directs attention to the important issue of the conversion of the senatorial aristocracy, which has long been seen as an important index of Christianisation (cf. 2.13, 6.9; Barnes 1995). It also appears to be a case of death-bed baptism, a not uncommon practice in this period, reflecting 'the early Christian sense of the absoluteness and finality of baptism' (Malbon 1990: 157 n. 9), especially when the individual in question held political office: 'fearing that they could not avoid mortal sin in the course of an active secular life [they] postponed baptism until they could sin no more' (Jones 1964: 110; cf. 980–1). On the importance of baptism as a Christian rite more generally, see 14.6.

Junius Bassus, a man of senatorial rank, who lived for 42 years, 2 months, went to God, newly baptised (*neofitus*), during his own prefecture of the city [of Rome], on the 8th day before the Kalends of September, when Eusebius and Hypatius were consuls [25 August 359].

5.3 Julian's religious reforms: Julian *Letters* 84 and 89

In these extracts from letters to provincial priests (the identity of the recipient of the second is unknown), Julian sets out some of the strategies by which he hopes to revive paganism. For the role of the priests, see Athanassiadi 1992: 181; for the differences between Julian's scheme and the earlier one of Maximinus (3.8), see Nicholson 1994; for the importance of hymns, cf. 1.5, 1.6.

(a) Julian Letter 84 (429c–431b)

(429c) Letter of the emperor Julian to Arsacius, high priest of Galatia. The Hellenic religion (*ho Hellēnismos*) is not yet progressing as expected, on account of us who adhere to it. The affairs of the gods are magnificent and mighty, better than we could have hoped or prayed for (may Adrastea forgive these words of mine); (429d) for not long ago, no-one dared to pray for so great and dramatic a change. So what is the problem? Do we think this is enough? Do we not realise that what has really contributed to the growth of atheism [i.e., Christianity] is their generosity towards strangers, their care for the burial of the dead, and the dignified way of life that they feign? (430a) I think we ought genuinely to be making each of these areas our business. Nor is it enough for you alone to behave in this way, but all who are priests in Galatia, without exception. Get them to take this seriously, whether by shaming them or by persuasion, and relieve them of their priestly responsibilities if they do not approach the gods accompanied by their wives, children and slaves, but allow their slaves or daughters or Galilaean wives to be disrespectful towards the gods (430b) and to give more honour to atheism than to the worship of the gods. Then advise them that priests are not to frequent the theatre and are not to drink in taverns or manage any trade or form of work that is disreputable or unbecoming. Honour those who do as you say, but dismiss those who do not.

Establish numerous hospices (*xenodocheia*) in each city, so that strangers experience generosity at our hands, (430c) not only our co-religionists but also others, whoever is in need. In the meantime I have made the following arrangements so that you will be well-supplied with resources. I have instructed 3,000 measures of grain and 60,000 measures of wine to be supplied each year for the whole of Galatia. It is my wish that a fifth of this be spent on the poor who assist the priests, while the remainder is to be distributed to strangers and those who beg from us. (430d) For it is disgraceful that, when no Jew has to beg and the ungodly Galilaeans support their own needy and ours, our people are seen to lack assistance from us. Teach those who adhere to the Hellenic religion to make their contribution to these responsibilities, and Hellenic villages to offer the first fruits of their labour to the gods. (431a) Accustom the Hellenes to these acts of generosity, teaching them that these have been our practice from ancient times. For Homer makes Eumenes say, 'Stranger, it is not right, not even if someone more wretched than you were to come, (431b) to show disrespect for a stranger. For all strangers and beggars are from Zeus. What little I have I willingly give' [*Odyssey* 14.56–8]. Let us not, through indifference, bring dishonour on our cause, or rather abandon worship of the gods entirely, by allowing others to outdo us in good deeds. If I learn that you are doing these things, I will be very happy.

(b) *Julian* Letter 89 (301d-302b)

The hymns of the gods ought to be learnt thoroughly. There are many beautiful ones composed by ancient writers and by more recent ones. But one should at least try to learn the ones that are sung in the temples. (302a) Most of them in fact have been given by the gods themselves when approached by suppliants, though a few are the work of men, composed in honour of the gods by divine inspiration and a soul untouched by evil. It is worth taking trouble over this, and praying to the gods both on an individual basis and in public, ideally three times a day, but if not, then at least at dawn and in the evening. (302b) For a worthy priest cannot go through a day or a night without making an offering to the gods. Dawn is the beginning of the day and evening the beginning of the night. It is right to offer the beginning of both periods of time to the gods, whenever it happens that we are not performing our priestly duties. When we are in the temples, it is fitting to observe all that the law of our forefathers lays down, and one must do neither more nor less. For the things of the gods are eternal, so we need to imitate their nature and thereby dispose them to be more favourable. ...

5.4 A defence of sacrifice: Sallustius *On the Gods and the Universe* 14–16

The following passage derives from a short treatise strongly influenced by features of Neoplatonic thought associated with Iamblichus (*c.* 245–*c.* 325) (Nock 1926: ch. 3). Since the emperor Julian was also an admirer of Iamblichus, and a portion of one chapter (4) owes a clear debt to a passage in one of the Julian's theological works (*Speech* 5.167ff.), it is generally accepted that the author is to be identified with Julian's friend and adviser Saturninius Secundus Salutius (Nock 1926: ci–civ; Bowersock 1978: 125) and the treatise placed in the context of Julian's attempted religious reforms. 'We see an attempt to distil the emperor's impassioned but not always easily comprehensible doctrine into guidelines for the priests and teachers who were to propagate the restoration' (Fowden 1998: 546). In this extract, a defence of sacrifice is offered, which helps one to understand the theoretical underpinnings of this aspect of Julian's reforms, while also presenting an interesting contrast with the views of another Neoplatonic thinker, Porphyry, on the same subject (1.13). It is also worth noting the treatise's subsequent veiled allusion to Christianity: 'the fact that unbelief has arisen in certain parts of the earth and will often occur hereafter should not disturb men of sense' (18) – a remark which has been seen as betraying 'lordly indifference to [Christianity's] spread' (Fowden 1998: 546). On offerings of hair to the gods (16), see, e.g., Pausanias 2.11.6. Further reading: Athanassiadi 1992: 68, 154–60.

(14) If any man thinks it is a reasonable and correct view that the gods are not subject to change, and then is unable to see how they take pleasure in the good and turn their faces away from the bad, are angry with sinners and propitiated by service, it must be replied that a god does not take pleasure (for that which does is also subject to pain) or feel anger (for anger is also an emotion), nor is he appeased by gifts (for that would put him under the dominion of pleasure), nor is it right that the divine nature should be affected for

good or evil by human affairs. Rather, the gods are always good and do nothing but benefit us, nor do they ever harm us: they are always in the same state. We, when we are good, have union with the gods because we are like them; if we become bad, we are separated from them because we are unlike them. If we live in the exercise of virtue, we cling to them; if we become bad, we make them our enemies, not because they are angry but because our sins do not allow the gods to shed their light upon us and instead subject us to spirits of punishment. If by prayers and sacrifices we obtain release from our sins, we do not serve the gods nor change them, but by the acts we perform and by our turning to the divine we heal our vice and again enjoy the goodness of the gods. Accordingly, to say that the gods turn their faces away from the bad is like saying that the sun hides himself from those bereft of sight.

(15) These considerations settle the question concerning sacrifices and the other honours which are paid to the gods. The divine nature itself is free from needs; the honours done to it are for our good. The providence of the gods stretches everywhere and needs only congruity for its enjoyment. Now all congruity is produced by imitation and likeness. That is why temples are a copy of heaven, altars of earth, images of life (and that is why they are made in the likeness of living creatures), prayers of the intellectual element, letters of the unspeakable powers on high, plants and stones of matter, and the animals that are sacrificed of the unreasoning life in us. From all these things the gods gain nothing (what is there for a god to gain?), but we gain union with them.

(16) I think it worthwhile to add a few words about sacrifices. In the first place, since everything we have comes from the gods, and it is just to offer to the givers the first fruits of what is given, we offer the first fruits of our possessions in the form of votive offerings, of our bodies in the form of hair, of our life in the form of sacrifices. Secondly, prayers divorced from sacrifices are only words, prayers with sacrifices are animated words, the word giving power to the life and the life animation to the word. Furthermore, the happiness of anything lies in its appropriate perfection, and the appropriate perfection of each object is union with its cause. For this reason also we pray that we may have union with the gods. So, since though the highest life is that of the gods, yet man's life also is life of some sort, and this life wishes to have union with that, it needs an intermediary (for objects most widely separated are never united without a middle term), and the intermediary ought to be like the objects being united. Accordingly, the intermediary between life and life

should be life, and for this reason living animals are sacrificed by the blessed among men, and were sacrificed of old, not in a uniform manner, but to every god the fitting victims, with much other reverence. (tr. A.D. Nock)

5.5 Julian's policy towards Christians: Julian *Letter* 114 (437b, 438a-c)

These passages come from a letter Julian wrote in Antioch on 1 August 362 to the inhabitants of the city of Bostra, in the province of Arabia. It was occasioned by public disturbances between pagans and Christians, prompting Julian to reiterate his policy towards the Christians (or 'atheists' and 'Galilaeans' as he liked to call them) – namely, toleration. Julian appreciated that open persecution had not worked in the past, and preferred to attack the church by other, more subtle means (e.g., 5.6), though individual instances of violence nevertheless did occur, such as the lynching of George, bishop of Alexandria. Julian's reference (438c) to the Christians having turned from the gods to 'the dead and their relics' is an allusion to Christ and the martyrs and their associated cults (cf. 16.13).

(437b) I have therefore decided to let all people know through this decree and by public proclamation that they [the Christians] are not to join with the clergy in fomenting trouble or be persuaded by them to take up stones and disobey the magistrates. But they may gather together whenever they wish to offer prayers for themselves as they are accustomed to do. However, if their clergy try to persuade them to cause public disturbances, they are not to agree, otherwise they will be punished ...

(438a) ... You who have gone astray are to respect those who worship the gods correctly and rightly according to the traditions passed down to us from past ages, and you who worship the gods are not to damage or loot the houses of those who have gone astray from ignorance rather than intent. (438b) We need to teach and persuade people by reason, not by blows or brutality or physical violence. I repeatedly advise those who are enthusiastic adherents of true religion not to commit injustices against the numerous Galilaeans, not to attack or abuse them. We should take pity on those who have gone wrong in this important matter, not express hatred. For reverence for the gods is truly the greatest of blessings, and disrespect for the gods the greatest of evils. The consequence is that those who turn from the gods to the dead and their relics reserve this penalty for themselves. We sympathise with those who are suffering, but we rejoice when they are set free and released by the gods.

5.6 Julian's law on Christian teachers: Julian *Letter* 61c

The emperor Julian's most notorious measure against the church was his law forbidding Christians from practising as teachers, issued on 17 June 362. A short passage from the law itself is preserved in the *Theodosian Code* (13.3.5), but more informative is the following letter, apparently addressed to Christian teachers in the eastern half of the empire (the usual introductory title has not been preserved). This sets out the formal justification for the measure, while also allowing Julian to indulge in polemic against Christianity (the gap in the manuscript at 423d is assumed to be a point at which a later copyist found Julian's anti-Christian sentiments too strongly worded to bear repeating). It might seem strange that a measure such as this should provoke such controversy (even the moderate pagan historian Ammianus Marcellinus, otherwise an admirer of Julian, found it repugnant: *History* 22.10.7, 25.4.20). What needs to be appreciated, however, is the social consequences of Julian's law: 'A man without the benefit of the *enkyklios paideia* [a rounded education] would find himself virtually debarred from a public career in his city, and generally diminished in status in a milieu in which the claims of *paideia* clearly continued to count. Well-to-do Christians faced a stark choice: to put their sons at a severe social disadvantage in their prospects, or to let them be taught by pagans. Julian's own experience, it may be guessed, will have given him no small faith in the transforming power of such an education' (Smith 1995: 114).

In terms of immediate consequences, a number of leading Christian scholars quit their posts, notably Marius Victorinus at Rome and Prohaeresius at Athens. Others set about transforming parts of the Bible into classical genres – e.g., the Pentateuch was rendered in epic form, the gospels as Platonic dialogues (Socrates *Church History* 3.16; Sozomen *Church History* 5.18). After Julian's death the following year, however, the law was quickly repealed (*Theodosian Code* 13.3.6 [11 January 364]). More generally, the episode highlights the issue of the relationship between Christianity and classical literature and learning: like Julian, some Christians believed the two should have nothing in common, but those who argued for compatibility were to win the day (Markus 1974). Further reading: Wilken 1984: 171–6; Smith 1995: 212–14; Hunt 1998a: 66–7.

(422a) In my view a good education (*paideia*) is not a matter of splendid elegance in words and language, but of a healthy mental disposition and intellect, and of right judgement about good and evil, beauty and repugnance. Whoever thinks one thing and teaches another to his students seems to me (422b) to have abandoned good education as much as he has honesty. If the difference between what he thinks and what he says concerns minor matters, this is bad, but can to a certain extent be tolerated. But if a person has views on the major issues, yet teaches things at odds with those views, is this not the behaviour of petty traders, the life of men who are untrustworthy and disreputable, (422c) who speak most highly of those goods which they consider least valuable, deceiving and taking in by these recommendations those to whom they wish to pass on, I imagine, their shoddy stock?

Therefore all who claim to teach anything should be of good character and not carry in their soul convictions at odds with the public practice of their profession. This ought above all to be the case, in my view, with those who teach the young about literature, who act as interpreters of the writings of the ancients, (422d) whether they are rhetoricians or grammarians, and especially if sophists. For these want to be, among other things, teachers not only of how to speak, but also of ethics, and they claim political philosophy as their particular field.

Let me leave for the moment the question of whether this is true or not. I praise them for aiming for such a wonderful profession, but I would praise them even more if they did not lie and prove that they think one thing and teach their students another. (423a) What then? Was it not the gods who guided Homer and Hesiod, Demosthenes, Herodotus and Thucydides, Isocrates and Lysias in all their learning? Did some not consider themselves consecrated to Hermes, and other to the Muses? I think it absurd that those who interpret the writings of these men do not honour the gods whom the authors revered. But though I think this absurd, I do not say that those teaching the young must change their views. I give them a choice – either not to teach what they do not consider worthy of serious attention, or, if they wish to continue teaching, to do so first by example (423b) and persuade their students that neither Homer nor Hesiod nor any of those whom they interpret <were stupid, as they wanted them to believe> when they accused them of being impious, lacking in intelligence and in error with regard to the gods. Since they make their living and receive a salary out of the writings of these men, they acknowledge that they are the most greedy of men, ready to do anything for a little bit of money.

(423c) Until now, there were many excuses not to frequent the temples, and the universal sense of menacing fear justified concealing one's real opinions concerning the gods. But since the gods have given us freedom, it seems absurd to me for men to teach things which they do not consider good. But if they regard as wise the writers whom they interpret and for whom they have, as it were, the status of prophets, (423d) they should first of all emulate their reverence for the gods. If, on the other hand, they think these writers have gone astray with regard to the most esteemed gods, they should hasten to the churches of the Galilaeans and engage in interpretation of Matthew and Luke < ... > You lay down rules forbidding the partaking of sacrificial victims. I wish that your ears and your tongue might be born again, as you would say, <in

abstaining from> those things in which I hope to be involved always, along with those who think and do what is pleasing to me.

(424a) For professors and teachers, the general law stands as such. But young people wishing to frequent [the schools] are not prevented from doing so. For it would not be <fair> or reasonable to close off the best way to children who do not yet know in which direction to turn, out of fear of their being led involuntarily to our ancestral traditions. Moreover, it would be right to heal them, as one heals the insane, without their permission, (424b) except that one makes allowances for all of them with a disease of this kind. For we ought, I think, to enlighten, and not punish, those who are deranged in mind.

5.7 Epigraphic evidence for Julian's religious policies: *CIL* 8.18529, *ILAlg* II,2.4647, *AE* (1969–70) 631, *AE* (1983) 895, *ILS* 8946, *AE* (1907) 191

This set of short inscriptions are of interest for the way they demonstrate awareness throughout the empire of Julian's restoration of traditional pagan practices. However, it has also been argued that they are more than just polite formulae and reflect positive support and enthusiasm for those reforms on the part of the town councils and individuals responsible for setting them up (Lepelley 1979–81: vol. 2, 401, 482–3; Kotula 1994). It should be added that the relevance of the final two inscriptions to Julian's religious policies has been challenged: it has been argued that the 'failings' in (e) are administrative, not religious (Arce 1984: 147), while the restoration of 'superstition' in the damaged text of (f) has understandably provoked disagreement (see Smith 1995: 280 n. 133).

(a) CIL 8.18529 (Casae, Numidia)

To our lord Flavius Claudius Julian, devout, blessed, powerful in every kind of virtue, invincible leader, restorer of freedom and of the Roman religion (*restitutor libe<r>t<at>is et Ro<manae> religion<is>*), and conqueror of the world.

(b) ILAlg II,2.4647 (Thibilis, Numidia)

The most splendid town council of the Thibilitans set [this statue] up and dedicated [it] to our lord Flavius Claudius Julian, devout, blessed, victor and conqueror, ever Augustus, restorer of sacred rites (*restitutor sacrorum*).

(c) AE (1969–70) 631 (Ma'ayan Barukh, Jordan Valley, Israel)

To the liberator of the Roman world, the restorer of the temples (*templorum* <*re*>*staurator*), reviver of the town councils and of the state (*cur*<*ia*>*rum et rei publicae recreator*), destroyer of the barbarians (*barbarorum extinctor*), our lord Julian ever Augustus, mighty victor over the Alamanns, mighty victor over the Franks, mighty victor over the Sarmatians, chief priest (*pontifex maximus*), father of his country: the <provincial assembly> of the Phoenicians ordered <this to be set up>.

(d) AE (1983) 895 (Thessalonica)

In the time of one most beloved of god, renewer of the sacred rites (*ananeōtes tōn hierōn*), lord and victor over every barbarian people, Claudius Julian, all-powerful and sole ruler of the world, Calliopius, most distinguished consular, dedicated [this altar].

(e) ILS 8946 (Mursa, Pannonia)

To our lord Flavius Claudius Julian, born for the good of the state, greatest <of emperors?>, celebrator of triumphs, ever Augustus, on account of his having done away with the defects of times past (*ob deleta vitia temporum preteri*<*torum*>).

(f) AE (1907) 191 (Baalbek, Syria)

To the renewer (<*repara*>*tor*) <of the Roman world>, to the restorer (*rest*<*itutor*>) <of all> things and <of all happiness>, to the reviver (<*re*>*creator*) <of the cults and> the destroyer (*exstinctor*) <of superstition, to Flavius> Julian, ever <Augustus>, mighty victor over the Germans, mighty victor over <the Alamanns>, mighty victor over the Sarmatians <and the Franks>, chief priest (*pontifex maximus*), with < ... > his vow < ... >

5.8 A plea for religious toleration: Themistius *Speech* 5.67b–70a

The speech of which the following passage forms a part was delivered before the emperor Jovian (363–4) at Ancyra on 1 January 364 by the pagan orator and philosopher Themistius (*c.* 317–*c.* 388/9). Jovian had come to the throne six months earlier in the wake of the debacle of Julian's invasion of Persia; his first act had been to make concessions to Persia in an unpopular peace treaty to which Themistius makes (surprisingly favourable) reference below (69b). Although Jovian was a Christian and might have been expected to implement a backlash against pagans, he seems to have pursued a moderate policy, and Themistius in fact alludes to legislation to that effect (67b), though nothing is otherwise known about it. Against this background, Themistius' role was one of either ensuring that Jovian did not waver in his resolve or, if he was in reality a spokesman for imperial policy (Heather 1998: 145–6), helping to deflect criticism from Christians. At the same time, his arguments represent a 'moment of inventiveness' in the development of toleration theory (Garnsey 1984: 25) and make for interesting comparisons with those deployed by Symmachus and Libanius a few decades later (6.4, 6.6). On points of detail, Theramenes (67d–68a) was an Athenian politician of the late fifth century BC notorious for changing his political allegiances, and the Ten and the Thirty are references to oligarchic councils comprising these numbers of men who ruled Athens in the same period; Cheops and Cambyses (68b) were rulers of Egypt and Persia respectively (cf. Herodotus 2.124–9, 3.27–29). Further reading: Dagron 1968: 149–86; Daly 1971; Garnsey 1984: 21–7; Vanderspoel 1995: ch. 6; Ando 1996: 176–82.

(67b) … The opening statement of your care for people has been your legislation on religious matters (I return again to the starting point of my speech). For you are the only one, so it seems, who has recognised that it is not possible for the emperor to compel his subjects in all matters, (67c) but that there are things which have escaped compulsion and are above threats and commands – such as the whole area of virtue and especially devotion to the divine; you have recognised that you need to take the lead in these good things if you are truly to possess them; you have very wisely understood that the impulse of the soul is to be unforced, independent, and free to make its own choices. For if it is not possible even for you, O Emperor, to legislate kindness in someone who has not made an internal choice to be so, how much more is it impossible for someone to be devout and loving towards God (67d) through fear of human words, transient constraints and feeble bogeys, which time has often brought but has also often taken away? Most absurdly, we are guilty of showing reverence to the imperial purple [worn by the emperor], and not to God, and of changing our religious rites more easily than the tides in the Euboean channel [in Greece]. In former times there was only one Theramenes, but now everyone is a timeserver; yesterday, almost, it was necessary to be in the Ten, (68a) but today, in the Thirty; there are those who go to altars, to sacrifices, to statues of the gods, to sacred tables. But you are not like this, most godlike of emperors; absolute ruler that you are, and will be to the end, in everything else, you ordain by law that everyone is to have their share in religious worship, emulating God in this respect, who has made the inclination to appropriate religious devotion a common trait of human nature, but has made the way in which that worship is expressed dependent on the decision of each person. Employing compulsion deprives people of the power to choose, which was granted by God. (68b) For this reason, the laws of Cheops and those of Cambyses scarcely lasted as long as those who issued them, but the law of God, which is also yours, remains unchanged forever, setting free each person's soul for the path of religious devotion which they think best. No confiscation of property, no punishment, no burning has ever overcome this law; it may happen that the body is broken and dead, but the soul will depart, carrying with it the knowledge of the law of freedom, (68c) even if its expression has been constrained.

But I have been persuaded, O Emperor, that, having understood the reason for this divine legislation – that it is inherent in man – you are going to pursue it step by step; for things done from a sense of competition are seen through to completion with greater purpose, whereas things done without rivalry are carried out carelessly. Lack of competition in everything fills us with yawning and idleness, but the soul is always easily stirred into diligent action by a contest. (68d) So you do not stand in the way of healthy rivalry in religious devotion and you do not blunt the keenness of enthusiasm for the divine which comes from competition and vying with one another. Everyone competing in the stadium heads for the judge awarding the prize, but they don't all take the same route. Some start in one place, others in another, and those who don't win are not completely without honour; in the same way, you understand that there is one great and truthful judge of the contest, (69a) but that there is not just one route to him – there is the route that is very difficult to travel along and the more direct one, there is the rough route and the level one; but they all alike converge on the one destination. Rivalry and eagerness come to us from the same source, but we don't all walk the same route. But if you allow only one path, you block off the rest and restrict the scope for competition. This is the nature of man from ancient times: 'Each man sacrificed to a different god' [*Iliad* 2.400] is a truth older than Homer.

(69b) For it has never been displeasing to God to produce this harmony of voices among men. According to Heraclitus, nature delights in concealing itself, and before nature, the creator of nature, whom we especially revere and marvel at for this reason, because the knowledge of him is not straightforward – not immediately obvious or exposed to view, nor grasped without effort or care. I would not make less of a case for this law than I would for friendship with the Persians. Because of the latter, we will not be at war with the barbarians, because of the law [of toleration] we will live together without dissension. (69c) We were worse towards one another than the Persians; more serious than their incursions were the legal attacks of each religion against the other within the city; the passage of time, O Emperor most beloved by God, has provided you with clear examples. Allow the scales to remain in balance, don't load them down with weights on one side; allow prayers for your rule to be offered to heaven from all sides.

Your army, O Emperor, is not entirely organised on one and the same model, but there are infantry, cavalry, those who manufacture weapons, skirmishers; there are some troops attached to your person, some who are nearby, others who are a great distance from you; there are some who are happy if they are known to those in your bodyguard, and others for whom this is not possible. But all are likewise dependent on you and your decisions, and not only those in the army, but all the other people, all your subjects distant from the troops – (70a) the farmers, the orators, the town councillors, the philosophers. Consider how the founder of the universe rejoices in this diversity. He wishes the Syrians to choose one form of religion, the Greeks another, the Egyptians another; nor does he wish the Syrians themselves to be all the same, but henceforth to be divided into smaller groups. For no-one thinks about these things in exactly the same way as his neighbour; rather, one man does so in one way, and another in a different way. Why then do we try to achieve the impossible through force?

5.9 The religious policies of Valentinian I:
Ammianus Marcellinus *History* 30.9.5, *Theodosian Code* 9.16.9, Sozomen *Church History* 6.21.7

(a) Ammianus Marcellinus History *30.9.5*

Valentinian I (364–75) was notorious for his brutality and violence in political and military affairs, yet somewhat paradoxically his reign was also characterised by an enlightened policy of religious toleration which elicited praise from the moderate pagan historian Ammianus Marcellinus, a policy which must have helped to reduce the scope for any immediate Christian backlash after Julian's reign. At the same time, Ammianus' characterisation of Valentinian may also have been intended as a veiled criticism of the rather less tolerant religious policies pursued by the emperor Theodosius I (379–95) during whose final years Ammianus completed and published his history (cf. the reference below to 'threatening decrees' (in 5.9a and 6.7).

Finally, his reign became famous for its toleration, for he took up a neutral stance on matters of religious difference. He did not interfere with anyone by ordering that this or that cult was to be worshipped, and he did not force his subjects by means of threatening decrees to adopt his own religious observances. Rather, he allowed the different cults to remain undisturbed as he found them.

(b) Theodosian Code 9.16.9

This passage corroborates and amplifies Ammianus' testimony, through its reference to laws of religious toleration issued at the start of Valentinian's reign (though these laws themselves are no longer extant). While this law was issued in the name of three emperors, its place of issue makes clear that Valentinian was responsible for it.

The emperors Valentinian, Valens and Gratian, Augusti, to the senate: I rule that divination (*haruspicina*) has nothing in common with cases of magic (*maleficia*), nor do I consider this or, moreover, any other religious practice permitted by our forefathers to be a type of crime. The laws issued by me at the start of my reign, in which everyone was granted the freedom to practise whatever religious observances they have imbibed in their minds, are testimony to this. We do not condemn divination, though we forbid its practice with intent to harm. Issued on the 4th day before the Kalends of June at Trier, in the consulships of Gratian Augustus (for the second time) and of Probus [29 May 371].

(c) *Sozomen* Church History 6.21.7

This passage, by a fifth-century eastern writer, suggests an explanation for Valentinian's policy of toleration. Sozomen's pointed contrast between Valentinian (who ruled the west) and his brother and co-ruler Valens (who ruled the east), to the advantage of the former, is accounted for by the fact that the latter favoured Arianism; the incident referred to at the start was one in which an orthodox Nicaean bishop had caused Valens embarrassment.

Because of this incident, the whole clergy was tested by the anger of the emperor [Valens], except those of the churches in the western empire, for Valentinian, who ruled the Romans in the more distant parts, was a supporter of the creed of the council of Nicaea and was so respectful in religious matters that he never issued orders to the clergy or otherwise chose to introduce innovations, for better or worse, into the laws of the church. For although he was a very fine emperor and, on the strength of his deeds, was considered a capable ruler, he took the view that church affairs lay outside his scrutiny (*kreitto tēs autou dokimasias*).

5.10 Popular preoccupation with the Arian controversy: Gregory of Nyssa, *On the Divinity of the Son and of the Holy Spirit* (PG 46.557)

In this excerpt from a sermon of 381, Gregory of Nyssa discusses the predilection of the inhabitants of Constantinople, even those of low social standing and limited education, for theological speculation and discussion. Gregory is critical of this tendency, thereby betraying his social prejudices and his anxieties about the breakdown of social distinctions (Lim 1995: 149–50), but the passage remains a useful reminder that the seemingly rarified theological debate about the nature of the Trinity associated with the Arian controversy and other doctrinal disputes of the period were matters of keen interest and significance for many people from across the social spectrum, and helps one understand better the passions these theological controversies aroused in ordinary people.

The account of Paul's stay in Athens was read to us from the *Acts of the Apostles* [17.16–34], how the people in that city were mad about idols and addicted to offering sacrifices. Like a swollen river flooding into the soul of the Apostle, the Holy Spirit provoked the blessed Paul, and he did not find a way of escaping from amidst those unworthy practices. As a result there was a contest with the Stoics and with the Epicureans, and standing on the hill of Ares, he tried to lead them from their practices to the knowledge of God, for he used an altar there and its inscription as the start of his discourse. Why am I now reminding you of the reading? Because like those Athenians, there are those today who spend their time doing nothing else except discussing and listening to new things coming forth yesterday or a little earlier from craftsmen, off-hand pontificating on theology, perhaps servants and slaves and fugitives from domestic service, grandly philosophising to us about matters difficult to understand. You know whom this sermon is addressed to. Everywhere throughout the city is full of such things – the alleys, the squares, the thoroughfares, the residential quarters; among cloak salesmen, those in charge of the moneychanging tables, those who sell us our food. For if you ask about change, they philosophise to you about the Begotten and the Unbegotten. And if you ask about the price of bread, the reply is, 'The Father is greater, and the Son is subject to him.' If you say, 'Is the bath ready?', they declare the Son has his being from the non-existent. I am not sure what this evil should be called – inflammation of the brain or madness, or some sort of epidemic disease which contrives the derangement of reasoning.

6

PAGANS AND CHRISTIANS
IN THE LATE FOURTH
CENTURY

The final decades of the fourth century saw the room for manoeuvre allowed to pagans increasingly restricted by the imperial government. As late as 382, a law was issued which sought to maintain a balanced approach to the status of temples (6.1), but this soon proved to be a misleading guide to the future. Probably in the same year, Valentinian's son and successor Gratian (375–83) rejected the traditional imperial office of chief priest (*pontifex maximus*) that Constantine and his successors had continued to hold, apparently untroubled by its anomalous implications. This important symbolic gesture was accompanied by other measures with greater practical import – the termination of public subsidies for the maintenance of the ceremonies and priesthoods associated with the official pagan cults in Rome and of the stipends paid to the Vestal Virgins (Cameron 1968; Matthews 1990: 203–4).

Although the resolve of some was weakening (6.2), there remained a substantial body of senators who were committed to paganism, as attested by a number of inscriptions (6.3), and they set about trying to persuade the emperor to reverse these measures. In doing so, they focused on another important symbol – the altar of Victory, which had been placed in the senate house by Augustus after the battle of Actium in 31 BC and on which offerings were made at the start of senatorial sessions. Constantius had removed it from the senate house in 357, but it was soon reinstated, presumably by Julian. Gratian then removed it once more in 382, and attempts by pagan senators to induce first Gratian, and then his brother and successor Valentinian II (383–92), to restore it (and, by implication, state subsidies for traditional rites) proved in vain (6.4, 6.5). Meanwhile in the eastern provinces, where Theodosius I was now emperor (379–95), the destruction of pagan temples, though strictly illegal, went unchecked, despite the pleas of pagan spokesmen

(6.6). The culmination of this was the destruction of the famed temple of Serapis in Alexandria in 391/2, and Theodosius' issuing of laws placing a comprehensive ban on all forms of sacrifice (6.7). Expressions of pagan resistance continued, whether in the form of pagan support for the revolt of Eugenius in Italy in the early 390s (Matthews 1990: 238–52), or the issuing of subversive prophecies predicting the demise of Christianity (6.8). But whether one focused on the senatorial aristocracy or the barbarian peoples to the north now increasingly impinging on the empire's affairs, there could be no doubting the overall trend (6.9). These final decades of the fourth century also witnessed the initial stages of the Christianisation of rural areas in the west, exemplified here by the activities of Martin of Tours in Gaul (6.10, 6.11) and reflected in the poetry of the period (6.12). The final item – a lead curse tablet (6.13) – may at first sight seem out of place, but its use of the pagan/Christian antithesis as a way of categorising people is a telling feature that provides an appropriate conclusion to the chapter.

It remains to suggest some of the factors responsible for these changes and their timing. As noted in the previous chapter, Julian's reign was bound to make Christian leaders less inclined to adopt a tolerant attitude towards paganism – a point explicitly articulated in the debate over the altar of Victory (6.5a (4)). However, internal controversy over Arianism continued to monopolise attention in the church (cf. 5.10) – until Theodosius made concerted efforts to resolve it, commencing with the Council of Constantinople in 381 (Matthews 1990: 122–6). The 380s also saw a number of laws issued against individuals apostasising from Christianity (*Theodosian Code* 16.7.1–5) – a worrying trend which may well have been a further stimulus to action (cf. 6.5a (4)). Nor should the role of leading personalities be minimised: Theodosius was an emperor who took his Christianity very seriously, while circumstances contrived to place him and other emperors of the period in close proximity to a forceful exponent of how Christian rulers should act – Ambrose, bishop of Milan (*c.* 340–97).

Further reading: Matthews 1990: chs 5, 8–9; McLynn 1994; Williams and Friell 1994; Drake 1996; Fowden 1998: 548–60; Moorhead 1999; sourcebook: Croke and Harries 1982.

6.1 Temples as an issue: *Theodosian Code* 16.10.8

The primary interest of this law lies in its sanctioning of a temple remaining in use, albeit for non-religious purposes, only a few years before a notorious wave of violence against temples in the same region (it is possible that this very temple was one of the victims: Matthews 1990: 140–1). The formal justification given is akin to declaring the temple an art museum, but the reference to large crowds frequenting it perhaps betrays the underlying motive – a concern to avoid public unrest. At the same time, it contains a sinister hint of pressure from other quarters in favour of more drastic action.

The Emperors Gratian, Valentianian [II], and Theodosius [I], Augusti, to Palladius, General responsible for Osrhoene: We have decided, on the advice of the imperial consistory, to allow the temple, consecrated once in the presence of large crowds and now still frequented by people, in which there are said to be located images which deserve to be judged for their artistic worth rather than their religious associations, to continue to be open, and we do not allow any imperial ruling obtained by surreptitious means to interfere in this matter. So that the urban populace and the large crowds can see the temple, Your Skilfullness is to allow it to remain open, by the authority of our rescript, and maintain all the celebrations of festivities. But this opportunity to enter the temple is not to be taken as giving permission for the performance of sacrifices, which is prohibited there. Issued on the day before the Kalends of December, at Constantinople, in the consulates of Antonius and Syragrius [30 November 382].

6.2 Pagan disillusionment: Symmachus *Letters* 1.51

This letter of 383 by one leading pagan senator to another is of interest for its expression of concern about a growing unwillingness on the part of colleagues to take traditional religious responsibilities seriously, and the suggestion that the lack of enthusiasm in some stems from hopes of enhancing their chances of political advancement. The difficulties alluded to in the opening lines are a reference to famine conditions which affected Rome at this time. For the writer, see 6.4, for the recipient (who clearly owned an estate in Etruria), see 6.3b.

Symmachus to Agorius Praetextatus. We had decided to remain outside the city walls still, but news that our native city was faltering changed my plans, since concern for my personal safety seemed dishonourable given the difficulties affecting the whole community. Furthermore, oversight of the holy priesthood requires my attention and the performance of responsibilities for the specified month. For when there is so much neglect on the part of priests, I am not prepared to let a colleague take my place. Substitution in religious duties was once straightforward; now neglecting the altars is, for Romans, a way of furthering one's career (*genus ambiendi*). As for you – how long will Etruria detain you? We are already complaining that it must be important to take priority over your fellow citizens for so long. Although a stay in the country is more pleasant, it is impossible to enjoy tranquillity properly when one is anxious about absent friends. Farewell.

6.3 Pagan commitment: *CIL* 6. 510 and 1779

The implications of the previous item need to be set against the substantial body of inscriptions from the 370s and 380s attesting the close involvement of some pagan senators in a wide range of religious activities, of which two examples are presented below. The second (of which only the opening part is given here) was set up in 387, though Praetextatus, one of the most eminent pagans of his generation, had in fact died at the end of 384. A distinctive feature of this body of inscriptions compared with earlier periods is the multiple priesthoods and initiations in a wide range of cults of Roman, Greek and oriental origin, which has been seen as reflecting the determination of these pagan senators 'to stand for the potential unity of the old religion ... now that the emperor was a Christian' (Fowden 1998: 552). For the significance of the *taurobolium* and related rites, see McLynn 1996. Further reading: Bloch 1945; Matthews 1973.

(a) CIL 6.510 (= ILS 4152)

To the great gods, to the mother of the gods [Cybele] and to Attis, Sextilius Agesilaus Aedesius – a man of senatorial rank, a not undistinguished legal advocate in the African courts and in the imperial council, also *magister libellorum et cognitionum sacrarum, magister epistularum, magister memoriae* [all senior legal posts at the imperial court], deputy of the [praetorian] prefects in the Spanish provinces with responsibility for imperial appeals, father of fathers of the invincible sun god Mithras, priest (*hierofanta*) of Hecate, chief priest (*archibucolus*) of the god Liber [Bacchus] – dedicated this altar after being reborn into eternity (*renatus in aeternum*) through the sacrifice of a bull (*taurobolium*) and the sacrifice of a ram (*criobolium*), when our lord Valens was consul for the fifth time and our lord the younger Valentinian [II] for the first, on the Ides of August [13 August 376].

(b) CIL 6.1779 (= ILS 1259)

To the eternal shades. Vettius Agorius Praetextatus [was] augur, priest of Vesta, priest of the Sun, member of the Board of Fifteen, curial priest of Hercules, consecrated to Liber [Bacchus] and in the

the origins of the temples, marvelled at their founders, and although he himself followed different beliefs, he preserved these for the empire.

8. For each person has their own custom, each their own religious rite. The divine mind distributed different cults to cities to be their guardians. Just as souls are assigned to the newborn, so tutelary spirits of destiny are assigned to peoples. Besides this, there are the benefits which especially recommend the gods to men. For since all reasoning is shrouded in ambiguity, from where does recognition of the gods come more directly than from the recollection and proofs of circumstances that turned out favourably? Now if it is length of time that gives religions authority, we should keep faith with so many centuries and follow our parents who followed theirs with happy results.

9. Let us now imagine Rome standing here and addressing you with the following words: 'O best of emperors, fathers of your country, show respect for my years during which devout ritual has led me. Let me practise the ancestral rituals, for there is nothing to regret. Let me live by my own customs, for I am free. This cult brought the world under my rule, these sacred rites drove Hannibal from the walls [Livy 26.8–11] and the Senonian Gauls from the Capitol [Livy 5.47]. Have I been preserved for this – to have fault found with my longevity?

10. 'I will see what sort of arrangement is being contemplated, but imposing change late in old age is insulting.'

Therefore we request peace for the gods of our forefathers, for our patron deities. Whatever each person worships, it is reasonable to think of them as one. We see the same stars, the sky is shared by all, the same world surrounds us. What does it matter what wisdom a person uses to seek for the truth? It is not possible to attain to so sublime a mystery by one route alone (*uno itinere non potest perveniri ad tam grande secretum*). But these are matters for debate by men at leisure; we offer you now prayers, not a battle.

6.5 A bishop responds: Ambrose *Letters* 72 (17).3–4, 10, 13–15, 17, and 73 (18).3–8

When Ambrose's court contacts alerted him to the general import of Symmachus' memorandum, he promptly wrote to the emperor presenting general arguments against acceding to Symmachus' request and asking that he be sent a copy of the memorandum so that he could respond to Symmachus' arguments point by point (*Letter* 72 – 17 in older editions). He duly received a copy and *Letter* 73 (18 in older editions) was the result. As one reads through Ambrose's responses, with their mixture of persuasive argument and thinly veiled threat, it is important to remember that the emperor he was addressing was only 13 years old – a fact he was not afraid to exploit. Predictably, Symmachus' request was turned down.

(a) Letter 72 (17).3–4, 10, 13–15, 17

3. Since you, most Christian emperor, have an obligation to make clear your faith in the true God, your enthusiasm and concern for that faith, your dedication to it, I am amazed that certain people should entertain the hope that altars to pagan gods might be restored at your command and funds for the conduct of pagan sacrifices be provided. For it will look like these funds, appropriated to the treasury and imperial coffers some time ago now, are being contributed out of your own pocket rather than being returned from theirs.

4. These people complaining about expenses are the ones who never spared our blood, who even destroyed church buildings. These people asking you to grant them privileges, too, are the ones who denied us, in Julian's recent law [5.6], the ordinary right to speak and teach. Those privileges, too, are ones by which even Christians have often been led astray. For it was their intention to ensnare some through those privileges – some through a lack of caution, others through their concern to avoid the burdens of public responsibilities. And because not everyone is strong, many have lapsed even under Christian emperors. ...

10. But it is not possible to issue this decree [for the restoration of the altar and of funds] without committing sacrilege. Therefore I ask you not to issue or prescribe this decree, or approve a law of this kind. As a bishop of Christ, I appeal to your faith. All of us bishops would have done so, if what reached people's ears were not so unbelievable and unexpected – that something like this could be proposed in your advisory council or requested by the senate. But do not let it be said that the senate has made this request when a few pagans (*gentiles*) are exploiting the name of the whole body. For about two years ago when they tried to make this request, the holy Damasus, bishop of the Roman church chosen by the will of God, sent me a written statement given him by the many Christian senators, protesting that they had not instructed any such thing to be done, that they did not agree with any such requests by pagan senators, that they did not give their consent; and they also complained, both publicly and in private, that they would not assemble in the senate house if any such decree was approved. Is it worthy of your times, of these Christian times, that the honour of Christian

senators be compromised so that the realisation of an ungodly purpose may be granted to pagan senators? I forwarded this statement to Your Clemency's brother [Gratian], from which it was clear that the senate had not instructed its representatives to do anything concerning the expenses of superstition. ...

13. If this were a dispute in the law courts, there would be an opportunity for the other party to respond. It is a dispute about religion, so I as bishop claim that right. Let a copy of the memorandum sent be given to me, so that I too may respond more fully, and when Your Clemency's kinsman [Theodosius I] has been consulted on all points, he may see fit to give a response. Certainly, if something different is decided, we bishops cannot endure it with equanimity and disguise our dissatisfaction. You may come to church, but you will not find this bishop there, or you will find him uncooperative.

14. How will you reply when your bishop says to you: 'The church does not want your gifts, because you have adorned pagan temples with gifts. The altar of Christ spits on your offerings, since you have set up an altar to idols. For yours is the voice, yours the hand, yours the signature of approval, and yours the deed. The Lord Jesus rejects and refuses your worship since you have offered worship to idols. He has said to you: "You cannot serve two masters." Virgins consecrated to God do not receive those privileges of yours to which virgins consecrated to Vesta lay claim. Why do you need priests of God when you have given preference to the godless requests of pagans? We cannot associate ourselves with the error of another.'

15. How will you reply to these words? That you are a boy who made a mistake? In Christ every age is mature, in God every age is fully developed. Childishness is not allowed in the faith – even small children affirmed Christ undaunted in front of persecutors. ...

17. Therefore, emperor, since you appreciate that you would be inflicting harm, above all, on God, and then on your father [Valentinian I] and brother [Gratian] if you were to issue such a decree, I ask you to take the course of action which you know will be advantageous to your salvation in the sight of God.

(b) Letter 73 (18).3–8

3. The senator and prefect of Rome put forward in his memorandum three propositions which he considered potent – that Rome asks, as he puts it, for her traditional rituals, that stipends should be

assigned [again] to their priests and the Vestal Virgins, and that when the priestly stipends were refused, a general famine ensued.

4. In the first proposition, Rome weeps with tearful and plaintive voice for her traditional religious rituals, as she says, asking for their restoration. These rites, she asserts, drove Hannibal from the city walls and the Senonian Gauls from the Capitol. So while the power of those rites is vaunted, their weakness is betrayed. For Hannibal made a mockery of the Roman rites for a long time and while the gods fought against him, he reached the walls of the city undefeated. Why did they, on whose behalf the arms of their gods were fighting, allow themselves to be besieged?

5. What shall I say about the Senonian Gauls? The remnants of the Roman forces would not have driven them off as they were infiltrating the inner parts of the Capitol if the frightened squawk of a goose had not given them away. See what sort of guardians Roman temples have! Where was Jupiter at that time? Or was he speaking through the goose?

6. But why should I deny that the sacred rites fought for the Romans? Yet Hannibal also worshipped the same gods. So which side do they want? Let them choose. If the rites on the Roman side were victorious, then they were defeated on the Carthaginian side; if they were triumphant on the Carthaginian side, then they certainly did not give the Romans any advantage.

7. So let that hateful complaint of the Roman people be gone – Rome did not command it. She interrupts them with different words: 'Why do you spatter me every day with the futile blood of innocent animals? Victory trophies are found not in the entrails of cattle but in the strength of soldiers. I conquered the world by other means. Camillus, who brought back legionary standards taken from the Capitoline after slaughtering those who had triumphed on the Tarpeian Rock, waged war; his courage overthrew those whom religion did not remove. What shall I say about Atilius [Regulus] who pursued his military service even to death? [Scipio] Africanus did not find victory among the altars of the Capitoline but among the battle lines of Hannibal. ... [Reference is then made to examples of Roman setbacks in more recent centuries, despite the presence of the altar of Victory.] Why do you seek the voice of God in dead cattle? Come and learn service in the heavenly army on earth. We live here and fight there. Let the God who established it teach me the mystery of heaven, not man who does not even know himself. Whom should I trust more concerning God than God himself?

How can I trust you [pagans] who acknowledge you are ignorant of what you worship?'

8. 'It is not possible', he says, 'to attain to so sublime a mystery by one route alone.' What you are ignorant of we know from the voice of God, and what you seek through inklings we have found through the very wisdom and truth of God. Your approach, therefore, has nothing in common with ours. You ask the emperors for peace for your gods, we ask Christ for peace for those very emperors. You worship the works of your own hands, we consider it is an affront to regard as a god anything that can be made. God does not wish to be worshipped in the form of statues – in fact, even your own philosophers laughed at them.

6.6 In defence of temples: Libanius *Speech* 30.8–11, 28–9

Libanius (314–*c.* 393) was a native of Antioch, one of the foremost orators of his day and a committed pagan. The speech from which the following passages are extracted was produced in 386 and addressed to the emperor Theodosius I. It was prompted by the recent tour of inspection of the eastern provinces by the praetorian prefect Maternus Cynegius, during which he destroyed a number of temples with the assistance of bands of monks – the focus of his invective in 8–12. Just how seriously Libanius viewed the situation is apparent from his concluding remarks: 'If these people without your permission proceed to attack anything that has escaped them or has been hastily restored, you may be sure that the landowners will defend both themselves and the law' (55). Further reading: Liebeschuetz 1972: 237–9; Gassowska 1982; Matthews 1990: 140–2; Fowden 1978; Trombley 1993: vol. 2, ch. 8.

(8) You then have neither ordered the closure of temples nor banned entrance to them. From the temples and altars you have banished neither fire nor incense nor the offerings of other perfumes. But this black-robed tribe, who eat more than elephants and, by the quantities of drink they consume, weary those that accompany their drinking with the singing of hymns, who hide these excesses under an artificially contrived pallor – these people, Sire, while the law yet remains in force, hasten to attack the temples with sticks and stones and bars of iron, and in some cases, disdaining these, with hands and feet. Then utter desolation follows, with the stripping of roofs, demolition of walls, the tearing down of statues and the overthrow of altars, and the priests must either keep quiet or die. After demolishing one, they scurry to another, and to a third, and trophy is piled on trophy, in contravention of the law. (9) Such outrages occur even in the cities, but they are most common in the countryside.

Many are the foes who perpetrate the separate attacks, but after their countless crimes this scattered rabble congregates and calls for a tally of their activities, and they are in disgrace unless they have committed the foulest outrage. So they sweep across the countryside like rivers in spate, and by ravaging the temples, they ravage the estates, for wherever they tear out a temple from an estate, that estate is blinded and lies murdered. Temples, Sire, are the soul of the countryside: they mark the beginning of its settlement, and have been passed down through many generations to the men of today. (10) In them the farming communities rest their hopes for husbands, wives, children, for their oxen and the soil they sow and plant. An estate that has suffered so has lost the inspiration of the peasantry together with their hopes, for they believe that their labour will be in vain once they are robbed of the gods who direct their labours to their due end. And if the land no longer enjoys the same care, neither can the yield match what it was before, and, if this be the case, the peasant is the poorer, and the revenue jeopardized, for whatever a man's willingness, surely his inability frustrates him. (11) So the outrages committed by these hooligans against the estates bear upon vital matters of state. If the victims of this looting come to the 'pastor' in town [the bishop of Antioch] – for that is the title they give to a fellow who is not all that he should be – if they come and tearfully recount their wrongs, this pastor commends the looters and sends the victims packing with the assurance that they are lucky to have got off so lightly. (12) Yet, Sire, these victims are your subjects too, and as workers are more useful than idlers, so are they more useful than their oppressors. These are as the bees, those the drones. ...

(28) And if they tell you that some other people have been converted by such measures and now share their religious beliefs, do not overlook the fact that they speak of conversions apparent, not real. Their converts have not really been changed – they only say they have. This does not mean that they have exchanged one faith for another – only that this crew have been bamboozled. They go to their ceremonies, join their crowds, go everywhere where these do, but when they adopt an attitude of prayer, they either invoke no god at all or else they invoke the gods. It is no proper invocation from such a place, but it is an invocation for all that. In plays, the actor who takes the part of the tyrant is not a tyrant, but just the same as he was before putting on the mask: so here, everyone keeps himself unchanged, but he lets them think he has been changed. (29) Now what advantage have they won when adherence to their

doctrine is a matter of words and the reality is absent? Persuasion is required in such matters, not constraint. If persuasion fails and constraint is employed, nothing has been accomplished, though you think it has. It is said that in their very own rules it does not appear, but that persuasion meets with approval and compulsion is deplored. Then why these frantic attacks on the temples, if you cannot persuade and must needs resort to force? In this way you would obviously be breaking your own rules. (tr. A.F. Norman)

6.7 A comprehensive ban on sacrifice: *Theodosian Code* 16.10.10

This law, issued by Theodosius in 391 to officials in Rome (with a matching one to Alexandria later in the year: *Theodosian Code* 16.10.11) represents a comprehensive ban on pagan sacrifice. 'The two cities thus singled out were potent symbols, both of catholic Christian dogma and, embarrassingly, of surviving polytheism. But the constitutions were also intended for universal application. And they were much more thorough than earlier ones' (Fowden 1998: 553). The laws also show particular concern about officials who might continue practising pagan rites on the sly and propose a strategy for uncovering them by putting pressure on their staff to inform. The influence of Ambrose has usually been seen here, particularly following his famous stand-off with Theodosius over the Thessalonican massacre (details in Matthews 1990: 234–7), though this – and indeed the importance usually attached to these laws – has been challenged (McLynn 1994: 315–33). The efficacy of the legislation certainly remains open to doubt (Errington 1997).

The Emperors Valentinian [II], Theodosius [I], and Arcadius, Augusti, to Albinus, Praetorian Prefect: No-one is to stain themselves with sacrifices, no-one is to slaughter harmless sacrificial animals, no-one is to enter shrines, no-one is to undertake the ritual purification of temples or worship images crafted by human hand – otherwise they will be liable to divine and human penalties. This ruling also applies to magistrates (*iudices*): if any of them is an adherent of pagan rituals and enters a temple anywhere to worship, whether while travelling or in the city, they will immediately be required to pay fifteen pounds of gold, and their staff will pay the same amount with comparable speed, unless they have acted against the magistrate and reported him without delay in a formal deposition. Consular governors and their staff are to pay six pounds, special commissioners (*correctores*) and [other] governors (*praesides*) four pounds, and their staff the same amount in equal shares. Issued on the 6th day before the Kalends of March, at Milan, in the consulates of Tatian and Symmachus [24 February 391].

6.8 Pagan prophecies against Christianity: Augustine *The City of God* 18.53–4

In this extract from one of his most famous works, Augustine, bishop of north African Hippo and one of the most influential church leaders of Late Antiquity (354–430), highlights an interesting form of pagan opposition to Christianity in the late fourth century. The strategy is self-explanatory, though it is perhaps worth highlighting the significance of the one-year old boy – his 365 days corresponded to the 365-year time-span predicted for Christianity. Further reading: Chadwick 1984.

(53) ... 'It is not for you to know the times which the Father has fixed by his authority' [Acts 1.7]. But since this is the statement of the evangelist [Luke], it is not surprising that it has not held back worshippers of the many false gods from inventing oracles from the evil spirits whom they revere as deities, oracles which set down limits for the time that the Christian religion would continue. For when they saw that so many severe persecutions could not destroy it but rather served to enlarge it wonderfully, they contrived Greek verses of some sort or other supposedly issued by a divine oracle to some enquirer. To be sure, these verses make Christ innocent of this crime of sacrilege, but they add that Peter had performed magical rites (*maleficia*) so that the name of Christ would be worshipped for three hundred and sixty-five years, and then when the specified number of years was completed, it would without delay come to an end. ... What sort of gods are these who cannot prevent those things that they can predict, gods who are so subordinate to the sorcery of one man and to one item of criminal magic – a magic whereby a one-year-old boy, so they say, was killed and hacked into pieces and buried according to a foul rite – that they allowed the sect opposed to them to grow in strength over such a lengthy period of time, to overcome the awful brutalities of so many severe persecutions, not by resisting, but by submitting, and to achieve the overthrow of their own idols, temples and sacred oracles? ... (54) I might have gathered together these oracles and many of their kind if the year itself had not passed which the false prophecy promised and which deluded pride believed. But since three hundred and sixty-five years from the time when the worship of the name of Christ was established through his physical presence and through the apostles were completed a few years ago, what else do we need to look for to refute that falsehood?

6.9 Aristocratic and barbarian converts: Jerome *Letter* 107.2

The following passage, part of a letter which the prominent Biblical scholar and ascetic Jerome (*c.*347–420) wrote in 403 to a young woman of Roman aristocratic birth (see Kelly 1975: 273–5 for the context), contains many points of interest, particularly the expectation that male senators will be won to Christianity through their womenfolk (cf. Brown 1961), and the specific example of Gracchus' conversion in the mid 370s and his treatment of a Mithraic shrine (cf. 1.14; Nicholson 1995; in the list of Mithraic grades, the second is usually *nymphius* ('bridegroom') rather than *cryphius*, which may well be a copyist's error). While the latter half of the passage becomes steadily overoptimistic in tone, it alludes to a number of important developments, especially the notorious destruction of the temple of Serapis in Alexandria in 391, and the acceptance of Christianity by the Goths (on which see further Heather and Matthews 1991: chs 4–7). Two additional points deserve mention in connection with this last item: the Goths were first exposed to Christianity through Roman prisoners of war carried off north of the Danube during the mid-fourth century, rather than through organised missionary endeavour; and Jerome omits to mention that the Goths converted to *Arian* Christianity.

Let this be said, Laeta, most devout daughter in Christ, so that you do not give up hope of your father's salvation, and so that by the same faith which has merited you a daughter, you may also win your father and rejoice in the blessing of your whole household, knowing what God has promised: 'Things which are impossible for men are possible for God' [Luke 18.27]. It is never too late to change. The robber passed from the cross to paradise; after becoming like an animal in heart and body and living with the wild beasts in the desert, Nebuchadnezzar, king of Babylon, regained human reason; and to pass over events of old which might seem like tall tales to sceptics, did not your relative Gracchus (whose name makes plain his aristocratic lineage) only a few years ago when he was in charge of the urban prefecture [of Rome, in 376/7], overthrow, destroy and burn the cave of Mithras and all the monstrous images by which the grades are initiated – Raven, Secret (*cryphius*), Soldier, Lion, Persian, Sun-runner, and Father – and send these ahead like hostages to gain the baptism of Christ? Even in the city [of Rome] paganism (*gentilitas*) is undergoing abandonment. Those who were once gods of the nations have been left on isolated heights with owls and birds of the night. The standards of the soldiers are emblems of the cross, the purple robes of the emperors and the glowing gems of their diadems are adorned with a representation of the cross of salvation. Egyptian Serapis has now become a Christian, Marnas at Gaza weeps at the closure of his temple, and trembles constantly at the prospect of its destruction. From India, Persia and Ethiopia, we welcome crowds of monks every day. The Armenians have laid aside their quivers, the Huns are learning the psalmbook, the cold regions of the Scythians are warmed by the ardor of their faith; the Goths, with ruddy complexion and blond hair, carry tented churches around with their army, and perhaps the reason they fight against us on equal terms is because they put their trust in the same religion.

6.10 Christianising the countryside (1): Sulpicius Severus, *Life of St Martin* 12–15

Martin was one of the most renowned holy men and bishops in the late fourth-century west (he was bishop of Tours, *c.* 371–97). This excerpt from the influential *Life* written by his follower Sulpicius Severus in 396 provides some insight into traditional pagan practices in rural areas of the western empire, while also illustrating how Martin set about converting the countryside. Despite the tendency for a work of hagiography such as this to exaggerate the magnitude of the obstacles faced by its hero, it is evident that the Christianisation of these predominantly rural parts had made little progress prior to the arrival of Martin. As the following passage makes clear, a key element in Martin's strategy was an uncompromisingly aggressive attitude towards the physical manifestations of non-Christian cults (for archaeological evidence of the destruction of pagan sites in Gaul in this period, see Fontaine 1967–9: vol. 2, 762; Stancliffe 1983: 332–5), though the passage is also of interest for what it indicates about pagan resistance to change. At the same time it highlights another element in Martin's strategy: 'Realising the powerful attraction of the sanctuaries and the periodic celebrations which brought together there the population of the surrounding countryside, Martin had the astuteness not to change traditional customs, but to substitute *in situ* the Christian chapel for the pagan shrine' (Fontaine 1967–9: vol. 2, 760). From a different perspective, the extract is a fine example of the sort of well-written and often exciting narrative one sometimes finds in hagiographies, features that help to explain the popularity of the genre. Further reading: Fontaine 1967–9: vol. 2, 713–807 (detailed commentary in French); Stancliffe 1983: esp. ch. 23; Van Dam 1985: ch. 6; Fletcher 1997: ch. 2, esp. 140–8.

12. On a subsequent occasion, it happened that while Martin was making a journey, he encountered the corpse of a pagan (*gentilis*) being taken to its tomb to the accompaniment of superstitious funeral rites. When he saw the approaching crowd from a distance, he did not realise what the occasion was and he stopped for a moment; for the intervening distance was about five hundred paces, making it difficult for him to make out clearly what he saw. (2) However, since he could see that it was a group of peasants and the linen clothes draped over the body were fluttering in the wind, he

thought pagan rituals of worship were taking place – for it is the practice of Gallic peasants, in their pitiful state of derangement, to carry through their fields images of demons covered in white cloth. (3) So making the sign of the cross against those confronting him, he ordered the crowd not to move from that spot and to put down their burden. Then, in an extraordinary manner, you would have seen these wretches first of all rooted to the spot like rocks. (4) Then when they tried with all their might to move forward but were unable to advance any further, they did an about-turn in an absurd whirling movement until, defeated, they put down the burden of the corpse. Struck dumb and staring at one another in turn, they silently wondered what had happened to them. (5) But when the holy man discovered that the gathering was for a funeral procession, not for religious rites, he raised his hand again and restored their ability to move and carry the corpse. So he compelled them to stand still when he wished, and he allowed them to depart when it suited him.

13. In the same way, when he was destroying a very old temple in a certain village and he started cutting down a pine tree next to the shrine, the priest (*antistes*) of that place and a crowd of other pagans began to offer resistance. (2) And although, by the will of the Lord, these same people took no action while the temple was being demolished, they would not allow the tree to be cut down. He earnestly pointed out to them that there was nothing worthy of reverence in a tree trunk; rather, they should follow the God whom he himself served; the tree had to be cut down because it was consecrated to a demon. (3) Then one of them, who was more impudent than the rest, said, 'If you have any confidence in your god whom you claim to revere, we will ourselves cut down this tree and you sustain the force of its fall; and if your Lord is with you, as you claim, you will escape unscathed.' (4) Then Martin, fearlessly trusting in the Lord, agreed to do so, and the whole crowd of pagans accepted an arrangement of this kind, regarding the sacrifice of their tree as easy to bear if by its downfall they could crush the enemy of their sacred rites. (5) And so since the pine tree leant in one direction and there could be no doubt as to where it would land when cut, Martin was bound and positioned in accordance with the peasants' judgement, on the spot where everyone was certain the tree was going to fall. (6) Then they began to cut down that pine tree with great gladness and joy, and there was present a crowd of astonished observers, at a distance. The tree now gradually began to give way and, being on the point of crashing down, was threatening

to destroy him. (7) From a distance, the monks grew pale and, terrified as the danger now came closer, they abandoned all hope and trust as they anticipated only the death of Martin. (8) But he trusted in the Lord and waited fearlessly, and when the falling pine had already produced a cracking sound and was already dropping, already descending headlong on top of him, he raised his hand in its path and interposed the sign of salvation. Then indeed – you would think the pine had been driven backwards by a whirlwind of some sort – it rushed in the other direction and almost laid low the peasants who had been standing in a safe position. (9) Then a clamour ascended to the heavens and the pagans were stupified with amazement, the monks wept for joy and the name of Christ was proclaimed by everyone together; and it was plain to see that salvation had come to that region on that day. For there was virtually no-one from that great crowd of pagans who did not abandon their misguided sacrilege and, desiring the laying on of hands, trusted in the Lord Jesus. And indeed, before Martin, very few, or rather, virtually no-one in those regions had accepted the name of Christ. That name has achieved such influence through his miracles and example that now there is no place there that is not well-endowed with crowded churches and monasteries. For it was his practice to build churches or monasteries without delay wherever he had destroyed pagan shrines.

14. About the same time and in the same way, he performed a miracle no less great. For when he had set fire to a very old and renowned pagan shrine in a certain village, dense masses of flames were being carried by the force of the wind towards a neighbouring, or rather adjoining, house. (2) When Martin realised, he rapidly scaled the roof of the house and positioned himself in the path of the advancing flames. But then, in an extraordinary manner, you could see the fire turn back against the force of the wind, so that a contest seemed to be taking place between the battling elements. And so through Martin's authority the fire did only what it was commanded. (3) In another village by the name of Leprosum [Levroux], he wanted likewise to destroy a temple which the false religion has richly endowed, but a crowd of pagans opposed him so strongly that he was driven off, not without injury. (4) So he withdrew to a spot nearby, where for three days he wore a hair-shirt and covered himself in ashes and, fasting and praying the whole time, he beseeched the Lord to demolish by divine power that temple which human efforts had been unable to destroy. (5) Then suddenly two angels armed with spears and shields like heavenly troops presented

themselves to him, saying that they had been sent by the Lord to put the crowd of peasants to flight and to provide protection for Martin, so that no-one could oppose him while the temple was destroyed; so he was to go back and devoutly finish the job he had begun. (6) So he returned to the village and while the crowd of pagans looked on passively, he demolished the sacrilegious temple down to its foundations and reduced all its altars and images to powder. (7) When they saw this, the peasants realised that a divine power had stunned and unnerved them to prevent them resuming their resistance to the bishop, and nearly all of them put their trust in the Lord Jesus, openly shouting and admitting that it was Martin's God who should be revered, whereas their idols, which had been unable to look after themselves, did not deserve their worship.

15. I will also record what happened in a district of the Aeduan region. While he was destroying a temple in the same way there, a mob of enraged pagan peasants rushed at him. When one of them, more impudent than the rest, attacked him with a drawn sword, Martin threw off his cloak and presented his bare neck for the blow. (2) The pagan had no hesitation about striking, but when he raised his right hand too high, he fell flat on his back and, disconcerted by the fear of God, he begged for forgiveness. (3) Here is another incident not unlike the previous one. While he was destroying an idol, someone wanted to strike him with a knife, but in the very act the weapon was removed from his hand and vanished. (4) In general, however, when hostile peasants tried to dissuade him from demolishing their shrines, he so mollified the hearts of these pagans through his holy preaching that, when the light of truth was shown to them, they threw down their temples themselves.

6.11 Corroboration of Martin's activities: *RICG* 15.39

This epitaph, from Vienne in the Rhone valley, southern Gaul, commemorates a woman named Foedula, literally 'the shameful one'. Although this could imply a lowly social origin, the verse form of the epitaph and the quality of the inscribing and of the marble imply rather a woman from the local elite, in which case her name was presumably intended to make a statement about Christian humility. The 'mighty Martin' with whom she credits her baptism must be Martin of Tours, so this inscription provides independent corroboration for his activities. Although mainly active in the neighbourhood of Tours, he is known to have visited Vienne in the late 380s (Paulinus of Nola *Letter* 18). The epitaph also associates her with the martyr cult of Sts Gervasius and Protasius, in whose church at Vienne she was buried. In 386, at a critical juncture in his episcopacy, Ambrose of Milan had fortuitously discovered their remains, and their popularity had then spread rapidly into

Gaul. Foedula's epitaph therefore epitomises two important aspects of the early stages in the Christianisation of Gaul at the end of the fourth century. Further reading: Descombes 1985: 268–73.

(cross between doves and palms)

Foedula, who by the mercy of the Lord has left this world,
Lies here in this tomb, which a holy faith has provided.
Previously baptised by the right hand of the mighty Martin
    (*Martinus procer*),
She left her sins in the font, reborn of God.
Now that the martyrs have provided her with this fitting resting-place,
It is they, the mighty Gervasius and Protasius (*Cerbasius procer*
    Protasiusque), whom she reveres.
By her faith she has gained deserved rest in this tomb,
She who lies associated with the saints has borne witness.

6.12 Christianising the countryside (2): Endelechius, *On the Deaths of the Cattle* 101–120

The 132-line poem from which this passage derives is the only surviving work of Severus Sanctus Endelechius, an orator at Rome in the late fourth century. A friend of Paulinus of Nola and Sulpicius Severus, he may have come from Gaul, which is also a possible setting for the poem. It is uncertain whether the subject matter is pure literary creation or was prompted by an actual outbreak of disease: there is a clear debt to Virgil's first *Eclogue* (including a nice inversion of that poem's lines [42–3] about offering sacrifice in honour of Octavian) and to his third *Georgic* with its description of a cattle plague (thereby providing an illustration of the appropriation of Classical literature by Christian writers). Nevertheless, Tityrus' remedy is suggestive both of the way in which Christianity slowly infiltrated rural life and of the way the new faith had to accommodate itself to traditional habits of warding off evil with charms and incantations. Further reading: Schmid 1960: 1–3; Trout 1995: 284 n.17 (with further references).

BUCOLUS: ... Now tell me, Tityrus, which god rescued you from this disaster, so that you do not suffer from this cattle plague which has ravaged your neighbours?

TITYRUS: There is a sign, which they say is that of the cross of the deity who alone is worshipped in the great cities, Christ, the glory of the eternal divinity, whose only son he is. This sign applied to the middle of their foreheads was the sure salvation of all the cattle. Thus indeed the god, powerful through this name, is called Saviour. Immediately the fierce pestilence

and pass away, and when pagan worship was going to recover. However, the outcome of their consultation of these oracles showed they were false, like those given by Apollo to Croesus the Lydian and to Pyrrhus the Epirote. You know also what happened when subsequently we sacrificed in those places outside the city: not a single sign or apparition or response was given, even though we had been accustomed previously to become aware of some such illusion. (p. 41) We were at a loss as we enquired and pondered much about what this meant. We changed the places of sacrifice. In spite of that, the supposed gods remained mute and everything to do with them remained ineffective. We thought they were angry with us and finally had the idea that perhaps one of our group had a will opposed to what we wanted to achieve. We asked each other whether we were all of the same sentiment, and discovered a young man who had made the sign of the cross in the name of Christ and that our concern was thereby rendered vain and our sacrifices ineffective, since the supposed gods often flee at the name of Christ and the sign of the cross. We were at a loss to explain this, and Asclepiodotus, the others sacrificing and the magicians inquired into the matter. One of them thought he had a solution to the problem and said, 'The cross is a sign indicating that a man has died by violence, so it is understandable that the gods loathe shapes of this sort.'

7.2 Persecution of pagans in sixth-century Antioch: *Life of the Younger St Symeon the Stylite* 161, 164

The younger Symeon was a holy man who lived on one of the mountains near Antioch (521–92), and the modern editor of his biography considers it to have been written by one of Symeon's disciples. Although this episode, probably from 555, is couched in high-flown language, the official at the centre of the investigations, Amantius, is known from an independent source which describes his involvement in the suppression of a Samaritan revolt (John Malalas *Chronicle* p. 487), and suppression of paganism is certainly a general feature of the emperor Justinian's religious policies, as is book-burning (Maas 1992: ch. 5). Further reading: Trombley 1994: 182–95.

(161) Within a four month period of the holy man predicting all these events, that official arrived. His name was Amantius, and before coming to the city of Antioch, he destroyed many of the unrighteous found en route, so that men shuddered with fear at his countenance. For everywhere he suppressed all evil-doing whether

in word or deed, inflicting punishment, including death, on those who had gone astray, so that from then on even those living a blameless life feared his presence. For he removed, as much as was possible throughout the east, all quarrelling, all injustice, all violence, and all wrongdoing. When this had happened, God showed his servant another vision, which he reported to us: 'A decision has come from God against the pagans (*Hellēnes*) and heretics (*heterodoxoi*), that this official will reveal the idolatrous errors of the atheists and gather together all their books and burn them.' When he had foreseen these things and reported them, zeal for God took a hold of that official and after investigating, he found that the majority of the leaders of the city and many of its inhabitants were preoccupied with paganism (*hellēnismos*), Manichaeism, astrological practices, automatism, and other hateful heresies. He arrested them and put them in prison, and after gathering together all of their books – a huge number – he burned them in the middle of the stadium. He brought out their idols with their polluted accoutrements and hung them along the streets of the city, and their wealth was expended on numerous fines. ... (164) ... Then the judge took his seat on the tribunal and subjected to special punishments some of them, who had confessed to having committed many terrible crimes on account of their ungodliness; some he ordered to do service in the hospices, while others, who called themselves clerics, he sent to receive instruction in monasteries; still others he sent off into exile, while some he condemned to death. But by imperial command, the majority of them, who pleaded ignorance as an excuse and promised to repent, he released without further investigation. And so it came about that after being corrected, everyone was dispersed and none of them remained in prison, with the exception of one who had caused many disturbances during times of public unrest, on account of which he deserved punishment. So it was an appropriate time to recall the judgements of God and to sing the praises of his inexpressible benevolence towards us.

7.3 Persecution of pagans in sixth-century Sardis: *I. Sardis* 19

This damaged inscription corroborates evidence in other sources (e.g., 7.2) of stringent action undertaken by Justinian against those identified as pagans in the mid-sixth century. The second title of the investigating officer is a post established in 539 (Justinian *Novels* 82, on which see further Roueché 1989: 147–8), so this enquiry must have taken place after that date. The phrase used to describe pagans also features in an imperial law of the late fifth/sixth century (*Justinianic Code*

1.11.10), and it is a reasonable assumption that Hyperechius' activities were designed to enforce this legislation. It also appears that the partially preserved name of the individual punished by Hyperechius was the first in a list on further blocks of stone that have not survived. The punishment imposed is of interest in the light of the language of disease that features so strongly in religious polemic during Late Antiquity (though those sent to hospices in 7.2 (164) go not to recuperate, but to serve). Further reading: Trombley 1994: 180–1.

+ List of the decisions reached and of the unholy and loathsome pagans (*Hellēnes*) banished by Hyperechius, the highly esteemed judicial officer (*referendarius*) and imperial judge (*theios dikastos*). < ... >ipos was <banished> to the hospice for the sick (*ton tōn arostōn xenona*) for ten years< ... >

7.4 Christianisation in rural Egypt: Besa *Life of Shenoute* 83–84

During his long life (*c.* 355–466?), Shenoute, abbot of the White Monastery at Atripe in southern Egypt, gained a well-deserved reputation as a forceful opponent of paganism and heresy. This extract, from the Coptic biography written by his successor, Besa, illustrates the persistence of pagan practices in rural areas of a region of the empire long exposed to Christianity, and Shenoute's blunt strategy in response (cf. **6.10**). On this specific episode, see Trombley 1993: vol. 2, 207–19; Frankfurter 1998a: 68–9; for Shenoute more generally, see Timbie 1986.

(83) Another time, our holy father *apa* Shenoute arose to go to the village of Pleuit in order to throw down the idols which were there. So when the pagans came to know of this, they went and dug in the place which led to the village and buried some [magical] potions [which they had made] according to their books because they wanted to hinder him on the road. (84) Our father *apa* Shenoute mounted his donkey, but when he began to ride down the road, as soon as the donkey came to a place where the potions had been buried, it would stand still and dig with its hoof. Straightaway the potions would be exposed and my father would say to the servant: 'Pick them up so that you can hang them round their necks'. Time and time again the servant who was going with him would beat the donkey, saying: 'Move!' But my father would say to him: 'Let him be, for he knows what he is doing!', and again he would say to the servant: 'Take the vessels and keep them in your hand until we enter the village so that we can hang them round their necks.' When he entered the village, the pagans saw him with the magical vessels which the servant had in his hands. They immediately fled away

and disappeared, and my father entered the temple and destroyed the idols, smashing them one on top of the other. (tr. D. Bell)

7.5 The fate of a temple in Carthage: Quodvultdeus *The Book of the Promises and Prophecies of God* 3.38 (44)

Quodvultdeus, bishop of Carthage from *c.*437 to the early 450s, here recounts how the Christian authorities dealt with a temple in Carthage dedicated to the goddess Caelestis – the Romanised version of the important Punic deity Tanit (Halsberghe 1984). Initially, the temple was closed, presumably as part of the more general shutting of pagan sanctuaries in north Africa in 399 known from other sources. Then, probably in 407/8, the Christian community gathered there for some sort of ceremony. Quodvultdeus' account seems to indicate that this marked the conversion of the temple to a church, but the eventual demolition of the building *c.* 421 gives pause for thought. At any rate, it is this denouement which is particularly significant, since it was apparently inspired by worries about the temple building remaining a focus for pagan hopes and implies that pre-Christian religious traditions still commanded wide support (cf. Augustine *Letters* 91.8).

A few points of detail warrant comment. The author's wordplay on the name Caelestis – which means 'heavenly' in Latin – is not easy to preserve in translation, while the point of the inscription is that the temple must originally have been dedicated during the reign of Marcus Aurelius (161–80) who, like all pagan emperors (and indeed some fourth-century Christian ones), held the office of chief priest (*pontifex maximus*). Finally, although the reference to the temple land becoming a place for burial of the dead is usually taken to mean a cemetery, the 'dead' here could be the dispossessed pagan deities themselves. Further reading: Braun 1964: 70–4, 574–8; Lepelley 1979–81: vol. 1, 42–4; vol. 2, 354–7; Hanson 1978.

In Africa, at Carthage, Caelestis – as they called her – had a temple of very substantial size ringed around by sanctuaries of all their gods. Its precinct was decorated with mosaic pavements and expensive columns and walls, and extended nearly 1,000 paces. When it had been closed for a long time and, from neglect, thorny thickets invaded the enclosure, and the Christian inhabitants wanted to claim it for the use of the true religion, the pagan inhabitants (*gentilis populus*) clamoured that there were snakes and serpents there to protect the temple. This only aroused the fervour of the Christians all the more and they removed everything with ease and without suffering any harm so as to consecrate the temple to the true celestial king and master. And in fact when the solemn feast of holy Easter was celebrated and a great crowd had gathered there and was approaching from every direction full of curiosity, the father of many priests and a man worthy of remembrance, the bishop

Aurelius – now a citizen of the heavenly homeland – placed his chair there on the spot [previously occupied by the cult statue] of Caelestis and sat down. I myself was there at the time with companions and friends, and while, in our youthful impatience, we were turning in every direction and inquisitively studied each detail according to its importance, something amazing and unbelievable confronted our gaze: on the façade of the temple, in very large letters of bronze, an inscription was written – 'Aurelius the chief priest (*pontifex*) dedicated [this]'. When they read this, the people marvelled at this deed inspired by the prophetic Spirit in a former time, which the prescient ordering of God had brought to this appointed outcome. And when a pagan made known a false prophecy, as if from the same Caelestis, to the effect that the sacred way and the temples would once again be restored to the ancient ritual of their ceremonies, God, the true God, whose prophetic utterances do not know how to lie or deceive at all, brought it about, under Constantius [III] and the empress [Galla] Placidia – whose son, the devout and Christian Valentinian [III], is now emperor – and by the efforts of the tribune Ursus, that all those temples were razed to the ground, leaving, appropriately, a piece of land for the burial of the dead; and the hand of the Vandals [who occupied Carthage in 439] has now destroyed that sacred way without leaving any reminder of it.

7.6 The temple of Isis at Philae in the mid-fifth century: *IGPhilae* 197 and Priscus *History* fr. 27.1

By the mid-fifth century, many temples had either been destroyed or converted into churches, and open celebration of pagan rites at cult centres was the exception. One location where such rites continued to be practised, however, was the temple of Isis at Philae, on the Nile in southern Egypt (cf. 1.8), illustrated here by an inscription placed by one of the priests at the entrance to the shrine of Osiris on the roof of the temple of Isis (celebrations in honour of Osiris were held during the month of Choiak, when this inscription was carved [Bernand 1969: 246]). Relative geographical isolation no doubt played a part in Philae's apparent immunity from enforced changes in other parts of the empire, but it would appear from the second extract, by the important fifth-century historian Priscus, that political considerations were also a major factor – in this case, maintaining good relations with the Blemmyes and Nobades, the peoples who replaced the kingdom of Meroe as the empire's neighbours to the south of Egypt. For detailed discussion of the inscription, see Bernand 1969: 237–46. On this phase of Philae's history, see more generally Trombley 1993: vol. 2, 225–35; Frankfurter 1998a: 105–6.

(a) IGPhilae 197

The act of worship of Smetchem, the chief priest (*protostolistēs*), whose father is Pachoumios, prophet (5) and whose mother is Tsensmet. I became chief priest in [the year] 165 [of the era] of Diocletian [448/9]. I came here (10) and carried out my function at the same time as my brother Smeto, successor of the prophet (15) Smet, son of Pachoumios, prophet. We give thanks to our mistress Isis and to our lord Osiris (20) for a blessing today, 23[rd day of the month] Choiak, [the year] 169 [of the era] of Diocletian [20 December 452].

(b) *Priscus* History *fr. 27.1*

When the Blemmyes and Nobades were defeated by the Romans, both peoples sent envoys to Maximinus on the subject of peace, wishing to conclude a treaty, and they said they would observe it while Maximinus remained in the region of Thebes. But when he would not agree to a treaty for this period of time, they said they would not bear arms during his lifetime. But when he would not accept this second proposal of their embassy, they agreed to a hundred year treaty. By its terms, Roman prisoners were to be released without ransom, whether captured in that incursion or another; cattle which had been carried off were to be returned, and compensation paid for those which had been consumed; and hostages of good birth were to be handed over by them as a guarantee of the treaty. For their part, they were to have unhindered access to the temple of Isis in accordance with traditional custom, while the Egyptians were to be responsible for the river boat in which the statue of the goddess was placed and transported. For at a specified time the barbarians bear the wooden image to their own country to consult it for oracles, before restoring it to the island. Maximinus considered the temple at Philae a suitable location in which to formalise the treaty, and certain men were sent there. When the representatives of the Blemmyes and the Nobades who had negotiated the treaty reached the island, the agreement was committed to writing and the hostages were handed over. ...

7.7 The end of the cult of Isis at Philae: Procopius *Wars* 1.19.31–5 and *IGPhilae* 203, 201

The first passage is the account by the important sixth-century historian Procopius of Justinian's termination of the cult of Isis at Philae, on the Nile in southern

Egypt, which has been dated to the mid-530s (Nautin 1967: 3–8). Although Justinian was well-known for his willingness to enforce conformity with his Christian convictions, it is possible that in this instance political considerations also contributed to his decision, namely a breakdown in peaceful relations with the neighbouring Blemmyes and Nobades (Nautin 1967: 6). Despite Procopius' statement that the temple was destroyed, it is clear that it remained standing (to the present day) and transformed into a church dedicated to Stephen, the very first martyr. The first inscription, on the wall of the main entrance to the temple of Isis, is one of a number recording the role of the local bishop Theodore (in post from *c.* 525 to at least 577 [Nautin 1967: 8]) in this process; the image of Stephen with which this inscription was associated was visible in the early nineteenth century, but has since been destroyed by the action of the Nile waters (Bernand 1969: 264–5). The second inscription, beside the entrance to the sanctuary of the temple of Isis, has been seen as having an apotropaic function *vis-à-vis* the demons believed to inhabit pagan shrines. For detailed discussion of the two inscriptions, see Nautin 1967: 14–16, 17–20; Bernand 1969: 256–9, 263–7; for more general context, see Nautin 1967; MacCoull 1990.

(a) Procopius Wars 1.19.34–37

(34) When this emperor [Diocletian] found there was an island in the River Nile very close to the town of Elephantine, he built a very strong fortress on it, and established there some shared temples and altars for the Romans and these barbarians, and placed priests from each people in the fortress, confident that their sharing in things sacred to them would result in friendliness (*philia*) between them. (35) For this reason he named the place Philae. Both these peoples, the Blemmyes and the Nobades, reverence all the other gods which the pagans (*Hellēnes*) acknowledge, as well as Isis and Osiris, not to mention Priapus. (36) The Blemmyes are also in the habit of sacrificing humans to the sun. These barbarians have used these temples on Philae until my own day, but the emperor Justinian decided to demolish them. (37) So the commander of the troops there, Narses – a Persarmenian by origin, whose desertion to the Romans I have previously mentioned – pulled down the temples at the emperor's command. He placed the priests in prison and sent the cult statues to Constantinople.

(b) IGPhilae 203

+ The very faithful friend of God, Father Theodore, bishop, who through the generosity of our Lord Christ has transformed this temple into a church of the holy Stephen, (5) [dedicated this image]. A blessing on him through the power of Christ. + [This inscription was put up] by Posios, deacon and warden. +

(c) IGPhilae *201*

The cross + has conquered – it always conquers. + + +

7.8 Gregory the Great's strategy in Britain: Bede *Church History of the English People* 1.30

Although Christianity had had a presence in Roman Britain (Thomas 1981), the arrival of pagan Anglo-Saxon settlers from the Continent during the fifth century meant that much of the island had to be re-evangelised, a task which Pope Gregory the Great (590–604) organised at the end of the sixth century. Bede (*c.* 672/3–735), a monk at Jarrow in northern England, preserved the famous letter Gregory wrote in July 601 to his missionaries there with instructions on how they should deal with pagan shrines. Further reading: Markus 1970; Wallace-Hadrill 1988: 44–5; Mayr-Harting 1991: ch. 3; Fletcher 1997: 111–19.

To my most beloved son, Abbot Mellitus, Gregory, servant of the servants of God. Since the departure of our companions and yourself I have felt much anxiety because we have not happened to hear how your journey has prospered. However, when Almighty God has brought you to our most reverend brother Bishop Augustine, tell him what I have decided after long deliberation about the English people, namely that the idol temples of that race should by no means be destroyed, but only the idols in them. Take holy water and sprinkle it in the shrines, build altars and place relics in them. For if the shrines are well built, it is essential that they should be changed from the worship of devils to the service of the true God. When this people see their shrines are not destroyed they will be able to banish error from their hearts and be more ready to come to the places they are familiar with, but now recognizing and worshipping the true God. And because they are in the habit of slaughtering much cattle as sacrifices to devils, some solemnity ought to be given them in exchange for this. So on the day of the dedication of the festivals of the holy martyrs, whose relics are deposited there, let them make themselves huts from the branches of trees around the churches which have been converted out of shrines, and let them celebrate the solemnity with religious feasts. Do not let them sacrifice animals to the devil, but let them slaughter animals for their own food to the praise of God, and let them give thanks to the Giver of all things for His bountiful provision. Thus while some outward rejoicings are preserved, they will be able more easily to share in inward rejoicings. It is doubtless impossible to cut out everything at once from their stubborn minds: just as the man who is attempting to climb to the highest place, rises by steps and degrees and not by leaps ... (tr. B. Colgrave)

7.9 The problem of public shows: Jacob of Serugh *Homily* 5

Public entertainment in the Roman world was closely bound up with religion, whether it be that the games in question honoured a particular deity, or the plays included re-enactments of stories from mythology involving gods and goddesses. These features raised grave doubts in the minds of church leaders about the propriety of Christians attending such occasions, yet it is clear that many continued to find them irresistible (cf., e.g., Augustine *Sermon* 51). The sermon from which the following extracts derive is one of many in which clergy tried to dissuade their congregations from participation. Written in Syriac, its author was a prominent Syrian churchman of the late fifth and early sixth century (451–521) who ended his life as bishop of Batnae (Serugh). It is of particular interest because he discusses the arguments of those he is trying to dissuade. Further reading: Markus 1990: ch. 8.

[The defence of those who frequent the spectacles] 'It is a show', they say, 'not paganism. What will you lose if I laugh? And since I deny the gods, I shall not lose through the stories concerning them. The dancing of that place [the theatre] gladdens me, and, while I confess God, I also take pleasure in the play, while I do not thereby bring truth to nought. I am a baptised [Christian] even as you, and I confess one Lord; and I know that the mimings which belong to the spectacles are false. I do not go that I may believe, but I go that I may laugh. And what do I lose on account of this, since I laugh and do not believe? [As for] those things in the stories which are mimed concerning the tales of the idols, I know that they are false; and I see them – laughing. What shall I lose on account of this? I am of the opinion that I [shall lose] nothing. Why then do you blame him who is without blame?' ...

[Jacob's reply] 'Who can bathe in mud without being soiled? ... You are the assembly of the baptised, whose husband and God is Jesus; and how will he not become jealous, since you praise idols? ... These worthless spectacles which are mimed with dancing, I will tell [you] without shame from what source they come. When the physician lances a boil, he bespatters his hands with festering matter, and he makes his fingers swim in foul blood on account of the healing [of the patient]. He soaks his clean hands in loathsome pus, and he does not shrink, and he defies the foul smell that he may scrape away the matter of the boil. In accordance with this rule I approach the boil which the spectacles have caused, in order that, when the tongue lances it, and is bespattered with it, it may become clean. I will say concerning their plays how futile their stories are, lest any man suppose that rashly I bring shame upon their deeds.

'They say that the grandfather of their gods [Kronos] was devouring his sons, and as a dragon [swallows] a serpent, so he was swallowing the child of his belly. This is the beginning of the story of the dancing of the Greeks; this one thing alone is sufficient that you should despise all their tales. ... But his son [Zeus] who was saved from him [Kronos] became famous through adultery, and, under various forms, he committed fornication with many women ...' (tr. C. Moss).

7.10 Christian methods of divination: *Council of Vannes* Canon 16

The decisions of this Gallic council held some time between 461 and 491 included the condemnation of a form of divination known as the 'lots of the saints' (*sortes sanctorum*), which 'involved the random selection of oracular responses from a collection designed for the purpose' (Klingshirn 1994: 220). An analogous practice was the *sortes Biblicae*, in which books of the Bible were opened at random (ideally on the altar of a church) for guidance about the future. In this instance, it is note-worthy that clergy are singled out for resorting to the practice. The Council of Agde (506) repeated this canon virtually word for word, with the inclusion of the laity (Canon 42). Further reading: Metzger 1988; Klingshirn 1994: 219–21; Gamble 1995: 237–41; MacMullen 1997: 139, 237–8.

Lest something which very seriously infests the faith of the catholic religion should perhaps appear to have been overlooked, namely that quite a number of clergy concern themselves with augury and under the name of a false religion called the 'lots of the saints' (*sortes sanctorum*), they practise the art of divination and predict the future by the study of writings of any sort – any clergy found either carrying out or teaching this shall be treated as outside the church.

7.11 A Christian oracle: *P. Rendel Harris* 54 and *P. Oxy.* 1926

These two short papyri from sixth-century Egypt form a pair of requests for help in making a business decision. They were written by the same person on a single sheet of papyrus which was then cut in half; although there are some variations in phraseology, the only essential difference is that the first looks for an answer in the affirmative, the second in the negative (Youtie 1975). The individual seeking help directs their request to the Christian God and a Christian saint, yet the technique employed owes a clear debt to traditional Egyptian methods of consulting oracles, whereby the divine answer was obtained by lot (cf. Browne 1976: 56–8 for comparisons with 1.10). Although the survival of a matching pair like this is rare, many individual requests have been recovered, 'suggest[ing] that oracles were no 'behind-the-scenes' favour but rather a common service to the community that was offered by certain churches and monasteries' (Frankfurter 1998a: 194). On the reverse of both papyri are the Greek letters χμγ (chi-mu-gamma), written three times and interspersed with crosses, but their significance remains a matter for debate. Some scholars have seen them as an acrostic for 'Mary bore Christ' or the like, while others have proposed that they are an isopsephism – that is, they possess some sort of numerological significance, arising from the fact that the letters of the Greek alphabet could be used to represent numbers (in this case 643). Whatever the answer, the formula certainly occurs in contexts implying its use as a sort of protective amulet (see Llewellyn 1997 for further discussion).

(a) P. Rendel Harris 54

+ My Lord God Almighty and St Philoxenus my patron, I beg you by the mighty name of the Lord God, if it is your will and you are helping me to acquire the money-changing business, I beg that you bid me to know and to make an offer. +

(b) P. Oxy. 1926

+ My Lord God Almighty, and St Philoxenos my patron, I beg you by the mighty name of the Lord God, if it is not your will that I make an offer for the money-changing business and for the weighing office, bid me to know not to make an offer. +

7.12 A Roman calendar from the mid-fifth century: An extract from the *Calendar of Polemius Silvius*

The text below comprises the entries for one month from a calendar compiled in 448/9 by a Christian writer in Gaul, Polemius Silvius, and dedicated to Eucherius, bishop of Lyons. Its chief interest lies in its accommodation of many traditional Roman observances and festivities – some with distinctly religious significance – alongside Christian festivals. Most matters of detail are glossed below, but note, first, that 'games' (*ludi*) focused on various types of theatrical performance while 'circus games' (*circenses*) meant chariot-races, and second, that the Romans counted inclusively, so that, e.g., 'the second day before ...' is actually the day before. The periodic references to the weather are generally thought to reflect the influence of Columella's first-century treatise on agriculture. Further reading: Salzman 1990:

242–6; Degrassi 1963: 388–405 (for commentary on points of detail, though in Latin).

JANUARY
Named after Janus. It has 31 days. It is called Sebet by the Jews, Tybi by the Egyptians, Posideon by the Athenians, Edineus by other Greeks [i.e., the Macedonian month of Audinaios].

The Kalends [1 January]
Named from the Greek *kalein*, that is from 'calling', because at that
    time the people were called to an assembly at the rostrum in Rome
4th day before the Nones [2 January]
Privately funded circus games. Southerly wind, sometimes with rain
3rd day before the Nones [3 January]
Day suitable for divination. Birthday of Cicero. Games
2nd day before the Nones [4 January]
Compitalian Games [to appease guardian spirits of cross-roads]
The Nones [5 January]
So named because the ninth day (*nonus dies*) separates them from the
    Ides. Portends a storm
8th day before the Ides [6 January]
Epiphany, on which day in times past the star which announced the
    birth of the Lord was seen by the Magi. Wine was made from
    water and the Saviour was baptised in the River Jordan.
    Southerly wind sometimes, or westerly wind
7th day before the Ides [7 January]
First 'napkin' (*mappa*) of the consul [to start chariot-races in celebra-
    tion of gaining the consulship], which is so called for this
    reason, because when King Tarquin of Rome was taking lunch
    in the Circus on a day when circus games were held, he threw
    his own napkin from the table outside in order to give the
    signal for the charioteers to race after lunch
6th day before the Ides [8 January]
Southerly wind sometimes and hail
5th day before the Ides [9 January]
Prescribed meeting of the senate. Substitute consuls are designated
    and praetors
4th day before the Ides [10 January]
3rd day before the Ides [11 January]
[Festival of] the Carmentalia from the name of the mother of Evander
    [viz. Carmentis, who, in one tradition about Rome's origins,
    advised her son to settle at the subsequent site of Rome]

2nd day before the Ides [12 January]

Birthday of our Lord Theodosius [II] Augustus [408–50] on the previous day

The Ides [13 January]

Named from the Greek *eidein*, from 'seeing', because, before this present [type of] year was valid [viz. the solar year, which superseded the lunar cycle], in the middle of the month, the moon, which began on the Kalends and from which we learned that the months (*menses*) were named [from the Greek for moon, *mēnē?*], was seen to be full. Second 'napkin' [for chariot-races in honour of Jupiter the Protector]. Sometimes wind or a storm

19th day before the Kalends of February [14 January]

18th day before the Kalends [15 January]

Anniversary of [the accession of the emperor] Honorius [395–423]. Circus games. Sometimes a southerly wind and rain

17th day before the Kalends [16 January]

16th day before the Kalends [17 January]

Palatine Games [for three days, in memory of the emperor Augustus]

15th day before the Kalends [18 January]

Games

14th day before the Kalends [19 January]

Games

13th day before the Kalends [20 January]

Birthday of [the emperor] Gordian [238–44]. Circus games

12th day before the Kalends [21 January]

Games. South-westerly wind. Portends a storm

11th day before the Kalends [22 January]

Anniversary of the holy martyr Vincentius. Rainy day

10th day before the Kalends [23 January]

Prescribed meeting of the senate. Quaestors are designated in Rome

9th day before the Kalends [24 January]

Birthday of [the emperor] Hadrian [117–38] [cf. 1.1]. Circus games

8th day before the Kalends [25 January]

Sometimes a storm

7th day before the Kalends [26 January]

6th day before the Kalends [27 January]

Games of the Twin Gods in Ostia, which was the first colony established

5th day before the Kalends [28 January]

Games. Southerly or south-westerly wind. Sometimes a wet day

4th day before the Kalends [29 January]

Games

3rd day before the Kalends [30 January]

Portends a storm

2nd day before the Kalends [31 January]

Circus games for the victory [of Constantius II in 344] over the inhabitants of Adiabenica [a Mesopotamian region]. Sometimes a storm

Part II

OTHER RELIGIOUS GROUPS

8

JEWS

The land of Israel, and particularly Jerusalem, were of special importance to Judaism in Graeco-Roman antiquity, not least because it
was only in the temple at Jerusalem that acceptable sacrifices could
be offered. Nevertheless, for many centuries before Late Antiquity,
historical circumstances had resulted in the transplanting of Jewish
communities all over the Mediterranean world – the so-called
Diaspora; hence the broad geographical spread of the material
included in this chapter, the focus of which is Jews in their relations
with pagans and Christians.

Judaism occupied a unique position *vis-à-vis* both pagans and
Christians. Despite Jewish refusal to acknowledge any god other than
their own, and their disdain for cult images, the Roman authorities of
the late first century BC and early first century AD had generally been
prepared to allow Jewish religious practices to continue unhindered
and even conceded special privileges, at least partly out of respect for
the antiquity of Jewish traditions (cf. Feldman 1993: ch. 6). The
Jewish revolts of the mid-first and early second centuries resulted in
the destruction of the temple in Jerusalem – a cataclysmic blow, given
its centrality in Jewish ritual – and the curtailment of privileges, but
Judaism *per se* was not outlawed, while the geographical distance that
separated Diaspora Jews from Jerusalem meant the temple's destruction was less significant for many; at the same time, the hereditary
office of patriarch, established with Roman approval in the second
century, was instrumental in maintaining links between Palestine and
Diasporan communities. As for the Christians, they of course traced
their roots back to Judaism, though the need to establish an independent identity necessarily created an ambivalent attitude towards their
Jewish heritage – an ambivalence which became even more
pronounced in Late Antiquity.

The first two items that follow illustrate the social prominence and broad acceptance of Jews in the wider community, both in terms of the holding of public office (8.1) and the 'visibility' of synagogues (8.2). Moreover, at those times in the mid-third and early fourth centuries when the imperial authorities were requiring the inhabitants of the empire to demonstrate reverence for the traditional deities (cf. 2.11–12, 3.3–5), it is apparent that the Jews received special exemption (8.3). In the mid-fourth century, the emperor Julian emphasised the common ground between pagan and Jewish religious practices (8.4) and went so far as to initiate the (ultimately unsuccessful) rebuilding of the temple in Jerusalem (8.5).

Meanwhile, church authorities were becoming increasingly eager to emphasise the differences between Christianity and Judaism, and prevent too close a level of interaction between adherents, as shown by canons from a church council in the early fourth century (8.6) and the sermons of a leading clergyman of Antioch towards the end of the century (8.7). That Judaism continued to win converts in Late Antiquity is also illustrated by epigraphic evidence (8.8), and the church's ongoing concern was reflected at councils of the fifth and sixth centuries (8.9). Such attitudes sometimes found expression in violence against Jews and their property, most notoriously at Callinicum in 388 (8.10). At this stage the emperors, though Christian, nevertheless tried to protect the rights of Jewish communities (8.11), but a shift towards less sympathetic measures becomes evident during the early fifth century (8.12). A fascinating account of the conversion of the Jews on the island of Minorca provides illuminating insights into the changes afoot (8.13), for which there is also a little corroborative epigraphic evidence (8.14). The legal position of Jews did not deteriorate further in significant ways during the sixth century, unlike that of the related Samaritans – with disastrous consequences for Palestine (8.15) – but individual acts of overt discrimination against Jews continued (8.16).

For general discussions of Judaism in Late Antiquity, see Simon 1986, Millar 1992; for collections of source material in translation, see Stern 1974–84 (literary sources), Linder 1987, 1997 (legal sources), Noy 1993–5 (inscriptions from Italy, Spain and Gaul, nearly all of which are late Roman); Williams 1998 includes late Roman material down to the 420s.

8.1 Jews on the town council: *BE* 81 (1968) 478 (p. 517) and Robert *NIS* 14 (p. 55)

These inscriptions – the first dating from the late third century, the second from the second half of the fourth century or later – are two examples of a number testifying to the holding of public office by members of the Jewish community in the important city of Sardis in western Asia Minor. It was only at the beginning of the third century that Jews were granted permission to do so (*Digest* 50.2.3.3) and although not an unmixed blessing in so far as such civic responsibilities entailed increasingly heavy financial burdens, these texts also imply a sense of civic pride. Certainly the appearance of Jews in this role is an important indication of the social standing and acceptance some of them could enjoy. The inscriptions themselves record gifts by the individuals in question to their local synagogue (the first is explicit about the gift, the second relates to marble wall revetments; for the synagogue itself, see **8.2**). Besides corroborative inscriptions from elsewhere (Williams 1998: 108–11, 147), it is interesting to compare the prominence of the Jewish community at Smyrna in the *Martyrdom of Pionius* (**2.12**) and the example of Theodorus in fifth-century Minorca (**8.13**). Further reading: Trebilco 1991: 37–54; White 1997: 321–3.

(a) BE 81 (1968) 478 (p. 517)

Aurelius Alexander, also known as Anatolius, a citizen of Sardis and a town councillor (*bouleutēs*), had the third bay [of the synagogue] adorned with mosaics.

(b) Robert NIS 14 (p. 55)

Aurelius Hermogenes, a citizen of Sardis, a town councillor (*bouleutēs*), and a goldsmith: I have fulfilled my vow.

8.2 A late Roman synagogue: the synagogue at Sardis

Synagogues were community centres and places for public prayer and the reading and teaching of the Law of Moses, and served as the focal point of Jewish community life throughout the Roman world. Archaeological remains of many have been found (see Kraabel 1979 for a survey), and those at Sardis are among the most impressive (**Figure 8.2**). Indeed, the synagogue at Sardis is by far the largest one discovered to date, capable of holding about a thousand people. This, together with the absence of some features found in other examples (e.g., benches along the side of the assembly hall) make it atypical in some respects. On the other hand, its overall layout is similar to other cases and it certainly had a repository for the scrolls of the Law on the wall nearest Jerusalem. Moreover, 'the distinctiveness of the Sardis Synagogue should not be taken as proof that its builders departed from some canonical standard of design. It is, rather, part of the growing evidence that there was no clear-cut universal canon for synagogue architecture in the ancient world' (Seager and Kraabel 1983: 177). Finally, the size and prominent location of the synagogue at Sardis is an important indication of the high social profile of the Jewish community there in Late Antiquity. It appears to have remained in use until its destruction by Persian invaders in 616. Further reading on the Sardis

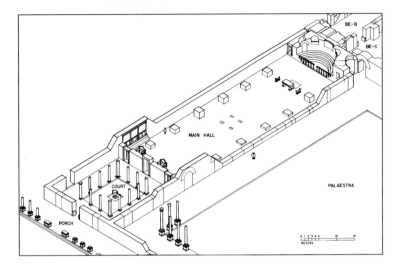

Figure 8.2   Reconstruction drawing of the Sardis synagogue

Source: By courtesy of the Archaeological Exploration of Sardis/Harvard University. Drawing by A.M. Shapiro, revised by A.R. Seager, 1966.

synagogue: Seager 1972; Seager and Kraabel 1983; Bonz 1990; Trebilco 1991: 40–43; White 1997: 310–21. Further reading on synagogues in Late Antiquity generally: Kraabel 1981; Levine 1987; Fine 1996, 1997.

8.3 Diocletian exempts Jews from sacrificing: *Palestinian Talmud, Abodah Zarah* 5.4

The Palestinian Talmud is a collection of sayings in Hebrew attributed to rabbis (religious teachers) and stories involving them over a period of several centuries, put together and edited in Palestine in the fifth century. The following excerpt is part of a discussion about Jewish relations with Samaritans, in the course of which incidental reference is made to imperial policy towards the Jews during the Diocletianic persecution (see further Smallwood 1976: 540). A similar exemption from sacrificing seems to have applied during the Decian persecution, judging by the evidence concerning Jews in the *Martyrdom of Pionius* (2.12) (Lane Fox 1986: 754 n. 16).

And there are those who wish to explain the reason [that the wine of the Samaritans was prohibited] as follows: When Diocletian the king came up here, he issued a decree, saying, 'Every nation must offer a libation, except for the Jews'. So the Samaritans made a libation. [That is why the] sages prohibited their wine. (tr. J. Neusner)

8.4 Common ground between pagans and Jews: Julian *Against the Galilaeans* fr. 72 (306B)

It is clear from elsewhere in his writings that the emperor Julian regarded Judaism as inferior to paganism, but he was also prepared to express approval of certain features, as indicated below. In part this was a tactical ploy in his campaign against the Christians (or 'Galilaeans' as Julian preferred), but it is also symptomatic of the importance of sacrifice to him. Indeed, a number of sources report him encouraging Jewish leaders to resume offering sacrifices to their god (Socrates *Church History* 3.20, Sozomen *Church History* 5.22, Theodoret *Church History* 3.15), and when they pointed out that this was impossible so long as the temple in Jerusalem lay in ruins, Julian proceeded to initiate its reconstruction (8.5). Further reading: Bowersock 1978: 88–9; Millar 1992: 106–8; Smith 1995: 193–6.

The Jews behave like the Gentiles (*tois ethnesin*) except that they acknowledge only one god. This is something distinctive to them, but alien to us. As for everything else, though, we share common ground – temples, sanctuaries, altars, rituals of purification, certain injunctions where we do not diverge from one another at all, or only in insignificant ways.

8.5 Julian's attempt to rebuild the temple in Jerusalem: Ammianus Marcellinus *History* 23.1.2–3

In this passage, the pagan historian Ammianus Marcellinus briefly describes Julian's plans to rebuild the temple in Jerusalem, and their failure (for details of other sources, see Levenson 1990). A number of pragmatic motives can be suggested for Julian's interest in this project – it would win him the support of Jews, large numbers of whom lived in southern Mesopotamia which he was soon to pass through during his invasion of Persia, and it would help to discredit Christianity, both by re-establishing the legitimacy of Judaism and by disproving Jesus' prophecy about the destruction of the temple. But it is also consistent with his firmly held belief in the importance of sacrifice (8.4). The fact that Ammianus makes no reference to the religious implications of the plan is not particularly significant in view of his generally low-key approach to religious controversy (on which see generally Matthews 1989: 435–51, recently challenged, though, by Barnes 1998: ch. 8). Further reading: Avi-Yonah 1976: ch. 8; Bowersock 1978: 88–9, 120–2; Wilken 1983: 138–48; Barnes 1998: 47–9.

(2) Although giving careful consideration to a variety of eventualities as, with keen enthusiasm, he pushed forward a vast range of preparations for the campaign [against Persia], Julian still extended his attention into every area. Eager to prolong the memory of his reign by the greatness of his works, he planned at great expense to restore the once admired temple in Jerusalem, which had with

difficulty been captured after many murderous encounters during its siege by Vespasian and subsequently Titus, and he had entrusted Alypius of Antioch – previously responsible to the praetorian prefects for the administration of Britain – with the task of bringing the matter to a speedy conclusion. (3) Although Alypius pressed ahead vigorously with the work, assisted by the governor of the province, terrifying balls of fire kept erupting near the foundations and made the site inaccessible to the workmen, some of whom were burned alive. Since this element resolutely opposed them in this way, the undertaking was halted.

8.6 Church prohibitions on associating with Jews: The *Council of Elvira*, Canons 49–50

These rulings from an early fourth-century church council in Spain (for the debate about the precise date, see 3.6) are among the earliest evidence for church authorities attempting to regulate Christian interaction with Jews (cf. 8.9).

49. It was decided to warn landowners not to allow their crops, which they receive with thanksgiving from God, to be blessed by Jews, for they might make our blessing ineffectual and impotent. If anyone presumes to do so after this prohibition, let them be completely excommunicated from the church.

50. If any member of the clergy or lay Christian (*fidelis*) has had a meal with Jews, it was decided that they should be prevented from receiving communion, in order to correct them.

8.7 Judaising Christians in Antioch: John Chrysostom *Sermons against the Jews* 1: 1.4–5; 3.2–5; 6.2–5

The following extracts come from the first of eight sermons which John Chrysostom (*c.* 354–407) began preaching towards the end of 386 during the period when he was a clergyman in Antioch. Although entitled *Against the Jews*, Judaising Christians were the primary target of the sermons, which provide valuable insights into the fluidity of the religious scene in late fourth-century Antioch; the virulence of his language betrays how worried he was by Christian fraternisation with Jews. The opening sentence refers to this Judaising as 'another disease' because John had recently begun a series of sermons against Arians, which he interrupted to deliver these sermons due to a major season of Jewish festivals being imminent. At 1.6.2, John refers to a synagogue at Daphne, a suburb of Antioch, where it seems that people (including some Christians) went to sleep, that is, a version of the practice of incubation where an individual stayed in a shrine for a number of days in pursuit of a response from the relevant deity, whether it be healing or guidance. Further reading: Wilken 1983; Simon 1986: 217–23; Feldman 1993: 369–82, 405–6; Kelly 1995: 62–6.

1. (4) ... Another very serious illness calls for any cure my words can bring, an illness which has become implanted in the body of the Church. We must first root this ailment out and then take thought for matters outside; we must first cure our own and then be concerned for others who are strangers. (5) What is this disease? The festivals of the pitiful and miserable Jews are soon to march upon us one after the other and in quick succession: the feast of Trumpets, the feast of Tabernacles, the fasts. There are many in our ranks who say they think as we do. Yet some of these are going to watch the festivals and others will join the Jews in keeping their feasts and observing their fasts. I wish to drive this perverse custom from the Church right now. ...

3. (2) ... The Jews say that they, too, adore God. God forbid that I should say this. No Jew adores God! Who says so? The Son of God says so. For he said: 'If you were to know my Father, you would also know me. But you neither know me nor do you know my Father' [cf. John 8.19]. Could I produce a witness more trustworthy than the Son of God? (3) If, then, the Jews fail to know the Father, if they crucified the Son, if they thrust off the help of the Spirit, who should not make bold to declare plainly that the synagogue is a dwelling of demons? God is not worshipped there. Heaven forbid! From now on it remains a place of idolatry. But still some people pay it honour as a holy place. (4) Let me tell you this, not from guesswork, but from my own experience. Three days ago – believe me, I am not lying – I saw a free woman of good bearing, modest, and a believer. A brutal, unfeeling man, reputed to be a Christian (for I would not call a person who would dare to do such a thing a sincere Christian) was forcing her to enter the shrine of the Hebrews and to swear there an oath about some matters under dispute with him. She came up to me and asked for help; she begged me to prevent this lawless violence – for it was forbidden to her, who had shared in the divine mysteries, to enter that place. I was fired with indignation, I became angry, I rose up, I refused to let her be dragged into that transgression. I snatched her from the hands of her abductor. I asked him if he was a Christian, and he said he was. ... (5) After I had talked with him at great length and had driven the folly of his error from his soul, I asked him why he rejected the Church and dragged the woman to the place where the Hebrews

assembled. He answered that many people had told him that oaths sworn there were more to be feared. ...

6. (2) ... Even if there is no idol there [in the synagogue], still demons inhabit the place. And I say this not only about the synagogue here in town but about the one in Daphne as well. ... I have heard that many of the faithful go up there to sleep beside the place. (3) But heaven forbid that I call these people faithful. ... Is not the dwelling place of demons a place of impiety even if no god's statue stands there? Here the slayers of Christ gather together, here the cross is driven out, here God is blasphemed, here the Father is ignored, here the Son is outraged, here the grace of the Spirit is rejected. Does not greater harm come from this place since the Jews themselves are demons? In the pagan temple, the impiety is naked and obvious; hence, it would not be easy to deceive a man of sound and prudent mind or entice him to go there. But in the synagogue there are men who say they worship God and abhor idols, men who say they have prophets and pay them honour. But by their words they make ready an abundance of bait to catch in their nets the simpler souls who are so foolish as to be caught off guard. (4) So the godlessness of the Jews and the pagans is on a par. But the Jews practise a deceit which is more dangerous. In their synagogue stands an invisible altar of deceit on which they sacrifice not sheep and calves, but the souls of men. (5) Finally, if the ceremonies of the Jews move you to admiration, what do you have in common with us? If the Jewish ceremonies are venerable and great, ours are lies. But if ours are true, as they *are* true, theirs are filled with deceit. ...
(tr. P.W. Harkins)

8.8 Converts to Judaism: *JIWE* 2.62 and 577 (= *CIJ* 1.462 and 523)

These two epitaphs, both from third- or fourth-century Rome, are among a number attesting conversions to Judaism (for others, see Williams 1998: 172; for other types of evidence, Feldman 1993: 385–411; Goodman 1994: 134–41). It has been suggested that the first, a freed slave, may have owed her conversion to her patron (i.e., former owner) (Noy 1995: 55), but unfortunately he chose not to include the most obvious item of evidence that might have provided corroboration – his name. The second example (which was accompanied by representations of the *shofar* (trumpet), *lulab* (palm-branch) and *menorah* (seven-branched candelabrum)) is also of interest for the title 'mother of the synagogues' – 'the only one attested for Jewish women at Rome' (Noy 1995: 426) – where 'synagogue' is 'likely to mean the Jewish community rather than the synagogue building' (Noy 1993: 7). For further detail on these inscriptions, see Noy 1995: 54–5, 457–9; for the 'mother of the synagogue', see Brooten 1982: 57–60; on Jewish proselytising more generally, see Simon 1986: ch. 10; Goodman 1994: ch. 7; Feldman 1993: ch. 11.

(a) JIWE 2.62

Felicitas, a convert (*proselita*) for 6 years <with the name?> Peregrina, who lived for 47 years. Her patron [set this up] for his well-deserving [freedwoman].

(b) JIWE 2.577

Veturia Paula, laid in her eternal home, who lived for 86 years and 6 months, a convert (*proselyta*) for 16 years with the name Sara, mother of the synagogues of Campus and Volumnius. May her sleep be in peace.

8.9 Further church prohibitions on associating with Jews: *The Council of Vannes* Canon 12

The Council of Vannes, held some time between 461 and 491, was the first church council since Gaul had come under Frankish rule to issue a pronouncement on relations with Jews. It is similar to one of those issued at the Spanish Council of Elvira in the early fourth century (8.6), though the earlier prohibition had included laity as well as clergy – an omission soon rectified at the Frankish Council of Agde in 506 (Canon 40).

In future all clergy should avoid dining with Jews, nor should anyone welcome them to a meal; for since they do not eat the food partaken by everyone else when at Christian homes, it is shameful and sacrilegious for Christians to eat their food. Since those things which we eat with apostolic approval are regarded by them as unclean, the clergy may begin to be inferior to the Jews, if we eat what is served by them while they condemn the food provided by us.

8.10 Intercommunal violence between Christians and Jews: Ambrose *Letter* 87 (40). 6–7, 10–15

These extracts from a letter of Ambrose, bishop of Milan, to the emperor Theodosius I in 388 (*Letter* 40 in older editions) highlight a theme of growing importance in the second half of the fourth century – intercommunal violence between Christians and Jews. The specific incident which prompted Ambrose's letter was the destruction by Christians of the Jewish synagogue in the frontier town of Callinicum on the Euphrates, though this was not an isolated incident in these years, and is consistent with the growing tide of Christian violence against pagan temples (cf. 6.6), while it seems that Jews had previously taken the opportunity during Julian's reign to attack churches. Far from condemning the actions of the Christians, Ambrose's purpose was to berate the emperor for ordering the punishment of those responsible and the rebuilding of the synagogue. It has recently been argued that Ambrose was merely using the incident as a convenient way of placing pressure on the emperor over another, quite different issue (McLynn 1994: 302), but even if so, his attitudes towards the Jews are hardly atypical of this period. Theodosius, whose presence in Milan following his defeat of the usurper Maximus brought him into direct contact with Ambrose, eventually rescinded his order, with the result that the episode has usually been seen as symptomatic of the growth of episcopal power *vis-à-vis* imperial authority (for an alternative reading, see McLynn 1994: 298–315). On points of detail, the burning of prefects' houses alluded to in (13) was a regular occurrence in late fourth-century Rome, often prompted by food shortages (cf. Ammianus Marcellinus *History* 27.3), while the destruction of the bishop of Constantinople's house in 388 was the result of Arian riots in that city. Further reading: Homes Dudden 1935: 371–9; Simon 1986: 226–7; Matthews 1990: 232–4.

6. There has been a report from the count responsible for military affairs in the east that a synagogue has been burnt down and that this was done at the instigation of the bishop. You have ordered the others [responsible] to be punished and the bishop himself to rebuild the synagogue. I do not add that the bishop's formal statement should have been waited for, for priests restrain disturbances, their concern is for public order, except when they are provoked by insults to God or by injury to the church. It may be that the bishop was too impetuous in setting the synagogue on fire, too timid in exercising his authority – are you not afraid, O Emperor, that he may accept your decision, do you not fear that he may betray his faith?

7. Are you not also afraid – as will happen – that he will refuse your count? So then he will have to make him either an apostate or a martyr – both alien to your times, both characteristic of persecution, if he is forced either to betray his faith or to undergo martyrdom. You see which way the outcome of this case is headed. If you regard the bishop as resolute, beware of making a martyr of one resolute in the faith; if you regard him as weak-willed, avoid the lapsing of one weak in the faith; for there is a greater responsibility on the one who forces one weak in the faith to lapse. ...

10. Is a place for the unbelief of the Jews to be created from the spoils of the church? Is the inheritance acquired by Christians through the favour of Christ to be handed over to the treasuries of the unbelievers? We read how temples of old were established for idols from the spoils of the Cimbri and from plunder taken from other enemies. This is the inscription the Jews will write on the

front of their synagogue: 'The temple of godlessness, built from the spoils of the Christians.'

11. But it is considerations of public order that motivate you, O Emperor. So which is more important – a semblance of public order, or the interests of true religion? Judicial strictness should give way to religion.

12. Have you not heard, O Emperor, that when Julian had ordered the temple in Jerusalem to be restored, those who were clearing out the debris were consumed by fire? Are you not wary of the same thing happening again now? You should not have ordered what Julian ordered.

13. But what is it that concerns you – that a public building of any sort has been burnt down, or that it was the location of a synagogue? If you are concerned by the burning of an insignificant building – for what else could it be in such an obscure fortress town? – do you not remember, O Emperor, how many houses of the Prefect of Rome have been burnt down without anyone being punished? To be sure, if any emperor had wished to punish this deed severely, he would have aggravated the difficulties faced by the one hit by so great a loss. So which is considered more worthy of punishment, if it should be – the burning of buildings in some quarter of the fort of Callinicum or in the city of Rome? Only recently the house of the bishop of Constantinople was burnt down and the son of Your Clemency interceded with his father so that you did not punish this insult to the son of the emperor and the burning of the episcopal house. ...

14. So there is no reasonable justification for such action [by you] to punish people so severely for burning a building, and even less so for burning a synagogue – a place of unbelief, a house of godlessness, a refuge for madness, which God himself has condemned; for so we read, when God our Lord speaks through the mouth of Jeremiah ... [Jer. 7.14–17]. God forbids anyone to intercede with him for those whom you think ought to be avenged.

15. But certainly if I were arguing my case according to the law of nations (*ius gentium*), I would mention how many basilicas of the church the Jews burned down in the time of Julian's reign. Two in Damascus, of which one has barely been restored – but with funds from the church, not the synagogue – while the other basilica presents an awful sight with its hideous ruins. Church buildings were burned in Gaza, Ascalon, Beirut, and in nearly all those parts, and no one sought revenge. A basilica in Alexandria, which alone surpassed the others, was also burned down by pagans (*gentiles*) and

Jews. That church was not avenged, so why is a synagogue being avenged? ...

8.11 Imperial protection for Jews:
Theodosian Code 16.8.9

Despite the outcome of the Callinicum episode – or perhaps because of it – emperors during the late fourth and early fifth century issued a number of imperial laws officially recognising the right of the Jews to meet without hindrance, and instructing imperial officials to prevent extremist Christians from attacking synagogues. The example below is the first in the series (cf. *Theodosian Code* 16.8.12 (397), 16.8.20 (412), 16.8.21 (420), 16.8.25 (423)), initiated, interestingly, by Theodosius I himself (also noteworthy for its opening confirmation that Judaism was not an outlawed religion). How effectively these laws were policed, however, is another matter (cf. **8.13**) – the very frequency with which the injunction was repeated suggests the difficulties involved. At the same time, a new theme begins to emerge in some of the later laws in this series, namely that the Jews are not allowed to build any new synagogues (a restriction reiterated in the sixth century by Justinian in *Novel* 131.14 (545) – though there is archaeological and epigraphic evidence which implies it was not always enforced: Gray 1993: 261–4). Further reading: Simon 1986: 227–9; Linder 1987: 86, 189–91; Millar 1992: 117–18.

The emperors Theodosius [I], Arcadius and Honorius, Augusti, to Addeus, Count and Master of both parts of the army [i.e., infantry and cavalry] in the east. It is well enough known that the religious group of the Jews is not prohibited by any law, so we are gravely disturbed that their gatherings have been prevented in some places. Therefore when Your Lofty Greatness has received this instruction, you will, with appropriate severity, restrain the excesses of those who, in the name of the Christian religion, dare to commit illegal acts and try to destroy and plunder synagogues. Issued in Constantinople on the 3rd day before the Kalends of October when the consuls were Theodosius (for the third time) and Abundantius [29 September 393].

8.12 Official discrimination against Jews:
Theodosian Code 16.8.24

In addition to the prohibition on the building of new synagogues (see introduction to **8.11**), the early fifth century also saw the initiation of other measures which discriminated against Jews, the most notable being the following prohibition on the employment of Jews in important areas of the imperial administration and in the army. It is, however, rather surprising to find the imperial authorities in the west (where the law was issued) feeling able to dispense with a source of recruits at a time when soldiers were in short supply – a case of religious principle prevailing over pragmatism? Another noteworthy feature is the use of the derogatory term *superstitio* for Judaism instead of the hitherto customary *religio* (Linder 1987: 57–8). This period also saw the introduction of laws against conversion to Judaism. Further reading: Linder 1987: 281–3.

The emperors Honorius and Theodosius [II] to Palladius, Praetorian Prefect [of Italy].

Those living according to the Jewish superstition (*superstitio*) shall be barred from trying to enter the imperial service (*militia*) from now on. To those who have already taken the oath of service among the inspectors of the imperial transport system (*agentes in rebus*) or the palace bureaucracy (*palatini*), we concede the right to carry on and complete their specified term of service, overlooking what is happening rather than approving it – but what we wish to be relaxed for a few at the present moment shall not be permitted in future.

Furthermore, we decree that those who, trammelled by the wrong-headed character of this people (*gentis huius perversitas*), are shown to have entered the armed forces (*armata militia*), are to be dismissed from military service (*absolvi cingulum*) without hesitation and with no protection being afforded by a favourable view of previous good service.

However, we do not deny Jews educated in the liberal studies the freedom to practise as legal advocates and we allow them to enjoy the honour of duties as town councillors, which they gain by the privilege of birth and by the splendour of family. Since these [concessions] ought to satisfy them, they should not regard the prohibition of imperial service as a mark of infamy.

Issued in Ravenna on the 6th day before the Ides of March when Honorius was consul for the twelfth time and Theodosius for the eighth [10 March 418].

8.13 A Jewish community and its conversion: Severus of Minorca *Letter concerning the Jews* 4–8, 12–14

Despite its relative insignificance in the overall context of the Roman empire, the small island of Minorca produced one of the most valuable documents for under-standing Jewish–Christian relations in Late Antiquity. Written by the local bishop Severus, it describes the process by which the Jewish community on the island was converted to Christianity in February 418. Two recent discussions (Hunt 1982b, Bradbury 1996 – the latter includes a translation of the whole letter) provide excellent commentaries on this document, but a few points of detail from the excerpts below warrant explanatory comment: the presbyter in 4.1–2 was the Spaniard

Orosius, an associate of Augustine, while the Jewish leader Theodorus' secular post of 'Defender' (6.2) involved responsibility for hearing local minor lawsuits (Jones 1964: 144–5); his standing within the Jewish community as 'Father of Fathers' is consistent with his role as leader, but the precise significance of the expression remains unclear (for discussion see Noy 1993: 91). Martyr relics and their impact are another important theme of interest (cf. 16.13), even if, somewhat surprisingly, they do not feature explicitly after 4.2.

4. (1) At about the same time that I, though unworthy, assumed the title of so great a priestly office [that of bishop], a certain presbyter, outstanding for his holiness, came from Jerusalem and stayed a short time in [the Minorcan town of] Magona. When it proved impossible to cross over to Spain, as he wished, he decided to return again to Africa. (2) Since it had been his intention to take to Spain some remains of the blessed martyr Stephen, recently discovered, he deposited them in the church of the aforementioned town [Magona] – no doubt at the prompting of the martyr himself. (3) No sooner had this been done than there was kindled the fire of His love which the Lord 'came to send forth into the earth' [Lk. 12.49] and which he desires to burn strongly. (4) Indeed immediately our lukewarm attitude began to grow hot and, as it is written, our hearts were 'burning on the way' [Lk. 24.32]. For now zeal for the faith was consuming our hearts, now the hope of many coming to salvation was aroused.

5. (1) As a result, even the courtesy of greeting [the Jews] was promptly discontinued, and not only was our habit of sociability [with them] done away with, but the detrimental sight of our longstanding friendliness was temporarily transformed into hatred – but out of love for eternal life. (2) In every street, contests over the Law were waged against the Jews, and in every home, battles over the faith.

6. (1) The Jewish inhabitants were particularly reliant on the influence and experience of a certain Theodorus who was the foremost man of the time in both wealth and honour, not only among the Jews but also among the Christians of the same town [Magona]. (2) For among the Jews he was a teacher of the Law and – to use their own expression – 'Father of Fathers' (*pater pateron*), (3) while in the town, he had discharged all responsibilities associated with the town council (*curia*), and had already been Defender (*defensor*), and was also now regarded as patron of the community. (4) But the Christians, humble in heart and in strength, but mightier in the power of truth, prayed for the help of their patron Stephen, until both sides withdrew, after agreeing a day for the contest and then arranging a truce.

7. (1) The Jews were very keen that Theodorus, on whose strength the whole synagogue depended, should return from the island of Majorca to which he had by chance gone at that time to inspect a property. (2) He returned as soon as a delegation was sent to him and alarmed many by his authority and, without extinguishing it, he damped down a little the flame of dispute. Then flaring up there with greater strength, the flame of faith also swept into the neighbouring town [of Jamona]. (4) And so the saying of Solomon was fulfilled, 'A brother helping a brother will be lifted up like a strong and towering city' [Prov. 18.19]. Many servants of Christ, not at all unwilling to undertake the hardship of the journey [from Jamona to Magona], decided to give all the strength of their hearts to this war.

8. ... (4) Then the Jews encouraged one another with examples from the time of the Maccabees, and were also willing to die in defence of their precepts. (5) And so they began not only to read over their books but also to bring to the synagogue stakes, stones, spears and all kinds of weapons, in order to drive back with physical force – if circumstances demanded it – the battle-line of the Christians protected by the power of the Holy Spirit. [Severus then relates various dreams shown by subsequent events to be significant.]

12. ... (3) So we reached Magona and immediately I sent clergy to announce my arrival to the Jews, and I asked them to see fit to come to the church. (4) But they sent back to us an unexpected message, saying that it was not proper for them to enter the church on that day (lest, I dare say, they be defiled); for it was, they said, the Sabbath day and if they marred that festival by any actions, they would be committing a very serious crime of violation. (5) Again I asked that they wait for me at the synagogue, if they preferred, since their entering the church seemed a defilement. They were not being forced by us to engage in servile work on the Sabbath day (6) but rather there would be a very restrained debate about the Law. It would not be a case of stirring up quarrels, but of engaging in conversation. ... [When the Jews persisted in their reluctance to meet, Severus decided to resolve the impasse with decisive action.]

13. (1) So we set out for the synagogue, singing a hymn to Christ en route, so great was our joy. (2) It was, moreover, a psalm, which the Jews were also singing with amazing cheerfulness – 'The memory of them has perished with a crash and the Lord abides forever' [Ps. 9.6–7]. (3) But before we arrived at the synagogue, some Jewish women (at the instigation of the Lord, I believe) had

the audacity to begin throwing enormous stones at us from an elevated position – no doubt to provoke the gentle attitude of our people. (4) Although these stones fell like hail on the tightly packed crowd, it is marvellous to report that not one of our people was even touched, let alone suffered a blow. (5) Then that awesome Lion removed a little of his lambs' gentleness. (6) While I vainly remonstrated, everyone took up stones and – ignoring the warning of their shepherd [Severus], since enthusiasm for Christ rather than anger suggested the same course of action to everyone – they decided that the wolves must be attacked with force, although it cannot be doubted that this was done with the approval of Him who alone is the true and good shepherd. (7) Then, so that He should not seem to have been responsible for a bloody victory for his flock, none of the Jews pretended to have been so much as touched, not even from ill-will, as is their habit. ... (12) After the Jews had withdrawn and we took possession of the synagogue, I do not say no-one took nothing from it, but no-one considered plundering it. (13) Apart from their books and silver, fire consumed it and all its accoutrements. We took away the holy books so they did not suffer harm among the Jews; but we returned the silver to them so they could not complain about our plundering or their loss.

14. And so while all the Jews were stunned at the destruction of the synagogue, we went to the church singing hymns and giving thanks to the one responsible for our success, and with tears flowing we beseeched the Lord to conquer the true lairs of falsehood and overwhelm with light the lack of faith in their dark hearts. [Over the ensuing days, increasing numbers of Jews (including Theodorus) agree to convert to Christianity, mindful particularly of the risk of further violence if they did not. By the end of Severus' letter, the tally of Jewish converts has reached 540 and the Jews are busy constructing a new church on the site of their former synagogue.]

8.14 A Jewish convert to Christianity: *JIWE* 1.8 (= *CIJ* 1².643a)

This inscription from Grado in northern Italy is one of the few attesting the conversion of a Jew to Christianity (for others, see Williams 1998: 159). It is a mosaic inscription, replete with picture of a vase sprouting grape-laden vines on which perch birds, discovered under the floor of Grado cathedral, and probably dating to the first half of the fifth century. The phrase 'out of his people' could refer either to his family or to the Jewish community in Grado, while 'the grace of Christ' is probably an allusion to baptism. For detailed discussion and full bibliography, see Noy 1993: 13–16 (including a photograph [Plate V]).

Here rests Petrus, also known as Papario, son of Olympius the Jew, who alone out of his people (*ex gente sua*) was worthy to attain the grace of Christ and was fittingly buried in this holy church on the day before the Ides of July [14 July] in the 4th year of the indiction.

8.15 Justinian and the Samaritans: *Justinianic Code* 1.5.17 and Procopius *Secret History* 11.24–28

The origins of the Samaritans and their relationship to the Jews were, and remain, matters of dispute. Although monotheistic and claiming descent from some of the tribes of Israel, they were by no means viewed favourably by Jews, as implied by 8.3. Roman legislation, however, often bracketed them with Jews – hence their inclusion in this chapter. Despite his fervour for religious conformity, the emperor Justinian did not significantly increase the disabilities of Jews, but for reasons which remain unclear, he pursued an aggressive policy of discrimination against Samaritans, as reflected in the first item, from a law issued in the late 520s. The Samaritans had a reputation for being rebellious which they duly lived up to on this occasion, launching a major revolt in northern Palestine. Although Procopius' *Secret History* is notorious for its polemical portrayal of Justinian and Theodora (see Cameron 1985: ch. 4 for general discussion), his outline of the Samaritan revolt is corroborated by the contemporary *Chronicle* of John Malalas (pp. 445–7), which Procopius supplements with the interesting, if unsurprising, detail about the superficiality of their conversion. The prohibition on their making wills was subsequently revoked – intriguingly, in response to an appeal by the bishop of Caesarea (Justinian *Novel* 129 of 551) – but in 555 there was a further revolt (in which some Jews also participated: John Malalas *Chronicle* pp. 487–8; cf. 7.2) and his successor Justin II reactivated Justinian's law in 572 on the grounds that 'some of them, after gaining baptism which grants salvation, have become so mad as to turn back again to that evil from which they had departed' (included among Justinian's *Novels* as 144 [preface]). Further reading: Crown 1986–87; Gray 1993: 249–59; Moorhead 1994: 25–6; Evans 1996: 116–17, 247–9.

(a) Justinianic Code *1.5.17*

The synagogues of the Samaritans are [to be] destroyed and, if they attempt to build others, they are [to be] punished. Whether they make a will or they die without a valid one, they are not able to have successors other than orthodox Christians, and they are not to make gifts or otherwise alienate property to anyone who is not orthodox. Instead the imperial treasury claims it for oversight by the bishops and the governors.

(b) *Procopius* Secret History *11.24–28*

(24) When a similar law was then laid down for the Samaritans as

well, utter confusion overtook Palestine. (25) All those living in my native Caesarea and in the other cities thought it silly to undergo any suffering in the name of senseless religious principles and took the name of Christians in exchange for their designation at that time, a pretence which enabled them to rid themselves of the danger posed by the law. (26) And all those who had some commonsense and reason did not disdain remaining loyal to the [new] religion, but the majority, angry that they had changed their ancestral beliefs, not voluntarily, but under legal compulsion, very quickly deserted to the Manichaeans and the so-called Polytheists. (27) But all the peasants came together en masse and decided to mount an armed rebellion against the emperor, putting forward as their own emperor a brigand by the name of Julianus, son of Sabarus. (28) They held out for some time when they came to blows with soldiers, but subsequently they proved the weaker in battle and were wiped out along with their leader. (29) One hundred thousand men are said to have been killed in this calamity, and the countryside – the best in the whole world – became bereft of peasants as a result.

8.16 Expulsion of Jews from Antioch in the late sixth century: Agapius of Membij *Universal History* Part 2, pp. 439–40

Agapius, bishop of Hierapolis (Membij) in Osrhoene in the tenth century, wrote a history in Arabic which preserves portions of earlier histories, now lost. Expulsion of the Jewish community from a city was certainly not a novelty (it had happened in Alexandria in 415: Williams 1998: 140–1; Haas 1997: 299–304), nor was the accusation of their showing disrespect for the religious practices of others. Stigmatising them by shaving their heads, however, does appear to be a disturbing innovation, while episodes like this help explain Jewish willingness to assist Persian invaders in the early seventh century (see Whitby 1988: 335 for references).

In the eleventh year of his reign [592/3] [the emperor] Maurice decreed the banishment of the Jews who were in Antioch, and they were driven from the city. This was the reason: A Christian had rented a house in order to live there. When he vacated it, he left behind an image of Mary. After him, a Jew rented the house, and when he (p. 440) entered it, he found this image and urinated on it. News of this incident reached the emperor, who ordered the expulsion of the Jews from Antioch and made them shave the middle of their heads so that they would be recognised by this mark. (tr. A.A. Vasiliev)

9

ZOROASTRIANS

Unlike Jews and Manichaeans, who could be found in most parts of the Roman empire during Late Antiquity, Zoroastrians were a geographically and numerically restricted religious group, confined to certain eastern provinces, especially in Asia Minor. This explains the relative brevity of this chapter, while also raising the question of whether they warrant separate consideration in a book about late Roman religious life. Perhaps not, but it seemed worth drawing attention to the fact that the spectrum of religious beliefs and practices encompassed by the Roman empire in this period included adherents of the ancient credal religion dominant in the regions to the east of the empire, a religion, moreover, actively supported by the rulers of the empire's chief rival in Late Antiquity, the Sasanian Persians. (It is also worth noting that, of the various religions that flourished during Late Antiquity, Zoroastrianism takes its place alongside Judaism and Christianity as the only ones still practised today.)

Zoroastrianism takes its name from Zoroaster (the westernised form of Zarathushtra), the details of whose life remain controversial. He was a prophet or religious reformer, probably active in eastern Iran, perhaps as early as the late second millennium BC or possibly not until the early centuries of the first millennium BC. In due course his teachings were taken up and supported by the Achaemenid dynasty of Persia – Cyrus, Darius, Xerxes and their successors – whose expansion into Asia Minor in the sixth century BC resulted in the establishment of Zoroastrianism there. After the conquest of the region by Alexander the Great and then the Romans, enclaves of Zoroastrian adherents maintained their traditional practices, and the following passages attest their continuing presence in Roman territory in the third (9.1), fourth (9.2) and fifth (9.3) centuries, respectively, while also alluding to distinctive elements of

Zoroastrian religious practice and belief. A key feature of Zoroaster's teaching was its dualistic emphasis: the world had been created by one eternal, uncreated and beneficent god, Ahuramazda (or Ohrmazd), aided by six lesser deities or yazads, but Ahuramazda was opposed by an evil spirit, Ahriman, with whom he engaged in an ongoing cosmic struggle – a struggle in which humans could play their part by choosing to do good. This included observance of various rituals of purification, daily prayers, respect for the earth and living creatures, and special reverence for fire, the symbol of righteousness. This last feature in due course assumed architectural expression in the form of fire altars and fire temples. Further reading: Boyce 1979.

9.1 Zoroastrians in third-century Asia Minor: *Inscription of Kirder 5–8*

The following passage is part of a late third-century inscription in Persian from Persepolis recounting the achievements of the Zoroastrian high priest Kirder. The first half of the passage relates events within the Sasanian Persian empire – including, interestingly, persecution of Jews, Christians, and other religious groups in Persia – while also providing a taste of the Zoroastrian worldview. In the second half, Kirder recalls the Persian invasion of the Roman empire by Shapur I in 260, in the course of which Persian forces penetrated deep into Asia Minor, where they encountered groups of Zoroastrians whom Kirder proceeded to re-organise and strengthen. Further reading: Boyce and Grenet 1991: 254–5.

(5) And after Vahram [I], King of kings, son of Shapur, had departed to the Place of the Gods, Vahram [II], King of kings, son of Vahram, was in the land, who in rule is generous and upright and kind and beneficent and virtuous. And for love of Ohrmazd [the supreme deity] and the yazads [beneficent deities], and for his own soul's sake, he increased my dignity and honour yet more. He gave me the dignity and honour of a nobleman; ... and throughout the empire I was made more authoritative and independent than formerly over religious matters. And I was Mobad [head priest] and Judge of the whole empire, and I was made Master of Ceremonials and Warden of the Fires of Anahid–Ardashir and Anahid the Lady [one of the yazads] at Istakhr. (6) And I was styled 'Kirder by whom Vahram's soul is saved, Mobad of Ohrmazd'. And in every province and place of the whole empire the service of Ohrmazd and the yazads was exalted, and the Mazda-worshipping religion and its priests received much honour throughout the land. And the yazads, and water and fire and cattle, were greatly contented, and Ahriman [the evil spirit] and the devs [demons] suffered great blows and

170

harm. And the creed of Ahriman and the devs was driven out of the land and deprived of credence. (7) And Jews and Buddhists and Brahmins and Aramaic- and Greek-speaking Christians and Baptisers and Manichaeans were assailed throughout the land. And images were overthrown, and the dens of demons were [thus] destroyed, and the places and abodes of the yazads [i.e., their fire temples] were established. ... (8) And from the first I, Kirder, underwent much toil and trouble for the yazads and the rulers, and for my soul's sake. And I caused many fires and priestly colleges to flourish in Iran, and also in non-Iranian lands. There were many fires and priests in non-Iranian lands which were reached by the armies of the King of kings. The provincial capital of Antioch and the province of Syria, and the districts dependent on Syria; the provincial capital Tarsus and the province of Cilicia, and the districts dependent on Cilicia; the provincial capital Caesarea and the province of Cappadocia, and the districts dependent on Cappadocia, up to Pontus, and the province of Armenia, and Georgia and Albania and Balasagan, up to the 'Gate of the Alans' – these were plundered and burnt and laid waste by Shapur, King of kings, with his armies. There too, at the command of the King of kings, I reduced to order the priests and fires which were in those lands. And I did not allow harm to be done them, or captives made. And whoever had thus been made captive, him indeed I took and sent back to his own land. And I made the Mazda-worshipping religion and its good priests esteemed and honoured in the land. (tr. M. Boyce)

9.2 Zoroastrians in fourth-century Cappadocia: Basil of Caesarea *Letters* 258.4

In the following passage from a letter he wrote in 377, Basil, bishop of Cappadocian Caesarea, responds to a request from Epiphanius, bishop of Salamis in Cyprus and author of a guide to heresies entitled the *Panarion* or *Medicine-chest for the Cure of All Heresies* (375), for information about a Cappadocian religious group known as *Magousaioi*. Features of Basil's description indicate they were adherents of Zoroastrianism – the role of fire in their ritual, and their practice of 'unlawful' (i.e., close-kin) marriage (cf. Lee 1988). The reference to 'Zarnuas' as their ancestor is probably a corruption of Zurvan, a deity identified with Time whom some Zoroastrians in the late Achaemenid period elevated as the begetter of both Ahuramazda and the evil spirit Ahriman; although this seriously compromised the dualism of Zoroastrianism, Zurvanite views were popular in Sasanian Persia. Further reading: Boyce and Grenet 1991: 277–9; Mitchell 1993: vol. 2, 73 (with references to further evidence of a continuing Persian legacy in Roman Anatolia, including Iranian names being common in Cappadocia).

The Magousaian people (about whom, in a previous letter, you considered it appropriate for us to inform you) is numerous and widely dispersed among us throughout almost all of the region, as a result of colonists from Babylonia being settled here long ago. They observe their own practices, and do not associate with other people; it is completely impossible to reason with them since they have been ensnared by the devil to his will. They have no books or teachers of their tenets, but are raised in this unreasoning way of life, children learning ungodliness from their parents. Besides these features, observable by all, they reject the slaughter of animals as a pollution and kill the animals they need through the hands of others. They have a passion for unlawful marriages and regard fire as a god, and the like. None of the magi, down to the present day, has told us tales of their being descended from Abraham; instead they name a certain Zarnouas as the founder of their people. There is nothing further I can communicate to your Honour about them.

9.3 Persian complaints about Roman treatment of Zoroastrians in the mid-fifth century: Priscus *History* fr. 41.1

The following extract from one of the surviving portions of the important fifth-century historian Priscus provides details about diplomatic exchanges between the Roman government in Constantinople and the Persians in 464/5, in which one of the issues was Roman treatment of Zoroastrians living in Roman territory. It is difficult to know what to make of Persian and Roman claims and counter-claims (e.g., was there legitimate cause for complaint, or were the Persians creating an issue to put pressure on the Romans over other matters?), but the passage certainly attests the continued presence of Zoroastrian communities in the empire's eastern regions in the latter half of the fifth century – and presumably communities of sufficient size to attract the attention of the two governments. In a subsequent portion of his history (fr. 41.3), Priscus says that although the Roman envoy (whose name must actually have been Constantinus – see *PLRE* 2: 317–18) had an audience with the Persian king Peroz, his mission resolved nothing.

An embassy from the Persian king also arrived with complaints about those of their own people fleeing from them [to the Romans] and about the Magians living in Roman territory from ancient times – that the Romans, wanting to divert the Magians from their ancestral practices and laws, were harassing them over their sacred rites and not allowing them to keep the so-called unquenchable fire alight at all times in accordance with their law. ... The Romans responded that they would send someone to discuss everything with the Parthian [*sic*] king, for there were no fugitives among them and they were not harassing the Magians over their religious observances. ... Constantius, who was prefect for the third time, and was of consular rank and a patrician, was sent as envoy to the Persians.

10

MANICHAEANS

Like Zoroastrianism, Manichaeism had its origins in Persia, but unlike Zoroastrianism, Manichaeism was a very recent development about whose founder much more evidence is available. Mani (216–274/6) was born and grew up in Babylonia as part of a Judaising Christian community which placed particular emphasis on ritual purification, but in his mid-20s he claimed to receive special revelations that prompted him to break with this religious group and begin teaching these revelations to any who would listen. Mani's teaching presented world history in terms of a struggle between Light and Darkness, between Good and Evil. Although this dualism, together with his geographical context, might suggest the influence of Zoroastrianism, he also taught that the material world was evil and corrupt – a view which shows that his fundamental debt was to Gnosticism (cf. 2.9 and Lieu 1992: 7–32, 51–70). According to Mani, the self-styled 'apostle of Jesus Christ' and 'Paraclete' or 'helper' (a term used in the New Testament of the Holy Spirit), every individual had within him or herself particles of Light that could be released by following a strict ascetic lifestyle involving abstention from sex and adherence to a vegetarian diet (certain kinds of vegetable were believed to contain particularly strong concentrations of these particles). The 'Elect' who adhered to this regime would facilitate the gradual triumph of Light over Darkness at a cosmic level, while also ensuring their own salvation after death. There was also a second grade of adherent – 'Hearers' – whose task was to serve the Elect but who were not expected to live up to such high standards (the most famous example being the young Augustine). Mani's message gradually gained followers within Persia, from where it was actively spread further afield both eastwards to India and eventually China, and westwards into the Roman empire. Mani himself travelled widely and was also viewed favourably within Persia during the reigns of Shapur I (240–72) and Hormizd I (272–3), but probably at the instigation of the Zoroastrian chief priest Kirder (cf. 9.1), he was imprisoned by their successor Vahram I (273–6) and executed. The appeal of his message, however, remained undiminished (for the nature of its appeal, see Lieu 1992: ch. 5).

The passages which follow begin with extracts from the *Cologne Mani Codex*, a remarkable document of enormous importance for understanding Mani's early life (10.1). Extracts from some Manichaean psalms discovered in Egypt illustrate various aspects of Mani's teaching (10.2), as also does a letter, likewise from Egypt, written against Manichaeism (10.3). This latter item is also indicative of the spread of Manichaeism into the eastern provinces of the Roman empire during the late third century, while the next item – a short epitaph from the Balkans – shows it moving further west (10.4). The Roman imperial authorities, both pagan and Christian, were very hostile towards Manichaeism, as shown by Diocletian's famous edict (3.2) and subsequent legislation (10.5), but the very need for such legislation during the fourth century shows that Manichaeans remained a religious group of importance, as also does the controversy over Jovinian's views on asceticism (11.8) and over Priscillian of Avila (on whom see Chadwick 1976; Burrus 1995). For further reading on Manichaeism in general, see Lieu 1992; Brown 1969; Lane Fox 1986: 561–71; Gardner and Lieu 1996.

10.1 Mani's early life: Extracts from the *Cologne Mani Codex*

The initial publication of the *Cologne Mani Codex* in 1970 and the years immediately following was an event of major importance for Manichaean studies because of the detail it contained about Mani's early life. Entitled 'On the Origin of his Body' (the final term is assumed to refer as much to his followers as to his person), it detailed the revelations he received, the conflict this produced with the 'Baptists' among whom he had grown up (generally thought to be Elchasaites, a Judaising Christian group known from other sources), his break with them, and his initial missionary journeys (especially notable is the reference to Mani's divine 'twin', another tell-tale sign of Gnostic influence). No less remarkable was the format of the codex: comprising nearly 200 pages measuring only 38 x 48 mm, with each page containing an average of 23 lines of text with letters no more than 1 mm high, it was the smallest ancient codex discovered up to that point in time. Its tiny size and the consequent difficulties for reading raised the possibility of its being intended as an amulet with symbolic value, but the fine scribal work revealed by closer inspection suggested other possibilities. Presumably it was written – and so could be read – with the aid of some form of magnification (such as a water-filled glass bottle), so perhaps it was 'miniaturised' to facilitate concealment – an understandable motive given the enthusiasm of the Roman authorities for burning Manichaean writings (cf. **3.2** (6)). Although the circumstances of its discovery and acquisition have never been made public, it is known to have come from Lycopolis in Egypt, an important Manichaean centre in Late Antiquity. The date of the codex is debated – possibly fourth century, or perhaps later – but the Syriac original of which it is a Greek translation could well have been produced much closer to Mani's own lifetime. As will be readily apparent from the extracts below, the codex has not survived undamaged. Further reading: Lieu 1992: 37–50, 70–3; Gardner and Lieu 1996: 154–61.

(a) The Cologne Mani Codex pp. 17–23

'When I was twenty-four (p. 18) years old, in the year in which Dariardaxar [Ardashir I], the king of Persia, subdued the city of Hatra, and in which king Sapores [Shapur I], his son, assumed the great crown, in the month of Pharmouthi on the eighth <?> day of the moon [17/18 April 240], the most blessed Lord took compassion on me and called me into his grace and sent me < ... > my twin (*syzygos*) in great splendour < ... > (p. 19) < ... he is> the mindful one who brings word of all the best counsel from our Father and from the good first right hand.'

And again he [Mani] spoke thus: 'When my Father was pleased and had mercy and pity on me so as to release me from the error of the sectarians, he had consideration for me through his innumerable <revelations> and sent <me my twin ... > (p. 20) <He brought me the best hope and> deliverance for those suffering and the truest instruction and insights and the laying on of hands from our Father. When he now came, he freed me and separated [me] and drew [me] away from the midst of that rule (*nomos*) in which I was brought up. In this way he called me and chose [me] and drew [me] and separated [me] from their midst. He drew me to the side < ... >

(p. 21) <The twin taught me ... > who I am and what my body is, and in what way I have come and how my arrival in the world came about, and who I am among those who are most distinguished in their excellence, and how I was born into this fleshly body or what kind of woman it was by whose help I was delivered and born according to this flesh and by whose <love?> I was conceived < ... > (p. 22) and how < ... > came into being, and who my Father on high is or in what way I was separated from him and was sent out according to his purpose, and what command and counsel he has given me before I was clothed in this instrument and before I was led astray in this disgusting flesh and before I put on its drunkenness and way of life, and who <he is> who is <my vigilant twin ... >

(p. 23) <The twin taught me ... > the secrets and the <thoughts> and the pre-eminence of my Father, and who I am and who my inseparable twin is; moreover, about my soul, which is the soul of all worlds – what it itself is or how it came to be. Besides these things, he revealed to me the boundless heights and the fathomless depths. He showed me everything which < ... >

(b) The Cologne Mani Codex *pp. 104–5*

Then the most glorious one himself said to me, 'You were not sent only to this creed [viz., the 'Baptists'], but to all people and every school, and to every city and place. For <by you> will <this> hope be made plain and be declared in all <regions> and districts of <the world>. And very many <people will receive> (p. 105) your word. So go forth and travel about. For I am with you as your helper and defender in every place in which you make known everything which I have revealed to you. So do not be downcast or distressed.'

Then he said a great deal more to me, emboldening me and instilling confidence in his hope. I prostrated myself before him and my heart rejoiced at the exquisite glimpse of that most blessed twin of mine, most pre-eminent and distinguished.

(c) The Cologne Mani Codex *pp. 121–3*

< ... > but I did <not> remain <in any village>. I travelled from <the land> of the Medes <to the brethren in> Gounazak. <In that place> there is tin-ore. When we came into the city of Ganazak, those with the brethren were anxious about the <daughter ... > (p. 122) < ... Her father said to me> 'Who are you? <What power> do you have?' <I said ... > to him, 'I am <a doctor>'. And he <replied> to me, '<If> you are willing, come into my house. For my daughter is tossed about by illness.' I went with him <and found> the girl was <deranged> and < ... > by <illness ... > (p. 123) < ... > and <he threw himself down> before me <in the presence of> other < ... > men. He said, '<Ask of me> what you wish' <Then I> said to him, 'I have <no need of> material possessions of <gold> and silver.' I took from him only <food> for the daily needs of the brethren with me.

(d) The Cologne Mani Codex *pp. 144–5*

< ... > There was < ... > in Pharat a man by the name of Og<gias?>, well-known for his <power> and influence over men, whose < ... >. <I saw> how the merchants who <sailed in> the ships to Persia and to India were sealing up his <goods> but were not <setting sail> until he came on board. < ... > When Og<gias? ... > (p. 145) Then <he said to> me, 'I want <to board> a ship and <travel> to India <in order to> obtain < ... > if this < ... >. But I said <to him>, 'I < ... >'.

10.2 Manichaean psalms: Extracts from *The Manichaean Psalmbook*

Nearly half a century before the discovery of the *Cologne Mani Codex* was made known, another discovery in Egypt gave a similar impetus to Manichaean studies. On this occasion, the site of the discovery was Narmouthis (modern Medinet Madi), and it involved not one, but seven codices (see Gardner and Lieu 1996: 148–54 for a convenient summary). One of them was a set of Manichaean psalms in a Coptic translation from Syriac via Greek. The translation has been dated to the late fourth century, but the original psalms were probably written in the late third century. The psalmbook is valuable for two reasons: first, because the psalms were part of the aesthetic appeal of Manichaeism (on which see Lieu 1992: 175–7), and second, because they present aspects of Manichaean theology. Thus, the extracts below include an extensive poetic exposition of the cosmic conflict between Light and Darkness, and also make reference to the Elect. The Bema was a platform erected at the time of a special festival to commemorate Mani's death, while it is thought that the names at the end of each psalm are probably those of other Manichaean martyrs.

(a) Psalm 223

Let us worship the Spirit of the Paraclete.
Let us bless our Lord Jesus who has sent to us
   the Spirit of Truth. He came and separated us from the Error
  of the world, he brought us a mirror, we looked, we
  saw the Universe in it.
When the Holy Spirit came he revealed to us
  the way of Truth and taught us that there are two
  Natures, that of Light and that of Darkness, separate
  one from the other from the beginning.
The Kingdom of Light, on the one hand, consisted in five
  Greatnesses, and they are the Father and his twelve
  Aeons and the Aeons of the Aeons, the Living Air,

the Land of Light; the great Spirit breathing in them,
    nourishing them with His light.
But the Kingdom of Darkness consists of five store-
    houses, which are Smoke and Fire and
    Wind and Water and Darkness; their Counsel
    creeping in them, moving them and inciting them to
    make war with one another.
Now as they were making war with one another they dared
    to make an attempt on the Land of Light, thinking that they
    would be able to conquer it. But they know not that which
                                  they have
    thought to do they will bring down on their own heads.
But there was a multitude of angels in the Land of the Light,
    having the power to go forth to subdue the enemy
    of the Father, whom it pleased that by his Word that
    he would send, he should subdue the rebels who desired
    to exalt themselves above that which was more exalted than
                                    they ...

This whole world stands firm for a season, here
    being a great building which is being built
    outside this world. So soon as that builder shall finish,
    the whole world will be dissolved and set on fire
    that the fire may smelt it away.
All life, the relic of Light wheresoever it be, he will
    gather to himself and of it depict an image.
    And the counsel of death, too, all the Darkness,
    he will gather together and make a likeness of its very self,
    it and the Ruler.
In a moment the living Spirit will come < ... >
    < ... > he will succour the Light. But the counsel of death
    and the Darkness he will shut up in the dwelling
    that was established for it, that it might be bound in it
                                   forever ...

This is the Knowledge of Mani, let us worship him
    and bless him. Blessed is every man that shall trust in him,
    for he it is shall live with all the Righteous.
Glory and victory to you our Lord Mani, the Spirit of
    Truth that comes from the Father, who has revealed to us
    the Beginning, the Middle and the End. Victory to the
    soul of the blessed Mary, Theona, Pshaijmnoute.

(b) Psalm 228

Our Lord the Paraclete has come, he has sat down upon his Bema;
let us all pray, my brethren, that he may forgive us
our sins.
The < ... > whom he sent in the counsel
of the Aeons of immortality. Implore him all.
He anointed him in his power, he made him perfect by the Spirit
of his love. Implore him all.
He appointed him to three powers, to tribulation, to a right
hand, to bliss. Implore him.
He gave into his hands the medicine of life that he might heal
the wounded. Implore him.
He gave light with his Light to our lamps. Put oil into
them by your faith. Implore him.
He gave the helmsman to the ships: the butter he brought to
the naked. Implore him.
He gave the bread of life to the hungry: the clothing he brought
to the naked. Implore him.
He gave light by his love to our Intelligence: he made his
faith shine in our Reason. Implore him.
He brought perfection to our Thought: long-suffering to our
Counsel. Implore him...
Let us bless him now, my brethren, and sing to him
in our spirit. Implore him.
We pray you all of us together, the Elect
and the Believers. Implore him.
Do not make reckoning with us now, our Lord, according to the
multitude of our sins.
Glory to the Father, who sent you for the salvation of your
holy Churches. Implore him.
Glory and victory to the Paraclete, our Lord, our Light,
Mani and the soul of Mary. Implore him.

(tr. C.R.C. Allberry)

10.3 Early anti-Manichaean polemic: *P. Ryl.* 3.469

The following damaged document is part of a Christian critique of Manichaean
ideas and practices – in the view of its editor and translator, probably a general
letter from the bishop of Alexandria to the churches of Egypt in the late third
century (the dating is based on letter forms). As such, it is evidence for the early
penetration of Manichaeism into the eastern provinces of the Roman empire, while
its content illustrates, on the one hand, important Manichaean doctrines, and on

the other, Christian efforts to counter them. Reference is made to Manichaean opposition to marriage – part of their antipathy to the human body and sexuality – while the 'Apology to the Bread' reflects Mani's belief that activities such as the sowing and reaping of grain and the making of bread risked doing damage to the particles of Light which existed in the material world despite the latter's inherent corruption. The author, who cannot resist playing on the verbal similarities between 'Manichaean' and 'madness' in Greek, is also familiar with the terminology of the Manichaean hierarchy, but his implausible allegations about the behaviour of female Manichaeans are better seen as a measure of his anxiety about the threat posed by Manichaeism. For a useful survey of other late Roman anti-Manichaean literature, see Lieu 1985–86 and 1986–87.

< ... > Again the Manichees speak falsely against marriage saying that he does well who does not marry. Paul says that the man who does not marry does better [1 Cor. 7.8]; but that the adulterer and the fornicator are evil is manifest from Holy Scriptures, from which we learn that 'marriage is honoured' by God, but that 'He abominates fornicators and adulterers' [Heb. 13.4]. Whereby it is manifest that He condemns them also that worship the creation [cf. Rom. 1.25] who < ... > 'have committed adultery with wood and stones' [i.e., idols] [Jer. 3.9]. Not but what God commands us to chastise the man who does evil, in these words: 'If there be found man or woman in one of the cities which the Lord your God gives you that has wrought wickedness in the sight of the Lord your God and has worshipped the sun or any of the host of heaven, it is an abomination to the Lord your God. Everyone that does these things is an abomination to the Lord your God' [Deut. 17.2–3]. And the Manichees manifestly worship the creation <? and that which they say> in their psalms is an abomination to the Lord < ... saying> 'Neither have I cast it [sc. the bread] into the oven: another has brought me this and I have eaten it without guilt'. Whence we can easily conclude that the Manichaeans are filled with much madness (mania), especially since this 'Apology to the Bread' is the work of a man filled with much madness. As I said before, I have cited this in brief from the document of the madness (mania) of the Manichaeans which fell into my hands, that we may be on our guard against these who with deceitful and lying words steal into our houses, and particularly against those women whom they call 'elect' and whom they hold in honour, manifestly because they require their menstrual blood for the abominations of their madness. We speak what we would not, 'seeking not our own profit, but the profit of many that they may be saved' [1 Cor. 10.33]. May therefore our God, the all good and the all holy, grant 'that you may abstain from

all appearance of evil' [1 Thess. 5.22] and that 'your whole spirit and soul and body be preserved blameless in the presence of the Lord Jesus Christ [1 Thess. 5.23]. Greet one another with a holy kiss' [2 Cor. 13.12–13]. The brethren with me greet you. I pray that you may be well in the Lord, beloved, 'cleansing yourselves from all filthiness of the flesh and spirit' [cf. 2 Cor. 7.1]. (tr. C.H. Roberts)

10.4 The westward spread of Manichaeism: *TzM* no. 67

This short (and incomplete) epitaph in Greek from Salona in Dalmatia, inscribed in either the late third or early fourth century, commemorates a female adherent of Manichaeism who originated from Lydia in Asia Minor and was 'a virgin', that is one of the Elect. Presumably it was set up by fellow Manichaeans and is important for showing that the religion had reached the Adriatic relatively early. Since the same cemetery contains epitaphs indicating that some of the local Christian leadership originated from the Mesopotamia centre of Nisibis, it has been suggested that 'the church at Salona had close connections with Christian communities along the eastern frontier and the Manichaeans might have exploited the link for their own ends' (Lieu 1992: 116).

Bassa, a virgin (*parthenos*), a Lydian, a Manichaean (*Manichea*) < ... >

10.5 Imperial persecution of Manichaeans: *Theodosian Code* 16.5.3 and 18

The fullest and most vehement piece of anti-Manichaean legislation in the Roman empire is Diocletian's edict of the late third or early fourth century (3.2), but it was certainly not the last official attempt to curb Manichaean activities. The two laws below attest the existence of Manichaeans in the city of Rome during the 370s and 380s. It was during this period, in 383, that Augustine, then a Manichaean 'Hearer', came from north Africa and spent a year in Rome, where Manichaean contacts were instrumental in bringing him to the attention of Symmachus for appointment to the professorship of rhetoric in Milan (Augustine *Confessions* 5.13.23 with Brown 1967: 68–70) – which has interesting implications for the social rank of some Manichaeans in Rome.

(a) Theodosian Code *16.5.3*

The emperors Valentinian [I] and Valens, Augusti, to Ampelius, Prefect of the City [of Rome]. Wherever a gathering of Manichaeans or a rabble of this sort is discovered, their teachers are to be punished with a severe penalty, those disreputable and shameful persons meeting together are to be separated from the company of people, and the houses and dwellings in which this wicked form of instruction is taught shall most certainly be appropriated to the resources of the imperial treasury. Issued at Trier on the 6th day before the Nones of March when Modestus and Arintheus were consuls [2 March 372].

(b) Theodosian Code 16.5.18

The emperors Valentinian [II], Theodosius [I] and Arcadius, Augusti, to Albinus, Prefect of the City [of Rome]. Anyone who disturbs the world in the name of the Manichaeans is to be driven completely from the earth, but especially from this city, under threat of judicial investigation. Moreover the wills of these same people shall have no force as testaments, and their property shall be confiscated to the public, nor shall it be permissible for anything to be bequeathed by them or to them. In short, let them have nothing in common with this world. Issued in Rome on the 15th day before the Kalends of July when Timasius and Promotus were consuls [17 June 389].

Part III

THEMES IN LATE
ANTIQUE
CHRISTIANITY

11

ASCETICS

Christianity did not have a monopoly on asceticism in antiquity. The Greek word *askēsis* from which the term derives originally referred to the training of a soldier or an athlete, but it was soon applied in philosophical contexts, as early as the fifth century BC, to training in virtue. Christian writers on asceticism owe a clear debt to these earlier traditions (cf. Meredith 1976; Bremmer 1992), which continued to maintain their vitality within late antique philosophy as well (Fowden 1982). Nevertheless, there is no doubt that the growth of ascetic practices was one of the most important features of Christianity during Late Antiquity.

Christian asceticism traces it more immediate roots back to Egypt, and to two particular individuals – Antony (*c.* 251–356) and Pachomius (*c.* 290–346). Antony became the model for the 'eremetic', or solitary, ascetic life, while Pachomius pioneered the 'coenobitic', or communal, form. This chapter therefore begins with extracts from the highly influential *Life of Antony* (11.1) and from the *Life of Pachomius* (11.2a) and his *Precepts* (11.2b). These extracts illustrate not only how these men pursued their respective forms of asceticism, but also provide indications of the way their prestige posed a potential threat to the institutionalised church and how the church authorities sought to 'domesticate' their influence. However, to view the early history of Christian asceticism purely in terms of these two figures and their influence is misleading, for it is apparent that alternative expressions of the ascetic impulse were also available (11.3).

From the point of view of Roman law, a celibate lifestyle incurred penalties initiated by the emperor Augustus many centuries earlier. Constantine's decision to revoke that legislation in 320 (11.4) has usually been seen as a recognition on his part of the growing importance of asceticism in Christianity, though other interpretations are possible. Subsequent emperors also had reason to legislate on matters arising from the growth of asceticism, though the second law included here actually highlights their concern that many individuals were becoming monks in order to escape civic responsibilities (11.5). At the same time, there were many for whom it entailed difficult decisions about career and marriage, typified here by a well-known story from Augustine's *Confessions* (11.6), which also illustrates the profound influence exerted by the *Life of Antony* at the opposite end of the empire.

The next item directs attention both to the origins of asceticism in Asia Minor and to the extremes to which the ascetic life could be taken by over-enthusiastic individuals (11.7). By contrast (or perhaps in reaction to this sort of phenomenon?), there were some Christians who tried to resist the trend towards valuing asceticism so highly that it reduced ordinary Christians to second-class status in the church (11.8). It should be added that fourth-century monks also had their pagan critics, particularly because of the involvement of some in the destruction of temples (6.6); in view of this, it is perhaps worth noting that there were times when they also played constructive roles in civic life, such as their intercession with imperial officials on behalf of the city of Antioch following the 'Riot of the Statues' in 387 (Liebeschuetz 1972: 236–7; cf. Brown 1971 more generally on the holy man as patron).

As this implies, Syria was another important centre for the practice of asceticism, publicised by a set of lives written by the fifth-century bishop, Theodoret. The example chosen illustrates many points of relevance to this and other chapters, but particularly the way in which asceticism was absorbed into the church hierarchy through appointing monks as bishops (11.9). The chapter concludes with two items from the sixth century – first, extracts from the life of an eastern holy man whose behaviour seems to run counter to the usual paradigm (11.10), and second, a short extract from the *Rule of Benedict* (11.11), which has been seen as a synthesis of various fourth-century traditions and which was to be highly influential in the medieval period. (Chapter 15, on women, also includes material relevant to the theme of asceticism: see **15.7–10**.)

Further reading: Chitty 1966; Hackel 1981; Rousseau 1978, 1990, 1999, 2000; Brown 1971, 1988, 1998a; Bagnall 1993: 293–303; Elm 1994; Elm and Janowitz 1998; sourcebook: Wimbush 1990.

11.1 The model for solitary ascetics: Athanasius
Life of Antony 1–3, 5, 8, 14, 44, 46–7, 90–2

The *Life of Antony* was written soon after Antony's death in 356 by Athanasius, bishop of Alexandria (328–73) (for the debate about authorship, see Bartelink 1994: 27–35; Brakke 1998: 15 n. 31). According to Sozomen *Church History* 1.13.2, Antony was born in the village of Koma on the middle reaches of the Nile, and apart from visits to Alexandria, his life was spent in that general region. The selection below aims to illustrate important episodes from his life – his background and calling, his struggles with the devil and gradual withdrawal deeper and deeper into the desert, and the idea of the ascetic as the new martyr. From remarks in the preface, Athanasius seems to have envisaged an overseas audience for whom Antony could provide a 'suitable model' (preface (3)) – a plausible hypothesis given Athanasius' periods of exile in the west in 336–7 and 339–45 (Bartelink 1994: 46–7). At the same time, it is apparent from the final chapters and other parts of the life not included below that Athanasius also had another agenda – namely to harness Antony's prestige to strengthen his own position, especially in his struggles with Arians and other heterodox groups in the Egyptian church (Brennan 1985; Bartelink 1994: 57–61; Brakke 1998: ch. 4). See 11.6 for the impact of the *Life*.

1. Antony was Egyptian by birth; his parents were well-born and well-off. Because they were Christians, he himself was brought up in the Christian way. (2) As an infant, he was raised by his parents and knew nothing else beyond them and their home. He grew, became a child and progressed towards maturity, but he could not bear to learn his letters, for he didn't want to associate with children. (3) His one desire, as it is written [Gen. 25.27], was to live a simple life in his own home. He used to accompany his parents to the house of the Lord. He was not lazy as a child, or arrogant as he grew older, but obeyed his parents and was attentive to the readings [in church], conserving the benefits within himself. (4) As a child it happened that he was moderately well-off, but he did not pester his parents for varied or rich food, nor did he seek after the pleasures to be derived from it. He was content with what he had and did not seek after more.

2. After the death of his parents, he was left on his own with a very young sister. He was about eighteen or twenty years old when he assumed responsibility for the home and for his sister. (2) Six months had not yet elapsed since the death of his parents when, going to the house of the Lord as usual and collecting his thoughts together, he was reflecting on everything – how the apostles had left all to follow the Saviour, how others, according to the *Acts*, sold their possessions, brought the proceeds and laid them at the feet of the apostles for distribution to the needy [Acts 4.35–7], and what a great hope is stored up for them in heaven. (3) Pondering these

things, he entered the church where it happened that the gospel was then being read, and he heard the Lord say to the rich man, 'If you want to be perfect, go, sell all your possessions, and give to the poor, and come and follow me, and you will have treasure in heaven' [Matt. 19.21]. (4) As if the memory of the saints which he had recalled was from God, and as if the passage had been read for him, Antony immediately left the house of the Lord and gave away to the people of his village the property which he had from his forebears – there were 300 *arourai* of very good, fertile land – so that they would not trouble himself or his sister at all. (5) He sold all the other moveable possessions which they had and gave the considerable sum of money he received to the poor, except for a small amount which he kept for his sister.

3. But entering the house of the Lord another time, he heard the Lord say in the gospel, 'Do not be anxious about tomorrow' [Matt. 6.34]. He could not bear to remain any longer, but going out he gave away even this small amount to suitable people. He entrusted his sister to the care of well-known and faithful virgins to be brought up in their celibate way of life. As for himself, he committed himself henceforth to an ascetic life instead of to his house, paying heed to himself and pursuing a life of self-discipline (*askēsis*). (2) For Egypt did not yet have its numerous monasteries and the monk knew absolutely nothing about the great desert. Whoever wished to pay heed to himself trained (*askein*) alone, not far from his own village. (3) Now there was at that time in a neighbouring village an old man who from his youth had trained in the solitary life. When Antony saw this, he emulated him in goodness. (4) Initially he began by also living in the vicinity of the village. Then if he heard about some zealous man somewhere, he set off to find him, like the wise bee, and he did not return to his own place until he had seen this man and received from him the provisions he needed for his journey towards virtue (*aretē*). (5) Living there at the outset, he weighed his intentions so as not to turn back towards the things of his parents or the memory of his relatives, but to have all his desire and all his enthusiasm directed towards the effort of training (*askēsis*). (6) However, he worked with his hands, having heard, 'Don't let the idle person eat' [2 Thess. 3.10]. He spent some of his income on bread, and gave the rest to the needy. He prayed continually, understanding that it was necessary to pray without ceasing and alone [Matt. 6.6; 1 Thess. 5.17]. (7) For he was so attentive to what was read out that he did not allow anything from

the scriptures to fall to ground, but retained everything, so that his memory took the place of books. ...

5. The devil, who hates good and is jealous, could not bear to see such resolve in a young man, and set about implementing his usual ploys against him also. (2) First, he tried to lure him away from the disciplined way of life (*askēsis*) by reminding him of his possessions, his responsibility for his sister, his family ties, love of money, desire for public esteem, the varied pleasures of food, and the other enjoyments of life, and finally the harsh demands of virtue and the great hardship it entails. He also brought to mind the frailty of the human body and the length of life. (3) In short, he built up in his mind a great dust cloud of thoughts, in his desire to detach him from his set purpose. But when the enemy saw that he was weak relative to Antony's resolve and that he was himself being thrown to the ground by his steadfastness, that he was being overthrown by his faith and tripped up by Antony's unceasing prayers, then he placed his overweening confidence in those weapons located near the navel (for these are his foremost snares against youths). He proceeded against the young man by disrupting his nights and disturbing him during the day to such an extent that observers perceived the struggle taking place between the two of them. (4) The devil suggested impure thoughts, but Antony overturned them with his prayers. The devil tried to titillate, but when he appeared to blush, Antony strengthened his body by faith and fasting. (5) The devil, frustrated, undertook to take on, at night, the appearance of a woman and to imitate her in every way, solely with a view to seducing Antony. But by meditating on Christ and the moral excellence derived from him, and by contemplating the spirituality of the soul, he put out the deceitful fire of the devil. (6) Again, the enemy brought to mind the sensual allurement of indulgence, but Antony, appropriately angry and distressed, contemplated the threat of the fire [of judgement] and the torment of the worm [Mk 9.48], and by opposing him with these thoughts, he passed through these trials unharmed. The enemy, on the other hand, was humiliated by all this. (7) For he who aspired to become like God was now being made sport of by a youth, he who exults over flesh and blood was being brought low by a flesh-clothed man. For the Lord worked with Antony – he who was clothed in flesh for our sake and who gave to the body the victory over the devil, so that each of those who undertake this contest can say, 'It is not I, but the grace of God which is with me' [1 Cor. 15.10]...

8. Gathering himself together in this way, Antony went off to the tombs which lay some distance from the village. (2) After instructing one of his friends to supply him with bread from time to time, he went inside one of the tombs; his friend closed the door on him and Antony remained alone inside. The enemy could not stand his being there, but fearing that little by little he might colonise the desert with the disciplined way of life, he entered with a band of demons one night and rained down such intense blows on him that Antony was left lying on the ground speechless from the ordeal. (3) He maintained that the beating was so violent as to conclude that the blows of ordinary men could never have inflicted such pain. But by the providence of God (for the Lord does not overlook those who hope in him) his friend came the next day bringing him the bread. Opening the door and seeing him lying on the ground as though dead, he picked him up and carried him to the house of the Lord in the village where he laid him on the earth. (4) Many relatives and people from the village sat around Antony as they would a corpse. Around midnight, Antony came to his senses and awoke. When he saw that everyone was asleep and that only his friend was awake, he beckoned to him to come and asked him to pick him up again and carry him to the tombs without disturbing anyone. [After seeing off further attacks by the devil in the tomb, Antony took up residence in an abandoned fort.]

14. He remained there for nearly twenty years, practising the ascetic life on his own. He did not go out [of the fort] and was rarely sighted. (2) After this, many who eagerly desired to emulate his disciplined way of life and some of his friends came and pulled down the door [of the fort] by force to compel him to come out. Antony came forth as if from some sanctuary where he had been initiated into mysteries and received divine inspiration. It was then that he appeared from the fort for the first time to those who had come to him. (3) When they saw him, they marvelled at the sight of his body which remained unchanged – it was neither stout from lack of exercise nor attenuated from fasting and fighting with demons, but rather the same as they had known before his withdrawal (*anachōrēsis*). His soul was in a state of purity. (4) For it had not been shrouded in distress, nor slackened by indulgence, nor affected by laughter or dejection. When he saw the crowd, he was not alarmed, and when he was greeted by so many people, he did not become excited. Rather, he remained absolutely composed like someone guided by reason (*logos*) and in a perfectly natural state. (5) Through him the Lord healed the bodies of many of those present

and in pain, and cleansed others from demons. (6) He gave Antony grace in his words, as a result of which he consoled many who were grieving, while others who were at odds he reconciled. He told everyone not to prefer anything in the world to the love of Christ. (7) In his discoursing with them, he reminded them of future blessings and of the generosity of God towards us 'who did not spare his own son, but gave him up for us all' [Rom. 8.32], and he persuaded many to embrace the solitary life. And so from that time there were monastic cells (*monastēria*) in the mountains also, and the desert became like a city of monks who left their possessions and reproduced the heavenly way of life. [Antony himself withdrew to a mountain further into the desert to the east of the Nile, and the bulk of the following chapters comprises Antony's discourses to visitors on various subjects.]

46. After this the persecution which happened during the time of Maximinus [emperor 308–13] overtook the church. When the holy martyrs were being led away to Alexandria, Antony left his cell (*monastērion*) and followed them, saying, 'Let us go so that we may participate in the contest, if called, or observe those doing combat'. (2) He conceived a yearning to undergo martyrdom, but he did not want simply to hand himself over. So he served the confessors in the mines and in the prisons, and he showed great enthusiasm before the judicial tribunal, encouraging those called to join the combat, receiving them as they underwent martyrdom, and remaining with them until the end. (3) When the judge saw the fearless enthusiasm of Antony and those with him, he ordered that none of the monks were to appear before the tribunal, or even remain in the city at all. (4) All the others thought it best to make themselves inconspicuous that day, but Antony showed no concern: rather, he washed his cloak and on the following day, he stood in an elevated position clearly visible to the judge. (5) Everyone was astonished at this, and when the judge passed by him after the hearing and saw him, Antony stood there, calmly demonstrating the commitment of us Christians. (6) For as I have already mentioned, he longed to undergo martyrdom, so he seemed distressed when he was not martyred. But the Lord was protecting him for our benefit and that of others so that he might become a teacher to many in the disciplined way of life which he himself had learnt from the Scriptures. (7) For by observing his way of life alone, many became enthusiastic imitators of his lifestyle. So once again he served the confessors in his usual manner, and like one chained up with them, he suffered through his service.

47. When at last the persecution ceased and the blessed bishop Peter had been martyred, Antony left and returned once more to his cell. There each day he was a martyr in his conscience and he joined combat in the struggles of the faith. He devoted himself greatly to self-discipline in a very rigorous manner. (2) For he was always fasting, and he wore a garment which was hairy on the inside and animal skin on the exterior – he kept this until the end of his life. He did not wash his body with water for the sake of cleanliness, and he never washed his feet or even plunged them into water without good reason. (3) No one ever saw him undressed, and no one saw the naked body of Antony, except when, after his death, he was buried. [Soon after, Antony withdrew to another mountain even deeper into the desert – the 'inner mountain' – from where he returned periodically to visit and instruct those seeking to emulate him.]

90. When the brothers pressed him to remain with them and end his life there, he did not agree for many reasons, as he made clear while also keeping silent, and especially for this one. (2) When those who are full of zeal die, especially the holy martyrs, the Egyptians like to perform funeral rites for their bodies by wrapping them in linen; they do not bury them in the ground, but place them on couches and keep watch over them inside their houses, believing that this is the way to honour the departed. (3) Antony often asked the bishops to advise the people in this matter. (4) He also reproved laymen himself and reprimanded women, saying that this practice was not right and certainly not divinely approved, for the tombs of the patriarchs and the prophets have been preserved down to the present time, and the body of the Lord himself was laid in a tomb and it was hidden by a stone placed in front until he rose again on the third day. (5) Saying these things, he showed that it is contrary to the law not to bury the bodies of the deceased after death, even if they are holy. For what is greater or more holy than the body of the Lord? (6) So when they heard this, many thereafter buried their dead in the ground and gave thanks to the Lord for having been taught so well.

91. But knowing this practice, Antony feared that his own body might be treated thus, so he made haste after bidding farewell to the monks in the outer mountain. Reaching the inner mountain, where he was accustomed to living, he fell ill a few months later. He called those who were with him – there were two who remained with him in the inner mountain for fifteen years, practising a disciplined life and serving him on account of his old age – and he said to them: (2) 'I am setting out, as it is written, on the way of the

fathers [cf. Josh. 23.14], for I see that the Lord is calling me. As for you, live soberly, do not fall away from the disciplined life you have long practised, but take care to maintain your enthusiasm, as though you were starting out now. (3) You are familiar with demons and their tricks, you know how fierce they are, but how weak their power is. So do not fear them, but rather always draw inspiration from Christ and trust in him. Live as though dying each day, be attentive to yourselves and remember the advice you have heard from me. (4) Have no contact with the schismatics, and absolutely nothing to do with the Arian heretics. For you know how I too avoided them on account of their fighting Christ and their heterodox teaching. (5) Rather, always strive earnestly to join yourselves above all with the Lord, then with the saints, so that after death, they may welcome you as dear friends into the eternal tents. Think about these things, too, and reflect on them. (6) And if you care for me and remember me as a father, do not allow anyone to take my body to Egypt and place it in a house. It was for this reason that I returned to the mountain and have come here. (7) You also know how I have always reproved those who do this and encouraged them to stop this practice. So perform then funerary rites for my body yourselves and bury it in the ground, and observe what I say to you: no one is to know the place, except yourselves alone. (8) As for me, at the resurrection of the dead, I will receive it back in incorruptible form from the Saviour. Distribute my clothing: to Athanasius the bishop, give one of my sheepskins and the cloak on which I lie – he gave it me new, and it has grown old alongside me; (9) and to Serapion the bishop [of Thmuis], give the other sheepskin, and you keep the hair garment. And now, my children, God be with you – for Antony is passing on and is no longer with you.'

92. After these words, they embraced him, he drew his feet up off the ground, and as if rejoicing at the sight of friends coming towards him – for he was lying with a radiant expression on his face – he died and was also taken to the fathers. (2) Then in accordance with the instructions he had given them, they performed funeral rites and wrapped him in linen, before burying his body in the ground, and to this day no one, with the exception of those two alone, knows where he is buried. (3) Each of those who received a sheepskin from the blessed Antony, and the cloak used by him, looks after them as items of great value. For looking at them is like seeing Antony, and wearing them like contemplating his reproofs with joy. ...

11.2 The model for communal asceticism: *Life of Pachomius (Bohairic)* 26, 28 and *Precepts of Pachomius* 26–7, 31, 35, 49, 58, 138–40

Unlike Antony, Pachomius did not come from a Christian family, but when conscripted into the army of Maximinus Daia in 312 he experienced such kindness at the hands of local Christians that he was converted. After spending a number of years undertaking charitable work in his local community in southern Egypt, he pursued a more withdrawn, ascetic lifestyle in the company of an older hermit. During this period he claimed to have heard a voice telling him to establish a monastery in the deserted village of Tabennesi, which became the basis of his experiment in communal asceticism and eventually spawned six further monasteries by the end of the fourth century. Chapter 26 from the *Life* and the excerpts from the *Precepts* below give some idea of how life in the monastery was organised, the emphasis on manual work, the assumption that there will be contact with the outside world, and the importance of literacy. Chapter 28 of the *Life* highlights the issue of the relationship of asceticism to the institutionalised church – the eagerness of the authorities to ordain Pachomius and so bring him more closely under their authority, and his clear reluctance (cf. Brakke 1998: 113–20). The *Bohairic Life* (Bohairic is a dialect of Coptic) is one of a number of biographies of Pachomius; for discussion of its complex relationship to the other biographies, see Rousseau 1999: ch. 2. Further reading: Rousseau 1999; Goehring 1996.

(a) Life of Pachomius (Bohairic) 26, 28

26. He appointed some from among the capable brothers as his assistants to take care of their souls' salvation. [He appointed] one [of them] at the head of the first house, that of the lesser stewards, with a second to help him in preparing the tables and in cooking for [the brothers]. [He appointed] another brother also, with his second – men who were faithful on every score – to look after the food and the care of the sick brothers. If anyone wanted to abstain from what was served at table or from what was served to the sick, there was no-one to prevent him from doing so. And at the doorway [he appointed] other brothers whose 'speech was seasoned with salt' [Col. 4: 6] to receive visitors according to each one's rank. [These porters] also instructed those who came to become monks, for their salvation, until he clothed them in the monk's habit. Similarly, [he appointed] other faithful [brothers] noted for their piety to transact sales and make purchases. In each house the brothers in service were replaced every three weeks, and a new class was appointed. They performed 'in fear and trembling' [Phil. 2:12] the task assigned them by the housemaster. He appointed still others with a housemaster and a second to work at the shops and at the mat-making and to be ready for every obedience. He likewise established three instructions a week: one on Saturday and two on the

holy Sunday, while the housemasters gave some, if they wished, on the two fastdays...

28. After his appointment as archbishop of Alexandria, Apa Athanasius came south to the Thebaid with the intention of proceeding as far as Aswan to give comfort to the holy churches. When our father Pachomius saw him with an escort of bishops walking before him, he also took the brothers and escorted him a long way. They chanted psalms while escorting him until they brought him inside the monastery, where he prayed in their assembly room and in all their cells. Apa Sarapion, bishop of Nitentori, grasped the archbishop's hand, kissed it, and said, 'I beg Your Piety to ordain to the priesthood Pachomius, father of the monks, so that he should be set over all the monks in my diocese, for he is a man of God. Alas! he refuses to obey me in this matter.' At once Pachomius disappeared into the midst of the crowd so as not to be discovered. When the archbishop had seated himself, as did the great crowd that was with him, he opened his mouth to speak and said to Sarapion, 'Indeed I have learned about the renown of the faith of this man Apa Pachomius of whom you speak to me, since I have been in Alexandria and even before my consecration'. Then he rose, prayed, and said to [Pachomius'] sons, 'Greet your father and say to him, 'So, you hid from us, fleeing from that which leads to jealousy, discord and envy, and you chose for yourself that which is better and will always abide in Christ! Our Lord, therefore, will accede to your wish. ...' (tr. A. Veilleux)

(b) Precepts of Pachomius 26–7, 31, 35, 49, 58, 138–40

26. When they are working at mats, the ministers shall ask each of the housemasters in the evening how many rushes are required per house. And so he shall dip the rushes and distribute them in the morning to each in order. If in the morning he notices that still more rushes are needed, he shall dip them and bring them around to each house, until the signal is given for the meal.

27. The housemaster who is completing the weekly service and the one taking up the service for the coming week and the superior of the monastery shall have the responsibility of observing what work has been omitted or neglected. They shall have the mats that are usually spread out on the floor in the assembly shaken out. And they shall also count the ropes twisted per week, noting the sum on tablets and keeping the record until the time of the annual gathering, when an account shall be given and sins forgiven everyone.

31. Each master shall teach, in his own house, how they must eat with manners and meekness. If anyone speaks or laughs while eating, he shall do penance and be rebuked there at once; and he shall stand until another of the brothers who are eating gets up.

35. The ministers shall eat nothing but what has been prepared for the brothers in common, nor shall they dare to prepare special foods for themselves.

49. When someone comes to the door of the monastery, wishing to renounce the world and be added to the number of the brothers, he shall not be free to enter. First, the father of the monastery shall be informed [of his coming]. He shall remain outside at the door a few days and be taught the Lord's prayer and as many psalms as he can learn. Carefully shall he make himself known: has he done something wrong and, troubled by fear, suddenly run away? Or is he under someone's authority? Can he renounce his parents and spurn his possessions? If they can see that he is ready for everything, then he shall be taught the rest of the monastic discipline: what he must do and whom he must serve, whether in the assembly (*synaxis*) of all the brothers or in the house to which he is assigned, as well as in the refectory. Perfectly instructed in every good work, let him be joined to the brothers. Then they shall strip him of his secular clothes and garb him in the monastic habit. He shall be handed over to the porter so that at the time of prayer he may bring him before all the brothers; and he shall sit where he is told. The clothes he brought with him shall be given to those in charge of this matter and brought to the storeroom; they will be in the keeping of the superior of the monastery.

58. When the signal is given to go to work, the housemaster shall lead them, and no-one shall remain in the monastery, except by order of the father. And those who shall go out shall not ask where they are going.

60. At work, they shall talk of no worldly matter, but either recite holy things or else keep silent.

64. If the brothers who are sent out on business or are staying far away eat outside the monastery, the weekly server who accompanies them shall give them food but without making cooked dishes, and he shall himself distribute water as is done in the monastery.

138. Everything that is taught them in the assembly of the brothers they must absolutely talk over among themselves, especially on the days of fast, when they receive instruction from their master.

139. Whoever enters the monastery uninstructed shall be taught

first what he must observe; and when, so taught, he has consented to it all, they shall give him twenty psalms or two of the Apostle's epistles, or some other part of the Scripture. And if he is illiterate, he shall go at the first, third, and sixth hours to someone who can teach and has been appointed for him. He shall stand before him and learn very studiously with all gratitude. Then the fundamentals of the syllable, the verbs, and nouns shall be written for him, and even if he does not want to, he shall be compelled to read.

140. There shall be no-one whatsoever in the monastery who does not learn to read and does not memorize something of the Scriptures. [One should learn by heart] at least the New Testament and Psalter. (tr. A. Veilleux)

11.3 Varieties of ascetic practice: Jerome *Letter* 22.34

Eustochium was a young woman of aristocratic birth who dedicated herself to a life of virginity, and in the mid-380s Jerome wrote her a long letter of instruction and advice about ascetic practices (Kelly 1975: 99–103). In the following excerpt he alludes not only to the solitary and communal forms of asceticism associated with Antony and Pachomius, respectively, but also to a third type (of which he has a very low opinion) – those who lived in small groups in an urban context. Their identity has been the subject of debate amongst modern scholars (Judge 1977; Morard 1980; Goehring 1992), but what is clear is that there was considerable variation beyond the two famous paradigms. For discussion of the Coptic terminology, see Horn 1994, while for ascetic variety and experiment more generally, see Elm 1994.

(1) Since I have mentioned monks and I know you are glad to hear about subjects relating to the holy, listen to this for a moment. In Egypt there are three kinds of monk. There are the 'coenobites', referred to as *sauhes* [lit. 'gathering'] in the indigenous language [Coptic], whom we may describe as living in community; there are the 'anchorites', who live alone in the desert and are known by this name because they have withdrawn from society; and there is a third category, whom they call *remnuoth* [lit. 'man living apart'], a most undesirable and detested kind, who are the only, or at least the main, type in our region [Palestine]. (2) These dwell together in twos or threes, not many more, living by their own decisions and authority, and part of what they earn they contribute to a common reserve so that they have shared food. For the most part they live in cities and villages, and whatever they sell is very expensive, as if it is their craftmanship which is holy, rather than their life. There is

frequent quarrelling among them because, supporting themselves as they do, they are not prepared to submit to any authority. (3) Indeed they often compete with one another in fasting and make what should be a private matter reason to boast. Among them everything is calculated to impress: loose sleeves, shoes that are too large, coarse clothing, frequent sighing, visits to virgins, bad-mouthing of clergy, and when a feast day comes around, they stuff themselves until sick.

11.4 Removal of legal handicaps on celibacy: *Theodosian Code* 8.16.1

For reasons that continue to be hotly debated by scholars, the emperor Augustus introduced legislation in the late first century BC, which penalised those who did not marry or, if married, did not have children, the penalty being loss of some or all inheritance rights outside the immediate family. The legislation proved particularly unpopular with the senatorial and equestrian elite, but it remained in force for more than three centuries. Its repeal by Constantine in the law below was at least symbolically important for the development of Christian asceticism, with its emphasis on the virtues of sexual abstinence, though some have seen Constantine's measure as more concerned to win the favour of the predominantly pagan senatorial aristocracy of Rome on whom Augustus' legislation had fallen most heavily. Moreover, 'even after that the legislators did not conceal that they were sympathetic towards fertile families … [and] the state for a long time afterwards showed clear reserve towards Christian asceticism, although it was outwardly tolerated' (Arjava 1996: 189). The second part of the law refers to the traditional prohibition in Roman law on husbands and wives giving one another gifts (on which see Treggiari 1991: ch. 11). Further reading: Evans Grubbs 1995: ch. 3; Arjava 1996: 77–80, 157–64.

The emperor Constantine Augustus to the people: Those who used to be classified as unmarried (*caelibes*) in the law of old are to be freed from the menacing terrors of the law and are to live as if numbered among the married and supported by the bond of marriage, and all shall enjoy the equal legal status of taking such inheritances as each is entitled to. Nor indeed is anyone to be classified as childless (*orbus*): the specified financial losses for this category shall not harm them. (1) We deem that this measure shall also apply to women, and we do away with the commands of the law imposed on their necks like yokes from everyone, without distinction. (2) But the exercise of this benefit shall not be available to husbands and wives *vis-à-vis* one another, since their deceitful allurements are for the most part scarcely discouraged by the strong opposition of the law, but the traditional force of the law shall remain in place between those people. Issued at Serdica on the day before the Kalends of February [31 January], and posted on the Kalends of April at Rome, when Constantine Augustus was consul for the sixth time and Constantine Caesar [one of Constantine's sons] for the first [1 April 320].

11.5 The ascetic life as escape: *Theodosian Code* 12.1.63

The following law suggests that non-spiritual factors could play a part in the decision by some individuals to adopt an ascetic lifestyle. The target of this particular law is the group known as *curiales* – town councillors who over the course of the fourth century faced increasingly onerous financial responsibilities within their communities. Particularly in Egypt, there was a long tradition of running away from excessive tax burdens (*anachōresis*), and joining a monastic community was one avenue of escape.

The Emperors Valentinian [I] and Valens, Augusti, to Modestus, Praetorian Prefect: Certain adherents of laziness have abandoned their responsibilities in the cities and gone off to uninhabited and secluded regions where, in the guise of religious devotion, they join companies of monks. Therefore we have ordered by this prudent law that any of their kind discovered within Egypt by the Count of the East are to be uprooted from their hiding places and recalled to undertake their duties in their home towns. Otherwise, in keeping with the tenor of our law, they are to be deprived of the attractions of their property, which we have decided should be claimed for those who take on the responsibilities of their public duties. Posted in Beirut on the Kalends of January when the emperors Valentinian and Valens were the consuls [1 January 370 or 373].

11.6 Conversion to the ascetic life: Augustine *Confessions* 8.6.15

In this passage from his autobiographical meditations addressed to God, Augustine relates a story he heard from a fellow north African named Ponticianus, which precipitated Augustine's conversion to Christianity while he was a professor of rhetoric at Milan in the mid-380s. The story concerns the circumstances that led two of Ponticianus' friends to abandon careers in the imperial bureaucracy for an ascetic life. Of particular interest is the crucial role played by Athanasius' *Life of Antony* in this decision, illustrating one of the media through which monasticism spread from Egypt to the west (Athanasius' own period of exile at Trier in the mid-330s was another important factor). Athanasius' *Life* first appeared in Greek in the late 350s, and was quickly translated into Latin, though verbal resemblances suggest that the version which features in this passage was the later translation of

Evagrius of Antioch which became available *c*.371 (O'Donnell 1992: vol. 3, 40–1). There has been speculation as to whether one of the two unnamed individuals in Ponticianus' story might in fact have been Jerome, though this intriguing possibility seems on balance unlikely (Matthews 1990: 50, 398; O'Donnell 1992: vol. 3, 39–40).

Then Ponticianus' talk turned to the communities living in monasteries and their way of life, fragrant to you, and the fruitful solitudes of the desert, of which we knew nothing. (There was a monastery at Milan beyond the walls of the city, full of good brothers and under the guidance of Ambrose, but we had not been aware of it.) Ponticianus continued talking, while we listened intently in silence. And so it happened that he told us how, at some point in time, he and three companions were in Trier and, while the emperor was busy for the afternoon with games at the circus, they had gone out walking in gardens adjacent to the city walls. Strolling there in pairs, one with Ponticianus separately from the other two, their paths gradually diverged. In their wanderings, the latter pair came upon a hut where there lived some of your servants, poor in spirit – 'of such is the kingdom of heaven' [Matt. 5.3] – and they found there a book containing the *Life of Antony*. One of them began to read it and to marvel; his heart was set on fire and while he read he contemplated adopting such a lifestyle and abandoning his secular career in the imperial bureaucracy to serve you (for they were employed as what they call *agentes in rebus* [inspectors of the imperial transport system]). Then suddenly, filled with holy love and a solemn sense of shame, he became angry with himself and turning his gaze on his friend, he said to him, 'Tell me, I ask you, what are we hoping to achieve through all this work of ours? What are we aiming for? For what purpose are we in the imperial service? Is there any greater goal for us in the palace than being friends of the emperor? And is that not a vulnerable position, full of risks? And through how many risks must one pass to achieve a position involving even greater risks? And how long will it take? By contrast, if I want to be a friend of God, I can do so now.' So he spoke and, in a state of turmoil as new life was birthed within him, his eyes returned to the pages. He read on and was being changed within, where you were observing, and his heart was being set free from the world, as soon became evident. For while he read, and pondered the waverings of his heart, he trembled from time to time as he made up his mind and resolved on the better course of action. Now yours, he said to his friend, 'I have now parted company with that ambition of ours and have decided to serve God, and I am making a start from this hour and in this place. If you don't want to do the same, at least don't oppose me.' The other replied that he would join him as a comrade for such great recompense and so great a calling. And now both yours, they began building their tower for the requisite cost of leaving behind all their possessions and following you [Luke 14.28–33]. Then Ponticianus and his companion, who were walking in other parts of the gardens looking for them, turned up at this same spot and finding them there, suggested they start back now that the day was drawing to a close. But when the other two told them of their plan and intention, and the way in which such a desire had arisen and become established within them, they asked them not to cause them trouble if they decided not to join them. Ponticianus and his companion did not change from their original paths, though they lamented for themselves, as he related. Congratulating them sincerely and entrusting themselves to their prayers, they set off with heavy hearts for the palace, while the other two, fixing their hearts on heaven, remained in the hut. Both men had fiancées who, after hearing of this, also dedicated their virginity to you.

11.7 Ascetic evolution and extremism in Asia Minor: Sozomen *Church History* 3.14.31–6

Basil of Caesarea has traditionally been seen as responsible for the establishment of asceticism as a significant phenomenon in Asia Minor, but the following passage from the church historian Sozomen (writing in the mid-fifth century) indicates that it had begun evolving there earlier and through the activities of another individual, Eustathius. The emergence of extremist tendencies among some of Eustathius' followers resulted in a church council at Gangra which condemned many practices associated with Eustathius (for a translation of the canons, see Yarbrough 1990); unfortunately, the date of the council remains uncertain – possibly as early as 343 or as late as 355 (Barnes 1989a). Eustathius himself seems to have accepted the council's discipline, and the fact that he became bishop of Sebaste in 355 implies that he did not lose all influence. It is certainly clear that the young Basil was an admirer. Further reading: Frazee 1981; Brown 1988: 287–8; Mitchell 1993: vol. 2, 111–14; Elm 1994: ch. 4; Rousseau 1994: 73–6.

(31) Eustathius, who was responsible for the church at Sebaste in Armenia, is said to have established a monastic regime among the Armenians, Paphlagonians and those living in Pontus, and to have been the initiator of a rigorous mode of life with regard to what food should be eaten and abstained from, what clothing should be worn, ethical standards and strict behaviour – so that some people

THEMES IN LATE ANTIQUE CHRISTIANITY

insist he was the author of the ascetic treatise written by Basil of Cappadocia. (32) But through his great strictness he is said to have fallen into extreme practices entirely at odds with the laws of the church. (33) Some people, however, exonerate him from this charge, instead blaming some of his disciples who disparaged marriage, refused to pray in the homes of married people, despised clergy who were married, fasted on the Lord's day, held church services in homes, declared that the wealthy had absolutely no part in the kingdom of God, detested the eating of meat, would not dress in the usual tunic and outer garment (*stolē*), instead wearing a strange and unusual garment, and introducing many other new practices. (34) As a result of this, many women were beguiled into leaving their husbands, and then, unable to maintain self-discipline, committed adultery; others cut their hair off in a false show of religious devotion and wore male clothing inappropriate for women. (35) On account of all this, neighbouring bishops gathered in Gangra, the chief city of Paphlagonia, and resolved that these people were outside the church at large, unless they publicly renounced each of the stated practices in accordance with the canons of the council. (36) It is said that henceforth Eustathius wore the outer garment (*stolē*) and went about his daily work like other priests, thereby proving that he had introduced and practised these novelties, not out of willfulness, but for the sake of godly discipline. ...

11.8 Criticism of rigorous asceticism: Jerome *Against Jovinian* 1.1, 3, 5 (excerpts) (*PL* 23.211–17)

Despite the growth of asceticism during the fourth century, there were some who were concerned that its more rigorist manifestations encouraged an undervaluing of 'ordinary' Christians and of marriage. One of those who articulated this criticism, was Jovinian who, though himself a monk, wrote some treatises on the subject in Italy in the early 390s. These have not survived, but Jerome's vitriolic rejoinder has, in the course of which he quotes extensively from Jovinian. The following excerpts are presented with three aims: first, to reproduce Jerome's summary of Jovinian's main propositions and provide a brief idea of how Jovinian used biblical quotation to support his stance; second, to give a taste of how Jerome responded, in terms of both argument and virulence of language; and third, to highlight Jovinian's apparent concern that excessive emphasis on ascetic abstention from marriage reflected Manichaean influence. Jovinian was condemned by a council convened by Siricius, bishop of Rome *c.* 393 (a decision endorsed by Ambrose), but it is evident that his views enjoyed widespread support in the west. Further reading: Kelly 1975: 180–9; Hunter 1987, 1989, 1993; Brown 1988: 359–61; Markus 1990: 38–41, 45–8, 75–7.

204

1. Only a few days have passed since holy brethren from the city of Rome sent me some short treatises by a certain Jovinian, asking me to respond to their absurdities and, through the authority derived from the gospels and the apostles, to make this Epicurus of the Christians tremble. ...

3. ... We are not adherents of the teachings of Marcion or of Manichaeus [i.e., Mani], we do not disparage marriage; nor have we been deluded by the error of Tatian, leader of the Encratites (who condemned and rejected not only marriage, but also food, which God has created to be consumed) into thinking that all sexual intercourse is impure. We know that in a great house there are not only vessels of gold and silver, but also of wood and clay, and on the foundation of Christ, which the master-builder Paul laid down, some put up a building of gold, silver and precious stones, while others do so with hay, wood and stubble [1 Cor. 3.10–13]. We are not unaware of the fact that 'marriage is honorable and the marriage-bed pure' [Heb. 13.4], we have read God's first instruction, 'Go forth and multiply and fill the earth' [Gen.1.28]. But although we accept marriage, we prefer virginity, which has its origins in marriage. Will silver no longer be silver if gold is more valuable than silver? Or is it an insult to the tree and the field if the fruit and the grain are preferred to the roots and leaves, the stems and husks? As fruit comes from the tree and grain from the stalk, so virginity comes from marriage. Although the harvests of a hundred-fold and sixty-fold and thirty-fold come from the same earth and from the same sowing, there is a large difference in quantity. The thirty-fold represents marriage ..., the sixty-fold widows, because they have been put in a tight and testing position. ... But the hundred-fold ... represents the crown of virginity. ...

I will briefly set out the opinions of our opponent, dragging them out from his dark books like snakes from their holes, and I will not allow their poisonous heads or coiled, filthy bodies any respite. What is harmful should be made known so it can be crushed when it has been revealed.

He says that 'virgins, widows, and married women who have been washed once in Christ, are of equal worth, if there is no difference between them in terms of other works.' He tries to show that 'those who are full of faith and have been reborn in baptism cannot be overthrown by the devil.' His third proposition is that 'there is no difference between abstaining from food and accepting it with thanksgiving.' The fourth and final is that 'there is one reward in the kingdom of heaven for everyone who has preserved their baptism'. ...

5. 'The first [proposition]', he says, 'is the view God takes: 'For which reason a man shall leave his father and mother and cleave to his wife and the two shall become one flesh' [Gen. 1.28].' And in case we might say this was written in the Old Testament, he declares that it is confirmed by the Lord himself in the Gospel: 'What God has joined, let no man put asunder' [Matt. 19.5, quoting Gen. 2.24], and he immediately adds, 'Go forth and multiply and fill the earth' [Gen. 1.28]. [Jerome then refers to numerous examples from the Old Testament adduced by Jovinian as evidence for positive approval of marriage.]

Suddenly he shifts to the gospel, and brings forward Zachariah and Elizabeth, Peter and his father-in-law, and the other apostles. And he introduces them, saying, 'If they want to adopt an empty defence and contend that it was when the world was new that it needed offspring, let them hear what Paul says: 'I want younger widows to marry and bear children' [1 Tim. 5.14]; and 'Marriage is honorable and the marriage bed undefiled' [Heb. 13.4]; and 'A wife is bound to her husband for as long as her husband lives. But if he dies, she may marry whomever she wishes, only in the Lord' [1 Cor. 7.39]... From this it is clear that you are adherents of the teaching of the Manichaeans who prohibit marriage and the eating of food which God has created to be consumed, and your consciences have been seared.'

And after many other arguments which it is tedious to discuss now, he works himself up as if for a rhetorical occasion and directs his comments at a generalised virgin, saying, 'I am not insulting you, virgin: you have chosen chastity because of the pressure of current circumstances. You have decided to do this in order to be holy in body and spirit. Do not be proud: you are a part of the same church as those women who are married!'

11.9 A monk-bishop: Theodoret *History of the Monks* 17 (Abraham)

This biography of a holy man from the early fifth century (the emperor in (9) is Theodosius II) – one of a collection by Theodoret, bishop of Cyrrhus (423–c. 460) – is of interest in relation to a wide range of subjects, from Christianisation to saints' relics. With specific reference to asceticism, it provides a good example of an increasing trend in Late Antiquity – the movement of monks into the episcopacy (cf. Markus 1990: ch. 13). It has also been seen as an illustration of the holy man as patron and mediator (Brown 1971: 86), though in fact 'far from bearing witness ...

to a solitary holy man acting as rural patron over a long period of time, Theodoret's account presents us with an established ascetic, accompanied by at least several others like himself, inspired by a specifically pastoral zeal, achieving status by an isolated ploy, and then exercising priestly authority in a quite customary way, still supported by ascetic colleagues, choosing in the end to return to a clearly defined ascetic establishment' (Rousseau 1997: 39–40). Further reading: Trombley 1993: 147–50.

1. It would not be right to pass over the memory of the excellent Abraham, on the pretext that after the monastic life he brought distinction to the office of bishop. For on account of this he is undoubtedly even more worthy of memory, because when compelled to change his status, he did not alter his manner of living, but took with him the labours of the ascetic and completed the course of life constrained by both the toils of the monastic life and the burdens of the episcopacy.

2. This man was also a product of the region of Cyrrhus, for it was there that he was born, grew up, and acquired the wealth which derives from ascetic virtue. For those who lived with him say that he subdued his body with such vigils, standing, and fasting that he remained immobile for long periods of time, not in the least able to move. Freed from this weakness by divine providence, he resolved to bear the dangers of piety for the sake of divine grace and made for the Lebanon after learning that a large village there was possessed by the darkness of ungodliness. He concealed his identity as a monk under the guise of a merchant and, together with his companions, carried sacks, as if to buy nuts – for this was the village's chief product. He rented a house after giving its owners a small sum of money, and for three or four days he kept quiet. Then gradually he began to celebrate the divine liturgy, using a moderate voice. When they realised he was singing psalms, the town crier called out to assemble everyone. Men, women and children gathered and blocked up the doors of the house from the outside, while they threw down from the roof a lot of earth they had collected. But when those inside saw they were being suffocated and entombed, they did not want to do or say anything other than offer prayer to God; then through the remonstrations of the elders, the villagers stopped their madness. They unblocked the doors and after dragging them clear of the mound of earth, they told them to leave immediately.

3. But in the midst of all this, tax collectors arrived to force them to pay their dues. Some of the villagers they put in chains, others they beat up. But forgetting all that had happened to them and

imitating the Master who, fastened to a cross, showed concern for those doing this, this godly man entreated the tax collectors to do their job with moderation. Then when the collectors sought guarantees of payment, he voluntarily accepted the judicial summons and promised to hand over one hundred pieces of gold in a few days' time. Full of amazement at the generosity of this man to whom they had done those terrible things, they asked his forgiveness for what they had dared to do to him, and invited him to become their patron (*prostatēs*). For the village did not have an owner – they themselves were farmers and owners. So he went to the city – it was Emesa – and found some friends who loaned him the hundred pieces of gold. Then he returned to the village and fulfilled his undertaking on the appointed day.

4. When they observed his commitment, the villagers extended their invitation to him more earnestly. When he promised to do so if they promised to build a church, they begged him to make an immediate start and took the blessed man around to show him the more suitable locations. One praised this spot, another that. Having chosen the better site, he positioned the foundations and a short time later he was putting the roof in place. Once the building was complete, he encouraged them to take on a priest. But when they said they would choose no one else, but begged to have him as father and shepherd, then he received the grace of the priesthood. He spent three years with them, guiding them well towards godly things. Then after preparing one of his companions to take his place, he resumed once more his monastic abode.

5. So as not to make my account overlong by describing everything he did – Abraham became well-known in these parts and accepted the office of bishop at Carrhae. It was a city inebriated with ungodliness and given over to the bacchic revelry of demons. But it was deemed worthy of cultivation by this man and when it received the fire of his teaching, it was freed completely from the thorny brambles of the past, and now prides itself on the harvests of the Spirit, offering to God sheaves of ripe grain. But this godly man did not undertake this cultivation without difficulty. He experienced much physical pain and imitated the technique of those entrusted with healing bodies, sometimes by easing it with compresses, sometimes by drawing it out with astringent remedies; on occasion he regained health by cutting and burning. The radiance of his life lent strong support to his teaching and his other expressions of concern. For illuminated by this radiance, the inhabitants listened to his words and gladly accepted what he did.

6. Throughout the whole of his time as bishop, he treated bread as unnecessary, and water too, and he never used a bed or fire. At night, he sang forty antiphonal psalms, doubling the length of the prayers which fall between them; for the remainder of the night, he sat on his chair and allowed his eyelids to rest for a short time. For Moses the lawgiver said, 'Man shall not live by bread alone' [Deut. 8.3], and the Lord remembered this saying when rebuffing the challenge of the devil [Matt. 3.4]. But we have not been taught anywhere in holy scripture that living without water is a possibility. For the great Elisha first satisfied this need from the stream, then when he reached the widow at Zarephath he asked her first to fetch him water, and then he requested bread [1 Kings 17.6, 10–11]. But during the period of his episcopacy this remarkable man consumed neither bread, nor beans, nor cooked vegetables, nor water, which according to those considered clever in these matters is regarded as the first of the four elements on account of its usefulness. But he derived his nutrition and fluids from lettuce, chicory, celery and similar plants, thereby demonstrating that the skills of the baker and the chef are redundant. When it was the season for fruit, this satisfied this need, but he partook of it after the evening liturgy.

7. While exhausting his body with these hardships, he extended inexhaustible hospitality to others. A bed was always ready for strangers who arrived; they were offered selected breads of high quality, wine with a sweet bouquet, fish, vegetables, and the other things which accompany them. In the middle of the day he himself sat with those eating, offering each helpings of what had been set before them, giving cups to everyone and encouraging them to drink up, thereby imitating his forebear of the same name – I mean the patriarch – who served his guests but did not himself eat [Gen. 18.1–8].

8. He spent the whole day dealing with the lawsuits of those quarrelling with one another, persuading some to be reconciled, compelling others unpersuaded by his sober instruction. No wrong-doer went away victorious over justice through effrontery. For by always giving the justice due to the one who had been wronged, he showed that they could never be overcome and were stronger than the one who wished to do wrong. He was like a very good doctor, always preventing an excess of humours and ensuring that the elements are in equilibrium.

9. The emperor had a longing to see this man – for rumour is winged, and easily makes known everything, both good and bad – and he called him to himself, embraced him on his arrival, and

considered his rough peasant attire more worthy of respect than his own purple robe. The choir of the empresses grasped his hands and his knees, and entreated a man who did not understand the Greek language.

10. Both for emperors and for all people, philosophy is something worthy of respect, and when those who love and care about it die, they gain greater acclaim. This can be learnt from many instances, but above all from the events surrounding this divinely inspired man. For when he died and the emperor learned this, he wanted to lay him to rest in one of the holy shrines. But when he realised that it would be appropriate to return the body of the shepherd to the sheep, he himself led the funeral cortege, followed by the choir of the empresses, and all the officials and the governed, soldiers and civilians. The city of Antioch, and those after it, received him with the same enthusiasm until he reached the great river. On the banks of the Euphrates, inhabitants of the towns and foreigners, all the country-dwellers and those from neighbouring parts, gathered together and pressed forward to gain a blessing (*eulogia*). Many men bearing rods were escorting the funeral bier in order to strike fear into those who tried to relieve the body of its clothing or loosen bits from it. Both singing of psalms and cries of lamentation could be heard. In her grief, one woman called him her patron, another her sustainer, yet another her shepherd and teacher; in tears, this man named him father, that upholder and protector. To the accompaniment of such commendations and wailings, they committed his holy and sacred body to the grave.

11. As for me, I marvel that, after changing his status, he did not alter his manner of life, that he did not acquire a taste for a less strict lifestyle in the episcopal office, but that he increased his ascetic labours – which is why I have included him in this *History of the Monks* and not separated him from the company that he loved, in the hope that I too may receive his blessings.

11.10 An anti-social holy man? John of Ephesus
Lives of the Eastern Saints 4

The extracts below come from another collection of lives of holy men, this time written in the sixth century by John of Ephesus, a Monophysite cleric (*c.* 507–*c.* 589). Since John alludes to the fact that he was a baby when the two brothers who are the subject of this section, Abraham and Maro, were active, they can be placed in the early sixth century. Maro is an intriguing example of a holy man because he seems intent on resisting social engagement – a feature which, in combination with other evidence, suggests a need to nuance the influential analysis of the holy man

210

by Peter Brown (Brown 1971; Elm and Janowitz 1998) with an appreciation of the scope for variation in involvement on the part of such ascetics. Further reading: Whitby 1987; Rousseau 1997: 46–9.

(p. 56) ... These two holy brothers were by birth from a village called Kalesh, in the territory of Amida; and the elder whose name was Abraham was first moved by zeal, and he went and dwelt in a monastery called Ar'a Rabtha in the territory of Ingila [in northern Mesopotamia]. Now there was a high stone column to which the men used to come in order to stand upon it in that monastery; and (p. 57) after he had broken himself for a space of ten years by great labours he himself ascended the column. And, when his brother whose name was Maro had seen it, he also came and entered upon the road from the first mile and began to walk soundly, while those two brothers were thenceforward illustrious for mighty labours of abstinence, until they received gifts of the Spirit also, the blessed Abraham receiving the power of working healings and driving out demons, he being above, while his brother the blessed Maro shunned these things, saying, 'Sir, I will have nothing to do with things that gain very vain glory for someone but deceive certain persons.' And many would seek assistance with these, but when he saw these persons coming to be healed he would shut his door and remain silent. For from the very beginning also he had made a great segment from a hollow tree and set himself up inside it, having taken it inside the enclosure in a certain corner; and he used to stand in it. ... [After Abraham died, Maro left his hollow tree and assumed his brother's position on top of the stone column.]

(p. 64) ... And from that time the multitude began to gather together to the saint in numbers many times as great as came to his brother Abraham; it was also very hateful to him that anyone should come and bring him a sick person or one possessed with a demon, but he would at once drive him out, saying these words, 'O wretched men, what has misled you into leaving God's altar and his great power which took up its dwelling in the saints who were slain in his name, and loved him and did his will, and coming to me the wretched man and provoker of God? Indeed, if I were one who pleased and loved God and did his will, you ought not to have come to me and neglected the saints, let alone when I provoke and irritate God. And there is another thing that you should know and understand, that it was because of my sins that I came up here to ask mercy like every man, not because of my righteousness. To (p. 65) myself the madman and man of evil life why do you come?' And so this wonderful man as if to drive arrogance from him and avoid the vain praise of men, even though he was gentle and kind, would violently and with anger drive away those who came to gaze at him as a great and righteous man. ... (tr. E.W. Brooks)

11.11 Western monasticism in the sixth century: *The Rule of Benedict* 48.1–9

Despite the prestige of Antony and other solitary ascetics during Late Antiquity, it was communal asceticism which proved to have the greater impact both then and subsequently. The *Rule of Benedict*, drawn up by the Italian monk Benedict of Nursia (*c.* 480–*c.* 550) and first implemented in his monastery at Monte Cassino, epitomises this. It drew upon and synthesised principles articulated by earlier advocates of the superiority of the communal life – Caesarius of Arles, John Cassian, and Augustine in the west, Basil of Caesarea and Pachomius in the east. Benedict's formulation imposed an austere and tightly ordered regime, but one tempered by humanity – features reflected in this short extract. The assumption of literacy is again also notable. At the same time, his *Rule* came to acquire such prestige that it was to exert a profound influence on the subsequent development of monasticism in western Europe. Further reading: Lawrence 1989: ch. 2.

Concerning daily manual labour. (1) Idleness is the enemy of the soul, and for this reason the brethren ought to be occupied at certain times with manual labour, and at other times again with reading about holy matters. (2) This is why we think times for both should be organised according to the following arrangement, (3) namely that from Easter until the Kalends of October they should go out in the morning and from the first hour until about the fourth do the work that needs doing. (4) From the fourth hour to about the sixth they should devote themselves to reading. (5) After the sixth hour, when they have finished eating, they should rest on their beds in absolute silence; if anyone wishes to read by themselves, let them read so that they disturb no one else. (6) Prayer at the ninth hour should be said earlier than usual, at half past eight. Then once again, they should work at what needs doing until evening prayer. (7) If necessity or poverty means that they must work at gathering the harvest themselves, they should not be despondent, (8) because then they are truly monks, if they live by the work of their own hands, like our fathers and the apostles. (9) But let everything be done in moderation, out of consideration for those who are weak.

12

BISHOPS

One of the most striking differences between late Roman society and that of earlier centuries is the increasing prominence of bishops within their communities. In part this was a result of the extra-ecclesiastical powers that Constantine bestowed on them (e.g., 12.5). It was also a reflection of their continuity – the fact that they usually held office in the same community until their death, unlike senior imperial officials who could expect to serve in a province for perhaps two to three years before moving on elsewhere. That stabilising role became even more important as the infrastructure of government began to crumble in the west during the fifth century. Finally, there is the fact that bishops were increasingly drawn from the local elites who had been used to providing community leaders for centuries.

The passages in this chapter direct attention to various themes relating to bishops. After considering an episcopal career inscription that epitomises some of those themes (12.1), the issue of selection of bishops is examined through the requirements laid down by a church council in the mid-fourth century (12.2), while a cautionary tale from the experience of Augustine shows why and how things could go wrong when such elementary principles were ignored (12.3). Another document, from the late fifth century, implies concern about the priorities of those being appointed bishops (12.4).

The most important extra-ecclesiastical power Constantine gave bishops was the right to hear court cases (12.5) – a responsibility that could prove to be a mixed blessing, at least for those bishops who took their duties seriously (12.6; cf. 11.9 (8)).

Much of the surviving epigraphic evidence about bishops reflects their role as builders, whether of churches (12.7) or of other structures of benefit to the wider community (12.8). This leads naturally into the other charitable activities of bishops, whether it be relieving a famine (12.9) or organising institutions to provide the needy with help in the longer-term (12.10) (cf. 13.9 for the ransoming of prisoners). It is perhaps not surprising that these final items derive from the post-Roman west.

Further reading: Jones 1964: ch. 22; Chadwick 1980; Lane Fox 1986: ch. 10; Brown 1992: 96–103; Barnes 1993: ch. 19; Hunt 1998b.

12.1 An episcopal career: *MAMA* 1.170

This inscription presents the interesting case history of a bishop in Asia Minor during the early fourth century. Significantly, his family background was in the local elite. He spent a period of time in imperial service – most scholars assume in the army, though since *militia* could mean service in the civilian administration in Late Antiquity, this is an alternative possibility (cf. Wischmeyer 1990: 235). By this stage he was a Christian (for Christians in the army of this period, see Tomlin 1998: 23–5) and he duly suffered persecution at the hands of Maximinus Daia's associates. Subsequently he went to live in the city of Laodicea in Phrygia (his place of origin may have been a village in its territory) where he was appointed bishop. In this capacity he engaged in – and advertised – construction activities analogous to those which his non-Christian forbears might have been expected to do on behalf of their city in times past. (It has been suggested that he might in fact have been bishop of a heterodox Christian group, but the evidence is circumstantial.) Further reading: Wischmeyer 1990; Mitchell 1993: vol. 2, 82, 102; Tabbernee 1997: 426–44; White 1997: 171–7.

I, Marcus Julius Eugenius, son of Cyrillus Celer of Kouessa, town councillor (*bouleutēs*), did military service in the office of the governor of Pisidia and married Flavia Julia Flaviana, the daughter of the senator Gaius Nestorianus. I served with distinction, and during the period when the order was issued by Maximinus for the Christians to sacrifice and not be released from the army, I stood firm through very many tortures at the hands of the governor Diogenes. I was eager to be released from the army and defend the faith of the Christians. After spending a short time in the city of the Laodiceans, I was appointed bishop by the will of almighty God, and served with great distinction as bishop for twenty-five whole years. I rebuilt the whole church from its foundations and all the adornments around it – porticos, four-sided porticos, paintings, mosaics, a fountain, a gateway – and I put up all the stone work – in a word, everything. When I was about to depart this human life, I made a tomb and sarcophagus for myself on which I had these words inscribed for the enhancement of the church and of my family.

12.2 Qualifications of would-be bishops:
Council of Serdica Canon 10

The Council of Serdica was called by the emperors Constans and Constantius II in 343 primarily to determine the orthodoxy or otherwise of Athanasius, bishop of Alexandria, but since the eastern and western bishops disagreed so strongly on this issue that the former refused to attend, the council ended up being a western affair presided over by the experienced Spanish bishop Ossius. Among its conclusions was the following which set out expectations as to the prior experience of anyone being considered for appointment as a bishop, and 'appears to be the earliest enactment of its kind' (Hess 1958: 105). Needless to say, the fourth century subsequently produced some prominent exceptions to this rule, most famously Ambrose of Milan. On the background to the council, see Barnes 1993: ch. 8; for this canon, see Hess 1958: 103–8.

Ossius the bishop said, 'And I think very careful consideration needs to be given to the following. If any wealthy man or lawyer from the courts or the bureaucracy should be requested as bishop, he should not be appointed unless he has first carried out the responsibility of reader and the offices of deacon and presbyter, and he may advance through each grade (if he is worthy) to the highest rank – the episcopate. For by holding the ranks for a considerable length of time, he can be tested as to his faith, moderation, seriousness, and modesty, and if he is deemed worthy, he can be honoured with the holy episcopate. For it is not appropriate, nor do good sense or order allow, for someone who is newly baptised to be ordained casually or lightly as bishop or presbyter or deacon – especially since the teacher of the gentiles, the blessed apostle [Paul] is seen to have forbidden this and commanded that it not be done [1 Tim. 3.6]. But those whose life as been tested over a long period of time and whose worth has been proven [are to be appointed].' Everyone said that they approved this.

12.3 A cautionary tale: Augustine *Letter*
20*.2.3–5.4

The following extract from the longest of the recently discovered letters of Augustine presents a cautionary tale on the need for great care in the selection of bishops. Augustine openly acknowledges his responsibility for the problems that resulted from the over-hasty ordination of the young man in question, while also indicating the part played by contemporary circumstances, namely the great influx of former Donatists into the church following the Council of Carthage in 411. At the same time, the letter contains much interesting detail relevant to other subjects, such as the existence of formal registers of the poor in receipt of church support (cf. Rouche 1974; Waha 1976), and the fact that Punic – the language of the Phoenician settlers who had founded Carthage in the eighth century BC – was still widely spoken in rural north Africa and was a consideration in the appointment of clergy (cf. Brown 1968; Millar 1968). Further reading: Frend 1982.

2. ... (3) Antoninus came to Hippo as a small boy with his mother and stepfather. They were so poor that they lacked the means to feed themselves on a daily basis. Then when they had thrown themselves on the resources of the church and I had discovered that Antoninus' natural father was still alive and that the mother had joined herself to this other man after separating from her husband, I persuaded both of them to observe continence. (4) The man entered the monastery with the boy, and she was placed on the register of the poor (*matricula pauperum*) whom the church supports, and in this way, by the mercy of God, they all came to be under our care. (5) Then with the passage of time – I won't linger on the many details – the man died, the mother grew old, the boy grew up. He took on the position of reader among his fellows, and began to show such potential that brother Urbanus (at that time a presbyter with us and in charge of the monastery, but now bishop of the church at Sicca) wanted him to be made presbyter on a certain large rural estate in our diocese; I was absent at the time, but before setting out I told him to provide someone whom a neighbouring bishop could ordain for that place, if my return was not imminent. (6) In the event this was not able to happen because Antoninus was unwilling. But when I learned about this later, I began to consider him capable of such a responsibility, not because I knew him as well as I should, but on the recommendation of head of the monastery.

3. Meanwhile I was finding it hard to manage such a large diocese in the way circumstances demanded, since many people had joined the church from the Donatists not only in the city but also in the countryside. After careful deliberation with the brothers, it seemed best to me that in the settlement of Fussala (which came under the see of Hippo) someone should be ordained bishop who could take responsibility for that region. (2) I sent a message to the senior bishop, he agreed to come, but at the last minute the priest whom I had thought suitable deserted us. What then was I to do, if I were not to postpone such an important business? (3) I was afraid that when the holy old man who had with difficulty come to us from far away returned home from us without having accomplished anything, the hearts of all those for whom this was of vital importance would be broken and there would be found those whom the enemies of the church would deceive with mockery of our failed

efforts. So I believed it would be best to propose for ordination someone who was at hand, whom I had heard knew the Punic language, and when I proposed him, the responsibility rested with me. For they did not request him on their own initiative, but in the same way they did not dare to reject someone from my people of whom I approved.

4. In this way I imposed such an enormous responsibility on a young man not much more than twenty years of age who was unproven in the work of the successive grades of clergy and was unknown to me with regard to matters about which I ought to have known beforehand. (2) My great error will be obvious to you. Observe what followed. The heart of the young man took fright at his sudden elevation to the rank of bishop when he had done nothing previously to warrant it. Then realising that the clergy and people submitted to him in whatever he instructed, he became puffed up with the arrogance of power and instead of teaching by word, he compelled by command in everything. He was glad to see himself feared when he did not see himself loved.

5. So that he might fill out the role, he sought out like-minded men ... 6. ... (3) Anyone who fell into their hands lost money, furniture, clothing, livestock, produce, wood, even stones. (4) The homes of some people were seized, and were even torn down in certain cases, so that they could be carried away for the construction of new buildings he was demanding. Some things were bought without being paid for. The fields of some people were invaded and left stripped of several years' produce. Some of them were retained and occupied pending an episcopal decision. ...

12.4 Appropriate conduct for a bishop: *Ancient Statutes of the Church* Canons 1–10

The document from which the following extract comes was written with a view to reforming the western church in the final decades of the fifth century. Although its authorship is uncertain, it was written in southern Gaul and its most recent editor has argued that it was the work of Gennadius of Marseilles. It ranges quite widely, but it begins by focusing on the lifestyle appropriate to bishops, which suggests that the author saw this as a fundamental problem in this period in the west. Its advocacy of ascetic principles reflects the influence of monasticism, and implies that contemporary bishops were seen as not being sufficiently separated from worldly concerns. The document is also of interest since it anticipates many of the reforms of the Gallic church championed by Caesarius of Arles in the early decades of the next century. Another theme is the need for the bishop to show due deference to his clergy. Further reading: Munier 1960; Klingshirn 1994: ch. 3.

(1) A bishop should have a humble dwelling not far from his church.

(2) A bishop should occupy a more elevated seat in a meeting of presbyters in church, but at home he should acknowledge the presbyters as his colleagues.

(3) A bishop should not make his personal property a matter of concern for himself, but should give his time only to reading, prayer, and preaching the word of God.

(4) A bishop's furniture should be of minimal cost and his tableware and food simple, and he should acquire the authority of his rank from his faith and his upright living.

(5) A bishop should not read pagan books (*gentilium libros*), and should only read heretical writings from necessity or circumstance.

(6) A bishop should not undertake the legal protection of wills.

(7) A bishop should not himself directly administer the support of widows, orphans, and travellers, but should do so through a senior presbyter or archdeacon.

(8) A bishop should not go to court when provoked over trivial matters.

(9) A bishop prevented from attending a synod by a sufficiently serious constraint should nevertheless send a representative in his place, adopting with the saving truth of faith whatever the synod decides.

(10) A bishop should not ordain clergy without the advice of his fellow presbyters, so that he can enquire into their reputation among the populace.

12.5 The judicial power of bishops: *Sirmondian Constitutions* 1

In this law, Constantine reiterates an earlier edict of his (cf. *Theodosian Code* 1.27.1 (318)) establishing a judicial role for bishops, but because it has been preserved in a manuscript independent of the edited version in the *Theodosian Code*, it includes a fuller exposition of its background and rationale. One of the most interesting features of this document is the fact that the reiteration was prompted by the disbelief of a senior official (and a Christian, at that) that Constantine had really intended to give bishops such wide-ranging powers. Although changes designed to reduce the scope of episcopal power in this area were introduced during the first half of the fifth century, Constantine's initiative marks a dramatic step in the enhancement of bishops' community-wide role. Further reading: Lamoreaux 1995; Hunt 1998b: 272–6.

The Emperor Constantine Augustus to Ablabius, Praetorian Prefect:

We are very surprised that Your Gravity, who is replete with justice and the true religion, wished to make certain from Our Clemency what Our Moderation had previously decided concerning the judicial rulings of bishops and what we now wish to be observed, Ablabius, dearly loved 'father'. And so because you wanted us to provide you with this information, we are again promulgating the programme of the salutary law we previously issued. As the provisions of our edict made clear, we decree that judicial rulings of any kind made by bishops are to be treated as unalterable and imperishable, irrespective of the age [of the litigants]. In other words, whatever has been finalised by the decision of bishops is to be regarded as forever inviolable and worthy of respect.

Accordingly, whether a case involves minors or adults, we wish responsibility for the implementation of decisions made by bishops to rest with you, who holds the highest position in judicial matters, and with all other judicial authorities. Whoever is involved in a case, whether plaintiff or defendant, may opt for the court of the bishop's holy law and, irrespective of whether the case is in its initial stages or has been under way for a period of time, whether it is in its concluding stages or judgement has already begun to be pronounced – immediately, without any question, the litigants are to be directed to the bishop, even if the other party objects. For the innate authority (*auctoritas*) of the holy religion searches out and makes known many matters which the deceitful snares of legal technicalities do not allow to be brought into the open. All cases, therefore, whether dealt with under praetorian law or civil, are to be confirmed by the law of lasting permanence when finalised by the judgements of bishops, and a matter decided by the judgement of a bishop shall not be re-examined.

Furthermore, every judge is to accept a bishop's testimony beyond all doubt, and other testimony is not to be heard when that of a bishop has formally been promised by one of the parties. For that testimony is upheld by the authority of truth, that testimony is not open to improper influences when it is the product of the morally sound conscience of a holy man.

We decreed this in our previous salutary edict, and we confirm it in lasting law, thereby suppressing the malicious seeds of litigation, so that wretched men caught up in the lengthy, almost endless snares of legal action may escape from unprincipled law suits or from misguided greed through a timely resolution. Therefore, Your Gravity and everyone else shall observe what Our Clemency has decreed concerning the rulings of bishops and has now encompassed in this law, produced for the lasting benefit of all. Issued on the 3rd day before the Nones of May, at Constantinople, in the consulates of Dalmatius and Zenophilus [5 May 333].

12.6 The judicial burdens of bishops: Augustine *Commentaries on the Psalms* 25.13

The bishop's responsibility to hear legal cases not only imposed on his time, it also tested his patience and placed him in an invidious position *vis-à-vis* the litigants, as Augustine explained in the course of elucidating a psalm for his congregation. (Note that the numbering of *Psalms* in the old Latin Bible differed slightly from that in modern Bibles: hence Augustine's *Psalm* 25 is equivalent to *Psalm* 26 in modern versions.) For the experience of another bishop, cf. 11.9 (8).

For example, it happens that two people bring a case before a servant of God. Both of them say their case is a legitimate one, for if either of them thought there were no grounds for their case they would not ask for a judge. So this party considers their case to be justified, and so does the other party. They come before the judge. Before the verdict is given, they both say, 'We accept your decision; whatever you decide, God forbid that we should reject it.' What are you to say? 'Decide the case how you wish, but just make a decision; if I should take exception to anything at all, let me be excommunicated.' Both parties love the judge before he gives judgement. Nevertheless, when the decision has been pronounced, it will go against one of them, though neither of them knows against whom it will go. ...

But if the party against whom the decision has gone cannot now undo it – for as it happens it is not upheld by the law of the church, but by the law of the authorities of this world who have granted to the church that whatever verdict is reached there cannot be annulled – if therefore the decision cannot be undone, the losing party does not now want to reflect on their own role, but turn their blinded eyes against the judge, disparaging him as much as they can. 'He wanted to favour the other party,' they say. 'He has taken the side of the wealthy – either he has accepted something from them, or he was afraid of offending them.' They accuse him as though he has taken bribes. Moreover, if someone poor has brought a case against someone wealthy, and the decision has gone in favour of the poor person, then the wealthy person likewise says, 'He has taken bribes.' What bribes can be had from a poor person?! 'He saw the poor person,' they say, 'and to avoid being criticised for acting against the poor, he has suppressed justice and given a verdict contrary to the truth.' Since these accusations will necessarily be made, understand that only in the presence and sight of God, who alone sees who takes bribes and who does not, is it possible for those who do not take bribes to say, 'But I have walked in my integrity; redeem me and have mercy on me. My foot has stood firm on righteousness' [Ps. 26.11–12]. I have been harassed on every side by the disputing and provocation of those who, with human recklessness, have found fault with my judgement, but 'my foot has stood firm on righteousness.' Why 'on righteousness'? Because he has earlier said, 'And trusting in the Lord, I will not be moved' [Ps. 26.1].

12.7 Episcopal church-building: *CIL* 12.5336 (= *ILCV* 1806)

The following inscription, from a damaged lintel lacking its right-hand end, records the building activity of a fifth-century Gallic bishop who oversaw the reconstruction of his church at Narbonne following its destruction by fire (possibly as a result of a Gothic attack in the 420s or 430s: Marrou 1970: 339). It is of interest, therefore, as another example of episcopal building activity, but also for the evidence it provides of an episcopal dynasty and for the prominent role of a pious layman of high status in encouraging the work and covering a substantial portion of its costs. From the data in the inscription, it can be deduced that Rusticus became bishop on 9 October 427; he is known from other sources to have died in 461/2 (Marrou 1970: 348–9). Further reading: Marrou 1970; Matthews 1990: 341–2.

By the mercy of God and Christ, this lintel was put in place in the 4th year [of the reconstruction work], when Valentinian [III] was consul for the sixth time, three days before the Kalends of December [29 November 445], in the 19th year of Rusticus' episcopacy < ... > In the 15th year of his episcopacy, on the 5th day of that year, three days before the Ides of October [13 October 441], with Ursus the presbyter and Hermes the deacon and their assistants supervising, Bishop Rusticus – son of Bishop Bonosus and of the sister of Bishop Arator, companion of Bishop Venerius in the monastery and his fellow-presbyter in the church at Marseilles – began setting up the wall of the church which had previously been burnt down. On the 37th day <of the episcopal year? of the work?>, the dressed blocks of stone began to be put in place. In the 2nd year [of the reconstruction work], seven days before the Ides of October [9 October 443], Montanus the sub-deacon completed the apse. Marcellus, Prefect of the Gauls, and a worshipper of God (*cultor Dei*), entreated the bishop to undertake this work, promising the required resources which he provided from the two years of his administration: 600 *solidi* as pay for the artisans, 1500 *solidi* for the other expenses. Contributions [were received] from the following: from the holy Bishop Venerius, 1< ... > *solidi*, from Bishop Dynamius 5< ... > *solidi*, from Oresius 2< ... > *solidi*, from Agroecus < ... > and Deconia< ... >, from Saluti< ... >

12.8 Other forms of episcopal building work: *AE* (1911) 90 and *IEJ* 13 (1963) 325

(a) AE *(1911) 90*

This is one example of episcopal building activity of practical benefit, though nothing further is known about the bishop in question, while the Zenonopolis of the inscription could be in either Isauria or Lycia. Further reading: Delehaye 1911 (though he wrongly dates the inscription to 488, rather than 487: cf. Bagnall *et al.* 1987: 509).

Firminianus, our most devout bishop of this famous city of Zenonopolis, has completely restored the whole aqueduct of the holy martyr Socrates [in the year] after the consulate of the illustrious Flavius Longinus, in the 11th year of the indiction, and it flowed for the first time in the fountain in the four-sided portico of the same victorious [martyr] in the month of February. So pray, you who benefit, that by the intercession of the holy martyr this [aqueduct] is preserved intact for many very long ages. Auxanon, aqueduct-builder from Prymnesseus, did the work.

(b) IEJ *13 (1963), p. 325*

This inscription, from Scythopolis in Palestine, records the charitable building activities of the local bishop ('shepherd' was a common term for the office in Late Antiquity) on behalf of a marginalised group in need of practical help. The inscription was found outside the ancient city walls; if this is a fair guide to the location of the baths, then it is consistent with the usual exclusion of lepers from society. Further reading: Avi-Yonah 1963.

Having repaired the baths, Theodoros the shepherd assigns them to those ill with the very serious disease of leprosy. In the time of the 7th year of the indiction, in the year 622 [558/9].

12.9 Episcopal crisis-management: Sidonius Apollinaris *Letters* 6.12

Despite its heavily eulogistic tone, there is much to be learnt from the following letter, written by one fifth-century Gallic bishop to another. Most obviously, it illustrates episcopal intervention of a very practical sort in a large-scale crisis – food shortage arising from war. But even the more standard catalogue of virtues enumerated in the opening sections shows what was expected of a good bishop: concern for the poor, the ability to influence secular authorities, an ascetic lifestyle, construction of churches, skilled preaching, and the conversion of pagans or heretics. The letter also highlights the aristocratic origins of many Gallic bishops in this period: the recipient, Patiens of Lyons, has sufficient personal wealth to be able to provide the grain needed to relieve the food shortage, while Sidonius' use of hunting metaphors and allusions to pagan mythology likewise reflects an aristocratic milieu (for the broader context to all this, see Mathisen 1993: esp. ch. 9). It is also worth noting that 'implicit in Sidonius' admiration for Patiens' demonstration of charitable largesse is an acknowledgement of more mundane considerations; in other years Patiens would not have handed out his stocks for nothing, he would have sold them' (Harries 1994: 227).

The crisis arose as a result of Gothic attempts to expand their Aquitanian kingdom north and north-east beyond the Loire and Rhone, as a result of which Sidonius' episcopal seat of Clermont in the Auvergne was repeatedly besieged during the early 470s. That Clermont survived was to a significant degree due to Burgundian aid, and it is their ruler Chilperic who is alluded to in (3) (for background, see Harries 1994: 222–7). Like most other barbarian peoples settled in the empire, the Burgundians adhered to the heretical Arian strand of Christianity, to which Sidonius' reference to Photinians (4) is an allusion (Photius was a fourth-century bishop whose heretical teachings had much in common with those of Arius).

Sidonius to the Lord Bishop Patiens, greetings. (1) People hold varying views, but I believe that a man really lives for his own benefit when he lives for the benefit of others and, taking compassion on the misfortunes and neediness of the faithful, accomplishes on earth the works of heaven. 'What are you getting at?', you ask. That maxim applies especially to you, blessed father, for whom it is not enough only to supply resources to those situations of need of which you are aware and who, by extending your pursuit of love to the far boundaries of Gaul, is accustomed to show concern for the interests of the needy before worrying about their identity. (2) No-one suffering from poverty or physical infirmity is disadvantaged if they are unable to seek you out, for you come first with open hands to those whose feet lack the strength to reach you. Your vigilance crosses into other provinces and in this way the breadth of your care is spread abroad so that the straitened circumstances of those situated far away receive attention; and it happens that because the diffidence of those at a distance moves you no less than the pleas of those nearby, you have often wiped away the tears of those whose eyes you have not seen.

(3) I say nothing of what you daily bear through unceasing

watchfulness, prayer and financial outlay on account of the needs of your impoverished townsfolk. I say nothing about the moderation with which you always behave, and the high regard for both your cultivated tastes and your self-restraint so that, as is well known, the present king is always praising your dinners, and the queen your fasting. I say nothing about your enhancing the church entrusted to you so attractively that an observer is unsure whether the new work rising up or the old being restored is better. (4) I say nothing of your responsibility for the emerging foundations of basilicas in many places and for their greatly increased adornment. And while the stature of the faith is increasing in many ways through your activities, the number of heretics alone is decreasing: as if on an apostolic hunt, you snare the wild hearts of the Photinians in the spiritual nets of your preaching, and the barbarians, compliant now whenever they are convicted by your word, follow your trail until you, ever trustworthy angler for souls, pull them out from the deep abyss of error.

(5) Credit for some of these deeds ought perhaps to be shared with other colleagues. But there is one item owed to your credit, by 'individual entitlement', as the jurists say, the truth of which your modesty cannot deny: after the Goths had finished their plundering and the cornfields had been consumed by fire, at your own personal expense (*peculiari sumptu*) you sent free grain to meet the general scarcity throughout the devastated parts of Gaul, although you would have been giving more than enough help to people wasting away from hunger if that produce had been for sale and not a gift. We have seen the roads congested with your grain; we have seen more than one granary along the banks of the Saone and the Rhone filled by you alone.

(6) Let the fictions of pagan myths give way, especially Triptolemus, supposedly received in heaven for discovering ears of grain for the first time – he whom his homeland of Greece, famous for its builders, artists and sculptors, consecrated temples to, made statues of and depicted in paintings. A tale of dubious worth presents him as travelling among the still uncivilised people of Dodona in two boats (to which the poets in time assigned the shape of serpents) distributing sowing seed which was unknown to them. I will say nothing about your generosity to the inland regions, but you filled two rivers rather than two boats from your granaries for distribution to the cities on the Tyrrhenian Sea. (7) But if as a man of religion you are perhaps displeased at being praised through examples drawn from the Hellenic superstition of Eleusis which you

consider inappropriate, let us draw comparisons with the histori-
cally attested diligence of the revered patriarch Joseph (setting to
one side respect for his mystical understanding); since he foresaw
the failure of the crops that was to follow the seven fruitful years, he
was easily able to provide relief. In keeping with the moral spirit of
the story, it is my view that a man who, without inspired fore-
knowledge, provides relief in an unexpected crisis of a comparable
kind is in no way inferior.

(8) I cannot conjecture the full extent of gratitude discharged to
you by the leaders of the communities of Arles, of Riez, of Avignon,
of Orange, of Alba, of Valence and of Tricastina, because it is difficult to measure in full the thanks of those to whom, as we know,
food has been supplied without any charge. However, I give you the
most profound thanks on behalf of the chief town of the Auvergne
[Clermont], to which you thought to bring aid without the induce-
ment of being in the same province, of geographical proximity, of a
convenient river, or of any offer of payment. (9) And so they relay
through me their great gratitude for having been fortunate enough
to achieve, through the abundance of your bread, a sufficiency of
their own. If I seem to have fulfilled adequately the duties of my
designated role, I will now become a messenger in place of an envoy.
I want you to know at once: your achievement is spoken of
throughout all Aquitania; in the hearts and prayers of everyone, you
are loved and praised, you are longed for and honoured. In the
midst of these evil times, you are a good priest, a good father, a
good year to those for whom it has been worthwhile to experience
their hunger and its risks, if they could not otherwise have experienced your generosity. See fit to remember me, Lord Bishop.

12.10 Episcopal organisation of charitable institutions: The *Lives of the Holy Fathers of Merida* 5.3

The following passage, probably written in the seventh century, provides a particularly interesting case of the deployment of church resources for the benefit of the
poor, in this instance in Gothic Spain during the late sixth century. It describes the
operation of a hospital and, even more intriguingly, a sort of ecclesiastical bank.
Further reading: Fear 1997: xxix–xxxiii (context), 72–6 (commentary).

At the very beginning of his episcopacy Masona established many
monasteries, enriching them with much land, he built several
churches of marvellous construction, and he brought many souls to

dedication to God there. Then he built a hospice (*xenodocium*) and endowed it with great estates, and after providing it with servants and doctors, he commanded them to devote themselves to the needs of travellers and the sick and he gave them the following precept, that the doctors should go unceasingly throughout the whole area of the city and whoever they found ill, whether slave or free, Christian or Jew, they should take them up in their own arms and carry them back to the hospice. After preparing a bed of fresh straw, they were to lay the sick person there and provide them with enough simple, nourishing food until with God's help they restored the invalid to their former healthy state. But whatever quantity of comforts were provided from the hospice's estates for the many ill brought in, the holy man still regarded it as insufficient. Adding even greater benefits to all these, he ordered the doctors to see to it with prudent care that they receive a half of all the rents brought to the church courtyard by all the accountants from all the church's estates, and that these be distributed to the patients.

Furthermore, if any inhabitant of the city or peasant from the countryside came to the church in need, and asked for wine, oil or honey from his stewards and produced a very small jar into which it could be poured, and the holy man saw him, then, always happy in appearance with a joyful face, he used to order the little jar to be smashed and provided a larger one.

God alone knows the full extent of his generosity towards the poor. However let me also recount one particular instance of this. So great was his concern for the afflictions of all the poor that he entrusted 2,000 *solidi* to the care of a respected deacon at the basilica of the most holy Eulalia by the name of Redemtus. Whenever anyone approached the deacon with a pressing need, after giving a guarantee [of repayment], he received as much as he wished from this fund without delay or difficulty and took care of his straitened circumstances. ...

13

MATERIAL RESOURCES

The fact that bishops were able to undertake charitable projects of the sort illustrated in the previous chapter is a reminder that Christianity in Late Antiquity was more than just a spiritual enterprise. This chapter aims to draw attention to the material basis of the church's activities by illustrating its sources of income and some of the problems involved.

Although the church obviously had income from members during the first three centuries (cf. 2.1 (5)), there can be no doubt that Constantine's decision to support Christianity made a dramatic difference to its material resources. For not only did the emperor ameliorate its legal status, he also began adding substantially to its wealth, the most graphic illustration of which is provided by the *Book of Pontiffs* (13.1). Over the years, other wealthy individuals followed suit (13.2, 13.3; cf. 15.5). Alongside this, a papyrus document provides interesting detail about what a humbler church in a rural area might expect to possess (13.4). Prominent among the property detailed in most of these initial four items are various types of metal objects used in church ritual, and actual examples from Late Antiquity have been recovered from various parts of the empire (13.5, 13.6).

Church leaders did not like to discourage giving by the wealthy, but it is evident that the latter often preferred to invest in buildings, rather than other more pressing needs, the meeting of which might not leave any obvious physical memorial (13.7). Churches could also find themselves facing legal difficulties if they needed ready cash and contemplated selling assets (13.8). Even disposal of church property for the legitimate purpose of ransoming captives could attract criticism (13.9).

The chapter concludes with a passage that bears on the issue of attitudes to wealth. An earlier extract (11.7) included reference to the fact that some Christians believed the wealthy could not expect entry to heaven, so it is of great interest to find one of the leading lights of fourth-century asceticism, Basil of Caesarea, expressing quite a balanced assessment of the role of material resources in the life of the Christian (13.10).

Further reading: Jones 1964: 894–910; Gould 1987; Leyerle 1994; MacCormack 1997; Janes 1998; Hunt 1998b: 257–62.

13.1 Constantine's endowment of the Lateran church, Rome: *The Book of Pontiffs* 34.9–12

The *Book of Pontiffs* (*Liber Pontificalis*) is a collection of biographies of bishops of Rome from St Peter through to the Middle Ages, first compiled in the sixth century and then regularly added to thereafter. The chapters dealing with the early centuries of the papacy are brief and of variable historical value (e.g., the beginning of the chapter from which this passage comes explains the conversion of Constantine in terms of his wishing to be healed of leprosy). However, the life of Silvester (314–35) includes extensive detail about Constantine's gifts to the church, and scholars are agreed that this portion is genuine. The following extract describes most of what Constantine gave to the 'Basilica of Constantine', i.e. the Lateran church (though for reasons of length the final portion concerning its baptismal font has been omitted). The rest of the chapter (not translated here) continues with details of gifts to St Peter's and other churches in Rome before moving on to bequests to churches in other parts of Italy. Although it soon makes for monotonous reading, it is an invaluable and striking indication of what Constantine's support for the church meant in practical, material terms. Further reading: Duchesne 1955–57: 191–2; Pietri 1976: 77–83; Davis 1989 (including a complete translation down to 715, and a very helpful glossary).

(9) In Silvester's time, Constantine Augustus constructed the following churches and adorned them:
The Basilica of Constantine, where he placed the following gifts:

- an altar canopy (*fastigium*) of beaten silver, which has in front the Saviour seated in a chair, 5 foot high, weighing 120 lb, and the twelve apostles, each 5 foot high and weighing 90 lb, with crowns of purest silver; (10) likewise, viewed from behind in the apse, the Saviour seated on a throne, 5 foot high, made from purest silver and weighing 140 lb, and four silver angels, each 5 foot high and weighing 105 lb, with gems from Alabanda [in Caria] for eyes, and holding spears; the canopy itself, made from polished silver, weighs 2025 lb
- vaulting of purest gold, and a light of purest gold which hangs

beneath the canopy with fifty dolphins of purest gold, weighing 50 lb, with chains which weigh 25 lb
– four crowns of purest gold with twenty dolphins, weighing 15 lb each
– the vault of the basilica with beaten gold across its width and its length, 500 lb
– seven altars of purest silver, each weighing 200 lb
– seven golden patens, each weighing 30 lb
– sixteen silver patens, each weighing 30 lb
– seven chalices (*scyphi*) of purest gold, each weighing 10 lb
– a single chalice of coral stone, adorned on all sides with emerald and jacinth gems, inlaid with gold, the whole of which weighs 20 lb and 3 oz
– twenty silver chalices, each weighing 15 lb
– two containers (*amae*) of purest gold, each weighing 50 lb and able to hold 3 measures of liquid
– twenty silver containers, each weighing 10 lb and able to hold 1 measure of liquid
– forty smaller chalices of purest gold, each weighing 1 lb
– fifty smaller serving chalices, each weighing 2 lb

(11) Decoration in the basilica:

– a chandelier (*farum cantharum*) made of purest gold, in front of the altar, in which burns oil of precious nard, with eighty dolphins, weighing 30 lb
– a silver chandelier with twenty dolphins weighing 50 lb, in which burns oil of precious nard
– forty-five silver chandeliers in the centre of the basilica, each weighing 30 lb, in which burns the oil described above
– on the right-hand side of the basilica, forty silver lights (*fara*), each weighing 20 lb
– twenty-five silver chandeliers on the left of the basilica, each weighing 20 lb
– fifty silver candlesticks (*cantara cirostata*) in the centre of the basilica, each weighing 20 lb
– three containers (*metretae*) of purest silver, each weighing 300 lb, able to hold 10 measures of liquid
– seven brass candelabra, in front of the altars, 10 feet high, decorated in silver with inlaid reliefs of the prophets, each weighing 300 lb

(12) For provision for the lights he designated:

– the estate (*massa*) Gargiliana, in the territory of Suessa, yielding 400 *solidi*
– the estate Bauronica, in the territory of Suessa, yielding 360 *solidi*
– the estate Auriana, in the territory of Laurentum, yielding 500 *solidi*
– the estate Urbana, in the territory of Antium, yielding 260 *solidi*
– the estate Sentiliana, in the territory of Ardea, yielding 260 *solidi*
– the estate Castis, in the territory of Catena, yielding 1,000 *solidi*
– the estate Trapeas, in the territory of Catena, yielding 1,650 *solidi*
– two censers of purest gold, weighing 30 lb
– a sweet-smelling gift in front of the altars, 150 lb each year

13.2 Endowment of a church by an imperial courtier: The *Cornutian Deed*

This legal document, preserved in a twelfth-century copy in the Vatican, sets out the provisions of the endowment of a church at Tibur (Tivoli) in central Italy in the final years of the western empire. The donor is not otherwise known (except that he owned a magnificent house on the Esquiline in Rome which he bequeathed to the church), though the second element in his name implies Germanic origin, which would not be unusual in a Roman army commander of this period. The content generally makes for interesting comparison with the previous item, especially because this document includes reference to textiles and books which are absent from Constantine's gifts in the *Book of Pontiffs*. On the other hand, the number of books is small compared with provincial churches in north Africa (3.3) and Egypt (13.4). The opening sentence is evidently the words of the twelfth-century copyist who wrote out what he could read of the original fifth-century document. Further reading: Duchesne 1955–57: cxlvi–cxlviii.

Authoritative copy of the charter of the church at Cornutia from the point at which we have been able to make sense of it.

< ... > namely that those who are subject to divine service might also be able to derive suitable sustenance from the place in which they serve; we also consider it appropriate that the temple of the divine religion be adorned every day with lights and that, when necessary expenses impinge with the passage of time, the costs involved in keeping the building in good order and repair are able to be met from this our gift. We are taking care of the requisite expenses for these items so that our service might be able to merit divine mercy. Moved by this consideration, I bequeath, by the terms of the present document, to the church of the Cornutan estate,

which is ours by law and which has been established and founded by me with the favour and help of God [the following]: Paternus Maranus Farm, Mount Paternus Farm, House of Mars Farm, Vegetes or Casa Proiectici Farm and Batilianus Farm – with the exception of Sigillosa, daughter of the tied tenants (*coloni*) Anastasius and Pica, whom we have retained and do retain as belonging to us by law – all situated in the province of Picenum, in the territory of Tibur, to be possessed clearly and directly with free title, with everything pertaining to them and in complete accordance with the law and the document drawn up, as I myself possess them, together with all the charges of formal registration and the expenses specified for the maintenance of lands tied to the aqueducts.

We also give to this same church the land on which it has been built with its surrounding grounds and by the aforementioned praetorian law we separate it and bequeath it to the clergy and guards to make gardens and houses. [There follows a description of the topographical features defining the area in question.]

Moreover I offer with the same generosity the [following] properties: that is, Callicianus Farm, New Cottage, Meadow Cottage, Martyr's Cottage, Crispinus' Cottage, Boaricus Farm, and Compact Cottage, situated in the province of Picenum, in the territory of Tibur, but retaining the use of the properties for myself for the rest of my life; by the generosity of this document I then transfer the properties to the same catholic church, on the legal requirement and condition that when, after my death, it shall also have acquired and laid legal claim to the income from them for itself, it will acknowledge in solemn manner its responsibility not only for the payment of taxes but also for the upkeep of the aqueducts, to the extent that it has been usual for these expenses to be defrayed by all owners of properties of this kind.

I also outlay silver for the adornment of the same church or for the celebration of the aforementioned holy mysteries, in the following forms, that is: a silver paten, one large silver chalice, two small silver chalices, one silver jug, a small vessel for offerings, a strainer, a censer, a silver cantharus lamp with eighteen chains and dolphins, four silver crown lamps with their own little chains, a silver lampstand; and in the burial place of martyrs (*confessio*), its two silver doors with their fastenings; all these items weigh in the city scales, by weight of silver, fifty-four pounds, seven ounces. Two bronze lamps, each with eight dolphins, and six large bronze vessels, twelve small ones, and two bronze lily-shaped lamps and two bronze lampstands; and also in textiles:

1 cape of pure silk, new with gold edging
1 cape of pure silk in four colours
[a further 8 capes of silk or linen]
and for archways 2 pure silk curtains, white with gold edging
2 purple curtains with gold edging
2 pure silk curtains, white with gold edging embroidered with
   feathers
2 curtains woven from silk, green and purple
2 curtains woven from silk, white and red
2 curtains woven from silk, white and purple
2 pure silk curtains, scarlet and green
[a further 58 curtains of silk or linen for various parts of the church]

also books (*codices*): the four gospels of the apostles, the psalmbook
and its companion.

[The donor then makes clear that none of his gifts are ever to be
alienated from the church and specifies penalties if this should
happen, namely that the donation reverts to his heirs.]

I have dictated this document of donation to my notary
Felicianus and, after it was read back, I have signed it in my own
hand in good faith and I, of my own will, have ordered that it be
entered in the official records, and with the concurrence of the
venerable presbyter, the deacons, and all the clergy of the aforementioned church, I have given my solemn promise concerning all the
aforementioned matters, on the 15th day before the Kalends of May
when our lord Leo, ever Augustus, was consul for the fourth time,
with the senator Probianus [17 April 471]. I, Flavius Valila, also
known as Theodorius, of senatorial rank, count, and master of both
branches of the army [infantry and cavalry], have consented to and
signed this donation, dictated by me and read back to me, of all the
abovementioned properties, of the silver and textiles, preserved and
guarded forever by the legal requirement and condition I have
imposed on this same donation, preserving for myself, to be sure,
the use of the abovementioned properties which I have preserved for
myself in the same document above.

13.3 The piety of a banker: *CIL* 11.288 and 294

The two most famous churches in Ravenna are S. Vitale and S. Apollinare in Classe,
noted for their beautiful mosaics, particularly those of Justinian and Theodora. The
inscriptions below show that the individual responsible for their construction was a
banker by the name of Julianus. Despite the havoc resulting from Justinian's long
campaign in the middle of the sixth century to reconquer Italy from the Goths,

Julianus clearly had plenty of money at his disposal, though perhaps he was based in the eastern Mediterranean. Further reading: Krautheimer 1965: 169–70; Deichmann 1969–89: vol. 2/2, 3–7, 21–7; Barnish 1985.

(a) CIL 11.288 (= ILCV 1795)

The basilica of the blessed martyr Vitalis, commissioned by the most blessed bishop Ecclesius [521–32], was built from the foundations, adorned and dedicated by Julianus the banker (*argentarius*), and consecrated by the very reverend bishop Maximianus [546–56] on the 12th day < ... > in the 6th year after the consulate of the younger Basilius [547].

(b) CIL 11.294 (= ILCV 695)

The basilica of the blessed priest Apollinaris, commissioned by the most blessed bishop Ursicinus [532–536], was built from the foundations, adorned and dedicated by Julianus the banker, and consecrated by the very reverend bishop Maximianus on the Nones of May in the 12th indiction, in the 8th year after the consulate of the younger Basilius [7 May 549].

13.4 Inventory of a village church: *P. Grenf.* 2.111

This papyrus document from the fifth or sixth century provides an interesting indication of what a church in a community of modest means (an Egyptian village) might be expected to possess when Christianity's legal status was assured (for church property before this was the case, see 3.3). Of special interest is the number of books (cf. 3.3, 13.2) and the fact that those made from parchment far outnumber those made of papyrus. As for some of the other items, the editors suggested that the curtains were 'either hangings of the altar canopy, or curtains in front of the sanctuary', while the iron rod was probably used for hanging the 'curtains over the central door of the sanctuary'; the linen cloths probably covered the altar, while the woollen cloths were perhaps the coverings for the eucharist. The repetition of 'bronze altar' half way down the list is presumably a case of scribal error.

+ Record of the holy treasures and other furniture of the holy church of Apa Psaios in the village of Ibion, assigned to the care of the very devout John, presbyter and steward, Choiak 15 [= 11 December], 13th year of the indiction, as follows:

silver cups 3
silver jug 1

curtains 2
iron rod 1
small one of the same 1
marble tabletop 1
bronze tripod for the tabletop 1
linen cloths for the table 23
woollen cloths 5
door curtains 6
old one of the same 1
woollen hanging 1
cloth hanging 1
bronze lampstands 4
iron lampstands 2
bronze altar 1
bronze altar 1
bronze basin 1
bronze flask 1
bronze baptismal fonts 2
lamps 6 wicks 6
bronze boat-shaped lamps 4 wicks 4
parchment books 21
papyrus books 3
cup 1
ladle 1
knife 1
bier 1
wooden table 1
leather cushions 2
censer 1
wooden chairs 3
benches 2
triple weaving web 1
cupboard 1
bronze vessel 1

[on the reverse] [Written] by me, Elias, archdeacon, for the holy
father George.

13.5 Church silverware from Syria (1):
The Hama treasure

The items pictured here (**Figure 13.5**) derive from sixth-century Syria. There is good reason to think that they formed part of a larger collection of silverware from the church in an ancient Syrian village known as Kaper Koraon, which probably lay about 50 miles south-east of Antioch; however, these particular items are part of what is better known as the Hama treasure, after the (supposed) location of their discovery in 1910 (for their complex history, see Mundell Mango 1986: ch. 2). The items in the photograph comprise two lampstands, a paten (or serving dish), two chalices, a flask, a box, and a strainer. As can be seen, a number of the items are inscribed with details of the individual(s) responsible for donating the item to the church – so, e.g., one of the lampstands has the following: 'Having made a vow, they fufilled their vow to [the church] of St Sergius and Bacchus. Sergius, Symeon, Daniel [and] Thomas, sons of Maximinus, village of Kaper Koraon.' For those who could never hope to have the means to fund the building of a church, this was the next best way of demonstrating piety and ensuring one's name was remembered. Finally, it is worth noting that this treasure is consistent with the archaeological remains of houses and churches from the region, which attest the considerable prosperity enjoyed there in Late Antiquity (for a useful summary of archaeological work in the region, see Foss 1995: 213–23; for excellent photographs, Peña 1997). Further reading: Mundell Mango 1986; Painter 1977.

Figure 13.5   Church silverware from the Hama treasure
Source: Walters Art Gallery, Baltimore.

13.6 Church silverware from Syria (2):
The Riha paten

This beautiful silver paten or serving plate (35 cm diameter) (**Figure 13.6**) was said to have been discovered near the modern Syrian village of Riha in 1908, though it is now thought to be another item which was once a part of the silverware belonging to the church at Kaper Koraon (cf. 13.5). The picture shows Christ twice behind an altar giving bread and wine to two groups of men, presumably the apostles, and the paten was itself presumably used in the eucharist at Kaper Koraon. The figures are gilded, enhancing the paten's value considerably, and stamps on the reverse allow it to be dated to the 570s. Around the rim is an inscription which reads: 'For the rest [of the soul] of Sergia, daughter of John, and of Theodosius, and for the salvation of Megas and Nonnos and of their children.' Further reading: Mundell Mango 1986: 165–70.

Figure 13.6   The Riha paten

Source: Dumbarton Oaks Collection, Washington DC.

13.7 Where are the resources of wealthy Christians best directed? Jerome *Letter* 130.14

Demetrias was a teenage girl of high aristocratic birth who in 413 decided to dedicate herself to a life of virginity, and Jerome was asked by her family to provide her with guidance on how best to go about fulfilling her objective (Kelly 1975: 312–13). Jerome's lengthy response covers a range of subjects, including the following advice on material possessions. Despite Jerome having a personal interest in encouraging the direction of material resources towards monasteries such as his own, his remarks still provide a telling critique of the natural inclination on the part of Christian aristocrats to plough their money into bricks and mortar. Old habits died hard.

[Claiming that he has no need to warn Demetrias against avarice, Jerome proceeds to discuss various relevant New Testament texts, culminating in the cautionary story of Ananias and Sapphira (Acts 5.1–11); he then continues:] From the time you dedicate yourself to perpetual virginity, your possessions are no longer your own; or rather, they are truly yours, because they have begun to be Christ's. While your grandmother and mother are alive, they should be administered in accordance with their wishes. But if they die and rest in the sleep of the saints (for I know that it is their wish that you should outlive them), when you are more mature in years, and your will is sterner and your ability to make decisions more resolute, you will do with it what seems best to you, or rather, what the Lord commands – for you will know that you possess only those things which you have disbursed in good works. Other people may build churches and adorn their walls with marble façades, transporting masses of columns and gilding their capitals which are incapable of enjoying the costly decoration, embellishing the doors with ivory and silver, and golden altars with precious stones. I do not censure this, I do not oppose it. 'Let each person be fully persuaded in their own mind' [Rom. 14.5]. It is better to do this than to brood over wealth that has been stored away. But there is another possibility for you: to cloth Christ in the person of the poor, to visit him in the ailing, to feed him in the hungry, to welcome him in those who need shelter, especially those belonging to the household of faith [Gal. 6.10], to sustain monasteries of virgins, to take care of the servants of God and of the poor in spirit who serve the same Lord as you day and night. While on earth, they imitate the life of angels and speak only of the praises of God. If they have food and clothing, they rejoice as if these were riches, and desire nothing more, provided they can maintain their calling. For if they desire more, they prove themselves unworthy of even these things which are necessary.

13.8 Restrictions on the alienation of church property: Justinian *Novel* 120.1, 10

Issued in Constantinople in 544, this law is of interest for what it implies about the difficulties individual churches faced should they need to realise any of their assets. The use of church property for the redemption of captives (i.e., from foreign peoples) had a long and honourable pedigree, though was not always without controversy (cf. 13.9). Also of interest is the detail about the variety of charitable institutions run by the church in Constantinople. The 'Great Church' is Hagia Sophia (cf. 14.5).

Since many different laws about the alienation and leasing and hiring and the rest of the administration of church property have been set forth, we have decided that everything should be brought together in this present law.

(1) We therefore decree that those who administer the affairs of the most holy Great Church in the imperial city [Constantinople], or of the orphanage (*orphanotropheion*) or hostel (*xenodocheion*) or poor-house (*ptōchotropheion*) or hospital (*nosokomeion*), or of any other holy house in the imperial city or situated within its boundaries (with the sole exception of the holy monasteries), are not permitted to sell, or give, or exchange, or give as a reciprocal gift, or alienate in any way whatsoever, immovable property, or the right to receive the public grain dole, or rural slaves, with the sole exception of exchanges made with the imperial palace. ...

(10) Concerning the holy vessels and utensils (*skeuē*) belonging to the most holy Great Church in the imperial city or to other houses of prayer situated in whatever part of our state, we have generally decided that, except for the redemption of prisoners, these shall not otherwise be sold or mortgaged. But if there are more vessels and utensils in any of the aforementioned holy houses than there is need for, and it so happens that this holy place is burdened with debts and has no other movable property from which the debts might be discharged, we grant them permission either to sell – with a duly formulated deed of record (as previously stated) – to other holy places that have need of them vessels and utensils found to be in excess, or to melt them down and likewise sell them, and to hand over their value for the debt, so that immovable property is not alienated. ...

13.9 Using church property to redeem captives: *Life of Caesarius of Arles* 32–33

This passage, from the biography of the bishop of Arles in early sixth century, illus-

trates an important use to which church property was sometimes put in Late
Antiquity – redemption of individuals taken captive as a result of raids or war.
Although the law discussed in the previous passage allowed this as a good reason
for church vessels and utensils to be alienated, it is apparent from this case (and
others) that such action still attracted criticism, principally because many of these
items 'were donations or legacies from pious individuals for the salvation of their
souls [cf. 13.6], and it was not thought proper to alienate, as it were, the grounds
of their salvation' (Klingshirn 1985: 185). The context of this particular incident
was the Frankish and Burgundian siege of Arles in 508, relieved by Gothic forces
from Italy. The concern expressed at the end of (32) about captives perhaps
becoming Arians or Jews refers to the possibility of their being purchased by
someone of that creed, who might then persuade or coerce their slave to conform.
Further reading: Klingshirn 1985, 1994: 113–17.

32. The Goths returned to Arles with a huge number of captives,
who crowded into the holy churches; even the bishop's residence
was filled with a mass of unbelievers. The man of God [Caesarius]
distributed to those in great need a sufficiency of both food and
clothing until he could free individuals from captivity with a gift of
redemption. He spent all the silver which the reverend Aeonius, his
predecessor, had left for the church's altar, observing that the Lord
moistened bread in a clay dish, not a silver cup, and that he also
commanded his disciples not to own gold or silver. Indeed this most
holy work was carried on even to the extent of giving away the holy
eucharist vessels. And when the censers, cups, and serving plates
had been given to redeem them, the holy adornment of the church
was sold to buy back the true church. Even today, the blows of axes
can be seen on the daises and screens where the decorations of the
small columns made of silver were removed. The man of God said
that no person in their right mind and redeemed by the blood of
Christ should, through loss of their free status and on account of
captivity, perhaps become an Arian or a Jew, and become a slave
when freeborn, and the slave of a man when the servant of God.

33. Through his action the church was not disfigured, but
enhanced and preserved; he caused the womb of the mother [the
church] to give birth to children, not to be punished. He often used
to say, 'I would like those bishops of the Lord and other clergy –
they who from fondness for more than they need are reluctant to
give senseless silver and gold from the offerings received by Christ
to the servants of Christ – to tell me and explain their reasoning. I
would like them, I say, to tell me, if such adverse circumstances as
these by chance befell them, whether they would want to be set free
by those inanimate gifts; or perhaps they would consider it sacrilege
if someone came to their aid with these tiny consecrated vessels. I

do not believe it is contrary to God's will to redeem men from captivity with the eucharist vessels of him who gave himself for the redemption of mankind.' From this we see that some praised this deed of the holy man, but would not imitate him. For surely it was for us that the blood of Christ shone in that glass vessel and his most precious body hung upon the cross?

13.10 The right attitude to possessions: Basil of Caesarea *Short Rules* 92 (*PG* 31.1145c–1148a)

The following extract from one of Basil's treatises on the ascetic life presents a very balanced view of material possessions and the appropriate attitude towards them – in contrast with the views of other ascetics from the same region (11.7). It is also of interest for its assumption that giving to the poor results in forgiveness of sin. Further reading: Gould 1987.

Question 92: When the Lord commands us to sell our possessions, from what motive should we do this? Because material possessions are themselves harmful by their very nature, or because of the distraction which arises from them in the soul?

Response: In answer to this it must first be said that no material thing would have been created by God if it were bad in itself. 'For everything created by God', it says, 'is good, and nothing is to be rejected' [1 Tim. 4.4]. Next, the command of the Lord instructed us not to throw away possessions as evil and shun them, but to exercise stewardship of them. And a man is condemned, not simply for having possessions, but for having the wrong attitude towards them, or for not using them in the right way. For a dispassionate and healthy attitude towards them, and utilising them in accordance with the Lord's command, results in many very necessary benefits – on the one hand, the cleansing of our sins (for it is written, 'But give what you can to the poor, and look, everything will be clean for you' [Luke 11.41]), on the other, inheriting the kingdom of heaven and gaining inexhaustible treasure, in accordance with what is said is another place: 'Do not be afraid, little flock, for it has pleased your heavenly Father to give you the kingdom. Sell your possessions and give to the poor. Get yourselves purses which do not wear out, treasure in heaven that never runs out [Luke 12.32].'

14

CHURCH LIFE

The focus of this chapter is the simple question of what happened in churches, and the temporal and spatial context of those activities. Chapter 2 includes material relevant to these themes in the third century (2.1, 2.4); this chapter pursues them through the fourth century and beyond. It begins with an example of a church calendar preserved on papyrus (14.1), before turning to the physical setting of church life – first as prescribed in a handbook on church organisation (14.2), and then as reflected in the plans of churches and in an artistic representation (14.3, 14.4, 14.5). An extract from a sermon provides valuable evidence on the character of preaching, and also on the important ritual of baptism (14.6), further reflected in an inscription (14.7) and an example of a baptismal font (14.8). A further extract from a sermon illustrates some of the problems that a preacher could encounter during a service (14.9), while two examples of hymns highlight another dimension of services (14.10, 14.11). Finally, the issue of pictures and images in churches is raised with reference to a textile wall-hanging and a painted icon (14.12). Further reading: Krautheimer 1965; Dix 1945.

14.1 A calendar of church services:
P. Oxy. 1357

The sixth-century papyrus document from which the following extract comes lists church services in the Egyptian town of Oxyrhynchus from October 535 to March 536. It is unlikely to be an exhaustive list of all the services during this period, its editors suggesting that it refers to those at which the bishop of Oxyrhynchus was (expected to be) present. It is unclear whether it is a list of forthcoming events or a record of services held, but it is of interest for the types of service held and the number of different churches (at least twenty-six) in a provincial town. Some churches are named after 'principal' saints (e.g., Mary, Peter, Paul), some after Egyptian saints, usually martyrs (e.g., Cosmas, Justus, Menas, Victor).

+ Notice of services (*synaxeis*) after the patriarch (*papa*) went downstream to Alexandria, as follows:
14th year of the indiction [535] Phaophi 23 [21 October] in the [Church] of Phoibammon, the Lord's day [Sunday]

25 [23 October] in St Serenos', day of repentance
30 [28 October] in the [Church] of the Martyrs, the Lord's day

Hathur 3 [31 October] in the [Church] of Phoibammon, day of Epimachos

7 [4 November] in the Evangelist's, the Lord's day
12 [9 November] in St Michael's, his day
13 [10 November] in the same
14 [11 November] in St Justus', his day
15 [12 November] in St Menas', his day
16 [13 November] in the same
17 [14 November] in St Justus'
<6 lines lost>

<Choiak> 7 [4 December] in St Victor's

12 [9 December] in the [Church] of Anniane, the Lord's day

15 [12 December] in St Kosmas', day of Ision
19 [16 December] in the Evangelist's, the Lord's day
22 [19 December] in St Philoxenos', his day
23 [20 December] in the same
24 [21 December] in the same
25 [22 December] likewise in the same
26 [23 December] in St Serenos', the Lord's day
27 [24 December] in the same
28 [25 December] in St Mary's, the birth of Christ
29 [26 December] in the same
30 [27 December] in the same likewise

Tybi 1 [28 December] in St Peter's, his day, and likewise in St Paul's, his day

3 [30 December] in the [Church] of Phoibammon, the Lord's day
11 [6 January] in the [Church] of Phoibammon, the epiphany of Christ ...

14.2 Church layout and conduct of services:
Apostolic Constitutions 2.57.1–9

The *Apostolic Constitutions* was a handbook on church organisation probably compiled in Syria in the late fourth century, and drawing heavily on a third-century work known as the *Teaching of the Apostles* (*Didascalia Apostolorum*). It provides guidance on the role of bishops, clergy and others involved in church ministry; here, it offers advice on the layout of the church building and the conduct of services.

(1) As for you, bishop, be holy and blameless, neither quarrelsome nor prone to anger nor harsh, but someone who knows how to edify, to discipline, and to teach; forebearing, gentle, mild, patient, someone who knows how to exhort and encourage, like a man of God. (2) When you gather together the church of God, like a helmsman of a great ship, command the congregation to behave with great discipline, instructing the deacons, like sailors, to assign the places to the brethren, like passengers, with great care and dignity. (3) And first, the church (*oikos*) should be oblong, facing the east with the sacristries on each side facing the east, resembling a ship. (4) Place the bishop's throne in the middle, seat the presbyters each side of him, and the deacons should stand nearby, ready for action and properly attired, for they are like the sailors and those in charge of the rowers. Under their supervision, the layfolk should sit in the other part [of the church] in a very orderly and quiet manner; the women should sit separately and maintain silence. (5) The reader, standing in the middle on something raised, should read the books of Moses and Joshua the son of Nun, of the Judges and the Kings, of the Chronicles and the Return from Exile, then the books of Job and Solomon and the sixteen Prophets. (6) After every two readings, let another person sing the hymns of David and the people reply by singing the refrains. (7) After this, our Acts should be read and the letters of Paul, our fellow labourer, which he sent to the churches by the inspiration of the Holy Spirit; after this, a presbyter or deacon should read the Gospels which we, Matthew and John, have passed on to you, and which the fellow workers of Paul – Luke and Mark – received and bequeathed to you. (8) And while the Gospel is being read, all the presbyters and deacons and all the people should stand in complete silence; for it is written, 'Be silent and hear, O Israel' [Deut. 27.9], and again 'But you, stand here and listen' [Deut. 5.31]. (9) And the presbyters should encourage the people, one after another, but not all of them, and last of all the bishop, who is like the helmsman. ...

14.3 A basilica church: St Paul's Outside the Walls, Rome

As church membership expanded beyond the capacity of house churches such as that at Dura-Europos (2.4), it became necessary to construct purpose-built structures able to hold large numbers. Both ideological and practical considerations ruled out anything derived from Roman religious architecture – 'the temples of the old gods ... had been designed to shelter an image, not to accommodate a congregation' (Krautheimer 1965: 19). Instead, the model adopted was the basilica or secular audience hall used by Roman officials in the fourth century. Although many variations on this were possible, its essence was a nave with aisles and a rostrum at the far end on which the relevant official was seated. The churches built by Constantine in Rome and elsewhere followed this pattern, but another good example from later in the fourth century is the church of St Paul Outside the Walls, Rome (**Figure** 14.3), constructed on the initiative of the emperors Theodosius I, Valentinian II and Arcadius to provide for the shrine of St Paul a structure comparable to St Peter's. Further reading: Krautheimer 1965: 17–21, 63–4.

14.4 A provincial church: The Tabarka mosaic

St Paul's was a structure designed for use by some of the population of a large metropolis. By contrast, this mosaic (**Figure** 14.4, a and b) from a tomb at Tabarka in north Africa, conveys some idea of the appearance of a smaller provincial basilica church in the early fifth century, though it is not necessarily a depiction of an actual church, so much as a representation of an ideal. The line drawings accompanying it convey the essentials of the mosaic more clearly and how such a church might have looked in three dimensions. The inscription reads, 'Mother church. Valentia, in peace'. Further reading: Krautheimer 1965: 141–2.

14.5 A domed church: Hagia Sophia, Constantinople

Following the devastation of the city centre of Constantinople during the Nika riot of 532, the emperor Justinian set about rebuilding the church of Holy Wisdom – Hagia Sophia – in magnificent style (**Figure** 14.5) (cf. **15.4**). Although its design was based on that of the basilica church, it incorporated a feature that required great engineering skill – the addition of a dome. This feature had been used in smaller churches in recent decades, but it had not previously been attempted on anything like this scale. The effect is very impressive, creating a light, airy space that draws the eyes heavenward. For a contemporary description (including detail of the church's lavish internal decoration), see Procopius *Buildings* 1.3.23ff. Further reading: Krautheimer 1965: ch. 9; Mainstone 1988.

14.6 Preaching and baptism: Ambrose *On the Sacraments* 1.4–5, 8–15

Baptism was one of the most important rituals in church life, the essential

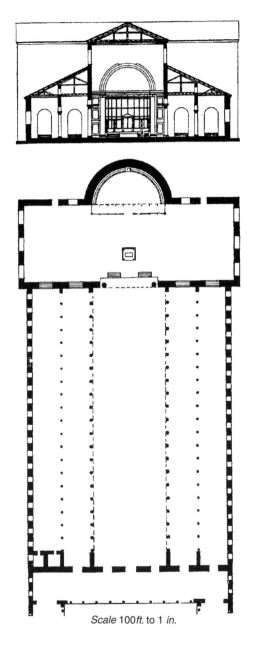

Scale 100*ft.* to 1 *in.*

Figure 14.3   The church of St Paul Outside the Walls, Rome

Source: C. Stewart, *Early Christian, Byzantine and Romanesque Architecture* (London, New York, Toronto: Addison Wesley Longman, 1954): 25.

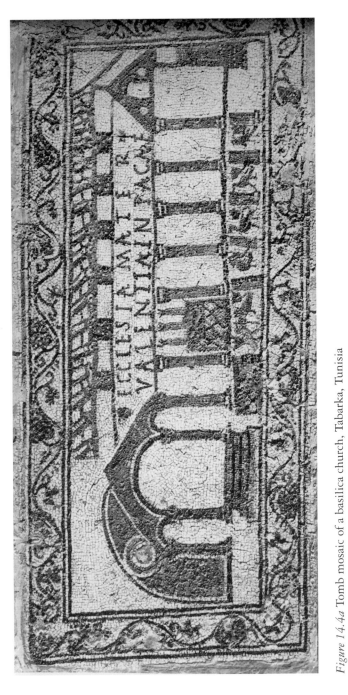

ECCLESIÆ MATERI
VATNIAIN PACHE

Figure 14.4a Tomb mosaic of a basilica church, Tabarka, Tunisia

Source: Photograph by Koppermann, InstNegNo 61.535. Reproduced by permission of the German Archaeological Institute, Rome.

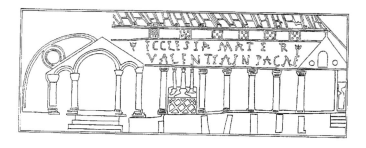

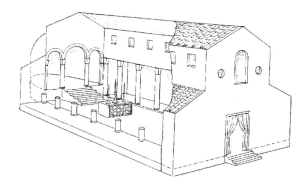

Figure 14.4b Line drawing of the tomb mosaic and reconstruction drawing
of a basilica church, Tabarka, Tunisia

Source: From *Archaeologia* vol. 95 (1953): Fig. 28. By courtesy of the Society of
Antiquaries of London.

qualification which allowed a Christian to partake of the eucharist. Infant baptism
was not unknown in Late Antiquity, but it seems to have been used primarily when
children were close to death (Ferguson 1979). Although this will have been a
common enough occurrence in a society with high mortality rates, most people
will have been baptised as adults. This involved becoming a catechumen (literally
'one who is instructed') for a period of preparation. The baptism itself usually took
place on the evening before Easter Sunday, and the sermons that comprise
Ambrose's work *On the Sacraments* were addressed to the newly baptised during the
week after Easter. They are of interest not only for their description of the steps
involved in baptism, but also as an example of preaching. There is good reason to
think they are the verbatim text of what Ambrose said, copied down by someone in
the congregation, and therefore not embellished subsequently. As will be evident,
the style is very accessible and Ambrose uses a variety of techniques to ensure that
his audience maintain their concentration and follow the argument. For the
baptismal process, see Homes Dudden 1935: 336–42, Van der Meer 1961: ch. 12,
Yarnold 1994; on Ambrose's preaching, see Cramer 1993: ch. 2, Rousseau 1998
(*contra* MacMullen 1989). Cf. also **5.2, 6.11, 15.3**.

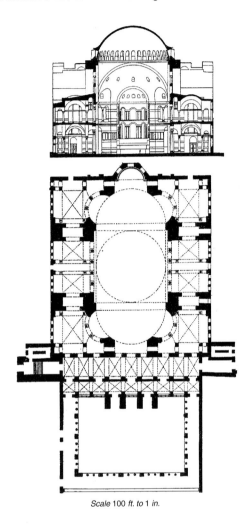

Scale 100 ft. to 1 in.

Figure 14.5 Hagia Sophia, Constantinople

Source: C. Stewart, *Early Christian, Byzantine and Romanesque Architecture* (London, New York, Toronto: Addison Wesley Longman, 1954): 68.

4. We have come to the font, you have entered, you have been anointed. Think about whom you have seen, reflect on what you have said, recall it carefully. A deacon [lit. 'Levite'] meets you, a presbyter comes to you. You are anointed like an athlete of Christ, as if you are about to engage in a contest in this world. You have committed yourself to the exertions involved in your contest. Those

who contend have what they hope for, for where there is a contest, there is a crown. You contend in the world, but you are crowned by Christ, and it is on account of the struggles in the world that you are crowned. For although your reward is in heaven, the earning of that reward takes place here.

5. When you were asked, 'Do you renounce the devil and his works?', how did you respond? 'I renounce them.' 'Do you renounce the world and its lusts?' How did you respond? 'I renounce them?' Recall what you said, and never forget the implications of the undertaking you have given. If you've given a written undertaking to someone, you are legally bound in order to receive their money; you are obligated and the money-lender can constrain you if you show reluctance. If you object, you go to a judge and there you'll be convicted on the basis of your undertaking. ...

8. So you have renounced the world, you have renounced the spirit of this age. Be alert! Those who owe money always keep in mind their undertaking. And you, who owe your faith to Christ, preserve that faith which is much more valuable than money. For faith is an eternal inheritance, whereas money is only temporary. So always remember what you promised: you will be more prudent. If you hold to your promise, you will also keep your undertaking.

9. Then you drew nearer, you saw the font, you saw the bishop near the font. I have no doubt that the same thought which occurred to Naaman crossed your mind, for even though he had been made clean, he still doubted at first. Why? I will tell you – listen.

10. You entered, you saw the water, you saw the bishop, you saw the deacon. In case someone perhaps says, 'Is that all?', it certainly is – where there is complete innocence, complete devotion, complete grace, complete holiness. You saw what you could see with physical eyes and with human perception; you didn't see what was being done, but what could be seen. The things that cannot be seen are much greater than what can be seen, 'because the things that can be seen are temporary, but the things that cannot be seen are eternal' [2 Cor. 4.18].

11. Let us then say this first – keep in mind the promise I speak and demand its fulfilment. We marvel at the mysteries of the Jews given to our fathers, outstanding first in the antiquity of their sacraments, then in their holiness. But I promise you this, that the sacraments of the Christians are more divine and of greater antiquity than those of the Jews.

12. What is more extraordinary than the passage of the Jewish

people through the sea (since we are talking about baptism at the moment)? Yet all the Jews who passed through died in the desert. But those who pass through this font, that is, from earthly things to heavenly – for this is a passage, and hence Easter (that is, Passover), a passing from sin to life, from guilt to grace, from impurity to holiness – those who pass through this font do not die but rise again.

13. So Naaman was a leper [2 Kgs. 5.1–14]. A slave girl said to his wife: 'If my master wants to be clean, he should go to the land of Israel and find a man there who can free him from leprosy. The slave girl told her mistress, the wife told her husband, Naaman told the king of Syria; as one of his most highly valued men, the king sent him to the king of Israel. The king of Israel heard that he had been sent to him to heal his leprosy, and he tore his garments. Then the prophet Elisha sent word to him: 'Why have you torn your garments, as though God does not have the power to heal leprosy?' Send him to me.' He sent him and the prophet said to the man when he arrived: 'Go down into the Jordan, immerse yourself, and you will be healed.'

14. Naaman began to reflect on this and say to himself: 'Is that all? I have come from Syria to the land of Judaea and I am told: 'Go into the Jordan, immerse yourself, and you will be healed?' As if there aren't better rivers in my homeland!' But his servants said to him: 'Master, why not carry out the prophet's instruction? Try it and see what happens.' So he went into the Jordan, immersed himself, and emerged healthy.

15. So what does this mean? You saw the water, but it is not any water that heals, but water which has the grace of Christ. There is a difference between the element and its consecration, between the act (*opus*) and its efficacy (*operatio*). The act is carried out with water, but its efficacy comes from the Holy Spirit. The water does not heal unless the Holy Spirit has descended and consecrated that water. As you have read, when our Lord Jesus Christ established the pattern for baptism, he came to John and John said to him: 'I ought to be baptised by you and you come to me.' Christ replied to him: 'Let it be so now, for it is fitting for us to fulfill all righteousness.' [Matt. 3.14–15] See how all righteousness is established in baptism.

14.7 Baptism and burial: *ILCV* 1516

This inscription from Lyons, which has been dated on stylistic grounds to the fifth or sixth centuries (Le Blant 1856–65: 552–3), is of interest, first, for its implication that baptism was able to offset the perceived handicap of barbarian birth (line 3) (cf. Brown 1972: 54 n. 1), and second, for the way the bereaved parents are presented as coping with their grief (lines 7–8).

Here twin brothers, side by side, give their bodies to the
    grave;
The soil has brought together these whom merit united.
Born of barbarian stock, but reborn from the baptismal font,
They give their spirits to heaven, they give their bodies to
    the earth.
Sorrow has come to Sagile their father and his wife,
Who without doubt wished to predecease them.
But with Christ's calming influence, great grief can be borne:
They are not childless – they have given gifts to God.

14.8 A baptistery: The Kélibia font

This beautiful baptismal font, now in the Musée du Bardo in Tunisia, comes from the Church of St Felix near Kélibia, on the north African coast about 150 km east of Carthage, and dates from the sixth century (see **Figure** 14.8). The inscription can be read as follows (though there is debate about interpretation of the first half: Duval 1982: 54–8): 'When the holy and most blessed Cyprian was bishop and priest, with the holy Adelfius presbyter of this [church] of the unity, Aquinius and his wife Juliana, with their children Villa and Deogratias placed this mosaic destined for the eternal water [of baptism]'. For the iconography employed, see Courtois 1955; Dunbabin 1978: 190. For the architecture of baptisteries and the range of possible shapes for fonts, see Davies 1962: ch. 1, and cf. 2.4.

14.9 Practical aspects of church services: Caesarius of Arles *Sermon* 78.1

This passage from a sermon contains a number of details of relevance to the conduct of church services in the west: the assumption that it was normal practice to stand during readings; the allusion to the fact that, in addition to passages from the Bible, martyr acts were sometimes read out (cf. Gaiffier 1954); and the common problem of clergy making themselves heard above the noise of congregational chatter (cf. Adkin 1985).

Moved by fatherly concern for those whose feet are in pain or who labour under some infirmity of body, I advised several days ago that when lengthy accounts of martrydoms (*passiones prolixae*) or some of the longer passages from Scripture are being read out, those who are unable to stand should humbly sit in silence and listen with attentive ears to what is being read. But now some of our daughters think that all of them, or at least the majority, ought to do this

Figure 14.8　Baptismal font from Kélibia, Tunisia

Source:　Reproduced by permission of Musée du Bardo, Tunisia.

regularly, even those who are sound in body. For when the reading of the word of God begins, they want to lie down as if in their own little beds. How I wish they would *only* lie down, and silently receive the word of God with a thirsty heart, instead of also spending their time in idle gossip, so that they do not hear what is being preached and also prevent others from hearing. So I ask you, esteemed daughters, and I remind you with fatherly concern, that when readings are being recited or the word of God is being preached, no-one is to lie down on the ground unless perchance forced to by some very serious illness; and then, do not lie down, but rather sit and receive with attentive ears and a hungry heart that which is preached.

14.10 Hymns in the west: Ambrose of Milan *Hymn* 4 ('God, creator of all things')

Although Ambrose's political interventions are the feature of his career which tends, understandably, to attract most attention (e.g., 6.5), another important legacy was his contribution to liturgy through his writing and use of hymns. Such was his impact in this sphere that his name literally became synonymous with 'hymn', often referred to as *ambrosianum* (e.g., *Rule of Benedict* 9.8). In a famous passage in his *Confessions* (9.7.15), Augustine describes Ambrose' use of hymns during his conflict with the Arians of Milan in 386, concerning which Ambrose himself made the following significant observations: 'They say that the people have been deceived by the lyrics of my hymns, and I certainly do not deny it, for there is nothing more powerful than elevated lyrics. For what is more powerful than confession of the Trinity, which is daily praised by the mouths of all the people? Everyone is eager to compete with one another in confessing the faith, for they know how to proclaim the Father and the Son and the Holy Spirit when it is in verse. In this way those who could scarcely have been students have all become teachers' (*Letter* 75a (21a).34; cf. McLynn 1994: 225–6; Moorhead 1999: 140–3).

Because of Ambrose's fame as a hymn-writer, it became increasingly difficult with the passage of time to distinguish genuine compositions from those wrongly attributed to him, but there are at least some about whose authenticity there is no doubt, and one of these is translated below. (Augustine makes frequent reference to it in his *Confessions*, notably at 9.12.32, where he quotes the first two stanzas.) This hymn was written to be sung in the evening and the meaning of the lyrics is generally clear and self-explanatory, but the underlying thought warrants elucidation at a few points: in the third stanza, 'the singers are regarded as having in the morning vowed to offer songs and prayers on being brought safely through the day. Now at evening, having obtained their petition, they acknowledge that the song and prayers are due' (Walpole 1920: 47); and in the final line of the sixth stanza, 'Ambrose seems to be thinking of the bodily warmth that accompanies sleep rising to overpower the soul and to set free the animal impulses' (Walpole 1920: 48).

God, creator of all things,
Ruler of the heavens, who clothes

The day in glorious light,
And the night in the gift of sleep,

So that rest may restore tired limbs
To gainful work,
Relieve weary souls,
And release torturing anxieties –

As we sing our hymn, we offer
Thanks for the day now over,
And prayers for the oncoming night:
Help us fulfil our vow.

Let the depths of our hearts celebrate you,
Let resonant voices acclaim you,
Let pure love cherish you,
Let sober souls adore you,

So that when the deep gloom of night
Envelops the day,
Our faith can eschew the shadows,
And the night shine with faith.

Do not let our souls go to sleep,
Rather, may sin fall asleep.
Let faith, which refreshes the pure,
Temper the warmth of slumber.

Released from impure thoughts,
Let the depths of our hearts dream of you,
Let not fear, by a trick of the jealous enemy,
Rouse us from our rest.

We ask Christ and the Father,
And the Spirit of Christ and the Father,
One being, powerful in everything -
Succour us who pray to you, Trinity.

14.11 Hymns in the east: Romanos the Melode
Hymn 49.1–4, 15–18 (Pentecost)

Ambrose was only one of a number of fine Christian hymn writers during Late Antiquity. The eastern half of the empire produced its fair share, of whom the most famous was Romanos the Melode, active during the reign of Justinian. His hymns, of which more than fifty survive, are known as *kontakia*. Thought to be influenced by Syriac hymn-writing (Romanos was a native of Syrian Emesa), distinctive features of the *kontakion* include a refrain at the end of each stanza linking it back to the Introduction and the use of 'bold imagery and vivid, almost theatrical, dialogue that dramatically recreates the scriptural texts set in the liturgical calendar' (Jeffreys 1991: 1148). The following extracts from his hymn for Pentecost illustrate these features, while also containing (in the final stanzas) an interesting expression of hostility towards classical (pagan) education, which perhaps reflects the generally rigorist attitude towards paganism that characterised Justinian's reign. It has been argued that the particular names singled out for denigration in Stanza 17 were carefully chosen to provide comprehensive coverage of the traditional classical syllabus – the *trivium*, comprising grammar (Homer), rhetoric (Demosthenes), and dialectic (Plato), and the *quadrivium*, comprising geometry, arithmetic and music (Pythagoras) and astronomy (Aratos) (Grosdidier de Matons 1981: 207 n. 2). Further reading: Carpenter 1970: Introduction; Topping 1976 (though Grosdidier de Matons (1981: 177–8, 203 n. 2) disagrees with Topping about linking the hymn to 529 and Justinian's closing of the Athenian Academy).

(Introduction)

When he came down and threw the languages (*glōssas*) into
    confusion,
The Most High divided the nations.
When he distributed the tongues (*glōssas*) of fire,
He called all people to unity,
And united in voice we glorify the Spirit all-holy.

(1)
Give your servants speedy and steadfast comfort, Jesus,
In the discouragement of our spirits.
Do not separate yourself from our souls in their afflictions,
Do not distance yourself from our hearts in their anxieties,
But come quickly to us always.
Draw near to us, draw near, you who are everywhere!
Just as you were always with the apostles,
So also unite yourself with those who long for you, Compassionate
    One,
So that, joined with you, we may sing hymns and glorify
The Spirit all-holy.

(2)
You were not separated from your disciples, Saviour, when you
    journeyed back to heaven;
For when you reached on high, you embraced the world below.
For no place is separated from you, whom no space can contain.
And if it comes into existence, it is destroyed and disappears,
And undergoes the fate of Sodom.

For it is you who maintains the universe, filling everything.
So the apostles had you in their souls;
Therefore they came down from the Mount of Olives, after your
    ascension,
Dancing and singing and glorifying
The Spirit all-holy.

(3)
The eleven disciples returned joyfully from the Mount of Olives.
For Luke the priest writes thus:
They returned to Jersualem,
They ascended to the upper room where they were staying,
And on entering, they sat down,
Peter and the other disciples.
Cephas [Peter], as their leader, said to them,
'We who are partakers of the kingdom – let us lift our hearts
Towards him who spoke this promise, "I will send you
The Spirit all-holy".'

(4)
Then after saying this to the apostles, Peter urged them to pray,
And standing in the midst, he cried out,
'Let us entreat on bended knee, let us implore,
Let us make this room a church,
For it is one and is becoming one.
Let us weep and cry out to God,
"Send us your wonderful Spirit,
So that he may guide all people to the land of righteousness
Which you have prepared for those who worship and glorify
The Spirit all-holy!"'

[Stanzas 5–14 recount the events of the Day of Pentecost]

(15)
But when those who had come there from everywhere saw them
    speaking in all the languages,
They were astonished and cried out, 'What does this mean?
The apostles are Galileans,
So how have they just now become, as we look on,
Fellow-countrymen of all nations?
When did Peter Cephas visit Egypt?
When did Andrew live in Mesopotamia?
How did the sons of Zebedee see Pamphylia?

How are we to make sense of this? What should we say? It is
　　entirely as desired by
The Spirit all-holy.'

(16)
Those who until recently were fishermen have now become learned
　　men (*sophistai*),
Now they are gifted speakers (*rhētores*), clearly comprehensible,
Who previously dwelt by the shores of lakes.
Those who started off stitching nets
Now unravel the snares of clever speakers and discredit them in
　　their unadorned speech.
For they speak *the* Word instead of a cloud of words,
They proclaim the one God, not one god among many.
They worship the One because he is one, the incomprehensible
　　Father,
The Son of the same nature, and, inseparable from them and like
　　them,
The Spirit all-holy.

(17)
Has it not been granted to them to prevail over everyone through
　　the languages they speak?
So why are the fools outside [the church] spoiling for a fight?
Why do the Hellenes bluster and drone on?
Why do they allow themselves to be deluded by the thrice-accursed
　　Aratos (*Araton ton triskataraton*)?
Why do they go astray in the company of Plato (*planōntai pros
　　Platōna*)?
Why are they fond of the feeble Demosthenes?
Why do they not realise that Homer is an idle dreamer?
Why do they babble on about Pythagoras who has rightly been
　　silenced?
Why do they not run with faith to those to whom has been revealed
The Spirit all-holy?

(18)
Let us praise, brothers, the tongues of the disciples, for it was
　　not with clever speech,
But with divine power that they caught every person.
They took his cross as a fishing rod, and they used words as a
　　line,
And they fished the world.

They had the Word for a sharp hook,
As bait they had
The flesh of the Lord of everything, not catching to kill,
But luring to life those who worship and glorify
The Spirit all-holy.

14.12 The church and images: A textile representation of Mary and a painting of Peter

The attitude of church authorities towards the use of Christian images in the third and fourth centuries was generally negative – no doubt as a result of the role of statues and other representations of the gods in pagan cults. In the early fourth century, e.g., a church council issued the following pronouncement: 'It was decided that there should be no pictures in church, for whatever is worshipped and reverenced might be depicted on the walls' (*Council of Elvira*, Canon 36; cf. Eusebius *Letter to Constantia* and Epiphanius *Letters* [translations in Mango 1986: 16–18, 41–3]). Yet it is apparent from the Dura baptistery (2.4) and the Roman catacombs that, in practice, decoration of Christian structures did occur, and by the latter half of the fourth century, artistic representations of Biblical themes were beginning to be accepted as having educative value, especially for Christians who were illiterate (e.g., Paulinus of Nola *Poem* 27.511–48). This, however, is still some distance from actual reverence for images, which becomes apparent during the sixth century and was to prove so controversial in the Byzantine iconoclastic controversy of the eighth and ninth centuries.

Figure 14.12a (178 x 110 cm) is a representation of Mary flanked by the archangels Michael and Gabriel, with Christ as a child in her lap and Christ as king above; the scene is surrounded by a decorative border with busts of the twelve apostles. The picture is woven in wool with a predominance of rich blues and reds, and was probably produced in sixth-century Egypt. Mary's special status developed particularly in the fifth century. One of the basic tenets of the Monophysite movement (which was especially strong in Egypt) was that Mary was the *Theotokos* ('the mother of God'), rather than the *Christotokos* ('the mother of Christ') – a distinction that emphasised Christ's essential divinity. In the late sixth century, Mary also became a particular object of devotion in Constantinople. On the tapestry, see Shepherd 1969; Weitzmann 1978: 46–7 (including colour photograph); on reverence for Mary, see Cameron 1978.

Figure 14.12b (92 x 53 cm) is an encaustic painting of the apostle Peter preserved in St Catherine's Monastery in the Sinai, though it is thought to have been executed in Constantinople, probably in the late sixth or early seventh century. It is of particular interest for the way in which it imitates late Roman consular diptychs (small representations of the office-holder carved in ivory), though with important differences: where the consul typically holds a sceptre of authority, Peter holds a staff topped with a cross, and where the consul holds the napkin to start the celebratory chariot races, Peter holds the keys of the kingdom. Above him in the three medallions where one would expect the emperor, empress and co-consul, there are representations of Christ, Mary and perhaps St John. On the painting, see Weitzmann 1978: 55–5 (including colour photograph); on icons more generally, see Cameron 1992.

Figure 14.12a   Icon of the Virgin. Egypt, Byzantine period, 6th century.
Tapestry weave, wool, 178 x 110 cm

Source: © The Cleveland Museum of Art, 1999, Leonard C. Hanna, Jr., Bequest,
1967.144.

Figure 14.12b   Encaustic icon of St Peter

Source: Reproduced through courtesy of the Michigan–Princeton–Alexandria Expedition to Mount Sinai.

15

WOMEN

The justification for including a separate chapter on women, if it is needed, is that they almost certainly constituted more than half the membership of the church during the third and fourth centuries (and probably beyond), and often played an important role in the spread of Christianity within families (15.1) – yet the scope for them to exercise leadership and authority within the church was very limited. As a result, they barely figure in the high-profile controversies of the fourth century considered in Chapters 3–6, and there is no role for them in Chapter 12 on bishops. Any sign of women usurping priestly prerogatives quickly resulted in condemnation by church authorities (15.2; cf. 2.10), though involvement in church life in certain strictly defined and subordinate capacities was allowed (15.3). Some women were in a position to make their presence felt, but usually only when they could draw on inherited wealth (15.4, 15.5; cf. 2.7).

For women more generally, Christianity was not without some positive benefits. Its emphasis on husbands adhering to the same standards of sexual behaviour as expected of wives (15.6) was an important break with the tradition of the 'double standard' in Roman society, even if discrepancies between principle and practice persisted on the part of some men. The development of asceticism also offered many women a legitimate alternative to marriage for the first time (15.7) – 'we have to remember how extraordinary it was, in Graeco-Roman terms, for a woman to opt not to marry' (G. Clark 1992: 51). On the other hand, more often than not it still left them subordinate to male authority (15.8). Moreover, it is apparent that families sometimes forced young girls to enter a monastery for less than commendable motives (15.9), and even for those who willingly embraced the ascetic life, the highest praise they could expect seems to have been couched in masculine terms (15.10). It remains to note that nearly all the surviving source material relating to women in late antique Christianity was written by men. One exception is Egeria's account of her travels in the Holy Land and adjacent regions (16.3) – a reminder of the way in which the growth of pilgrimage opened another avenue for female involvement in the wider world, at least for those who could afford travel; another is the fascinating and erudite Virgilian *Cento* of the aristocratic Proba (Clark and Hatch 1981).

Further reading: E. Clark 1990a, b; G. Clark 1992, 1995; Elm 1994; Arjava 1996; Cooper 1996; sourcebook: E. Clark 1983 (Kraemer 1988 and Lefkowitz and Fant 1992, while much broader in coverage, include material on women and late antique Christianity).

15.1 The role of women in Christianisation: *CIL* 8.12260

The role of females in the penetration of Christianity among the Roman aristocracy has often been discussed (cf. 6.9). This inscription from the north African town of Tepelte, near Carthage (presumed to date from Constantine's reign or later because of its overt reference to Christianity), reveals an analogous process occurring at the level of local elites in the provinces, and is corroborated by other north African evidence, including the well-known case of Augustine's mother, Monica. 'Aedile' and *duovir* were two positions of political importance at the local community level. (Because the father had the epitaph prepared when he was still alive, a space was left to fill in his age after he died – but the executors of his will clearly forgot to do so.) Further reading: Lepelley 1979–81: vol. 1, 361, vol. 2, 167.

Sacred to the eternal shades. Manilius Faustinianus, son of Manilius Victor and Fortunata, a former aedile and *duovir*, a man of honourable rank, devout, lived for <?> years. While still alive, he had this [epitaph] prepared for himself and his family.

Sacred to the eternal shades. Mecenatia Secundula, a faithful [or 'baptised'] Christian (*cristiana fidelis* [*sic*]), a woman of honourable rank, the wife of Manilius Faustinianus, <lived for ? years>, 2 months.

Sacred to the eternal shades. Manilius Fortunatianus, son of Manilius Faustinianus, former aedile and *duovir*, a man of honourable rank, devout, lived for 32 years, 1 month.

15.2 Female clergy? *Council of Nîmes* Canon 2 and Gelasius *Letter* 14.26

These two items – the first a ruling by a Gallic church council in the late fourth century, the second from a letter by the bishop of Rome to the bishops of the southern Italian regions of Lucania, Bruttium and Sicily in 494 – allude to situations where women had apparently been allowed to assume the role of clergy. The responses of the relevant authorities make clear that this was regarded as unacceptable and contrary to normal church practice (cf. 2.10). Further reading: Rossi 1991.

(a) Council of Nimes *Canon 2*

It has also been suggested by certain people that, contrary to apostolic teaching and unknown until this time, women seem to have been accepted into the priestly ministry (*ministerium leviticum*) somewhere. Church teaching does not allow this because it is unseemly and such ordination, carried out contrary to reason, should be done away with. Care is to be taken that no one presumes to do this in future.

(b) *Gelasius* Letter *14.26*

Nevertheless we have heard – it is intolerable – that contempt for divine matters has sunk so low that women are encouraged to minister at the sacred altars, and to carry out everything assigned only to the responsibility of the male gender, to which they do not belong.

15.3 Female involvement in ministry: *Ancient Statutes of the Church* Canon 100

Although excluded from being clergy, women were allowed to be deaconesses, a position sanctioned by the New Testament (Rom. 16.1, 1 Tim. 3.11). Their work including caring for the female poor and sick, but one of their most important tasks was – no doubt due to concerns about propriety – assisting in the baptism of women. This passage, from a treatise of the late fifth century that drew heavily on earlier handbooks about church organisation (cf. 12.4), reiterates their responsibilities in this respect. Further reading: Gryson 1976.

Widows or nuns who are chosen for the ministry of baptising women should be trained for that responsibility in such a way that they are able to explain in clear and sensible language to uneducated peasant women at the time of their baptism how they should reply to the questions of the person baptising them and how they should live after they have received baptism.

15.4 An eminent female benefactor: The *Greek Anthology* 1.10 (lines 42–50, 74–6)

Preserved in a Byzantine collection of ancient epigrams and short poems, the poem from which this extract comes is a description of a church commemorating the third-century martyr St Polyeuctus. The church was built in Constantinople during the mid-520s by Anicia Juliana, a prominent aristocratic lady whose family could claim blood ties to a string of fifth-century emperors. This poem was the main source of knowledge about this church until 1960, when construction work in Istanbul revealed its physical remains – including beautiful marble blocks bearing portions of the original inscribed version of the poem which had adorned the walls of the church. These and other finds have confirmed that it must indeed have been an impressive and richly decorated structure. Since Juliana's son, Anicius Olybrius, was a potential contender for the imperial throne on the death of the childless Anastasius in 518 (in addition to his distinguished descent, Olybrius was married to Anastasius' niece), Juliana's church has been seen not only as an expression of piety, but also as a pointed reassertion of family pride, badly bruised by the unexpected accession to imperial office of the backwoods-born guards officer Justin. The construction of the even more magnificent church of Hagia Sophia (14.5) in the 530s by Justin's nephew and successor Justinian can in turn be viewed, at least in part, as the new imperial family's riposte – a conclusion consistent with the tradition that Justinian exclaimed, on first entering his new church, 'Solomon, I have vanquished you!' (Harrison 1989: 40) and with his forbidding anyone thereafter to build a church without imperial sanction (Procopius *Buildings* 1.8.5). Further reading: Harrison 1989 (including superb photographs of the excavations).

What choir is capable of doing justice to the achievements of Juliana, who, after Constantine, embellisher of his Rome, and after the holy golden light of Theodosius [II], and after the imperial origins of so many forebears, in a few years brought to completion a project worthy of her lineage, indeed more than worthy? She alone overpowered time and surpassed the wisdom of renowned Solomon by erecting a temple fit for God. An eternity is not sufficient to celebrate the expertly fashioned splendour of its beauty. ... [A detailed description of the church follows.] After a vast host of exertions, Juliana realised an achievement on this scale for the sake of the souls of her parents and for her own life and the lives of those who are to come and those who already are.

15.5 The largesse of a Gothic lady: *P. Ital.* 13

Although papyri are normally associated with Egypt, a small number from northern Italy have been preserved, and this one (the beginning of which is damaged) records the donation to the church at Ravenna of substantial property and other assets by a Gothic lady named Ranilo. Its date, soon after the end of Justinian's protracted reconquest of the Italian peninsula from the Goths (535–52), explains the reference to 'these disturbed times' early in the document. The fact that the donor and her husband are Goths means they are likely to have been Arian in terms of original religious allegiance; 'the characteristic intertwining of emperor and church [in this document] might just suggest that Ranilo and her husband, wealthy people of high rank, had recently converted [to Catholicism] in accordance

with the imperial laws and were making a timely gift to prove their loyalty'
(Amory 1997: 409). On a more technical matter, it is unclear why the gift includes
the requirement that the church immediately hand some of it over to Aderit's illegitimate son, unless perhaps his illegitimacy created some difficulty in Ranilo
making the gift directly to him.

< ... > of my deceased father Aderit, one-time man of glorious rank
(*vir gloriosus*), 50 pounds of silver; 100 *solidi* of income, that is, six
twelfths of the Firmidian property, in the territory of Urbino, and of
the < ... >lian property, in the territory of Lucca, that is a half of
each of these properties with all of their equipment and accessories
and everything belonging to them, with all adjacent farmsteads and
surrounding areas, their boundaries and boundary-markers, with
their servants and slaves which are known to be on the specified
properties, and if any of these who have run away during these
disturbed times can be found, we grant permission for them to be
held and brought back, established as you are through this my deed
of gift as masters and agents of what is your property. We likewise
give jewelry and clothing to the value of 50 *solidi*, of which your
Holiness may claim power of ownership with full legal sanction
from this present day. All these things accrued to me as inheritance
from my father Aderit, one-time man of glorious rank, on whose
instruction I openly declare myself to be acting.

From the aforementioned items, you for your part shall give as a
gift to Ademunt, who is also called Andreas, my deceased father's
illegitimate son, 15 pounds of silver, one and a half twelfths of the
aforementioned properties with all that belongs to them, and 50
solidi worth of jewelry and clothing. And invoking the day of the
fearful Final Judgement and the safety of the victorious emperor
who rules the Roman empire, I promise that neither I myself nor
my descendants or successors will challenge this gift at any time or
for any reason, especially since I have done this on the instruction of
my father, and there can be no doubting that your defence and
protection shelters me, just as you will also keep me safe from
violent attacks in the future. Therefore, we have delivered the
things which required delivery, and formally conveyed the things
requiring formal conveyance. We promise that there is no bad faith
in this legally accomplished gift nor will be. For the formalisation
of the transfer we retain for ourselves the right to use and receive
revenue from the aforementioned assets for a period of 30 days.
With our agreement you also have full power to have this gift
entered in the public records that you wish, without needing any

further permission from us, and should it be necessary, I also promise that I will provide my response in the records, just as I have also at this time made my declaration to the councillors of this city.

With the full strength of the law and on the basis of considered deliberation, I have dictated [the terms of] this gift to Severus, public notary of the city of Ravenna, and since we do not know how to write, both I and my husband Felithanc, man of distinguished rank (*vir sublimis*), have imprinted our marks in our own hand, and I have provided witnesses to undersign. Confirmed by the formal request for and giving of a guarantee, I have made over [this gift] to you, most holy archbishop, and to your representatives in the presence of the undersigned, in the 27th year of the reign of our lord Justinian, on the day before the Nones of April, twelve years after the consulship of the younger Basilius, man of senatorial rank (*vir clarissimus*) [4 April 553]. Done at Ravenna, in the house of the donor's husband, in the 1st year of the indiction.

Mark + of the aforementioned donor Ranilo, woman of distinguished rank (*sublimis femina*).

Mark + of the Felithanc, husband of the aforementioned, man of distinguished rank, which I, the public notary Severus, have added.

+ At the request of the donor, Ranilo, woman of distinguished rank, and her husband, Felithanc, man of distinguished rank, to whom [the terms of] this gift have been read out in my presence and who have made their marks, I, Laurentius, man of respectable rank (*vir spectabilis*), have undersigned as a witness, and the gift has been made over in my presence.

[The same formula is repeated by four other witnesses – Arborius, *vir clarissimus*, Bassus, *vir clarissimus*, Amantius, *vir spectabilis*, and a fourth whose name cannot be deciphered due to damage to the papyrus.]

I Severus, public notary, have completed this gift in full on the day and twelve years after the consulship written above.

15.6 Christianity and the 'double standard': Jerome *Letter* 77.3

The view that different, less stringent moral standards applied to men than women when it came to sexual behaviour was an ingrained feature of traditional Roman values and social practice (Treggiari 1991: 299–309). By contrast, Christianity insisted that men adhere to the same high standards of conduct as women and have sexual relations only with their wives. Although the need for writers and preachers to reiterate this point regularly shows that male behaviour was often resistant to change, the fact that the principle was championed remains a significant innovation from the point of view of women. Further reading: E. Clark 1990a: 20–1; G. Clark 1992: 38–40.

The laws of the emperors and the laws of Christ are different. Papinian [a famous third-century jurist] advises one thing, our Paul another. Among them the reins of male chastity are relaxed, only sexual relations with respectable women, single or married, are condemned, and sexual gratification is allowed without restriction in brothels and with slave girls, as though guilt were a matter of the social rank [of the female], rather than of the lust [of the male]. Among us, what women are not permitted to do applies equally to men – both sexes serve [God] on the same terms.

15.7 Asceticism as a desirable alternative to marriage: *Life of Olympias* 2–6

The experiences of Olympias, a young woman of high birth in late fourth-century Constantinople, are of great interest for their illustration of the way the ascetic life could be a welcome alternative to marriage for some women, and the obstacles that might confront a woman of her status in achieving that objective. The identity of the author of the *Life* is uncertain, but is thought to be someone who knew Olympias. Further reading: Clark 1979: ch. 3 (including a full translation).

(2) She was the daughter according to the flesh of Seleucus, one of the *comites* [the emperor's 'companions'], but according to the spirit, she was the true child of God. It is said that she was descended from Ablabius who was governor and she was bride for a few days of Nebridius, the prefect of the city of Constantinople, but in truth she did not grace the bed of anyone. For it is said she died an undefiled virgin, having become a partner of the divine Word, a consort of every true humility, a companion and servant of the holy, catholic and apostolic church of God. Left an orphan, she was joined in marriage to a husband, but by the goodness of God she was preserved uncorrupted in flesh and spirit. ... [Her husband died after less than a year of marriage, and apparently without consummating it.]

(3) ... Through a certain demonic jealousy, it transpired that her widowhood became the subject of mischief. She was falsely accused before the emperor Theodosius of having dispensed her goods in a disorderly fashion. Since indeed she was his relation, he took pains to unite her in marriage with a certain Elpidius, a Spaniard, one of his own relatives. He directed many persistent entreaties to her and when he failed to achieve his goal, he was annoyed. The pious

Olympias, however, explained her position to the emperor Theodosius: 'If my King, the Lord Jesus Christ, wanted me to be joined with a man, he would not have taken away my first husband immediately. Since he knew I was unsuited for the conjugal life and was not able to please a man, he freed him, Nebridius, from the bond and delivered me of this very burdensome yoke and servitude to a husband, having placed upon my mind the happy yoke of continence.'

(4) She clarified these things to the emperor Theodosius in this manner, before the plot against the most holy John, patriarch of Constantinople [John Chrysostom]. The emperor, when he heard the testimony against the pious Olympias, commanded the man then prefect of the city, Clementius, to keep her possessions under guard until she reached her thirtieth year, that is, her physical prime. And the prefect, having received the guardianship from the emperor, oppressed her to such a degree at Elpidius' urging ... so that groaning under the the strain, she would meekly bear the option of marriage. But she, even more grateful to God, responded to these events by proclaiming, 'You have shown toward my humble person, O sovereign master, a goodness befitting a king and suited to a bishop, when you commanded my very heavy burden to be put under careful guard, for the administration of it caused me anxiety. But you will do even better if you order that it be distributed to the poor and to the churches, for I prayed much to avoid the vainglory arising from the apportionment, lest I neglect true riches for those pertaining to material things.'

(5) The emperor, upon his return from the battle against Maximus [391], gave the order that she could exercise control over her own possessions, since he had heard of the intensity of her ascetic discipline. But she distributed all of her unlimited and immense wealth and assisted everyone, simply and without distinction. ... She followed to the letter with intelligence the divinely-inspired teachings of the most holy archbishop of this sacred church, John, and gave to him for this holy church ... ten thousand pounds of gold, twenty thousand of silver and all her real estate situated in the provinces of Thrace, Galatia, Cappadocia Prima, and Bithynia; and more, the houses belonging to her in the capital city. ...

(6) Then by the divine will she was ordained deaconess of this holy cathedral of God and she built a monastery at an angle south of it. ... In the first quarter she enclosed her own chambermaids, numbering fifty, all of whom lived in purity and virginity. Next,

Elisanthia, her relative who had seen the good work pleasing to God, which God gave her to carry out, also herself a virgin, emulating the divine zeal, bade farewell to the ephemeral and empty things of life with her sisters Martyria and Palladia, also virgins. Then the three entered with all the others, having made over in advance all their possessions to the same holy monastery ... so that all those who gathered together according to the grace of God in that holy fold of Christ numbered two hundred and fifty. ... (tr. E.A. Clark)

15.8 The establishment of a female monastery: *Life of Pachomius (Bohairic)* 27

This passage from the *Life of Pachomius* (cf. 11.2) relates the decision of Pachomius' sister to emulate her brother and the resulting foundation of a female monastery. Significantly, however, the monastery is effectively under the authority of males, directly through the role of Peter and indirectly through Pachomius formulating their rules. Further reading: Elm 1994: 289–96.

(27) Pachomius' sister, whose name was Mary and who had been a virgin from childhood, heard about him and she came north to see him at Tabennesi. When he was told she had arrived, he sent the brother who watched the door of the monastery to tell her, 'I see you have learned I am alive. Do not be distressed, however, because you have not seen me. But if you wish to share in this holy life so that you may find mercy before God, examine yourself on every point. The brothers will build a place for you to retire to. And doubtless, for your sake the Lord will call others to you, and they will be saved because of you ...' When she heard these words from the lips of the porter she wept, and she accepted the advice. When our father Pachomius had found that her heart inclined to the good and right life, he immediately sent the brothers over to build a monastery for her in that village, a short distance from his own monastery; it included a small oratory. Later on many heard about her and came to live with her. They practised *ascesis* eagerly with her, and she was their mother and their worthy elder until her death. When our father Pachomius saw that the number of [these women] was increasing somewhat, he appointed an old man called Apa Peter, whose 'speech was seasoned with salt' [Col. 4.6] to be their father and to preach frequently to them on the Scriptures for their souls' salvation. [Pachomius] also wrote down in a book the rules of the brothers and sent them to them through [Peter], so that they might learn them. (tr. A. Veilleux)

15.9 Asceticism as a family strategy: Basil of Caesarea *Letters* 199.18

In this extract from a letter written in 375, Basil, bishop of Caesarea and a leading light in the development of ascetic practice, articulates the need for care and commonsense before allowing young girls to dedicate themselves to a life of virginity (a decision that the church regarded as irrevocable once made). In particular, he notes the practice of some families dedicating daughters for the wrong motives. He does not elaborate, but one can well imagine its attractiveness as a strategy for avoiding provision of a dowry or, in the case of poverty stricken families, as a way of reducing the pressure on meagre family resources. Further reading: Arjava 1996: 164–7.

Now we need to agree on this first – a virgin is defined as a female who has willingly offered herself to the Lord, renounced marriage, and preferred the life of holiness. We admit those who make their profession from the time they have reached an age when they fully understand. For it is not proper to regard the words of children as being fully authoritative in matters of this sort, but if a girl is older than sixteen or seventeen and is in possession of her reason, if she remains intent after being questioned at length and persists in her entreaties that she be accepted, then she should be entered on the list of virgins, her profession should be approved, and any violation on her part should be strictly punished. For parents, brothers, and other relatives present many girls [for dedication to virginity] before this age, not because the girl is eager to embrace celibacy on her own initiative, but because the family want to organise some means of living for themselves. Girls in this situation should not be readily admitted until we have clearly investigated their own wishes in the matter.

15.10 When is a woman a man? *Life of Melania the Younger* 39

The life of the younger Melania, a woman from a prominent and wealthy Roman aristocratic family in the early fifth century who pursued an ascetic lifestyle, presents many interesting parallels with the experiences of Olympias (15.7). This brief excerpt, from the period when Melania undertook a tour of monasteries and holy men in Egypt, directs attention to a more general point, namely the assumption that the highest praise one could give to a woman like Melania who had demonstrated outstanding ascetic discipline was to reclassify her as male (which, intriguingly, is further equated here with a heavenly state). Further reading: G. Clark 1992: 128–30 (and for a full translation of the *Life*, E. Clark 1984).

Leaving Alexandria, they went to the mountain of Nitria and the so-called 'Cells', where the fathers of the most holy men there received the blessed woman as though she were a man. For it is true that she had exceeded the limit of the female gender (*to gynaikeion metron*) and had acquired a masculine – or rather, a heavenly – mentality (*phronema andreion mallon de ouranion*).

16

PILGRIMS AND HOLY PLACES

Although Christianity was a religion originally grounded in a sense of time rather than place (Markus 1990: 139–42), it is understandable that some Christians should have developed an interest in visiting the locations where the Bible narratives were set. From the third century, there are the examples of Pionius (**2.12** (4.18–20)) and Alexander of Cappadocia who went to Palestine 'for the purpose of prayer and investigation of the [holy] places' (Eusebius *Church History* 6.11.2), among others (Hunt 1982a: 3–4). During the fourth century, such journeys became more common. Following Constantine's acquisition of the east in 324, it became much safer for Christians to travel to Palestine, Constantine himself took an interest in the region through his funding of church construction at various sites of Biblical significance, and his mother Helena popularised the idea through her pilgrimage there in the late 320s (Hunt 1982a: chs 1–2). The first surviving detailed first-hand account of a pilgrimage followed soon after (**16.1**). From the 360s or early 370s, there is evidence for a group of young women making the journey (**16.2**), while from the 380s there is the detailed record of the travels of a woman from the west (**16.3**). The particular part of her travels illustrated here was in the Sinai peninsula, and there is documentary evidence for this remaining a focus for pilgrimage in the late sixth century (**16.4**). Enthusiasm for and approval of pilgrimage was not, however, shared by all, and in the late fourth century, an eminent bishop wrote an articulate critique of the practice (**16.5**).

Pilgrimage, of course, had elements in common with tourism, most obviously the evident desire of pilgrims to return home with a memento of their visit. The most popular form of memento was the clay flask or *ampulla* containing oil from a holy site (**16.6**), but another possibility was a handful of soil (**16.7**). The diffusion of relics from the Holy Land is another reflection of this, illustrated here by the diffusion of fragments of the True Cross (**16.8**).

The Holy Land was not the only goal for pilgrims. Throughout the Mediterranean world holy men and women, living and deceased, also became objects of devotion, illustrated here by Symeon the Stylite in Syria (**16.9**) and the shrine of Felix of Nola in Italy (**16.10**). A common reason for making such a journey was the need for physical healing, which might be achieved by making votive offerings (**16.11**) or by carrying home a clay token (**16.12**). Out of this there also emerged a widespread interest in the physical remains, or relics, of martyrs and other holy men and women (cf. **8.13**, **11.9** (10)) – a development, however, that did not escape criticism (**16.13**). The chapter concludes with a representation of the arrival of relics at a city (**16.14**).

Further reading: Hunt 1982a; Ousterhout 1990; Dassmann *et al.* 1995 (a major conference devoted to late antique pilgrimage); Mango 1995; Frankfurter 1998b: 3–48.

16.1 The earliest first-hand account by a Holy Land pilgrim: The *Bordeaux Itinerary*

The text from which the following passage is extracted is the earliest surviving example of a detailed first-hand account of a pilgrimage, undertaken, in this case, from Bordeaux to Jerusalem (thence back to Milan) in the year 'when Dalmaticus and Zenophilus were consuls' (333). Much of the text comprises a simple listing of staging posts (*mutationes*) and resting points (*mansiones*) with distances between them – of interest to the student of place names and routes in the Roman empire, but not so much to the student of religious life (and so not translated here). The concern with distances (given in Roman miles, so somewhat shorter (*c.* 1500 m) than the modern mile (1609 m)) may imply that the author had a practical purpose in mind, namely to provide a guide for others who wished to follow in their steps, though this assumption has not gone unchallenged (Douglass 1996). When the pilgrim reaches Palestine, however, the text becomes more expansive, and among other things provides valuable evidence for the extent to which Constantine had already left his imprint on the landscape in the nine years since he had gained control of the eastern half of the empire. Also of interest is the way in which Old Testament sites outnumber New Testament ones, possibly a clue to Christian pilgrimage developing out of Jewish pilgrimage (Wilkinson 1990). It is noteworthy, however, in the light of later fourth-century practices, that this pilgrim says nothing about offering prayers or reading appropriate scriptures at any of the sites (Douglass 1996: 324–5). The writer's identity is unknown, but frequent comment on matters of special interest to women may point to female authorship (Taylor 1993: 313; Douglass 1996; but note also the more cautious conclusions of Weingarten 1999). Further reading: Wilkinson 1981: 153–63 (commentary); Hunt 1982a: 55–8, 83–5; Wilken 1992: 108–11.

(583) ... The city of Sidon: 8 miles. From there to Sarepta: 9 miles. There Elijah went up to the widow and sought food for himself [1 Kings 17.10ff.]. Staging post at Ad Nonum: 4 miles. (584) The city of Tyre: 12 miles. The distance from Antioch to Tyre is 174 miles, with 20 staging posts and 11 resting points. Staging post at Alexandroschene: 12 miles. Staging post at Ecdeppa: 12 miles. The city of Ptolomaida: 8 miles. Staging post at Calamon: 12 miles. Resting point at Sicaminos: 3 miles. (585) Mount Carmel is there. There Elijah offered sacrifice [1 Kings 18.19ff.]. Staging post at Certha: 8 miles. The boundary between Syria Phoenica and Palestina. The city of Caesarea in Palestina, that is Judaea: 8 miles. The distance from Tyre to Caesarea in Palestina is 73 miles, with 2 staging posts and 3 resting points. In that place is the bath of Cornelius the centurion who gave many alms. At the third milestone from there is (586) Mount Syna, where there is a spring: women who bathe in it fall pregnant. The city of Maximianopolis: 18 miles. The city of Isdradela [Jezreel]: 10 miles. There King Ahab resided and Elijah prophesied. In that place is the plain where David killed Goliath. The city of Scythopolis: 12 miles. (587) Aser, where the estate of Job was: 16 miles. The city of Neapolis [Nablus]: 15 miles. Mount Agazaren [Gerizim] is there: the Samaritans say Abraham offered sacrifice there, and 1300 steps rise up to the top of the mountain. There at the foot of that very mountain is the place whose name is Shechem. In that place is a tomb, where Joseph was buried, (588) on an estate which his father Jacob gave him [Josh. 24.32]. From there also Dinah the daughter of Jacob was seized by the sons of the Amorites [Gen. 34.2]. A mile from there is the place named Sechar, where the Samaritan woman went down to draw water from that same place, where Jacob dug a well, and our Lord Jesus Christ spoke with her [Jn. 4.5ff.]. Plane trees planted by Jacob are also there, and a bath which is filled from that well. 28 miles from there on the left-hand side going towards Jerusalem is an estate called Bethar. A mile from there is the place where Jacob slept, when he was going to Mesopotamia, and the almond tree is there, and he saw a vision and the angel wrestled with him [Gen. 28.12, 32.24]. King Jeroboam was there, to whom a prophet was sent to convert him to the most high God; (589) and the prophet was commanded not to eat with the false prophet whom the king had with him, and because he was led astray by the false prophet and ate with him, on his way back a lion met the prophet on the road and killed him [1 Kings 13.11–31].

Jerusalem is 12 miles from there. The distance from Caesarea in

Palestine to Jerusalem is 116 miles, with 4 staging posts and 4 resting points. In Jerusalem there are two large pools beside the temple – one on the right, the other on the left – which Solomon made, and inside the city are the twin pools with five porticos called Bethsaida. Those who had been ill for many years were healed there. These pools contain water whose turbulence gives it a scarlet appearance. In that place there is also a crypt in which Solomon used to torture demons. There is also the corner of (590) a very high tower, where the Lord ascended and said to the one tempting him, 'You shall not tempt the Lord your God, but serve him alone', and there is a large angular rock, concerning which it was said: 'The rock which the builders rejected has been made the chief corner-stone.' And below the parapet of that very tower are several rooms where Solomon had his palace. The room is also there in which he sat and wrote about wisdom; that very room is roofed with only one stone. Also in that place are great underground cisterns and pools built with much effort. And (591) in that very sanctuary, where the temple which Solomon built used to be, you might think the blood of Zacharias had just been shed today on the marble pavement before the altar [2 Chron. 24.20–2, Matt. 23.35]. Also visible throughout the whole area are the imprints of the hobnails of the soldiers who killed him, so that you might think they had been impressed into wax. Two statues of Hadrian are also there, and not far from the statues is a rock with a hole in it, to which the Jews come every year and anoint; with wailing they lament and rend their garments and so depart. The palace of Hezekiah king of Judaea is also there.

Furthermore, on the way out of Jerusalem to ascend Zion, on the left-hand side (592) down in a valley next to the wall is the pool called Siloam; it has a portico running around all four sides, and another large pool outside. Its spring flows for six days and nights, but the seventh day is the Sabbath, and it does not flow at all, either by day or by night. Zion is ascended by this same route from which is visible the place where the house of the priest Caiaphas was, and the column where they flogged Christ is still there. Inside Zion, within the wall, can be seen the place where David had his palace. And of the seven synagogues which were there only one remains, the others having been ploughed up and planted over as the prophet Isaiah (593) said [Is. 1.8]. From there as you proceed outside the wall from Zion towards the gate to Neapolis, down in the valley on the right-hand side are the walls where the house of Pontius Pilate was, and the praetorium where he listened to the Lord before he suffered. Moreover on the left-hand side is the hill of Golgotha, where the Lord was crucified. (594) Only a stone's throw away from there is the tomb where his body was laid and where on the third day he rose; in that same place there has now been built a basilica by order of the emperor Constantine, that is a house of the Lord, beside which is a very beautiful cistern from which water is raised, and behind which is a bath where infants are baptised. Moreover, proceeding to the Jersualem gate which faces the east to ascend Mount Olivet, there is a valley called Jehosophat's. On the left, there is a vineyard in which the rock where Judas Iscariot betrayed Christ is. On the right (595) is a palm tree, from which children took branches and laid them down for Christ when he came. Not far from here, only a stone's throw away, there are two very beautifully fashioned memorial tombs. The prophet Isaiah was placed in one, made from a single rock, and Hezekiah king of the Jews in the other. From there you ascend Mount Olivet, where the Lord taught the apostles before his suffering. A basilica has been constructed there by order of Constantine. Not far from there is the hill the Lord went up to pray and where Moses and Elijah appeared when he took Peter (596) and John with him [Matt. 17.2; Mk. 9.1; Lk. 9.28].

A mile and a half eastwards from there is the village called Bethany; in that place is the tomb where Lazarus was placed whom the Lord brought back to life. Moreover 18 miles from Jerusalem is Jericho. Descending the mountain, behind a tomb on the right, there is the sycamore tree which Zacchaeus climbed in order to see Christ. A mile and a half from that city is the spring of the prophet Elisha [2 Kings 2.19–22]. Previously if any woman drank from its water, she would not have children. Elisha brought a clay jar in which he placed salt, and came and stood above the spring and said: 'Thus says the Lord: he has healed these waters.' Thereafter any woman drinking from it will have children. Above that same spring is the house of Rahab the prostitute, where she hid the spies who entered [Josh. 2.1ff.], and when Jericho fell, she alone escaped [Josh. 6.20–23]. The city of Jericho used to be there, around whose walls the children of Israel marched with the ark of the covenant and the walls fell down. From that spot can be seen the place where the ark of the covenant was and the twelve stones which the children of Israel raised from the Jordan [Josh. 4.20]. In that same place Joshua the son of Nun circumcised the children of Israel and buried their foreskins [Josh. 5.3].

From Jericho it is 9 miles to the Dead Sea. Its water is extremely bitter, there are no fish of any kind in it at all, nor any boat, and if anyone goes to swim, the water turns him over. (598) From there to the Jordan, where the Lord was baptised by John, is 5 miles. Above the far bank of the river there is the hill where Elijah was taken up into heaven. Four miles on the road going from Jerusalem to Bethlehem, on the right, is the tomb where Rachel, the wife of Jacob, was laid. Two miles from there, on the left, is Bethlehem, where the Lord Jesus Christ was born; a basilica has been built there by order of Constantine. Not far from there is the tomb of Ezechiel. Going down into the tomb the names of Asaph, Job, Jesse, David, and Solomon are written in Hebrew letters low down on the wall. (599) From there to Bethasora is 14 miles, where the pool in which Philip baptised the eunuch is located [Acts 8.36–8]. It is 9 miles from there to Terebinth, where Abraham dwelt and dug a well under a terebinth tree, and spoke and ate food with the angels [Gen. 18.1ff.]; a very beautiful basilica has been built there by order of Constantine. It is 2 miles from there, Terebinth, to Hebron, where there is a very beautiful square tomb made of stones, in which were laid Abraham, Isaac, Jacob, Sarah, Rebecca and Leah. (600) The distances from Jersualem are thus: the city of Nicopolis, 22 miles, the city of Lydda, 10 miles, the staging post of Antipatris, 10 miles, the staging post at Betthar, 10 miles, the city of Caesarea, 16 miles. The complete distance from Constantinople to Jerusalem is 1,164 miles, with 69 staging posts, and 58 resting points. ... [From this point, the guide consists almost entirely of distances, etc. for the return journey, though with the occasional comment such as the following: (603) ... 'the city of Philippi, 10 miles, where Paul and Silas were imprisoned'.]

16.2 Group pilgrimage in the mid-fourth century: Athanasius *Letter to Virgins who Went and Prayed in Jerusalem and Returned* pp. 170–2

The main concern of this letter of Athanasius (*c.* 295–373), bishop of Alexandria, was to provide guidelines for the conduct of virgins living in community, but the opening sections (below), include important material for the subject of Holy Land pilgrimage. The date of the letter is uncertain – probably the latter stages of Athanasius' life and so the third quarter of the fourth century (Elm 1994: 332 n. 2; Brakke 1998: 271) – but it certainly predates Egeria's travels (16.3). It shows females travelling as a group to the Holy Land, and focusing their attention on the places of Christ's birth, death and ascension (this last, implied towards the end of the second paragraph below, is made explicit later in the letter). It is also significant for its articulation of reservations about pilgrimage, reservations which were to be more fully developed by Gregory of Nyssa (16.5). Further reading: Lebon 1928; Elm 1987; Elm 1994: 331–6; Brakke 1998: 36–41.

(p. 170) We grieve with you, maidservants of Christ, because as you were separating from the holy places you shed streams of bitter tears. As you were travelling, you were also weeping because you were leaving far behind the cave of the Lord, which is the image of Paradise or, rather, which surpasses it. For there 'the first human being, from the earth, a person of dust' was formed; but here 'the second human being, from heaven' was renewed [1 Cor. 15.47]. There he who had been 'in the image and likeness' [Gen. 1.26] was changed into something imperfect, but [here] the unchanging image of the Father appeared. The first person hid himself under the fig-tree, but the second person took shelter under the power of the Most High. There he was banished from the angelic glory, but here he was glorified by the angelic choir and worshipped by the magi. Bethlehem, where until today the echoes full of praise endure in every watch of the night! As you were leaving this holy Bethlehem, you travelled quite rightly in many tears from your heart's distress because you recalled that beautiful way of life: the true fast, the entirely pure prayers of that quiet and untroubled manner [of life], the prayers that are continually arising there, and especially (p. 171) the noble exhortations that you would hear from the holy ones as you sat at their feet like Mary in times of stillness [Lk. 10.38–42]. Because you were leaving these pearls, you were sorrowful. Hence as you were saying farewell to your sister virgins, upon your breasts the tears of each of you mingled with those of her companion.

You nonetheless had the hope of consolation in seeing the holy cave of the resurrection and the site of Golgotha, which also is not inferior to the excellence of Paradise. For there he who stretched out his hand toward the tree brought death on all, but here he who was stretched out on the tree of the cross bestowed salvation on all. He who was there was led astray by the serpent, but here that serpent was led astray. There the taste was sweet, but the act bitter; here, however, the food was bitter, but the result sweet. Not a little did the departure from the holy mountain grieve you. But just as the disciples were in groans as they descended from the mountain because the Saviour departed from them – 'For then they will fast', he said, 'when the bridegroom is taken from them' [Matt. 9.15] – likewise you too were in great distress as you departed from the holy places because you desire and long for the courts of the Lord [Ps. 84.3].

(p. 172) Now take heart and do not be grieved! You have not journeyed far from the holy places, for where Christ dwells, there is holiness. And where Christ's presence is, there too is an abundance of the joys of holiness. He lives also in our temple if we keep [its] holiness undefiled always [1 Cor. 6.19] ... (tr. D. Brakke [*Athanasius and Asceticism*, pp. 292–3. © 1998. David Brakke]).

16.3 A female pilgrim's travels in Sinai: The *Itinerary of Egeria* 1–5

The *Itinerary* from which the following passage comes is probably the best-known account of a pilgrimage from Late Antiquity. It has not, however, survived complete, and the loss of its opening and conclusion in particular mean that absolute certainty about authorship and precise date is impossible. The writer was undoubtedly a woman – a fact of cardinal significance – and the general consensus now is that her name was Egeria. She seems to have come from somewhere in the western provinces of the empire – the Rhone valley of Gaul is the most likely location (Sivan 1988a) – and to have undertaken her extensive travels in the early 380s. The work is addressed to female companions back home, and while it is often assumed that she and they were nuns, they may in fact have been layfolk (Sivan 1988b). She lived in the east for at least three years, during which she made a number of trips around Palestine, Syria, Egypt and the Sinai Peninsula. All this presupposes a background of some means, as also does her ability to read and write, though the deficiencies of her Latin style suggest that she was not of aristocratic upbringing. The following extract, which starts where the surviving manuscript begins mid-sentence, presents parts of the first five chapters, in which the author relates her visit to Mount Sinai and its environs, and it reflects many of the salient features of the work as a whole. Further reading: Wilkinson 1981; Hunt 1982a: 58–62, 86–8; Wilken 1992: 111–14.

1. < ... > were pointed out in accordance with the Scriptures. Walking on, we arrived at a place where the mountains through which we were proceeding opened out to create a long valley – large, very wide and particularly beautiful – and across this valley there came into view Sinai, the holy mountain of God. This place where the mountains opened out adjoins the spot where the 'Tombs of Craving' [Num. 11.34] are situated. (2) When we reached this place, our guides, the holy men who were accompanying us, advised us thus: 'It is usual for those who come here to offer a prayer when they first set eyes on the mountain of God from this spot.' And this we did. From this point to the mountain of God was a distance of perhaps four miles across the valley which, as I have said, was large.

2. The valley itself, lying below the side of the mountain of God, is large indeed, and according to what we could gauge with our own eyes and what they told us, it is perhaps sixteen miles in length and, they said, four miles wide. We had to travel along this valley to approach the mountain. (2) This large and very wide valley is the

one in which the children of Israel waited during those days when the holy Moses went up the mountain of God and was there for forty days and forty nights [Ex. 24.18]. This is also the valley in which the [golden] calf was made [Ex. 32] – the spot is pointed out to this day, for a large rock stands there embedded in the ground. This is the valley at the head of which is the place where the holy Moses, while grazing his father-in-law's livestock, heard God speak to him twice from the burning bush. ...

3. Late on the Sabbath we reached the mountain, and when we approached some cells the monks who live there welcomed us most warmly and showed us every kindness; there is also a church there with a presbyter. We stayed the night there, and then early on the Lord's Day we undertook the ascent of the various mountains, accompanied by the presbyter and the monks who live there. It is hard work climbing those mountains, for you do not ascend gradually in a circular manner – in a spiral, as we say – but you go up those mountains in a straight line as if up a wall, and you have to go down steep drops, until you reach the very foot of the mountain in the middle, which is Sinai itself. (2) Aided by Christ our God and assisted by the prayers of the holy men accompanying us, we undertook this hard work. I had to ascend on foot because it was completely impossible to do so in the saddle, yet it did not feel like work because I realised that, with God's help, I was fulfilling the desire I had. At the fourth hour [ten o'clock], we reached the summit of Sinai, the holy mountain of God, where the Law was given, and where the glory of the Lord came down on the day when the mountain was covered in smoke [Ex. 19.18]. (3) There is a church of modest proportions there, since the summit of the mountain does not encompass a very large area, but the church has considerable charm of its own. (4) So when, with God's help, we had climbed to the summit and reached the entrance of the church, the presbyter assigned to the church hurried out from his cell to meet us – a virtuous old man who had been a monk since his youth and, as they say here, an ascetic, and – what more can I say? – one who was worthy to be in that place. There also came to meet us other presbyters and all the monks, too, who dwell on the mountain, or at any rate those not prevented by old age or physical infirmity. (5) No-one actually lives on the summit of the middle mountain; there is nothing there other than the church and the cave in which the holy Moses had been [Ex. 33.22]. (6) After everything was read from the Book of Moses in that place and the offering had been made in the appropriate manner, and we had shared in the communion, we went out of the

church. ... (7) ... When we had gone outside the door of the church, I asked the holy men to point out for us the various features, and immediately they agreed to do so. They pointed out the cave where the holy Moses had been when he ascended the mountain the second time, to receive the tablets [of the Law] again, after he had broken the original set when the people sinned [Ex. 34]...

4. When we had achieved all we wished and for which we had hastened to ascend, we embarked on the descent from the summit of the mountain of God, then climbed another mountain adjacent to it. This place is called 'On Horeb', and there is a church there. (2) For this place is the Horeb where the holy prophet Elijah came when he fled from the presence of King Ahab, when God spoke to him, saying, 'What are you doing here, Elijah?', as is written in the Books of the Kingdoms [1 Kings 19.9]. The cave is also there in which the holy Elijah hid, which to this day can be seen in front of the door of the church which is there. Also pointed out was the stone altar which the holy Elijah placed there to make an offering to God. The holy men accompanying us kindly showed us these things. (3) Then we presented an offering of our own there, praying with great fervour, and the passage from the Book of the Kingdoms was read. For whenever we arrived anywhere, I always particularly wanted the relevant passage to be read to us from the Bible. ...

5. ... (5) Along the valley they also pointed out the dwellings each of the Israelites had had, made from stone in a circular shape, for even today the foundations are still visible. They also showed us the place where the holy Moses commanded the children of Israel to run from gate to gate after returning from the mountain [Ex. 32.27]. (6) They also indicated the place where the calf which Aaron had made for them was melted down, at the command of the holy Moses. They also pointed out the stream from which the holy Moses provided the children of Israel with water to drink, as was written in Exodus. (7) They also showed us the place where the seventy men received some of Moses' spirit [Num. 11.25]. They also indicated the place where the children of Israel had a craving for food [Num. 11.4]. They also showed us the place which is called 'Fire' because a part of the camp burned until the fire ceased at the holy Moses' prayer [Num. 11.1–3]. (8) They also showed us the place where manna and quails rained down on them [Num. 9.1–5]. And so in this way we were shown each event recorded in the holy books of Moses as having happened in that place, that is in that valley, which as I have said lay below the mountain of God, that is holy Sinai. It has taken a long time to describe all these things in

turn, and it is difficult to remember so much. But when you read the holy books of Moses, dear sisters, you will understand better everything which happened there. ...

16.4 The price of an escort to the Holy Mountain: *P. Ness.* 89

Excavations at the southern Palestinian site of Nessana uncovered a cache of papyrus documents, including a (damaged) account of expenditures by some traders in the late sixth century from which the following has been extracted. It is included here because among the sundry items purchased is a reference to the cost of hiring an escort to accompany the traders to 'the Holy Mountain', almost certainly Mt Sinai. 'While the present papyrus does not record a pilgrimage, ... it does incidentally partake of the nature of one, for the Christian traders did not fail to attend services and leave offerings in the church' (Kraemer 1958: 253). It is also of interest for the cost involved, since 'the amount is considerable – more than half that of a camel' (Kraemer 1958: 259 n. 22). The unit of money referred to in the text is the *solidus*.

... and other various wares – 1½ lbs.
The two of us smelted it (at the order?)

of his Holiness Father Mantheas – 1 lb. of iron (?)		5⅓ sol.
Paid as price of the slave girl	3 sol.	
plus camel worth	6 ⅓ sol.	
total		9 ⅓
as price of slave boy	6 sol.	
plus camel worth	4 ⅓ sol.	
total (including fee of man who drew up bill of sale)		10 ⅓

Paid to Arab escort who took us to the Holy Mountain		3 ½
Turned over to us by Father Martyrios		270 ½ sol.
We went to prayers in the Holy Mountain and		
made an offering of		1
Expenditures for you, also purchase of fish		
and almonds		1
Donation to Monastery in behalf of the group		
from your town	10 sol.	
also in behalf of ...	7 sol.	
total		17

(tr. C.J. Kraemer)

16.5 The case against pilgrimage: Gregory of Nyssa *Letter* 2

This letter is of interest as the most forthright argument from Late Antiquity against pilgrimage: 'he states with exemplary brevity the classical theological case against sacralization of place' (Wilken 1992: 117). Similar sentiments were sometimes expressed by Jerome, but elsewhere he approves of pilgrimage, and of course he himself ended up living in Palestine. The recipient of this letter is otherwise unknown, but the references throughout to ascetic life ('the loftier way of life', 'the perfect', etc.) imply a monastic context. The visit to Arabia and Palestine to which Gregory alludes in (12) took place in the early 380s, so the letter was obviously written at some point between then and his death *c*. 395. As quickly becomes apparent from the letter, Gregory was a native of Cappadocia (he was a younger brother of Basil of Caesarea). Ironically, his strictures about the risks to which travel exposed females are belied by Egeria's account of her journeys (**16.3**). Further reading: Elm 1987; Wilken 1992: 117–19.

Concerning those who go to Jerusalem, to Censitor. (1) Since you posed questions in your letter, my friend, I thought it appropriate to respond to you on each point in order. It is my view that those who have dedicated themselves once and for all to the loftier way of life do well to pay attention at all times to the words of the gospel. Just as those straightening out an object with a rule alter the crookedness of the thing in their hands into straight lines in conformity with the straightness of the rule, so it is appropriate, I think, for those who have taken upon themselves a sort of rule which is right and unchangeable – I am talking about the way of life prescribed by the gospel – to direct themselves straight towards God in accordance with it. (2) Since some of those who have entered into the solitary and separated life think it a part of their devotion to see the places in Jerusalem where evidence of the Lord's stay in the flesh can be observed, they do well to look towards the rule and, if the guidance of the commands requires this, to undertake this deed as a precept of the Lord. But if it is extraneous to the Lord's commands, I do not know what it means to wish to carry out a prescription which has become a requirement of blessing for oneself.

(3) When the Lord calls the blessed to their inheritance in the kingdom of heaven, he does not count journeying to Jerusalem among their good deeds. When he preaches the Beatitudes, he does not include any such exertion among them. Why pursue something which does not make us blessed or fit for the kingdom? Let him who has understanding think about this. (4) And if this undertaking was advantageous, it would not be a good thing, even so, for the perfect to pursue. But as we observe clearly that this activity

also causes spiritual damage in those engaged in the virtuous life, it no longer deserves to be a matter of great urgency but rather of great caution, so that those choosing to live in conformity with God's ways are not wounded by something harmful.

(5) What then is harmful in this? The holy way of life is available to all, both men and women, and decorum is the distinctive feature of the life according to its philosophy. It is achieved by living a separated life away from society, where the sexes do not mingle or have dealings with one another, for neither men among women nor women among men are inclined to guard against indecency. (6) But the constraints of the journey are always disrupting the scrupulous observance of virtue among them and leading to indifference with regard to those observances. For it is impossible for a woman to undertake such a journey unless she has someone to protect her and, on account of her physical weakness, to help her up onto her mount and to dismount, and to support her across rough terrain. But whatever we may suppose – either she has a friend looking after her or she hires someone to provide service – in neither situation does her conduct escape blame. For whether she is supporting herself on a stranger or on a friend, she is not observing the law of chastity. (7) Moreover, when the inns and lodgings and cities throughout the eastern regions contain so much impropriety and indifference towards evil, how can eyes avoid smarting while moving through smoke? Where the ear is defiled, where the eye is defiled, the heart is defiled as it takes in improprieties through eye and ear. How is it possible to travel through places of sensuality without having one's senses aroused?

(8) Why should he who has been to those places have any advantage, as if the Lord were living physically in those places right up until this very day but was not present among us, or as if the Holy Spirit was with the inhabitants of Jerusalem in abundance yet was unable to come to us? (9) Indeed, if it were possible to recognise the presence of God from what is visible, one might think that God dwells among the people of Cappadocia rather than in places elsewhere; for there are so many sanctuaries in these parts, through which the name of the Lord is glorified, that one can scarcely count more sanctuaries in the whole world. (10) If the grace of God was greater in the places near Jerusalem, then sin would not be common among those living there; but today there is no kind of depravity which they do not have the effrontery to engage in – fornication, adultery, theft, idolatry, poisoning, envying, murder. This last evil is especially prevalent, so that there is no-one who is not ready to

murder in these places, with those of the same race attacking one another like wild animals for paltry gain. When these things happen, what proof is there that grace is greater in those places?

(11) But I know the objection of many to what I am saying. For they say, 'Why did you not also abide by these prescriptions yourself? For if there was no advantage in being there for the person who makes the journey in the name of God, why did you undertake such a journey for no purpose?' (12) Let them hear my defence on these matters. It was on account of this [episcopal] responsibility with which I am obliged to live by the One who orders our life that there came an instruction from the holy council for me to go to those parts so as to set in order the church in Arabia. And since Arabia is adjacent to the area around Jerusalem, I promised that I would also undertake, with the leading men of the holy church in Jerusalem, an investigation into those affairs of theirs that were in disorder and in need of someone to act as a mediator. (13) Since the most devout emperor offered the opportunity for an easier journey through the imperial system of carriages, there was no need for us to undergo those things which we have observed in the case of others, for the carriage was like a church and a monastery for us, and throughout the whole journey we all sang psalms and fasted together in the Lord. (14) So our journey should not cause anyone offence; rather, our advice should gain credence, for it is these things which we have observed with our own eyes about which we are giving advice. (15) For we have confessed that Christ who appeared on earth is the true God, both before we were at the place and after, and our faith was neither diminished nor increased after this; we knew for a fact the incarnation through the Virgin before we saw Bethlehem, we knew for a fact the resurrection from the dead before we saw the tomb, and we assented to the truth of the ascension into heaven without seeing the Mount of Olives. We derived only one benefit from this trip – the knowledge that, in comparison, our own places are much more holy than those elsewhere.

(16) So 'You who fear the Lord, praise him' [Ps. 22.23] in the places where you are. For a change of location does not result in God drawing near; rather, God will come to you wherever you may be, if the resting-place of your soul is found to be such that the Lord can dwell and move about in you. (17) But if your 'inner man' [Rom. 7.22; Eph. 3.16] is full of wicked thoughts, even if you are at Golgotha, even if you are on the Mount of Olives, even if you are in the tomb of the Resurrection (*Anastasis*), you are as far from receiving Christ in yourself as those are who have not even begun to

confess him. (18) So advise the brothers, dear friend, to leave their bodies to approach the Lord [2 Cor. 5.8], and not to leave Cappadocia to go to Palestine. But if anyone should put forward as an excuse the words of the Lord commanding the disciples not to leave Jerusalem [Acts 1.4], let him understand what is being said. Since the grace and gift of the Holy Spirit had not yet been given to the apostles, the Lord commanded them to remain in that place until they had been clothed with power from on high [Lk. 24.49]. (19) So if what happened from the beginning continues to the present day – that the Holy Spirit in the guise of fire distributes gifts of grace to each one – then everyone needs to be in that place where the dispensing of grace occurred; but if 'the Spirit blows where it wills' [Jn. 3.8], believers here also are partakers of grace 'in proportion to their faith' [Rom. 12.6], and not by virtue of their having travelled to Jerusalem.

16.6 Mementos (1): a clay pilgrim flask

Judging by the considerable numbers found around the Mediterranean, the most popular form of pilgrim memento was the small flask or *ampulla*, sometimes made of metal, more often of clay (as here). The flask usually bore some sort of iconography appropriate to the particular site or shrine, and was designed to carry earth, water or lamp oil from the location. The one illustrated in **Figure 16.6** (15 x 11 cm) is from the shrine of St Menas in northern Egypt (Abu Mena). Although not in the Holy Land, it serves as a reminder that other locations also attracted pilgrims, and indeed this shrine is the source of the greatest number of surviving *ampullae*. Menas was a military martyr of uncertain date, and his shrine developed at the spot where the two camels (flanking Menas on the flask) carrying his body supposedly stopped and refused to proceed any further. For the associated pilgrimage centre, see Grossmann 1998. Further reading: Hunt 1982a: 130–1; Vikan 1982.

16.7 Mementos (2): Augustine *The City of God* 22.8

Pilgrims to the Holy Land often brought back treasured mementos of their visit; little clay containers of oil (*ampullae*) were particularly popular (16.6). In the following anecdote, however, Augustine recounts a rather different sort of memento carried back to north Africa, and its consequences. A pocketful of Palestinian soil is both an obvious souvenir – literally a bit of holy land – and yet also a peculiar choice, because its association with Christ is so tenuous and generalised. However, 'Christ's sojourn on earth, it seems, had sanctified not only the specific places where he lived and died, but the very soil of the land itself' (Wilken 1992: 125). (For epigraphic confirmation of Augustine's story, see **16.8a** below.) Augustine's attitude is also interesting. Elsewhere, he expresses views consistent with Gregory of Nyssa's opposition to the sacralisation of place, but here he 'tolerated,

Figure 16.6   St Menas pilgrim flask
Source: Photograph by R. Cortopassi. © The Louvre, Paris.

even approved, the transporting of soil from the holy land all the way to North Africa as a talisman against evil spirits and balm for healing. ... Here, as elsewhere, Augustine's piety collides with his theology' (Wilken 1992: 125). Further reading: Hunt 1982a: 129–30.

A man of tribunician status named Hesperius lives near us; he has a farm in the district of Fussala, called Zubedi. When he discovered, through the troubles experienced by his animals and slaves, that his home was suffering from the harmful influence of evil spirits, he asked our priests, in my absence, if one of them could go to him and pray for the removal of the spirits. One of them went and offered there the sacrifice of the body of Christ, praying to the best of his ability that this harassment would cease, and by the mercy of God, it did cease immediately. Hesperius had also received from a friend of his some holy soil (*terra sancta*) carried back from Jerusalem where Christ was buried and rose again on the third day, and he hung this in his bedroom to ensure that he himself did not also experience anything evil. Then when his house had been cleansed from that disturbance, he thought about what he should do with that soil – for, due to his sense of awe, he was reluctant to keep it in his bedroom for too long. It so happened that I and a colleague of mine,

Maximinus, bishop of the church at Sinita, were in the neighbourhood at that time. Hesperius asked us to come, and we did so.
When he had told us the whole story, he also made the following
request – that the soil be buried somewhere and a place for prayer
be established on the spot where Christians could also gather to
celebrate the things of God. We did not object, and it was done.
There was a young peasant there who was paralysed. When he heard
about this, he asked his parents to carry him to that holy place
(*locum sanctum*) without delay. When he had been carried there, he
prayed, and he promptly left the place healthy and on his own two
feet.

16.8 The diffusion of relics from the Holy Land: *ILCV* 2068 and 1822

These important inscriptions from relatively unimportant towns in western north
Africa illustrate the way in which relics from the Holy Land could circulate widely
and reach distant and peripheral parts of the empire. Both confirm the early diffusion of the cult of the True Cross reported by Cyril of Jerusalem in his *Catechical
Lectures* (4.10, 10.19, 13.4) of 350. The first inscription is precisely dated to 359;
linguistic features suggest a fourth-century date for the second, and Flavius Nuvel
has been plausibly identified with the Nubel mentioned briefly by Ammianus
Marcellinus in a Mauretanian context (*History* 29.5.2), implying a date in the
middle of the century for the inscription. The first inscription also makes reference
to soil from the Holy Land, confirming **16.7**, and to the cult of martyrs – in this
case, honouring a combination of figures of empire-wide stature (Peter and Paul),
well-known African saints (Cyprian), and local heroes. Further reading: Hunt
1982a: 38–42, 128–30; Duval 1982: 331–7, 351–3; Matthews 1989: 371–3.

(a) ILCV 2068 (= CIL 8.20600) (Tixiter, Mauretania)

Holy memorial of earth of the promise where Christ was born
(*memoria sacta de tera promisionis ube natus est Christus* [*sic*])[and] of the
apostle Peter and of Paul. Names of the martyrs Datianus,
Donatianus, Cyprian, Nemesanus, Citinus and Victoria. In the year
of the province 320 [359], Benenatus and Pequaria set it up.
Victorinus, Miggin, on the 7th day before the Ides of September [7
September] < ... > and Dabula and a fragment from the wood of
the cross (*de lignu crucis*).

(b) ILCV 1822 (= CIL 8.9255) (Rusguniae, Mauretania)

A fragment of the holy wood of the cross of Christ the Saviour (*de
sancto ligno crucis Christi Salvatoris*) having been carried and placed

here, Flavius Nuvel, former commander of the *Armigeri Iuniores* (literally 'younger weapon-bearers') unit of cavalry, son of Saturninus, a man of very high rank (*vir perfectissimus*) and a former count, and of Colecia, a very honourable woman, great-grandson (?) of Elurus Laconicus (?), has dedicated this basilica which he promised in a vow and offers (*basilicam voto promissam et oblatam*) with his wife Nonnica and all their household.

16.9 Pilgrimage to a holy man: Theodoret *History of the Monks* 26.11–12 and the pilgrim complex at Qal'at Sem'an

Symeon the Stylite (died *c.* 459) was one of the most famous holy men of the fifth century, acquiring his reputation in part as a result of his unusual form of ascetic extremism – sitting on top of a pillar (cf. Harvey 1988; Frankfurter 1990). Theodoret, bishop of Cyrrhus (423–*c.* 460), naturally included him in his collection of stories about Syrian ascetics (composed *c.* 444), and here describes the way he attracted large numbers of pilgrims. No doubt there is a significant element of hyperbole here, but there is corroborative evidence of Symeon's reputation in sixth-century Gaul (Nasrallah 1974) and the scale of the complex that grew up around his pillar at Qal'at Sem'an (see **Figure** 16.9b) likewise confirms his popularity (albeit posthumously).

(a) *Theodoret* History of the Monks *26.11–12*

(11) As his reputation spread in every direction, people from everywhere flocked to him, not only those living nearby, but also those separated by a journey of many days. Some brought those weakened in body, others requested health for the sick, still others asked for help to become fathers and sought to receive through him what they could not obtain by natural means. When they received it and their requests were granted, they returned home rejoicing, proclaiming the blessings they have chanced upon, and thereby prompting many, many more to set out with their needs. So with everyone arriving from all directions and every route resembling a river, a sea of people is to be seen gathered in that place which receives these rivers from all around. For not only were those living in our empire flowing there, but also Ishmaelites, Persians and Armenians subject to them, Iberians, Homerites, and people living further inland from them. Many came who live in the most westerly regions – Spaniards, Britons, and Gauls who live between them. And there is no need to talk about Italy, for it is said that the man was such a topic of conversation in great Rome that in all the entrances to

shops little images of him have been set up as a kind of protection for them, providing security there. (12) Since incalculable numbers were now arriving, all trying to touch him and to gain some blessing from his clothing of skins, he thought at first that this excessive honouring was absurd, then becoming unhappy with the disturbance caused by the practice, he contrived to stand upright on his column. Initially he ordered a column of six cubits to be cut, then of twelve, and after that twenty-two, and now thirty-six. For he longs to fly to heaven and to escape from his stay on this earth.

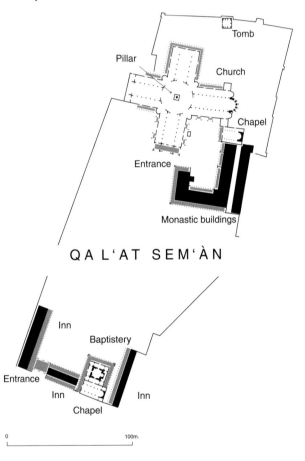

Figure 16.9b   The pilgrimage complex at Qal'at Sem'an in the late fifth century

Source: After G. Tchalenko, *Villages antiques de la Syrie du Nord*, vol. 2 (1953), Pl. 50.1.

16.10 Pilgrimage to a saint's shrine: Paulinus Of Nola *Poem* 18.154–84, 198–205

Paulinus of Nola (*c*. 353–431) was a Gallic aristocrat who initially followed a traditional career in imperial service (he was governor of the Italian region of Campania
in the early 380s), before renouncing his wealth in 394 to pursue an ascetic lifestyle
at Nola in Campania, where he subsequently became bishop. The focus of his
attention in Nola was the shrine of Felix, a third-century cleric and confessor (for
the uncertainty surrounding Felix's life, see Trout 1999: 31 n. 53). The shrine had
already been the object of devotion before Paulinus' arrival, but under his care its
reputation expanded significantly. Every year Paulinus celebrated the anniversary of
Felix's death (14 January) by reading a poem in his honour; the following extract
comes from the one written for the year 400, and conveys some sense of the evolution of the site, the pilgrims who flocked there, and their reasons for doing so.
Further reading: Brown 1981: 53–7; Saxer 1995: 46–51; Trout 1999: ch. 7 (with
plans of the complex on pp. xviii–xx [figs 1a–c]); Van Dam 1993: ch. 4 (for
another important pilgrimage centre in the west).

When the due ceremonies had been carried out [following Felix's
death], they united the blessed corpse with its tomb, but the divine
grace implanted in those holy limbs could not die or be buried with
his flesh. Instead, there shone forth immediately from the bones laid
to rest a light which, from that time until now, has never ceased to
give proofs of Felix's potent virtue through its healing powers. (160)
And this same light will continue to shine for as long as the world
exists, a guardian of the saint's remains throughout the centuries.
This demonstrates the vitality of the dead martyr, and by bringing
the blessings of Christ to the tomb of Felix, the marvellous name of
Felix is spread far and wide to every land; it enhances the renown of
Nola before all towns as the only one worthy of so great a guest. By
the grace of Christ, Nola has become so widely known through the
benefits of Felix that, as you can see, the town has grown with new
inhabitants and buildings where originally there was just a poor
tomb which (170) had, with difficulty, been built by the Lord's
people, fearful of swords and fire in that harsh period when the true
religion, menaced by the ungodly, was a crime (as an earlier generation has relayed to more recent descendants). They had enclosed a
great light under that little structure and that holy nook then had
possession of a great deposit. Aware of the hidden light, it has
projected forth, like a fountain, splendid shrines; it remains like a
precious gemstone set amongst the buildings, diffusing [its light]
throughout the five basilicas and their spacious rooms around the
holy tomb, whose roofs, (180) seen from afar, create the impression
of a great city to viewers. But though substantial, these buildings

are overwhelmed by crowds because as faith increases the grace of Christ overflows and proves to people through his healing gift that Felix is alive. ...

You can also see peasants from the countryside not only carrying children in fatherly arms, (200) but often leading sick cattle with their hand, freely committing them to the saint as if he were visible; then, believing that healing has been granted in response to their prayers, they rejoice in God whom they know from experience, and trust their animals are now healthy. Indeed many are quickly healed crossing the threshold, and they conduct their livestock home happy. ...

16.11 Saints and healing (1): Theodoret *The Healing of Pagan Diseases* 8.63–4 and examples of votive offerings

In his treatise entitled *The Healing of Pagan Diseases* – a detailed defence of Christianity against the arguments of pagans – Theodoret, bishop of Cyrrhus (*c.* 423–*c.* 460) describes the practice of bringing votive offerings for healing to the shrines of martyrs (cf. **1.9**). (It is also of interest apropos the theme of Christianisation that Theodoret felt the need to write such a work in the early fifth century, as also for its use of the metaphor of sickness and health in religious polemic (cf., e.g., **3.9** (11), **5.6** (424), **8.7**).) A collection of small metal plaques from sixth- or seventh-century Syria seem to be examples of such offerings. The two below in **Figure 16.11** (measuring 4 x 4.5 cm and 2.6 x 3.6 cm, respectively) are made of a mixture of copper and silver, and both bear a pair of eyes (cf. **1.9**); the text on the first reads, 'Lord, help + Amen +', that on the second, 'In fulfillment of a vow'. Further reading: Vikan 1982: 45–6, 1984: 66–7; Mundell Mango 1986: 242–5.

(a) Theodoret The Healing of Pagan Diseases 8.63–4

(63) ... Those who are well ask [the martyrs] to protect their good health, while those who are worn down by illness request release from their sufferings. The childless ask for children, infertile women call out to become mothers, and those who have received this gift request that it be kept perfectly safe for them. ... They do not approach them like gods – rather they entreat them as men of God and call on them to act as ambassadors on their behalf. (64) Those who ask with confidence gain what they request – their votive offerings clearly testify to their healing. For some offer representations of eyes, some of feet, others of hands; some are made of gold, others of wood. Their Master accepts these little items of little worth, valuing the gift according to the merit of the one offering it. The

display of these objects advertises deliverance from suffering – they have been left as commemorations by those who have regained their health. They proclaim the power of [the martyrs] laid to rest there – whose power proves that their God is the true God.

(b) Votive offerings (see Figure 16.11)

16.12 Saints and healing (2): a clay pilgrim token

This clay disk in **Figure 16.12** (measuring 3.4 x 3.3 cm) is one of several dozen examples of such tokens deriving from the shrine associated with the younger Symeon the Stylite (521–92), who attracted pilgrims to his pillar on the 'Miraculous Mountain' near Antioch in the same way that his fifth-century namesake had to Qal'at Sem'an (16.9). The token shows a bust of Symeon atop his pillar; angels bearing garlands approach from either side to crown the holy man, while a monk carrying a censer climbs the ladder on the left. To the right of the pillar, John the Baptist places his hand on the head of a child-like Christ, while the dove of the Holy Spirit descends from above. Though not easily discernible, the Greek word for 'health' is written across the middle of the token in reverse (the result of the mechanical process by which the tokens were stamped). From various episodes in the *Life of the Younger St Symeon the Stylite*, it is apparent that these tokens, or *eulogiai* (literally, 'blessings'), were made from clay at the foot of the saint's pillar and were given to pilgrims as medicinal amulets. Further reading: Vikan 1982, 1984: 67–70.

16.13 Controversy over the cult of martyrs' relics: Jerome *Against Vigilantius* 4–5 (PL 23.342–3)

As has become apparent from earlier passages (8.13, 11.9 (10)), a phenomenon related to pilgrimage to saints and their shrines was popular interest in the physical remains, or relics, of martyrs and other holy men and women which many believed were charged with spiritual power. This passage reflects both that development and the criticism it attracted in some quarters – in this case from a Gallic Christian named Vigilantius who, in the first decade of the fifth century wrote a treatise denouncing the practice of showing reverence to relics. As with Jovinian (11.8), Vigilantius' work has survived only indirectly, as quoted by Jerome in his vitriolic rebuttal (who cannot resist making awful jokes based on Vigilantius' name – literally 'the wide awake one'). Further reading: Kelly 1975: 286–90; Massie 1980; Hunt 1981; Stancliffe 1983: 301–11; Markus 1990: ch. 10; Hunter 1999.

4. ... Among other blasphemous remarks, he also says this: 'Why do you need not just to show great respect for, but also to worship whatever it is you reverence by carrying around in a little container?' And again in the same pamphlet: 'Why do you kiss and venerate dust wrapped in a linen cloth?' And in what follows: 'We

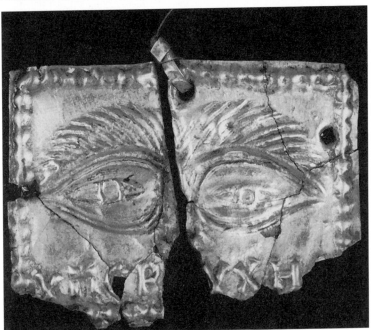

Figure 16.11 Silver plaquettes from Ma'aret en-Norman treasure

Source: The Walters Art Gallery, Baltimore.

Figure 16.12   Clay pilgrim token
Source: The Menil Collection, Houston.

see what is virtually a pagan rite (*prope ritum gentilium*) being brought into the churches under the pretext of religion. While the sun is still shining, vast numbers of candles are lit and everywhere they kiss and worship a little bit of dust, wrapped in a linen cloth inside an expensive little container. People of this sort confer great honour on the most blessed martyrs, thinking to make them conspicuous with cheap little candles – when it is the Lamb in the midst of the throne with all the brightness of his majesty who makes them conspicuous.'

5. You madman – who has ever worshipped the martyrs? Who has thought a man was God? When the Lycaonians believed Paul and Barnabas were Jupiter and Mercury and wanted to offer sacrifices to them, didn't Paul and Barnabas tear their clothes [in anger] and declare that they were men? [Acts 14.11–18] Not that they weren't superior to Jupiter and Mercury, men long dead and gone; but it was through the error of paganism that the honour due to God was offered to them. We also read this with reference to Peter, who raised Cornelius by the hand when the latter wanted to worship him, and said, 'Get up, for I too am a man.' [Acts 10.26]. And you dare to talk about 'whatever it is that you carry around in a small container and worship'? I would like to know what it is that you are calling 'whatever it is'! Explain more clearly what you mean by 'a little bit of dust, wrapped in a linen cloth inside an expensive little container' – even if it means blaspheming God without any restraint. It is the relics of the martyrs which he deplores being wrapped in a valuable piece of cloth, rather than their being gathered up in rags or a goatskin, or thrown out on the rubbish heap, so that the dissipated and dozy Vigilantius alone might be worshipped! Are

we then violating God's law when we enter the basilicas of the apostles? Did the emperor Constantius [II] transgress when he transferred the holy relics of Andrew, Luke and Timothy to Constantinople, in whose presence the demons wail and those possessing Vigilantius admit to feeling their impact. Should our emperor Arcadius also be called sacrilegious because now, after a long time, he has brought the bones of the blessed Samuel from Judaea to Thrace? Are all the bishops not only sacrilegious but to be considered fools because they carried that worthless item and disintegrated ashes in silk and a golden vessel? Are the people from all the churches stupid because they went to meet the holy relics and greeted them with joy, as if they saw the prophet alive and present with them, so that, from Palestine to Chalcedon, crowds of people came together and with one voice praised Christ. To be sure, they were honouring Samuel, and not Christ, whose priest and prophet Samuel was. You assume he is dead, and so blaspheme. Read the Gospel: '"I am the God of Abraham, of Isaac and of Jacob" – he is not the God of the dead, but of the living!' [Matt. 22.32]. If then they are alive, they are not, as you would have it, 'shut up in honourable custody'!

16.14 The arrival of martyrs' relics: The Trier ivory

This ivory carving (**Figure 16.14**) illustrates the sort of scene referred to by Jerome in the previous passage – crowds thronging the streets to watch the arrival of martyrs' relics. The relics are contained in the small box being carried by two bishops atop the carriage on the left. There has been considerable debate as to whether this carving depicts a specific event. An attractive argument has been made for identifying it as the arrival in Constantinople in 421 of relics of St Stephen, with the emperor Theodosius II himself leading the procession and being greeted by his sister Pulcheria (Holum and Vikan 1979), but other interpretations have been proposed (e.g., Wilson 1984). It is possible that the carving itself formed one side of a box for holding relics.

Figure 16.14   The Trier ivory

Source: Amt für kirchliche Denkmalpflege Trier (photograph: Ann Münchow)

EDITIONS

For editions of inscriptions and papyri, see Abbreviations on p. pp. xv–xvii. Where the most recent edition of a work remains that published in *PG* or *PL*, it is not included below since the reference to the relevant volume is given with the passage.

Agapius of Membij, *Universal History* Part 2, ed. and tr. A.A. Vasiliev, *PO* 8 (Paris: Firmin-Didot, 1912).

Ambrose, *Hymns*, ed. J. Fontaine (Paris: Editions du Cerf, 1992).

——, *Letters*, ed. M. Zelzer, *CSEL* 82 (1982).

——, *On the Sacraments*, ed. B. Botte, *SC* 25a (1961).

Ammianus Marcellinus, *History*, ed. W. Seyfarth (Leipzig: Teubner, 1978).

Ancient Statutes of the Church, ed. C. Munier, in *CCSL* 148 (1963), pp. 164–88.

Apostolic Constitutions, ed. M. Metzger, *SC* 320, 329, 336 (1985–87).

Ariphron of Sicyon, *Hymn to Hygeia*, ed. D. Page, *Poetae Melici Graeci* (Oxford: Clarendon Press, 1962): no. 813.

Athanasius, *Life of Antony*, ed. G.J.M. Bartelink, *SC* 400 (1994).

——, *Letter to Virgins who Went and Prayed in Jerusalem and Returned*, tr. D. Brakke, in Brakke *Athanasius and Asceticism* (Baltimore: Johns Hopkins University Press, 1998), pp. 292–302.

Augustine, *The City of God*, ed. B. Dombart and A. Kalb, *CCSL* 47–8 (1955).

——, *Commentaries on the Psalms*, eds D.E. Dekkers and I. Fraipont, *CCSL* 38–40 (1956).

——, *Confessions*, ed. J.J. O'Donnell (Oxford: Clarendon Press, 1992).

——, *Letters 1*–29**, ed. J. Divjak, Paris: Bibliothèque Augustinienne, vol. 46B (1987).

Basil of Caesarea, *Letters*, ed. Y. Courtonne (Paris: Budé, 1957–66).

Bede, *Church History of the English People*, ed. and tr. B.A. Colgrave and R.A.B. Mynors (Oxford: Clarendon Press, 1969).

Besa, *Life of Shenoute*, tr. D.N. Bell (Kalamazoo: Cistercian Publications, 1983).

Book of Pontiffs, ed. L. Duchesne (Paris: Boccard, 2nd edn, 1955–57).

Bordeaux Itinerary, eds P. Geyer and O. Cuntz, in *CCSL* 175 (1965), pp. 1–26.

Caesarius of Arles, *Sermons*, ed. G. Morin, *CCSL* 103–4 (1953).

Cologne Mani Codex, eds A. Henrichs and L. Koenen, Papyrologia Coloniensia 14 (Opladen: Westdeutscher Verlag, 1988).

Comparison of the Laws of Moses and the Romans, in P.E. Huschke, E. Seckel and B. Kuebler (eds) *Iurisprudentia Anteiustiniana* (Leipzig: Teubner, 1908–27), vol. 2, pp. 329–94.

Cornutian Deed, in the *Book of Pontiffs*, ed. L. Duchesne (Paris: Boccard, 2nd edn, 1955–57), vol. 1, pp. cxlvi–cxlvii.

Council of Elvira, in E.J. Jonkers (ed.) *Acta et Symbola Conciliorum quae saeculo quarto habita sunt* (Leiden: Brill, 1954), pp. 5–23.

Council of Nimes, ed. C. Munier, *CCSL* 148 (1963), pp. 50–1.

Council of Serdica, ed. C.J. Hefele, *Histoire des conciles* vol. 1.2 (Paris: Letouzy et Ané, 1907), pp. 759–804.

Council of Vannes, ed. C. Munier, *CCSL* 148 (1963), pp. 150–8.

Cyprian, *Letters*, ed. G.F. Diercks, *CCSL* 3B–C (1994–6).

Endelechius, *On the Deaths of the Cattle*, in F. Buecheler and A. Reise (eds) *Anthologia Latina* (Leipzig: Teubner, 1906), vol. I, 2, no. 893.

Eunapius, *Lives of the Philosophers and Sophists*, ed. J. Giangrande (Rome: Polygraphica, 1956).

Eusebius, *Church History*, ed. G. Bardy, *SC* 31, 41, 55 (1952–60).

——, *Life of Constantine*, ed. F. Winkelmann (Berlin: Akademie Verlag [*GCS Eusebius* 1/1], 1975).

Gelasius, *Letters*, ed. A. Thiel, *Epistolae Romanorum Pontificum* (Brunsbergae, 1868), pp. 285–613.

Gospel of Philip, tr. W.W. Isenberg in J.M. Robinson (ed.) *The Nag Hammadi Library in English*, 3rd edn (Leiden: Brill, 1988), pp. 141–60.

Greek Anthology, ed. H. Beckby (Munich: Heimeran, 2nd edn, 1965–8).

Gregory of Nyssa, *Letters*, ed. P. Maraval, *SC* 363 (1990).

Inscription of Kirder, tr. M. Boyce in M. Boyce, *Textual Sources for the Study of Zoroastrianism* (Manchester: Manchester University Press, 1984), pp. 112–13.

Itinerary of Egeria, eds A. Franceschini and R. Weber, in *CCSL* 175 (1965), pp. 37–103.

Jacob of Serugh, *Homily* 5, tr. C. Moss in C. Moss 'Jacob of Serugh's homilies on the spectacles of the theatre', *Le Muséon* 48: 108–12 (1935).

Jerome, *Letters*, ed. I. Hilberg, *CSEL* 54–6 (1910–18).

John Chrysostom, *Sermons against the Jews*, tr. P.W. Harkins, *FC* 68 (1979).

John of Ephesus, *Lives of the Eastern Saints*, ed. and tr. E.W. Brooks in *PO* 17–19 (Paris: Firmin-Didot, 1923–5).

Julian, *Letters*, ed. J. Bidez (Paris: Budé, 1924).

——, *Against the Galileans*, ed. E. Masaracchia (Rome: Ateneo, 1990).

Justinian, *Novels*, eds R. Schoell and G. Kroll, 7th edn (Berlin: Weidmann, 1963).

Justinianic Code, ed. P. Krueger, 14th edn (Berlin: Weidmann, 1967).

Lactantius, *On the Deaths of the Persecutors*, ed. J.L. Creed (Oxford: Clarendon Press, 1984).

Latin Panegyrics, ed. R.A.B. Mynors (Oxford: Clarendon Press, 1964).

Libanius, *Speech* 30, ed. and tr. A.F. Norman in *Libanius: Selected Works* vol. 2 (Cambridge, Mass., and London: Harvard University Press and Heinemann [Loeb Classical Library], 1977).

Life of Caesarius of Arles, ed. G. Morin, in *Sancti Caesarii Arelatensis Opera Omnia*, vol. 2 (Maredsous, 1942), pp. 293–345.

Life of Melania the Younger, ed. D. Gorce, *SC* 90 (1962).

Life of Olympias, tr. E.A. Clark in E.A. Clark *Jerome, Chrysostom and Friends: Essays and Translations* (New York: Edwin Mellen Press, 1979), pp. 127–42.

Life of Pachomius (Bohairic), tr. A. Veilleux in *Pachomian Koinonia* vol. 1 (Kalamazoo: Cistercian Publications, 1980).

Life of the Younger St Symeon the Stylite, ed. P. van den Ven (Brussels: Société des Bollandistes [Subsidia Hagiographica 32], 1962–70).

Lives of the Holy Fathers of Merida, ed. A. Maya Sanchez, *CCSL* 116 (1992).

Manichaean Psalmbook, vol. 2.2, tr. C.R.C. Allberry (Stuttgart: Kohlhammer, 1938).

Martyrdom of Felix of Thibiuca, ed. H. Delehaye, in *AB* 39 (1921), pp. 241–76 at 268–70.

Martyrdom of Pionius, ed. L. Robert (Washington DC: Dumbarton Oaks, 1994).

Optatus of Milevis, *Against the Donatists*, ed. C. Ziwsa, *CSEL* 26 (1893).

Origen, *Against Celsus*, tr. H. Chadwick (Cambridge: Cambridge University Press, 1953).

Palestinian Talmud, Abodah Zarah, tr. J. Neusner, *The Talmud of the Land of Israel* vol. 33 (*Abodah Zarah*), (Chicago and London: University of Chicago Press, 1982).

Paulinus of Nola, *Poems*, ed. W. Hartel, *CSEL* 30 (1894).

Polemius Silvius, *Calendar*, ed. A. Degrassi, *Inscriptiones Italiae* vol. 13.2 (Rome, 1963), pp. 263–76.

Porphyry, *On Abstinence from Animal Foods*, eds J. Bouffartigue, M. Patillon and A. Segonds (Paris: Budé, 1977–95).

——, *Against the Christians*, ed. A. von Harnack (Berlin: Abhandlungen der königlichen Preussischen Akademie der Wissenschaften, Philosophisch-historische Klasse, nr. 1: 1916).

Precepts of Pachomius, tr. A. Veilleux in *Pachomian Koinonia* vol. 2 (Kalamazoo: Cistercian Publications, 1981).

Priscus, *History*, ed. R.C. Blockley, *The Fragmentary Classicising Historians of the Later Roman Empire: Eunapius, Olympiodorus, Priscus and Malchus*, vol. 2 (Liverpool: Francis Cairns, 1983).

Procopius, *Secret History*, eds J. Haury and G. Wirth (Leipzig: Teubner, 1963).

——, *Wars*, eds J. Haury and G. Wirth (Leipzig: Teubner, 1962–3).

Quodvultdeus, *The Book of the Promises and Prophecies of God*, ed. R. Braun, *CCSL* 60 (1976).

Romanos the Melode, *Hymns*, ed. J. Grosdidier de Matons, *SC* 99, 110, 114, 128, 283 (1964–81).

Rule of Benedict, ed. R. Hanslik, *CSEL* 75 (1960).

Sallustius, *Concerning the Gods and the Universe*, ed. and tr. A.D. Nock (Cambridge: Cambridge University Press, 1926).

Severus of Minorca, *Letter concerning the Jews*, ed. S. Bradbury (Oxford: Clarendon Press, 1996).

Sidonius Apollinaris, *Letters and Poems*, ed. C. Luetjohann, *MGH.AA* 8 (Berlin, 1887).

Sirmondian Constitutions in *Theodosian Code*, ed. T. Mommsen, 2nd edn (Berlin: Weidmann, 1954), pp. 907–21.

Sozomen, *Church History*, eds J. Bidez and G.C. Hansen (Berlin: Akademie Verlag [*GCS* 50], 1960).

Sulpicius Severus, *Life of Saint Martin*, ed. J. Fontaine, *SC* 133–5 (1967–9).

Symmachus, *Letters*, ed. O. Seeck, *MGH.AA* 6 (Berlin, 1883).

——, *Memoranda ('Relationes')*, ed. O. Seeck, *MGH.AA* 6 (Berlin, 1883).

Tertullian, *Apology*, ed. E. Dekkers, *CCSL* 1 (1954), pp.85–171.

Themistius, *Speeches*, eds H. Schenkl, G. Downey and A.F. Norman (Leipzig: Teubner, 1965–74).

Theodoret, *The Healing of Pagan Diseases*, ed. P. Canivet, *SC* 57 (1958).

——, *History of the Monks*, ed. P. Canivet and A. Leroy-Molinghen, *SC* 234, 257 (1977–9).

Theodosian Code, ed. T. Mommsen, 2nd edn (Berlin: Weidmann, 1954).

Zacharias, *Life of Severus*, ed. M.A. Kugener, *PO* 2 (Paris: Firmin-Didot, 1903).

Zosimus, *New History*, ed. F. Paschoud (Paris: Budé, 1971–89).

BIBLIOGRAPHY

Adkin, N. (1985) 'A problem in the early church: noise during sermon and lesson', *Mnemosyne* 38: 161–3.

Amory, P. (1997) *People and Identity in Ostrogothic Italy, 489–554*, Cambridge: Cambridge University Press.

Ando, C. (1996) 'Pagan apologetics and Christian intolerance in the ages of Themistius and Augustine', *JECS* 4: 171–207.

Arce, J. (1984) *Estudios sobre el Emperador Fl. Cl. Juliano*, Madrid: Instituto Rodrigo Caro de Arqueologia.

Arjava, A. (1996) *Women and Law in Late Antiquity*, Oxford: Clarendon Press.

Athanassiadi, P. (1992) *Julian: An Intellectual Biography*, London: Routledge.

Avi-Yonah, M. (1963) 'The bath of the lepers at Scythopolis', *IEJ* 13: 325–6.

—— (1976) *The Jews of Palestine: A Political History from the Bar Kokhba War to the Arab Conquest*, Oxford: Blackwell.

Bagnall, R. (1993) *Egypt in Late Antiquity*, Princeton, NJ: Princeton University Press.

—— (1995) *Reading Papyri, Writing Ancient History*, London: Routledge.

Bagnall, R., Cameron, A., Schwartz, S., and Worp, K. (1987) *Consuls of the Later Roman Empire*, Atlanta: Scholars Press.

Baratte, F. (1992) 'Les trésors de temples dans le monde romain: une expression particulière de la piété', in S.A. Boyd and M. Mundell Mango (eds) *Ecclesiastical Silver Plate in Sixth-Century Byzantium*, Washington DC: Dumbarton Oaks, 111–21.

Barnes, T.D. (1981) *Constantine and Eusebius*, Cambridge, MA: Harvard University Press.

—— (1982) *The New Empire of Diocletian and Constantine*, Cambridge, MA: Harvard University Press.

—— (1984) 'Constantine's prohibition of pagan sacrifice', *AJP* 105: 69–72.

—— (1989a) 'The date of the Council of Gangra', *JTS* 40: 121–4.

—— (1989b) 'Christians and pagans in the reign of Contantius' in *L'Église et l'empire au IVe siècle*, Geneva: Fondation Hardt (*Entretiens* vol. 34), 301–43.

—— (1993) *Athanasius and Constantius: Theology and Politics in the Constantinian Empire*, Cambridge, MA: Harvard University Press.

—— (1994a) *From Eusebius to Augustine*, Aldershot: Variorum.

—— (1994b) 'Scholarship or propaganda? Porphyry *Against the Christians* and its historical setting', *BICS* 39: 53–65.

—— (1995) 'Statistics and the conversion of the Roman aristocracy', *JRS* 85: 135–47.

—— (1998) *Ammianus Marcellinus and the Representation of Historical Reality*, Ithaca and London: Cornell University Press.

Barnish, S.J.B. (1985) 'The wealth of Iulianus Argentarius: Late antique banking and the Mediterranean economy', *Byzantion* 55: 5–38.

Bartelink, G.J.M. (1994) *Athanase: Vie d'Antoine*, Paris: Editions du Cerf (*SC* 400).

Beard, M., North, J., and Price, S. (1998) *Religions of Rome*, Cambridge: Cambridge University Press (2 vols).

Beck, R.J. (1984) 'Mithraism since Franz Cumont', *ANRW* II.17.4: 2002–115.

—— (1996) 'Mithras', in S. Hornblower and A.J. Spawforth (eds) *The Oxford Classical Dictionary*, 3rd edn, Oxford and New York: Oxford University Press, 991–2.

Bernand, E. (1969) *Les Inscriptions grecques et latines de Philae*, vol. 2 (*Haut et Bas Empire*), Paris: CNRS.

Beskow, P. (1980) 'The portorium and the mysteries of Mithras', *Journal of Mithraic Studies* 3: 1–18.

Betz, H.D. (1991) 'Magic and mystery in the Greek Magical Papyri' in C.A. Faraone and D. Obbink (eds) *Magika Hiera: Ancient Greek Magic and Religion*, New York: Oxford University Press, 244–59.

—— (ed.) (1992) *The Greek Magical Papyri in Translation, including the Demotic Spells*, Chicago: University of Chicago Press.

Black, M. (1970) 'The chi–rho sign – Christogram and/or staurogram?' in W.W. Gasque and R.P. Martin (eds) *Apostolic History and the Gospel*, Exeter: Paternoster, 319–27.

Bloch, H. (1945) 'A new document of the last pagan revival in the west, 393–394 A.D.', *HTR* 38: 199–244.

Bonz, M.P. (1990) 'Differing approaches to religious benefaction: The late third-century acquisition of the Sardis synagogue', *HTR* 86: 139–54.

Bouffartigue, J., Patillon, M., and Segonds, A. (1979–95) *Porphyre: De l'Abstinence*, Paris: Budé (3 vols).

Bowersock, G. (1978) *Julian the Apostate*, London: Duckworth.

—— (1982) 'The imperial cult: perceptions and persistence', in B.F. Meyer and E.P. Sanders (eds) *Jewish and Christian Self-Definition*, London: SCM Press, vol. 3, 171–82.

—— (1986) 'From emperor to bishop: The self-conscious transformation of political power in the fourth century AD', *CPh* 81: 298–307.

—— (1990) *Hellenism in Late Antiquity*, Cambridge: Cambridge University Press.

—— (1995) *Martyrdom and Rome*, Cambridge: Cambridge University Press.

Boyce, M. (1979) *Zoroastrians: Their Religious Beliefs and Practices*, London, Boston and Henley: Routledge & Kegan Paul.

Boyce, M. and Grenet, F. (1991) *A History of Zoroastrianism* vol. 3, Leiden: Brill.

Bradbury, S. (1994) 'Constantine and the problem of anti-pagan legislation in the fourth century', *CPh* 89: 120–39.

—— (1996) *Severus of Minorca: Letter on the Conversion of the Jews*, Oxford: Clarendon Press.

Brakke, D. (1998) *Athanasius and Asceticism*, Baltimore: Johns Hopkins University Press.

Braun, R. (1964) *Quodvultdeus: Livre des promesses et des prédictions de Dieu*, vol. 1, Paris: Editions du Cerf (*SC* 101).

Breasted, J.H. (1922) 'Peintures d'époque romaine dans le désert de Syrie', *Syria* 3: 177–213.

Bremer, J.M. (1981) 'Greek hymns', in H.S. Versnel (ed.) *Faith, Hope and Worship: Aspects of Religious Mentality in the Ancient World*, Leiden: Brill, 193–215.

Bremmer, J.N. (1992) 'Symbols of marginality from early Pythagoreans to late antique monks', *G&R* 39: 205–14.

Brennan, B. (1985) 'Athanasius' *Vita Antonii*: a sociological interpretation', *VC* 39: 209–27.

Brock, S. (1994) 'Greek and Syriac in late antique Syria', in A.K. Bowman and G. Woolf (eds) *Literacy and Power in the Ancient World*, Cambridge: Cambridge University Press, 149–60.

—— (1998) 'Syriac culture, 337–425', in A. Cameron and P. Garnsey (eds) *The Cambridge Ancient History*, vol. 13: *The Late Empire AD 337–425*, Cambridge: Cambridge University Press, 708–19.

Brooten, B. (1982) *Women Leaders in the Ancient Synagogues: Inscriptional Evidence and Background Issues*, Chico, CA: Scholars Press.

Brown, P. (1961) 'Aspects of the Christianization of the Roman aristocracy', *JRS* 51: 1–11 (= Brown 1972: 161–82).

—— (1967) *Augustine of Hippo: A Biography*, London: Faber.

—— (1968) 'Christianity and local culture in late Roman Africa', *JRS* 58: 85–95.

—— (1969) 'The diffusion of Manichaeism in the Roman empire', *JRS* 59: 92–103 (= Brown 1972: 94–118).

—— (1971) 'The rise and function of the holy man in late antiquity', *JRS* 61: 80–101 (= Brown 1982a: 103–52).

—— (1972) *Religion and Society in the Age of Saint Augustine*, London: Faber.

—— (1981) *The Cult of the Saints: Its Rise and Function in Latin Christianity*, London: SCM Press.

—— (1982a) *Society and the Holy in Late Antiquity*, London: Faber.

—— (1982b) 'The last pagan emperor', in *Society and the Holy in Late Antiquity*, London: Faber, 83–102.

—— (1988) *The Body and Society: Men, Women and Sexual Renunciation in Early Christianity*, New York: Columbia University Press.

—— (1992) *Power and Persuasion in Late Antiquity: Towards a Christian Empire*, Madison, WI: University of Wisconsin Press.

—— (1995) *Authority and the Sacred: Aspects of Christianization in the Roman World*, Cambridge: Cambridge University Press.

—— (1998a) 'Asceticism: pagan and Christian', in A. Cameron and P. Garnsey (eds) *The Cambridge Ancient History*, vol. 13: *The Late Empire AD 337–425*, Cambridge: Cambridge University Press, 601–31.

—— (1998b) 'Christianization and religious conflict', in A. Cameron and P. Garnsey (eds) *The Cambridge Ancient History*, vol. 13: *The Late Empire AD 337–425*, Cambridge: Cambridge University Press, 632–64.

Browne, G.M. (1970) 'The composition of the *Sortes Astrampsychi*', *BICS* 17: 95–100.

—— (1974) *The Papyri of the 'Sortes Astrampsychi'*, Meisenheim am Glan: Verlag Anton Hain.

—— (1976) 'The origin and date of the *Sortes Astrampsychi*', *Illinois Classical Studies* 1: 53–8.

Burrus, V. (1995) *The Making of a Heretic: Gender, Authority, and the Priscillianist Controversy*, Berkeley: University of California Press.

Cameron, Alan (1968) 'Gratian's repudiation of the pontifical robe', *JRS* 58: 96–9.

Cameron, Averil (1978) 'The Theotokos in sixth-century Constantinople', *JTS* 29: 79–108.

—— (1983) 'Constantinus Christianus', *JRS* 73: 184–90.

—— (1985) *Procopius and the Sixth Century*, London: Duckworth.

—— (1991) *Christianity and the Rhetoric of Empire*, Berkeley: University of California Press.

—— (1992) 'The language of images: The rise of icons and Christian representation', in D. Wood (ed.) *The Church and the Arts*, Oxford: Blackwell (*SCH* 28), 1–42.

Cameron, A. and Hall, S.G. (1999) *Eusebius: Life of Constantine*, Oxford: Clarendon Press.

Carpenter, M. (1970) *Kontakia of Romanos, Byzantine Melodist*, vol. 1, Columbia: University of Missouri Press.

Chadwick, H. (1953) *Origen: Contra Celsum*, Cambridge: Cambridge University Press.

—— (1967) *The Early Church*, Harmondsworth: Penguin.

—— (1976) *Priscillian of Avila: The Occult and the Charismatic in the Early Church*, Oxford: Clarendon Press.

—— (1978) 'Conversion in Constantine the Great', in D. Baker (ed.) *Religious Motivation: Biographical and Sociological Problems for the Church Historian*, Oxford: Blackwell (*SCH* 15), 1–13 (= Chadwick 1991: Study 16).

—— (1979) 'The relativity of moral codes: Rome and Persia in Late Antiquity', in W.R. Schoedel and R.L. Wilken (eds) *Early Christian Literature and the Classical Intellectual Tradition*, Paris: Editions Beauchesne, 135–53 (= Chadwick 1991: Study 21).

—— (1980) 'The role of the Christian bishop in ancient society', in E.C. Hobbs and W. Wuellner (eds) *Protocols of the 35th Colloquy, Center for Hermeneutical Studies, Berkeley* (= Chadwick 1991: Study 3).

—— (1981) 'The church of the third century in the west', in A. King and M. Henig (eds) *The Roman West in the Third Century*, Oxford: British Archaeological Reports, 5–13 (= Chadwick 1991: Study 14).

—— (1984) 'Oracles of the end in the conflict of paganism and Christianity in the fourth century', in E. Lucchesi and H.D. Saffrey (eds) *Mémorial André-Jean Festugière: Antiquité païenne et chrétienne*, Geneva: Cahiers d'Orientalisme 10 (= Chadwick 1991: Study 8).

—— (1991) *Heresy and Orthodoxy in the Early Church*, Aldershot: Variorum.

Chastagnol, A. (1981) 'L'inscription constantinienne d'Orcistus', *MEFRA* 93: 381–416.

Chitty, D.J. (1966) *The Desert a City: An Introduction to the Study of Egyptian and Palestinian Monasticism under the Christian Empire*, Oxford: Blackwell.

Chuvin, P. (1990) *A Chronicle of the Last Pagans*, tr. B.A. Archer, Cambridge, MA: Harvard University Press.

Clark, E.A. (1979) *Jerome, Chrysostom and Friends: Essays and Translations*, New York: Edwin Mellen Press.

—— (1983) *Women in the Early Church*, Collegeville, Minnesota: Liturgical Press.

—— (1984) *The Life of Melania the Younger: Introduction, Translation and Commentary*, New York and Toronto: Edwin Mellen Press.

—— (1990a) 'Early Christian women: sources and interpretation', in L.L. Coon, K.J. Haldane, and E.W. Sommer (eds) *That Gentle Strength: Historical Perspectives on Women in Christianity*, Charlottesville: University Press of Virginia, 19–35.

—— (1990b) 'Patrons, not priests: Gender and power in late antique Christianity', *Gender and History* 2: 253–73.

Clark, E.A. and Hatch, D.F. (1981) *The Golden Bough, the Oaken Cross: The Virgilian Cento of Faltonia Betitia Proba*, Chico, CA: Scholars Press.

Clark, G. (1992) *Women in Late Antiquity: Pagan and Christian Life-styles*, Oxford: Clarendon Press.

—— (1995) 'Women and asceticism in Late Antiquity: The refusal of gender and status', in V. Wimbush and R. Valantasis (eds) *Asceticism*, New York: Oxford University Press, Part 2, ch. 3.

Clarke, G.W. (1971) 'Two Christians in the *familia Caesaris*', *HTR* 64: 121–4.

—— (1984) 'An illiterate lector?' *ZPE* 57: 103–4.

—— (1984–9) *The Letters of St Cyprian of Carthage*, New York: Paulist Press (4 vols).

—— (1998) 'Two mid-third century bishops: Cyprian of Carthage and Dionysius of Alexandria. Congruences and convergences', in T.W. Hillard, R.A. Kearsley, C.E.V. Nixon and A.M. Nobbs (eds) (1998) *Ancient History in a Modern University*, Grand Rapids, MI, and Cambridge: Eerdmans, vol. 2, 317–28.

Cooper, K. (1996) *The Virgin and the Bride: Idealized Womanhood in Late Antiquity*, Cambridge, MA: Harvard University Press.

Corcoran, S. (1996) *The Empire of the Tetrarchs: Imperial Pronouncements and Government, AD 284–324*, Oxford: Clarendon Press.

Courtois, C. (1955) 'Sur un baptistère découvert dans la région de Kélibia', *Karthago* 6: 98–123.

Cramer, P. (1993) *Baptism and Change in the Early Middle Ages, c. 200–c. 1150*, Cambridge: Cambridge University Press.

Creed, J.L. (1984) *Lactantius: De Mortibus Persecutorum*, Oxford: Clarendon Press.

Croke, B. (1984–5) 'The era of Porphyry's anti-Christian polemic', *Journal of Religious History* 13: 1–14.

Croke, B. and Harries, J. (1982) *Religious Conflict in Fourth-Century Rome*, Sydney: Sydney University Press.

Crown, A.D. (1986–87) 'The Samaritans in the Byzantine orbit', *BJRL* 69: 96–138.

Curran, J. (1996) 'Constantine and the ancient cults of Rome: The legal evidence', *G&R* 43: 68–80.

Dagron, G. (1968) 'L'Empire romaine d'Orient au IVe siècle et les traditions politiques de l'hellénisme: le témoignage de Themistius', *Travaux et mémoires* 3: 1–242.

Daly, L.J. (1971) 'Themistius' plea for religious tolerance', *GRBS* 12: 65–79.

Darling Young, R.A. (1990) 'Zacharias, *Life of Severus*', in V.L. Wimbush (ed.) *Ascetic Behaviour in Greco-Roman Antiquity*, Minneapolis: Fortress Press, 312–28.

Dassmann, E., Thraede, K., and Engemann, J. (eds) (1995) *Akten des XII. internationalen Kongresses für christlichen Archäologie*, Münster: Aschendorffe.

Davies, J.G. (1962) *The Architectural Setting of Baptism*, London: Barrie and Rockliff.

Davies, P.S. (1989) 'The origin and purpose of the persecution of AD 303', *JTS* 40: 66–94.

Davis, R. (1989) *The Book of Pontiffs ('Liber Pontificalis'): The Ancient Biographies of the First Ninety Roman Bishops to AD 715*, Liverpool: Liverpool University Press (TTH).

Degrassi, A. (1963) *Inscriptiones Italiae* vol. 13.2, Rome: Istituto Poligrafico dello Stato.

Deichmann, F.W. (1969–89) *Ravenna: Hauptstadt des spätantike Abendlandes*, Wiesbaden/ Stuttgart: Franz Steiner (3 vols).

Delehaye, H. (1911) 'L'aqueduc de S. Socrate à Zenonopolis', *AB* 30: 316–20.

Demarolle, J-M. (1970) 'Les femmes chrétiennes vues par Porphyre', *JAC* 13: 42–7.

Deschamps, G. and Cousin, G. (1891) 'Inscriptions du temple de Zeus Panamaros', *BCH* 15: 169–209.

Descombes, F. (1985) *Recueil des inscriptions chrétiennes de la Gaule* vol. 15 (Viennoise du Nord), Paris: CNRS.

de Ste. Croix, G.E.M. (1954) 'Aspects of the 'Great' Persecution', *HTR* 47: 75–113.

Dix, G. (1945) *The Shape of the Liturgy*, 2nd edn, Westminster: Dacre Press.

Douglass, L. (1996) 'A new look at the *Itinerarium Burdigalense*', *JECS* 4: 313–33.

Drake, H. (1996) 'Lambs into lions: explaining early Christian intolerance', *Past and Present* 153: 3–36.

Duchesne, L. (1955–57) *Le Liber Pontificalis, Texte, introduction et commentaire*, 2nd edn, Paris: Boccard (2 vols).

Dunbabin, K.M.D. (1978) *The Mosaics of Roman North Africa: Studies in Iconography and Patronage*, Oxford: Clarendon Press.

Duval, Y. (1982) *Loca Sanctorum Africae: Le Culte des martyrs en Afrique du IVe au VIIe siècle*, Rome: Collection de l'école française de Rome 58 (2 vols).

Eck, W. (1971) 'Das Eindringen des Christentums in den Senatorenstand bis zu Konstantin d. Gr.', *Chiron* 1: 381–406.

Elm, S. (1987) 'Perceptions of Jerusalem pilgrimage as reflected in two early sources on female pilgrimage (3rd and 4th centuries AD)', *Studia Patristica* 20: 219–23.

—— (1994) *'Virgins of God': The Making of Asceticism in Late Antiquity*, Oxford: Clarendon Press.

Elm, S. and Janowitz, N. (eds) (1998) *Peter Brown's Holy Man Twenty-five Years On* (= *JECS* 6: 343–539).

Errington, R.M. (1988) 'Constantine and the pagans', *GRBS* 29: 309–18.

—— (1997) 'Christian accounts of the religious legislation of Theodosius I', *Klio* 79: 398–443.

Evans, J.A.S. (1996) *The Age of Justinian*, London and New York: Routledge.

Evans Grubbs, J. (1995) *Law and Family in Late Antiquity: The Emperor Constantine's Marriage Legislation*, Oxford: Clarendon Press.

Fear, A. (1997) *The Lives of the Visigothic Fathers*, Liverpool: Liverpool University Press (TTH).

Feldman, L.H. (1993) *Jew and Gentile in the Ancient World: Attitudes and Interactions from Alexander to Justinian*, Princeton NJ: Princeton University Press.

Ferguson, E. (1979) 'Inscriptions and the origin of infant baptism', *JTS* 30: 37–46.

—— (1980) 'Spiritual sacrifice in early Christianity and its environment', *ANRW* II.23.2: 1151–89.

Filoramo, G. (1990) *A History of Gnosticism*, tr. A. Alcock, Oxford: Blackwell.

Fine, S. (ed.) (1996) *Sacred Realm: The Emergence of the Synagogue in the Ancient World*, New York: Oxford University Press.

—— (1997) *'This Holy Place': On the Sanctity of the Synagogue during the Graeco-Roman Period*, Notre Dame: Notre Dame University Press.

Fink, R.O., Hoey, A.S., and Snyder, W.F. (1940) 'The *Feriale Duranum*', *Yale Classical Studies* 7: 1–222.

Fishwick, D. (1988) 'Dated inscriptions and the *Feriale Duranum*', *Syria* 65: 349–61.

Fletcher, R. (1997) *The Conversion of Europe from Paganism to Christianity, 371–1386 AD*, London: HarperCollins.

Fontaine, J. (1967–9) *Sulpice Sévère: Vie de Saint Martin*, Paris: Editions du Cerf (*SC* 133–5) (3 vols).

Foss, C. (1995) 'The Near Eastern countryside in late antiquity: a review article', in J.H. Humphrey (ed.) *The Roman and Byzantine Near East: Some Recent Archaeological Research*, Ann Arbor, MI: JRA Supplement 14, 213–34.

Fowden, G. (1978) 'Bishops and temples in the eastern Roman empire A.D. 320–435', *JTS* 29: 53–78.

—— (1982) 'The pagan holy man in late antique society', *JHS* 102: 33–59.

—— (1987) 'Nicagoras of Athens and the Lateran obelisk', *JHS* 107: 51–7.

—— (1991) 'Constantine's porphyry column: the earliest literary allusion', *JRS* 81: 119–31.

—— (1998) 'Polytheist religion and philosophy', in A. Cameron and P. Garnsey (eds) *The Cambridge Ancient History*, vol. 13: *The Late Empire AD 337–425*, Cambridge: Cambridge University Press, 538–560.

Frankfurter, D. (1990) 'Stylites and *phallobates*: pillar religions in late antique Syria', *VC* 44: 168–98.

—— (1998a) *Religion in Roman Egypt: Assimilation and Resistance*, Princeton, NJ: Princeton University Press.

—— (ed.) (1998b) *Pilgrimage and Holy Space in Late Antique Egypt*, Leiden, Boston, Cologne: Brill.

Frazee, C.A. (1981) 'Anatolian asceticism in the fourth century: Eustathios of Sebastea and Basil of Caesarea', *Catholic Historical Review* 66: 16–33.

Frend, W.H.C. (1982) 'Fussala: Augustine's crisis of credibility (*Ep.* 20*)' in C. Lepelley (ed.) *Les Lettres de Saint Augustin découvertes par Johannes Divjak: Communications présentées au colloque des 20 et 21 septembre 1982*, Paris: Études augustiniennes, 251–65 (= Frend 1988: Study 10).

—— (1988) *Archaeology and History in the Study of Early Christianity*, London: Variorum.

Gager, J.G. (ed.) (1992) *Curse Tablets and Binding Spells from the Ancient World*, New York and Oxford: Oxford University Press.

Gaiffier, B. de (1954) 'La lecture des actes des martyrs dans la prière liturgique', *AB* 72: 134–66.

Galvao-Sobrinho, C.R. (1995) 'Funerary epigraphy and the spread of Christianity in the west', *Athenaeum* 83: 432–66.

Gamble, H.Y. (1995) *Books and Readers in the Early Church: A History of Early Christian Texts*, New Haven and London: Yale University Press.

Gardner, I.M.F. and Lieu, S.N.C. (1996) 'From Narmouthis (Medinet Madi) to Kellis (Ismant el-Kharab): Manichaean documents from Roman Egypt', *JRS* 86: 146–69.

Garnsey, P. (1984) 'Religious toleration in Classical Antiquity', in W.J. Shiels (ed.) *Persecution and Toleration*, Oxford: Blackwell (*SCH* 21), 1–27.

Gascou, J. (1967) 'Le rescrit d'Hispellum', *MEFRA* 79: 609–59.

Gassowska, B. (1982) 'Maternus Cynegius, Praefectus Praetorio Orientis, and the destruction of the Allat temple in Palmyra', *Archeologia* 33: 107–23.

Geffcken, J. (1978) *The Last Days of Greco-Roman Paganism*, tr. S. MacCormack, Amsterdam: North-Holland Publishing Company.

Gibbon, E. (1994) *The History of the Decline and Fall of the Roman Empire*, ed. D. Womersley, London: Penguin (3 vols).

Goehring, J. (1992) 'Through a glass darkly: Diverse images of the *apotaktikoi(ai)* of early Egyptian monasticism', *Semeia* 57: 25–45.

—— (1996) 'Withdrawing from the desert: Pachomius and the development of village monasticism in Upper Egypt', *HTR* 89: 267–85.

Goodman, M. (1994) *Mission and Conversion: Proselytizing in the Religious History of the Roman Empire*, Oxford: Clarendon Press.

Gordon, R.L. (1990) 'The veil of power: emperors, sacrificers and benefactors', in M. Beard and J. North (eds) *Pagan Priests: Religion and Power in the Ancient World*, London: Duckworth, 199–232.

—— (1996) *Image and Value in the Graeco-Roman World: Studies in Mithraism and Religious Art*, Aldershot: Variorum.

Gould, G. (1987) 'Basil of Caesarea and the problem of the wealth of monasteries', in W.J. Shiels and D. Wood (eds) *The Church and Wealth*, Oxford: Blackwell (*SCH* 24), 15–24.

Grabar, A. (1967) *The Beginnings of Christian Art, 200–395*, tr. S. Gilbert and J. Emmons, London: Thames and Hudson.

Grant, R.M. (1975) 'The religion of Maximin Daia', in J. Neusner (ed.) *Christianity, Judaism and Other Greco-Roman Cults*, Leiden: Brill, vol. 4: 143–66.

Gray, P.T.R. (1993) 'Palestine and Justinian's legislation on non-Christian religions', in B. Halpern and D.W. Hobson (eds) *Law, Politics and Society in the Ancient Mediterranean World*, Sheffield: Sheffield Academic Press, 241–70.

Gregory, T.E. (1986) 'The survival of paganism in Christian Greece', *AJP* 107: 229–42.

Grosdidier de Matons, J. (1981) *Romanos le Melode: Hymnes*, vol. 5, Paris: Editions du Cerf (*SC* 283).

Grossmann, P. (1998) 'The pilgrimage center of Abû Mînâ', in D. Frankfurter (ed.) (1998b) *Pilgrimage and Holy Space in Late Antique Egypt*, Leiden, Boston, Cologne: Brill, 281–302.

Gryson, R. (1976) *The Ministry of Women in the Early Church*, tr. J. Laporte and M.L. Hall, Collegeville, MI: Liturgical Press.

Haas, C. (1997) *Alexandria in Late Antiquity: Topography and Social Conflict*, Baltimore and London: Johns Hopkins University Press.

Hackel, S. (ed.) (1981) *The Byzantine Saint*, London: Fellowship of St Alban and St Sergius.

Hall, L.J. (1998) 'Cicero's *instinctu divino* and Constantine's *instinctu divinitatis*: the evidence of the Arch of Constantine for the senatorial view of the 'vision' of Constantine', *JECS* 6: 647–71.

Halsberghe, G.H. (1972) *The Cult of Sol Invictus*, Leiden: Brill.

—— (1984) 'Le culte de Dea Caelestis', *ANRW* II.17.4: 2203–23.

Hanson, R.P.C. (1978) 'The transformation of pagan temples into churches in the early Christian centuries', *JSS* 23: 257–67 (= Hanson 1985: ch. 16).

—— (1985) *Studies in Christian Antiquity*, Edinburgh: T&T Clark.

—— (1988) *The Search for the Christian Doctrine of God: The Arian Controversy 318–381*, Edinburgh: T&T Clark.

Harries, J. (1994) *Sidonius Apollinaris and the Fall of Rome, AD 407–485*, Oxford: Clarendon Press.

Harrison, M. (1989) *A Temple for Byzantium: The Discovery and Excavation of Anicia Juliana's Palace–Church in Istanbul*, London: Harvey Miller.

Harvey, S.A. (1988) 'The sense of a stylite: perspectives on Simeon the Elder', *VC* 42: 376–94.

Heather, P. (1998) 'Themistius: a political philosopher', in Mary Whitby (ed.) *The Propaganda of Power: The Role of Panegyric in Late Antiquity*, Leiden: Brill, 125–50.

Heather, P. and Matthews, J. (1991) *The Goths in the Fourth Century*, Liverpool: Liverpool University Press (TTH).

Hess, H. (1958) *The Canons of the Council of Sardica, AD 343*, Oxford: Clarendon Press.

Hillgarth, J.N. (1986) *Christianity and Paganism, 530–750: The Conversion of Western Europe*, Philadelphia: University of Pennsylvania Press.

Holum, K.G. and Vikan, G. (1979) 'The Trier ivory, *adventus* ceremonial, and the relics of St Stephen', *Dumbarton Oaks Papers* 33: 115–33.

Homes Dudden, F. (1935) *The Life and Times of St. Ambrose*, Oxford: Clarendon Press (2 vols).

Hopkins, K. (1998) 'Christian number and its implications', *JECS* 6: 185–226.

Horn, J. (1994) 'Tria sunt in Aegypto genera monachorum. Die ägyptischen Bezeichnungen für die "dritte Art" des Mönchtums bei Hieronymus und Johannes Cassianus', in H. Behlmer (ed.) *Quaerentes Scientiam: Festgabe für Wolfhart Westendorf zu seinem 70. Geburtstag*, Göttingen: Seminar für Ägyptologie und Koptologie, 63–82.

Horsley, G.H.R. (1982) *New Documents Illustrating Early Christianity* vol. 2, North Ryde, NSW: Macquarie University.

Hunt, E.D. (1981) 'The traffic in relics: some late Roman evidence', in S. Hackel (ed.) *The Byzantine Saint*, London: Fellowship of St Alban and St Sergius, 171–80.

—— (1982a) *Holy Land Pilgrimage in the Later Roman Empire AD 312–460*, Oxford: Clarendon Press.

—— (1982b) 'St Stephen in Minorca – an episode in Jewish–Christian relations in the early 5th century AD', *JTS* 33: 106–23.

—— (1993) 'Christianising the Roman Empire: The evidence of the Code', in J. Harries and I. Wood (eds) *The Theodosian Code: Studies in the Imperial Law of Late Antiquity*, London: Duckworth, 143–58.

—— (1998a) 'Julian', in: Averil Cameron and P. Garnsey (eds) *The Cambridge Ancient History*, vol. 13: *The Late Empire AD 337–425*, Cambridge: Cambridge University Press, 44–77.

—— (1998b) 'The church as a public institution', in Averil Cameron and P. Garnsey (eds) *The Cambridge Ancient History*, vol. 13: *The Late Empire AD 337–425*, Cambridge: Cambridge University Press, 238–76.

Hunter, D.G. (1987) 'Resistance to the virginal ideal in late fourth-century Rome: The case of Jovinian', *Theological Studies* 48: 45–64.

—— (1989) '*On the Sin of Adam and Eve*: A little-known defense of marriage and child-bearing by Ambrosiaster', *HTR* 82: 283–99.

—— (1993) 'Helvidius, Jovinian and the virginity of Mary in late fourth-century Rome', *JECS* 1: 47–72.

—— (1999) 'Vigilantius of Calagurris and Victricius of Rouen: ascetics, relics and clerics in late Roman Gaul', *JECS* 7: 401–30.

Isenberg, W.W. (1988) 'Introduction to the *Gospel of Philip*', in *The Nag Hammadi Library in English*, Leiden: Brill, 139–41.

Janes, D. (1998) *God and Gold in Late Antiquity*, Cambridge: Cambridge University Press.

Jeffreys, E.M. (1991) 'Kontakion', in A. Kazhdan (ed.) *The Oxford Dictionary of Byzantium*, Oxford and New York: Oxford University Press, p. 1148.

Jones, A.H.M. (1964) *The Later Roman Empire 284–602: A Social, Economic and Administrative Survey*, Oxford, Blackwell (2 vols [1986 reprint]).

Judge, E.A. (1977) 'The earliest use of the monachos for "monk" (P. Coll. Youtie 77) and the origins of monasticism', *JAC* 20: 72–89.

Kelly, J.N.D. (1975) *Jerome: His Life, Writings and Controversies*, London: Duckworth.

—— (1995) *Goldenmouth: The Story of John Chrysostom – Ascetic, Preacher, Bishop*, London: Duckworth.

Keppie, L. (1991) *Understanding Roman Inscriptions*, London: Batsford.

Keresztes, P. (1975) 'The Decian *libelli* and contemporary literature', *Latomus* 34: 761–81.

Klingshirn, W.E. (1985) 'Charity and power: Caesarius of Arles and the ransoming of captives in sub-Roman Gaul', *JRS* 75: 183–203.

—— (1994) *Caesarius of Arles: The Making of a Christian Community in Late Antique Gaul*, Cambridge: Cambridge University Press.

Knipfing, J.R. (1923) '*Libelli* of the Decian persecution', *HTR* 16: 363–90.

Kotula, T. (1994) 'Julien Auguste et l'aristocratie municipale d'Afrique: Réflexions méthodologiques', *Antiquités africaines* 30: 271–9.

Kraabel, A.T. (1979) 'The Diaspora synagogue: Archaeological and epigraphic evidence since Sukenik', *ANRW* II.19.2: 477–510.

—— (1981) 'The excavated synagogues of Late Antiquity from Asia Minor to Italy', *Jahrbuch des Österreichischen Byzantinistik* 32.2: 227–36.

Kraeling, C.H. (1967) *The Excavations at Dura-Europos, Final Report VIII, Part II: The Christian Building*, New Haven: Yale University Press.

Kraemer, C.J. (1958) *Excavations at Nessana*, vol. 3: *The Non-literary Papyri*, Princeton, NJ: Princeton University Press.

Kraemer, R.S. (1988) *Maenads, Martyrs, Matrons, Monastics: A Sourcebook on Women's Religion in the Graeco-Roman World*, Philadelphia: Fortress Press.

Krautheimer, R. (1965) *Early Christian and Byzantine Architecture*, Harmondsworth: Penguin.

Lamoreaux, J.C. (1995) 'Episcopal courts in Late Antiquity', *JECS* 3: 143–67.

Lane, E.N. (1971) *Corpus Monumentorum Religionis Dei Menis*, vol. 1, Leiden: Brill.

—— (1990) 'Mēn: a neglected cult of Roman Asia Minor', *ANRW* II.18.3: 2161–74.

Lane Fox, R. (1986) *Pagans and Christians in the Mediterranean World from the Second Century AD to the Conversion of Constantine*, Harmondsworth: Penguin.

Laumonier, A. (1958) *Les Cultes indigènes de Carie*, Paris: Boccard.

Lawrence, C.H. (1989) *Medieval Monasticism: Forms of Religious Life in Western Europe in the Middle Ages*, 2nd edn, London and New York: Longman.

Le Blant, E. (1856–65) *Inscriptions chrétiennes de la Gaule antérieures au VIIIe siècle*, Paris: Imprimerie impériale (2 vols).

Lebon, J. (1928) 'Athanasiana Syriaca II', *Le Muséon* 41: 169–216.

Lee, A.D. (1988) 'Close-kin marriage in late antique Mesopotamia', *GRBS* 29: 403–13.

Lefkowitz, M.R. and Fant, M.B. (1992) *Women's Life in Greece and Rome: A Sourcebook in Translation*, 2nd edn, London: Duckworth.

Lepelley, C. (1979–81) *Les Cités de l'Afrique romaine au Bas-Empire*, Paris: Études augustiniennes (2 vols).

Levenson, D. (1990) 'Julian's attempt to rebuild the temple: An inventory of ancient and medieval sources', in H. Attridge *et al.* (eds) *Of Scribes and Scrolls*, Lanham: University Press of America, 261–79.

Levine, L.I. (ed.) (1987) *The Synagogue in Late Antiquity*, Philadelphia: American Schools of Oriental Research.

Lewis, N. (1982) *The Compulsory Public Services of Roman Egypt*, Florence: Edizioni Gonnelli.

—— (1983) *Life in Egypt under Roman Rule*, Oxford: Clarendon Press.

Leyerle, B. (1994) 'John Chrysostom on almsgiving and the use of money', *HTR* 87: 29–47.

Liebeschuetz, W. (1972) *Antioch: City and Imperial Administration in the Later Roman Empire*, Oxford: Clarendon Press.

—— (1979) *Continuity and Change in Roman Religion*, Oxford: Clarendon Press.

Lieu, S.N.C. (1985–86) 'Some themes in later Roman anti-Manichaean polemics I', *BJRL* 68: 434–69.

—— (1986–87) 'Some themes in later Roman anti-Manichaean polemics II', *BJRL* 69: 235–75.

—— (1989) *The Emperor Julian: Panegyric and Polemic*, 2nd edn, Liverpool: Liverpool University Press.

—— (1992) *Manichaeism in the Later Roman Empire and Medieval China*, 2nd edn, Tübingen: Mohr.

Lieu, S.N.C. and Montserrat, D. (eds) (1996) *From Constantine to Julian: Pagan and Byzantine Views: A Source History*, London: Routledge.

Lieu, S.N.C. and Montserrat, D. (eds) (1998) *Constantine: History, Historiography and Legend*, London: Routledge.

Lim, R. (1995) *Public Disputation, Power, and Social Order in Late Antiquity*, Berkeley, Los Angeles, London: University of California Press.

Linder, A. (1987) *The Jews in Roman Imperial Legislation*, Detroit: Wayne State University Press.

—— (1997) *The Jews in the Legal Sources of the Early Middle Ages*, Detroit: Wayne State University Press.

Llewellyn, S.R. (1997) 'The Christian symbol XMΓ, an acrostic or an isopsephism?' in S.R. Llewellyn (ed.) *New Documents Illustrating Early Christianity*, vol. 8, Grand Rapids and Cambridge: Eerdmans, 156–68.

Maas, M. (1992) *John Lydus and the Roman Past: Antiquarianism and Politics in the Age of Justinian*, London and New York: Routledge.

MacCormack, S. (1997) 'Sin, citizenship and the salvation of souls: The impact of Christian priorities on late-Roman and post-Roman society', *Comparative Studies in Society and History* 39: 644–73.

MacCoull, L. (1990) 'Christianity at Syene/Elephantine/Philae', *Bulletin of the American Society of Papyrologists* 27: 151–62.

McKechnie, P. (1996) ' "Women's religion" and second-century Christianity', *JEH* 47: 409–31.

—— (1999) 'Christian grave-inscriptions from the "Familia Caesaris"', *JEH* 50: 427–41.

McLynn, N. (1994) *Ambrose of Milan*, Berkeley, Los Angeles, London: University of California Press.

—— (1996) The fourth-century *taurobolium*', *Phoenix* 50: 312–30.

MacMullen, R. (1968) 'Constantine and the miraculous', *GRBS* 9: 81–96.

—— (1981) *Paganism in the Roman Empire*, New Haven and London: Yale University Press.

—— (1984) *Christianizing the Roman Empire* AD 100–400, New Haven and London: Yale University Press.

—— (1989) 'The preacher's audience (AD 350–400)', *JTS* 40: 503–11.

—— (1997) *Christianity and Paganism in the Fourth to Eighth Centuries*, New Haven and London: Yale University Press.

Magie, D., *Roman Rule in Asia Minor to the End of the Third Century after Christ*, Princeton, NJ: Princeton University Press (2 vols).

Mainstone, R.J. (1988) *Hagia Sophia: Architecture, Structure and Liturgy of Justinian's Great Church*, London: Thames and Hudson.

Malbon, E.S. (1990) *The Iconography of the Sarcophagus of Junius Bassus*, Princeton, NJ: Princeton University Press.

Mango, C. (1980) *Byzantium: Empire of the New Rome*, London: Weidenfeld and Nicolson.

—— (1986) *The Art and Architecture of the Byzantine Empire 312–1453*, (reprint of 1972 edn) Toronto: University of Toronto Press.

—— (1995) 'The pilgrim's motivation', in E. Dassmann, K. Thraede, and J. Engemann (eds) *Akten des XII. internationalen Kongresses für christlichen Archäologie*, Münster: Aschendorffe, 1–9.

Markus, R.A. (1970) 'Gregory the Great and a papal missionary strategy', in G.J. Cuming (ed.) *The Mission of the Church and the Propagation of the Faith*, Oxford: Blackwell (*SCH* 6) 29–38.

—— (1974) 'Paganism, Christianity and the Latin classics in the fourth century', in J.W. Binns (ed.) *Latin Literature of the Fourth Century*, London: Routledge and Kegan Paul, 1–21.

—— (1990) *The End of Ancient Christianity*, Cambridge: Cambridge University Press.

Marrou, H.I. (1970) 'Le dossier épigraphique de l'évêque Rusticus de Narbonne', *Rivista di archeologia cristiana* 46: 331–49.

Massie, M. (1980) 'Vigilance de Calagurris face à la polémique hiéronymienne: Les fondements et la signification du conflit', *Bulletin de littérature ecclésiastique* 81: 81–108.

Mathisen, R.W. (1993) *Roman Aristocrats in Barbarian Gaul*, Austin, TX: University of Texas Press.

Matthews, J. (1973) 'Symmachus and the oriental cults', *JRS* 63: 175–95.

—— (1989) *The Roman Empire of Ammianus*, London: Duckworth.

—— (1990) *Western Aristocracies and Imperial Court AD 364–425* (reprint of 1975 edition with postscript), Oxford: Clarendon Press.

Mayr-Harting, H. (1991) *The Coming of Christianity to Anglo-Saxon England*, 3rd edn, University Park, PA: Pennsylvania State University Press.

Meredith, A. (1976) 'Asceticism – Christian and Greek', *JTS* 27: 313–32.

—— (1980) 'Porphyry and Julian against the Christians', *ANRW* II.23.2: 1119–49.

Metzger, B.M. (1988) 'Greek manuscripts of John's Gospel with "hermeneiai"', in T. Baarda *et al.* (eds) *Text and Testimony*, Kampen: Kok, 162–9.

Millar, F. (1968) 'Local cultures in the Roman empire: Libyan, Punic and Latin in Roman Africa', *JRS* 58: 126–34.

—— (1977) *The Emperor in the Roman World, 31 BC – AD 337*, London: Duckworth.

—— (1983) 'Inscriptions', in M.H. Crawford (ed.) *Sources for Ancient History*, Cambridge: Cambridge University Press, 80–136.

—— (1992) 'The Jews of the Graeco-Roman Diaspora between paganism and Christianity, AD 312–438', in J. Lieu, J. North, and T. Rajak (eds) *The Jews among Pagans and Christians in the Roman Empire*, London and New York: Routledge, 97–123.

Mitchell, S. (1988) 'Maximinus and the Christians in AD 312: a new Latin inscription', *JRS* 78: 105–24.

—— (1993) *Anatolia: Land, Men and Gods in Asia Minor*, Oxford: Clarendon Press (2 vols).

Moorhead, J. (1994) *Justinian*, London and New York: Longman.

—— (1999) *Ambrose: Church and Society in the Late Roman World*, London and New York: Longman.

Morard, F. (1980) 'Encore quelques réflexions sur monachos', *VC* 34: 395–401.

Moss, C. (1935) 'Jacob of Serugh's homilies on the spectacles of the theatre', *Le Muséon* 48: 87–112.

Mundell Mango, M. (1986) *Silver from Early Byzantium: The Kaper Koraon and Related Treasures*, Baltimore, MD: Walters Art Gallery.

Munier, C. (1960) *Les Statuta Ecclesiae Antiquae*, Paris: Presses Universitaires de France.

Musurillo, H. (ed. and tr.) (1972) *The Acts of the Christian Martyrs*, Oxford: Clarendon Press.

Nasrallah, J. (1974) 'Survie de Saint Simeon Stylite l'Alepin dans les Gaules', *Syria* 51: 171–97.

Nautin, P. (1967) 'La conversion du temple de Philae en église chrétienne', *Cahiers archéologiques* 17: 1–43.

Nicholson, O. (1994) 'The "pagan churches" of Maximinus Daia and Julian', *JEH* 45: 1–10.

—— (1995) 'The end of Mithraism', *Antiquity* 69: 358–62.

Nixon, C.E.V. and Rodgers, B.S. (1994) *In Praise of Later Roman Emperors: The 'Panegyrici Latini'*, Berkeley: University of California Press.

Nock, A.D. (1926) *Sallustius: Concerning the Gods and the Universe*, Cambridge: Cambridge University Press.

—— (1972) *Essays on Religion and the Ancient World*, ed. Z. Stewart, Oxford: Clarendon Press.

Noy, D. (1993) *Jewish Inscriptions of Western Europe*, vol. 1: *Italy (excluding the City of Rome), Spain and Gaul*, Cambridge: Cambridge University Press.

—— (1995) *Jewish Inscriptions of Western Europe*, vol. 2: *The City of Rome*, Cambridge: Cambridge University Press.

O'Donnell, J.J. (1977) ' "Paganus": Evolution and use', *Classical Folia* 31: 163–9.

—— (1992) *Augustine: Confessions*, Oxford: Clarendon Press (3 vols).

Ousterhout, R. (ed.) (1990) *The Blessings of Pilgrimage*, Urbana and Chicago: University of Illinois Press.

Pagels, E. (1979) *The Gnostic Gospels*, London: Weidenfeld and Nicolson.

—— (1991) 'The "mystery of marriage" in the *Gospel of Philip* revisited', in B.A. Pearson (ed.) *The Future of Early Christianity: Essays in honour of Helmut Koester*, Minneapolis: Fortress Press, 442–54.

Painter, K.S. (1977) *Wealth of the Roman World: Gold and Silver AD 300–700*, London: British Museum.

Pearson, B.A. (1990) 'Gnosticism in early Egyptian Christianity', in his *Gnosticism, Judaism and Egyptian Christianity*, Minneapolis: Fortress Press, 194–214.

Pekáry, T. (1986) 'Das Opfer vor dem Kaiserbild', *Bonner Jahrbücher* 186: 91–103.

Peña, I. (1997) *The Christian Art of Byzantine Syria*, trs E. Brophy and F. Reina, London: Garnett Publishing.

Penella, R.J. (1990) *Greek Philosophers and Sophists in the Fourth Century A.D.: Studies in Eunapius of Sardis*, Leeds: Francis Cairns.

Pestman, P.W. (1994) *The New Papyrological Primer*, 2nd edn, Leiden: Brill.

Pietri, C. (1976) *Roma Christiana: Recherches sur l'église de Rome, son organisation, sa politique, son idéologie de Miltiade à Sixte III (311–440)*, Rome: Bibliothèque des écoles françaises d'Athènes et de Rome (2 vols).

—— (1983) 'Grabinschrift II (lateinisch)', *RAC* 12: 514–90.

Pohlsander, H.A. (1969) 'Victory: the story of a statue', *Historia* 18: 588–97.

—— (1986) 'The religious policy of Decius', *ANRW* II.16.3: 1826–42.

Praet, D. (1992–93) 'Explaining the Christianization of the Roman Empire: Older theories and recent developments', *Sacris Erudiri* 33: 5–119.

Rea, J.R. (1979) '*P. Oxy.* XXXIII 2673.22: πυλην to "ὑλη!" ', *ZPE* 35: 128.

Richardson, L. (1992) *A New Topographical Dictionary of Ancient Rome*, Baltimore and London: Johns Hopkins University Press.

Rives, J.B. (1999) 'The decree of Decius and the religion of the empire', *JRS* 89: 135–54.

Robert, L. (1937) *Études anatoliennes*, Paris: Boccard.

—— (1994) *Le Martyre de Pionios, prêtre de Smyrne*, eds G.W. Bowersock and C.P. Jones, Washington DC: Dumbarton Oaks.

Rodgers, B.S. (1980) 'Constantine's pagan vision', *Byzantion* 50: 259–78.

Rossi, M.A. (1991) 'Priesthood, precedent, and prejudice: On recovering the women priests of early Christianity', *Journal of Feminist Studies in Religion* 7: 73–94.

Rouche, M. (1974) 'La matricule des pauvres: Evolution d'une institution de charité du Bas Empire jusqu'à la fin du Haut Moyen Age', in M. Mollat (ed.) *Études sur l'histoire de la pauvreté*, Paris: Publications de la Sorbonne, 84–110.

BIBLIOGRAPHY

Roueché, C. (1989) *Aphrodisias in Late Antiquity*, London: JRS Monographs 5.

Rousseau, P. (1978) *Ascetics, Authority and the Church in the Age of Jerome and Cassian*, Oxford: Clarendon Press.

—— (1990) 'Christian asceticism and the early monks', in I. Hazlett (ed.) *Early Christianity: Origins and Evolution to AD 600*, London: SPCK, 112–22.

—— (1994) *Basil of Caesarea*, Berkeley: University of California Press.

—— (1998) 'The preacher's audience: a more optimistic view', in T.W. Hillard, R.A. Kearsley, C.E.V. Nixon and A.M. Nobbs (eds) *Ancient History in a Modern University*, Grand Rapids, MI, and Cambridge: Eerdmans, vol. 2, 391–400.

—— (1999) *Pachomius: The Making of a Community in Fourth-Century Egypt* (reprint of 1985 edition with new preface), Berkeley: University of California Press.

—— (2000) 'Monasticism', in Averil Cameron, B. Ward-Perkins, and M. Whitby (eds) *The Cambridge Ancient History*, vol. 14: *Late Antiquity – Empire and Successors, A.D. 425–600*, Cambridge: Cambridge University Press, ch. 25.

Rudolph, K. (1990) 'Gnosticism', in I. Hazlett (ed.) *Early Christianity: Origins and Evolution to AD 600*, London: SPCK, 186–97.

Rutherford, I. (1998) 'Island of the extremity: space, language and power in the pilgrimage traditions of Philae', in D. Frankfurter (ed.) (1998b) *Pilgrimage and Holy Space in Late Antique Egypt*, Leiden, Boston, Cologne: Brill, 229–56.

Ryberg, I.S. (1955) *Rites of the State Religion in Roman Art*, New Haven: Memoirs of the American Academy in Rome 22.

Salzman, M.R. (1990) *On Roman Time: The Codex-Calendar of 354 and the Rhythms of Urban Life in Late Antiquity*, Berkeley: University of California Press.

Saxer, V. (1995) 'Pilgerwesen in Italien und Rom im späten Altertum und Frühmittelalter', in E. Dassmann, K. Thraede, and J. Engemann (eds) *Akten des XII. internationalen Kongresses für christlichen Archäologie*, Münster: Aschendorffe, 36–57.

Schmid, W. (1960) 'Endelechius', *RAC* 5: 1–3.

Seager, A.R. (1972) 'The building history of the Sardis synagogue', *American Journal of Archaeology* 76: 425–35.

Seager, A.R. and Kraabel, A.T. (1983) 'The synagogue and the Jewish community', in G.M.A. Hanfmann (ed.) *Sardis from Prehistoric to Roman Times*, Cambridge, MA: Harvard University Press, 168–90.

Segelberg, E. (1960) 'The Coptic–Gnostic Gospel according to Philip and its sacramental system', *Numen* 7: 189–200.

—— (1983) 'The Gospel of Philip and the New Testament', in A.H.B. Logan and A.J.M. Wedderburn (eds) *The New Testament and Gnosis: Essays in honour of R.M. Wilson*, Edinburgh: T. & T. Clark, 204–12.

Shepherd, D.G. (1969) 'An icon of the Virgin: A sixth-century tapestry panel from Egypt', *Bulletin of the Cleveland Museum of Art* 56: 90–120.

Sijpesteijn, P.J. (1980) 'List of nominations to liturgies', *Miscellanea Papyrologica* 7: 341–7.

Simon, M. (1986) *Verus Israel: A Study of the Relations between Christians and Jews in the Roman Empire (AD 135–425)*, tr. H. McKeating, Oxford: Oxford University Press.

Sivan, H. (1988a) 'Who was Egeria? Piety and pilgrimage in the age of Gratian', *HTR* 81: 59–72.

—— (1988b) 'Holy land pilgrimage and western audiences: some reflections on Egeria and her circle', *CQ* 38: 528–35.

Smallwood, E.M. (1976) *The Jews under Roman Rule From Pompey to Diocletian*, Leiden: Brill.

Smith, M. (1998) 'Coptic literature, 337–425', in Averil Cameron and P. Garnsey (eds) *The Cambridge Ancient History*, vol. 13: *The Late Empire AD 337–425*, Cambridge: Cambridge University Press, 720–35.

Smith, R.B.E. (1995) *Julian's Gods: Religion and Philosophy in the Thought and Action of Julian the Apostate*, London and New York: Routledge.

Snyder, G.F. (1985) *Ante Pacem: Archaeological Evidence of Church Life before Constantine*, Mercer: Mercer University Press.

Solmsen, F. (1979) *Isis among the Greeks and Romans*, Cambridge, MA: Harvard University Press.

Stafford, E.J. (2000) *Worshipping Virtues: Personification and Belief in Ancient Greece*, London: Duckworth and University of Wales Press.

Stancliffe, C. (1983) *St Martin and his Hagiographer: History and Miracle in Sulpicius Severus*, Oxford: Clarendon Press.

Stark, R. (1996) *The Rise of Christianity: A Sociologist Reconsiders History*, Princeton, NJ: Princeton University Press.

Stern, M. (1974–84) *Greek and Latin Authors on Jews and Judaism*, Jerusalem: Israel Academy of Sciences and Humanities (3 vols).

Tabbernee, W. (1997) *Montanist Inscriptions and Testimonia: Epigraphic Sources illustrating the History of Montanism*, Macon, GA: Mercer University Press.

Taylor, J.E. (1993) *Christians and the Holy Places: The Myth of Jewish-Christian Origins*, Oxford: Clarendon Press.

Thomas, C. (1981) *Christianity in Roman Britain to AD 500*, London: Batsford.

Thornton, J.C.G. (1986) 'The destruction of idols – sinful or meritorious?', *JTS* 37: 209–21.

Timbie, J. (1986) 'The state of research on the career of Shenoute of Atripe', in B.A. Pearson and J.E. Goehring (eds) *The Roots of Egyptian Christianity*, Philadelphia, PA: Fortress Press, 258–70.

Tomlin, R.S.O. (1988) 'The curse tablets', in B. Cunliffe (ed.) *The Temple of Sulis Minerva at Bath*, vol. 2: *The Finds from the Sacred Spring* (Oxford University Committee for Archaeology: Monograph No. 16), 59–278.

—— (1998) 'Christianity and the late Roman army', in S.N.C. Lieu and D. Montserrat (eds) *Constantine: History, Historiography and Legend*, London: Routledge, 21–51.

Topping, E.C. (1976) 'The Apostle Peter, Justinian and Romanos the Melodos', *Byzantine and Modern Greek Studies* 2: 1–15.

Trebilco, P. (1991) *Jewish Communities in Asia Minor*, Cambridge: Cambridge University Press.

Treggiari, S. (1991) *Roman Marriage*, Oxford: Clarendon Press.

Trombley, F. (1993) *Hellenic Religion and Christianization, c. 370–529*, Leiden: Brill (2 vols).

—— (1994) 'Religious transition in sixth-century Syria', *Byzantinische Forschungen* 20: 153–95.

Trout, D.E. (1995) 'Christianizing the Nolan countryside: animal sacrifice at the tomb of St Felix', *JECS* 3: 281–98.

—— (1999) *Paulinus of Nola: Life, Letters, and Poems*, Berkeley: University of California Press.

Van Dam, R. (1985) *Leadership and Community in Late Antique Gaul*, Berkeley, Los Angeles, London: University of California Press.

—— (1993) *Saints and Their Miracles in Late Antique Gaul*, Princeton, NJ: Princeton University Press.

Van der Meer, F. (1961) *Augustine the Bishop*, tr. B. Battershaw and G.R. Lamb, London: Sheed and Ward.

Vanderspoel, J. (1995) *Themistius and the Imperial Court: Oratory, Civic Duty, and Paideia from Constantius to Theodosius*, Ann Arbor: University of Michigan Press.

Van Minnen, P. (1994) 'The roots of Egyptian Christianity', *Archiv für Papyrusforschung* 40: 71–86.

Van Straten, F.T. (1981) 'Gifts for the gods', in H.S. Versnel (ed.) *Faith, Hope and Worship: Aspects of Religious Mentality in the Ancient World*, Leiden: Brill, 65–151.

Vikan, G. (1982) *Byzantine Pilgrimage Art*, Washington, DC: Dumbarton Oaks.

—— (1984) 'Art, medicine and magic in early Byzantium', *Dumbarton Oaks Papers* 38: 65–86.

Waha, M. de (1976) 'Quelques réflexions sur la matricule des pauvres', *Byzantion* 46: 336–54.

Wallace-Hadrill, J.M. (1988) *Bede's 'Ecclesiastical History of the English People': A Historical Commentary*, Oxford: Clarendon Press.

Walpole, A.S. (1920) *Early Latin Hymns*, Cambridge: Cambridge University Press.

Weingarten, S. (1999) 'Was the pilgrim from Bordeaux a woman? A reply to Laurie Douglass', *JECS* 7: 291–8.

Weitzmann, K. (1978) *The Icon: Holy Images, Sixth to Fourteenth Century*, London: Chatto and Windus.

Welles, C.B., Fink, R.O., and Gilliam, J.F. (1959) *The Excavations at Dura-Europos, Final Report*, vol. 5, part I (*The Parchments and Papyri*), New Haven: Yale University Press.

Whitby, M. (1987) 'Maro the Dendrite: an anti-social holy man?', in M. Whitby, M. Whitby, and P. Hardie (eds) *Homo Viator: Classical Essays for John Bramble*, Bristol: Bristol Classical Press.

—— (1988) *The Emperor Maurice and his Historian: Theophylact Simocatta on Persian and Balkan Warfare*, Oxford: Clarendon Press.

—— (1991) 'John of Ephesus and the pagans: Pagan survivals in the sixth century', in M. Salamon (ed.) *Paganism in the Later Roman Empire and in Byzantium*, Cracow: Byzantina et Slavica Cracoviensia 1, 111–31.

White, L.M. (1990) *Building God's House in the Roman World, Architectural Adaptation among Pagans, Jews and Christians*, Baltimore and London: Johns Hopkins University Press.

—— (1997) *The Social Origins of Christian Architecture*, vol. 2: *Texts and Monuments for the Christian 'Domus Ecclesiae' and its Environment*, Valley Forge PA: Trinity Press International (= *Harvard Theological Studies* 42).

Wilken, R.L. (1983) *John Chrysostom and the Jews: Rhetoric and Reality in the late 4th Century*, Berkeley and Los Angeles: University of California Press.

—— (1984) *The Christians as the Romans Saw Them*, New Haven and London: Yale University Press.

—— (1992) *The Land Called Holy: Palestine in Christian History and Thought*, New Haven and London: Yale University Press.

Wilkinson, J. (1981) *Egeria's Travels to the Holy Land*, Warminster: Aris and Phillips.

—— (1990) 'Jewish holy places and the origins of Christian pilgrimage', in R. Ousterhout (ed.) *The Blessings of Pilgrimage*, Urbana and Chicago: University of Illinois Press, 41–53.

Williams, M.H. (1998) *The Jews among Greeks and Romans: A Diaspora Sourcebook*, London: Duckworth.

Williams, R. (1987) *Arius: Heresy and Tradition*, London: Darton, Longman and Todd.

Williams, S. (1985) *Diocletian and the Roman Recovery*, London: Batsford.

Williams, S. and Friell, G. (1994) *Theodosius: The Empire at Bay*, London: Batsford.

Wilson, L.J. (1984) 'The Trier procession ivory: a new interpretation', *Byzantion* 54: 602–14.

Wimbush, V.L. (ed.) (1990) *Ascetic Behaviour in Greco-Roman Antiquity*, Minneapolis: Fortress Press.

Wischmeyer, W. (1990) 'M. Iulius Eugenius: Eine Fallstudie zum Thema "Christen und Gesellschaft im 3. und 4. Jahrhunderte"', *Zeitschrift für die neutestamentliche Wissenschaft* 81: 225–46.

Yarbrough, O.L. (1990) 'Canons from the Council of Gangra', in V.L. Wimbush (ed.) *Ascetic Behaviour in Greco-Roman Antiquity*, Minneapolis: Fortress Press, 448–55.

Yarnold, E. (1994) *The Awe-Inspiring Rites of Initiation*, 2nd edn, Edinburgh: T&T Clark.

Youtie, H.C. (1975) 'Questions to a Christian oracle', *ZPE* 18: 253–7 and Plate VIII.

INDEX OF SOURCES

This index provides details of all the sources translated in this volume, including a handful of short items which appear in the introductions to other sources; these have been marked with an asterisk.

1. LITERARY SOURCES

(a) Arabic

(b) Coptic

(c) Greek

(d) Hebrew

(e) Latin

Sulpicius Severus, *Life of St Martin* 12–15: **6.10**
Symmachus, *Letters* 1.51: **6.2**
——, *Memoranda* 3.3–10: **6.4**
Tertullian, *Apology* 39.1–6: **2.1**

(f) Syriac

Athanasius, *Letter to Virgins who Went and Prayed in Jerusalem and Returned* pp. 170–2: **16.2**
Jacob of Serugh, *Homily* 5 (extracts): **7.9**
John of Ephesus, *Lives of the Eastern Saints* 4, pp. 56–7, 64–5: **11.10**
Zacharias, *Life of Severus* pp.39–41: **7.1**

2. LEGAL TEXTS

(a) Roman law

Comparison of the Laws of Moses and the Romans 15.3: **3.2**
Cornutian Deed: **13.2**
Justinian, *Novels* 120.1, 10: **13.8**; 144 preface: **8.15***
Justinianic Code 1.5.17: **8.15a**
Sirmondian Constitutions 1: **12.5**
Theodosian Code 8.16.1: **11.4**; 9.16.9: **5.9b**; 12.1.63: **11.5**; 16.5.3: **10.5a**; 16.5.18: **10.5b**; 16.8.9: **8.11**; 16.8.24: **8.12**; 16.10.2: **5.1a**; 16.10.3: **5.1b**; 16.10.8: **6.1**; 16.10.10: **6.7**

(b) Church law

Council of Elvira, Canons 2–3, 55–7, 59–60: **3.6**; 36: **14.12***; 49–50: **8.6**
Council of Nimes, Canon 2: **15.2a**
Council of Serdica, Canon 10: **12.2**
Council of Vannes, Canon 12: **8.9**; 16: **7.10**

3. DOCUMENTARY TEXTS

(a) Inscriptions and graffiti

AE (1907) 191: **5.7f**; (1911) 90: **12.8a**; (1969–70) 631: **5.7c**; (1973) 235: **1.15**; (1983) 895: **5.7d**;
BE 81 (1968) 478 (p. 517): **8.1a**
CIJ 1.462: **8.8a**; 1.523: **8.8b**; 1^2.643a: **8.14**
CIL 3.4415: **3.1**; 3.4800: **1.14b**; 6.510: **6.3a**; 6.1139: **4.3**; 6.1779: **6.3b**; 6.8498: **2.5a**; 6.8987: **2.5b**; 6.31775: **1.16b**; 6.32004: **5.2**; 8.9255: **16.8b**; 8.12260: **15.1**; 8.18529: **5.7a**; 8.20600: **16.8a**; 11.288: **13.3a**; 11.294: **13.3b**; 11.5265: **4.10**; 12.5336: **12.7**
CIMRM 1438: **1.14b**; 2350: **1.14a**
CMRDM I.50: **1.3**
DT 286: **1.10**
IEJ 13 (1963), p. 325: **12.8b**
IGLT 1265: **4.7a**; 1889: **4.7b**
IGPhilae 168: **1.8a**; 178: **1.8b**; 180: **1.8c**; 197: **7.6a**; 201: **7.7c**; 203: **7.7b**
ILAlg II, 2.4647: **5.7b**

(b) Papyri

GENERAL INDEX

Ablabius (4th c. official) 89–92, 218–19, 267
Abraham (patriarch) 172, 209, 274, 276
Abraham, bishop of Carrhae 206–10
Abraham (Syrian holy man) 210–11
Abu Mena 286
Academy, Athenian, closure of 255
Achaemenids 169, 171
Adam and Eve 40, 45
Africa, north 4, 19, 30, 114, 133, 164, 286–7; Christianisation 138–40, 262; Christians 67–9, 71–2; churches 244, 246–7, 251–2, 288–9; Donatists 68, 215–16; Manichaeans 66, 182; temples 138–9
Ahuramazda/Ohrmazd (deity) 170
Alexander of Cappadocia (pilgrim) 272
Alexander, bishop of Alexandria 87
Alexandria 46, 134, 180, 189, 193, 241, 270; Arianism 87; Christian presence 38–9, 42–3, 161; Jews 162; temples 26–7, 123, 125
altars: church 228–30, 233–4; pagan 21, 58, 100, 114, 121, 131, 155; of Victory 111–12, 115–21; Zoroastrian 170; *see also* sacrifice
Amantius (6th c. official) 135–6
Ambrose, bishop of Milan 123, 129, 202, 204, 215; as hymn-writer 253–4; as polemicist 112–17, 159–60; as preacher 244, 247–50
Amida 211
Ammianus Marcellinus 102, 108–9, 155, 288
ampullae, pilgrim 286–7
amulets: Christian 293–4; pagan 145
Anastasius (emperor) 5, 264

Ancyra 105
Anglo-Saxons 142
Anicia Juliana 264
anointing 45, 248
Antioch 121, 135, 210, 235, 274; ascetics in/near 171, 188, 293; as imperial base 2, 78, 95, 101; Jewish community 156–8, 168
Antoninus Pius (emperor) 19
Antony (ascetic) 187–8, 189–95, 199, 201–2
Aphrodisias 134
Aphrodite 25, 31
Apollo 27, 80–1, 135
Apollonius of Tyana 32
aqueducts 222, 231
Aquitania 225
Arabia/Arabs 6, 17, 101, 282, 283, 285
Aratos 255, 257
Arcadius (emperor) 244, 296
arches, of Septimius Severus (Lepcis Magna) 19–21; of Constantine (Rome) 80, 83
Ardashir I (Persian king) 176
Arianism/Arians/Arius 81, 87–8, 96, 109, 110, 112, 125, 133, 156, 160, 189, 195, 223, 239, 253, 264
Arles 238–40
Armenia/Armenians 126, 203, 289
army, Roman 2, 3, 4, 16–17, 26, 33, 46–7, 83; exclusion of Jews 162–3; persecution of Christians in 214
Arsinoe 42
Artemis 28
asceticism/ascetics, Christian 187–212; and church hierarchy/authority 187, 195, 196–7, 200; variety 187, 199–200; 'coenobitic'/communal 187, 196–9, 212; criticism of 188,